CONTENT PAGE

INTRODUCTION..................2
SKULL TATTOOS..................3
ANIMAL TATTOOS..................13
DRAGON TATTOOS..................31
SAMURAI TATTOOS..................36
ROSE TATTOOS..................41
ANGEL WINGS TATTOOS..................46
LANDSCAPE TATTOOS..................51
SCARY TATTOOS..................56
ALIEN TATTOOS..................61
JOKER TATTOOS..................66
DIAMOND TATTOOS..................71
ANCHOR TATTOOS..................76
CROWN TATTOOS..................79
SNAKE TATTOOS..................84
MUSICAL TATTOOS..................88
BUTTERFLY TATTOOS..................92
VIKING TATTOOS..................95
PIRATE SHIP TATTOOS..................98
TRIBAL TATTOOS..................101
SPACE THEMED TATTOOS..................106
SPACESHIP TATTOOS..................111
TREE TATTOOS..................116
STAR TATTOOS..................121
ENGINE TATTOOS..................126
ALCOHOL TATTOOS..................131
STAIRWAY TATTOOS..................136
CITYSCAPE TATTOOS..................140
PHOENIX TATTOOS..................145
WAVE TATTOOS..................150
MONEY BAG TATTOOS..................153
TREASURE CHEST TATTOOS..................157
ROBOT TATTOOS..................162
LIPS TATTOOS..................168
HOURGLASS TATTOOS..................171
GLADIATOR TATTOOS..................175
TRANSPORT TATTOOS..................180
CHESS TATTOOS..................186
EYE TATTOOS..................190
DINOSAUR TATTOOS..................195
LOCK TATTOOS..................199
KEY TATTOOS..................202
FINAL THOUGHTS..................206

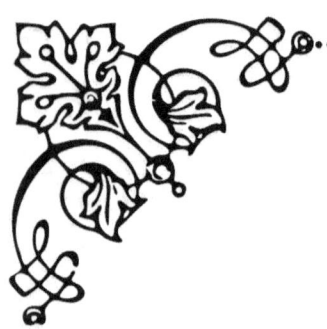

INTRODUCTION:

Thank you for purchasing this book. It's designed to inspire your next tattoo.

This book includes many different styles and themes of tattoos to choose from, ranging from dragon tattoos to skull tattoos. It's designed to give the reader a vast selection of ideas on the different types of AI tattoos, helping to decide your favourite style and design. This 200+ page book includes hundreds of tattoos and is designed for both the individual looking to get their next tattoo, as well as the tattoo artist looking for new ideas.

HOW TO USE THIS BOOK:

There is a wide range of tattoo designs within this book, and I hope it helps the viewer in the process of choosing their next tattoo. These tattoo designs should be used as a guide or tool for the tattoo artist to create their own work from. If you discover a tattoo design that you like, (which I'm sure you will!) I would recommend that the tattoo artist you choose, adds his or her own creative style to the design, and makes it their own.

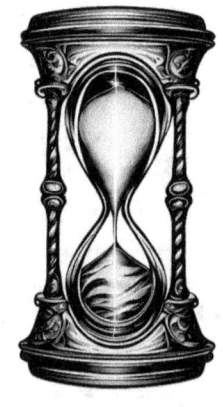
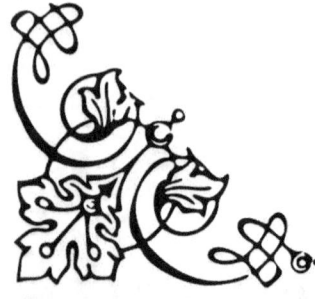

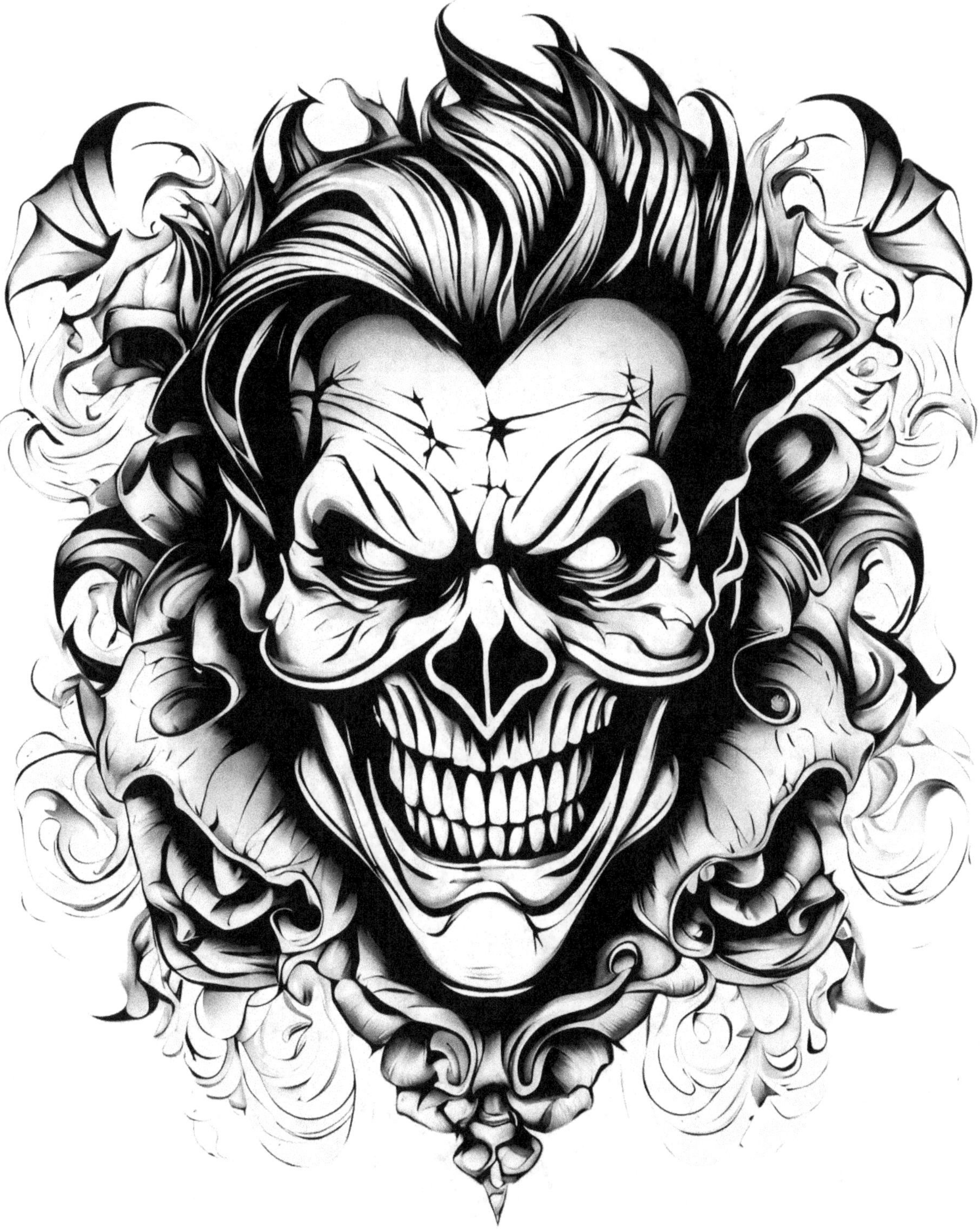

SKULL TATTOOS

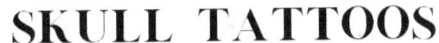

SKULL TATTOOS

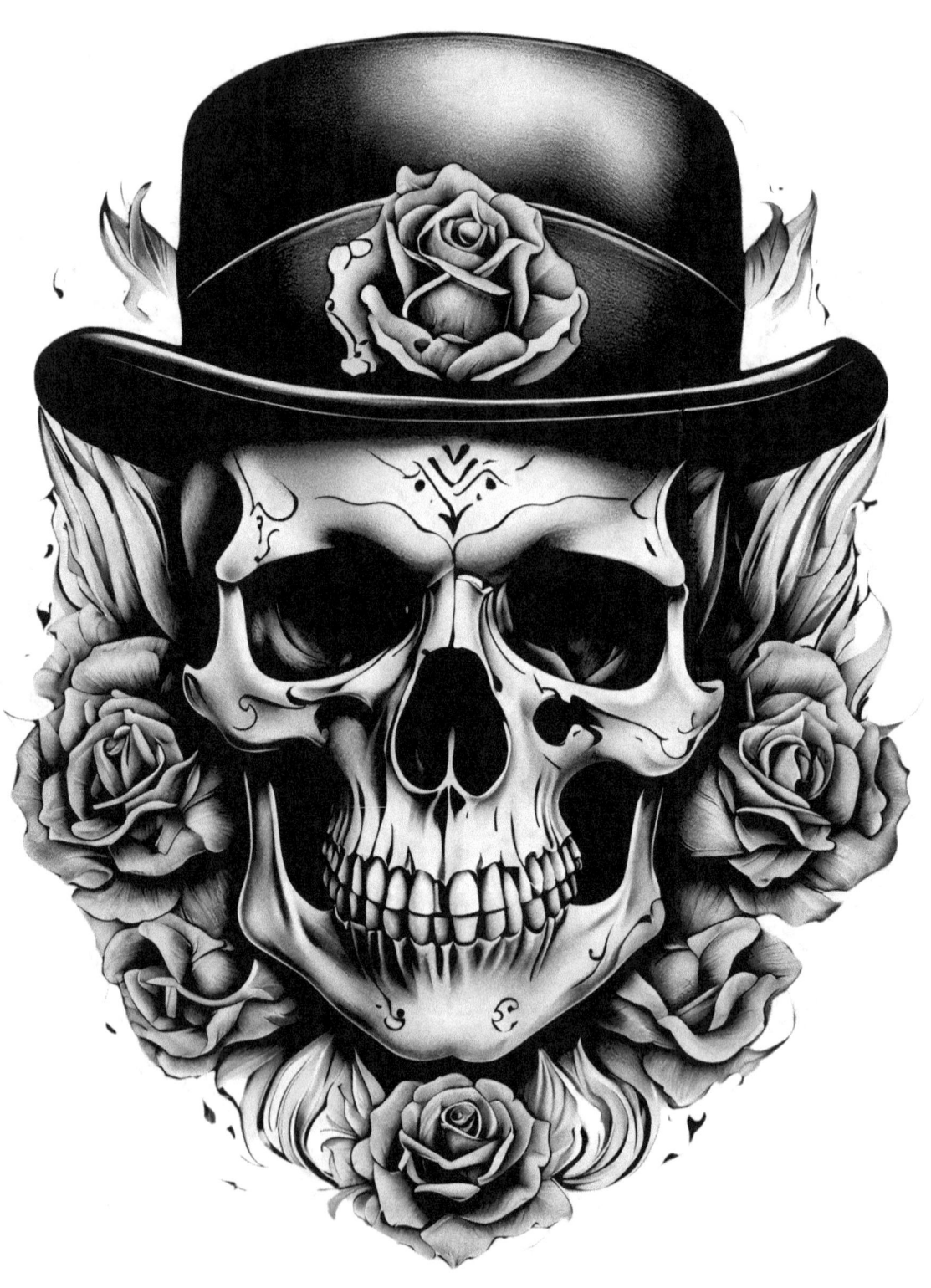

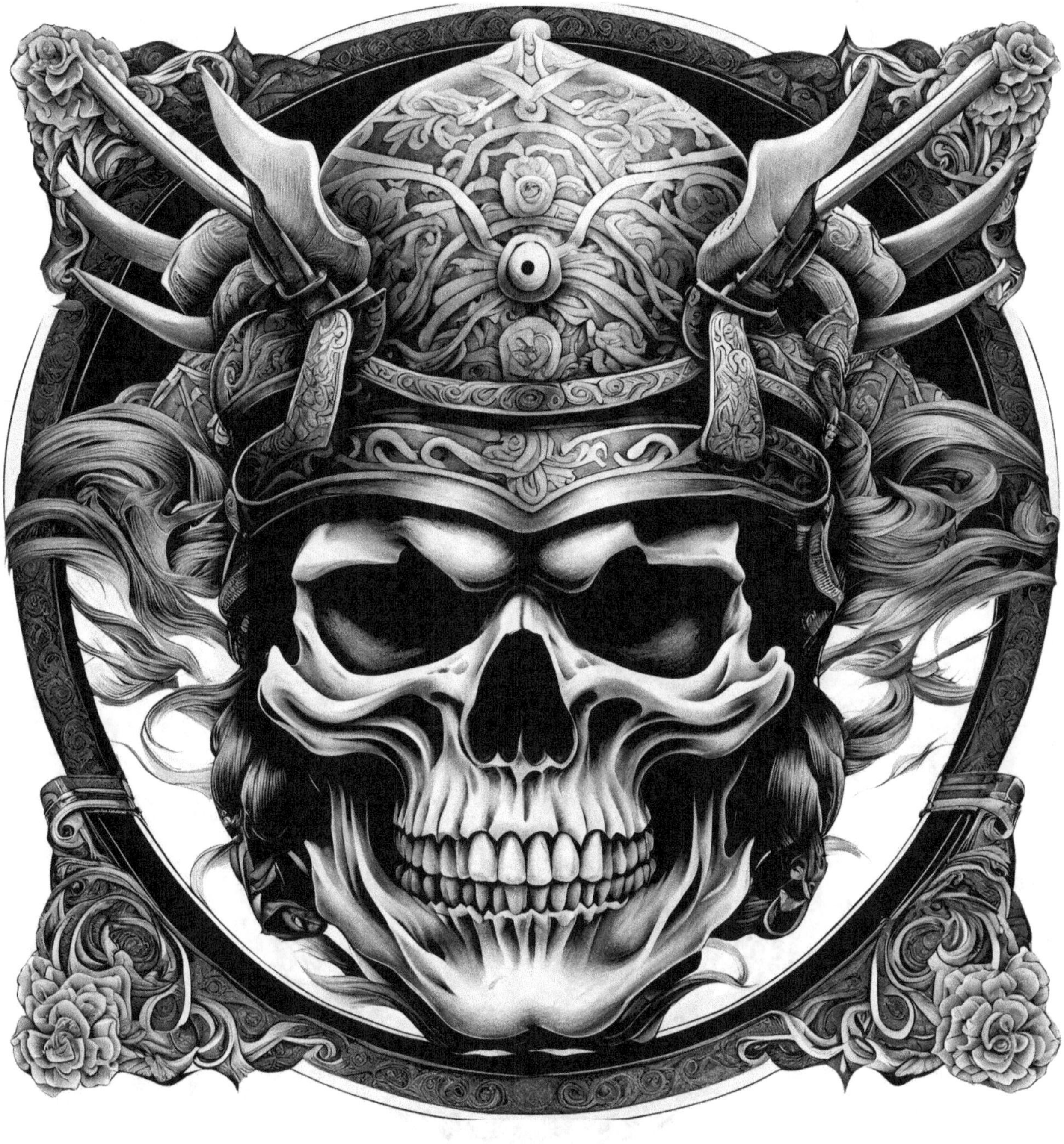

SKULL TATTOOS

SKULL TATTOOS

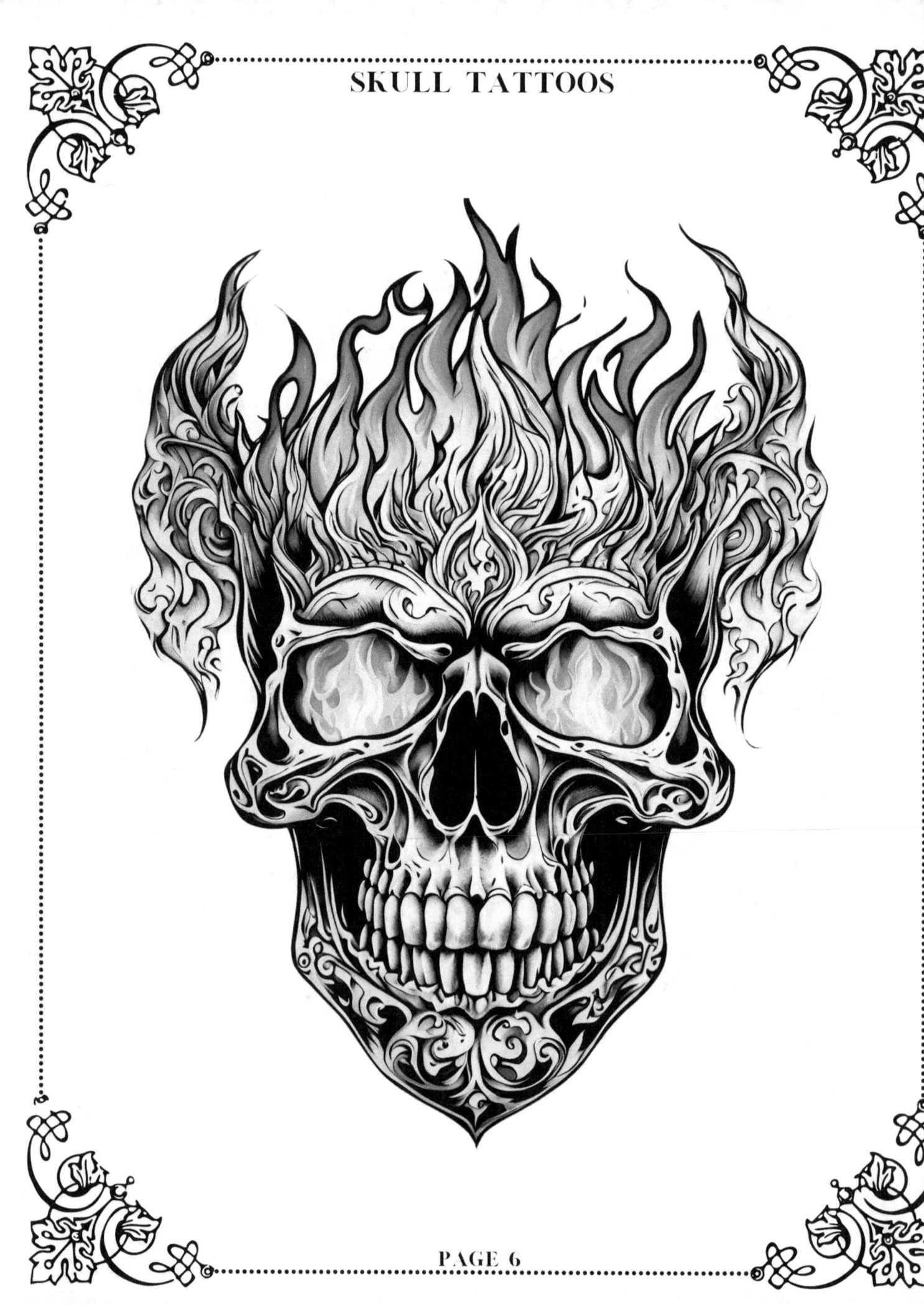

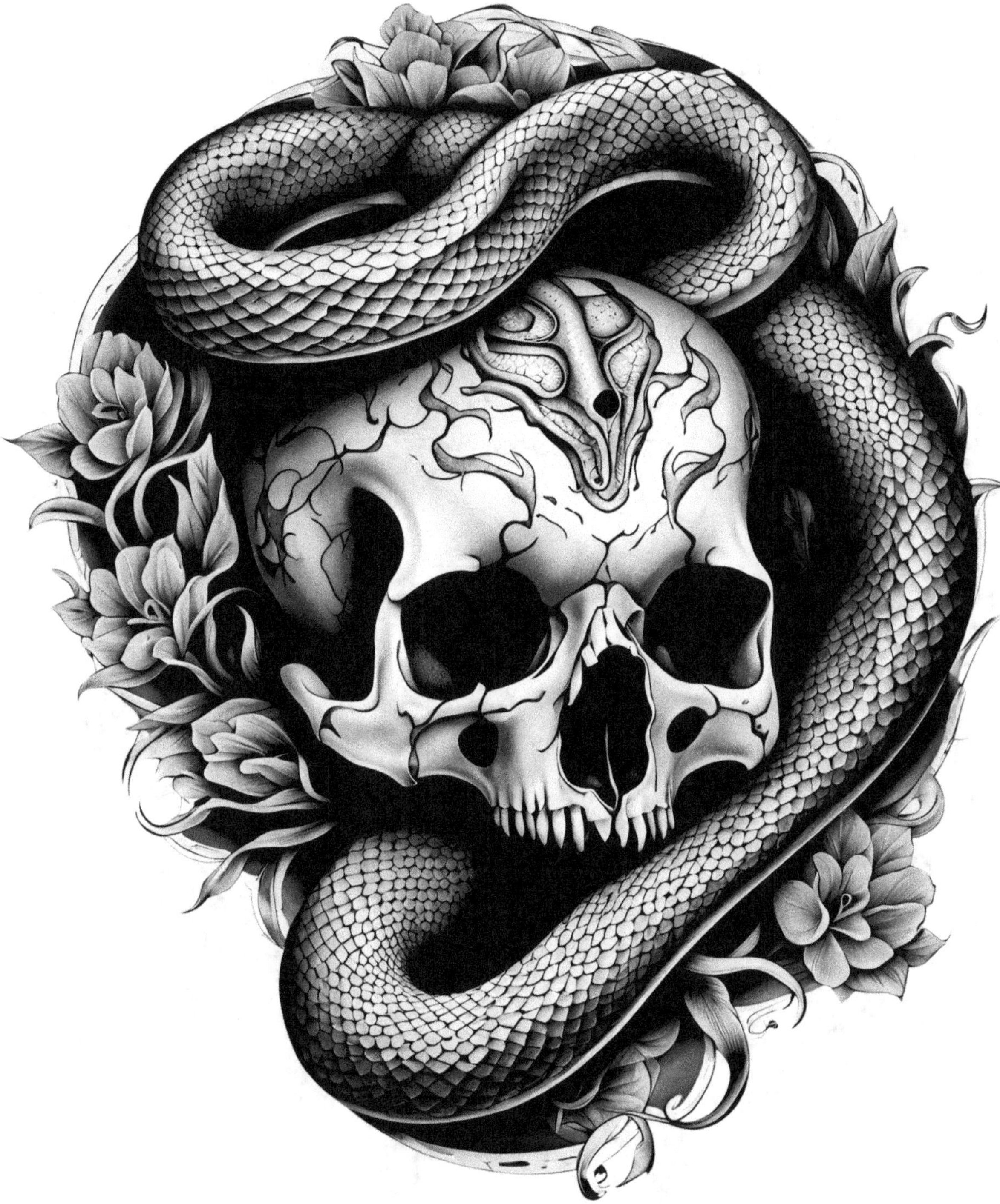

SKULL TATTOOS

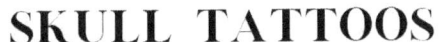

PAGE 7

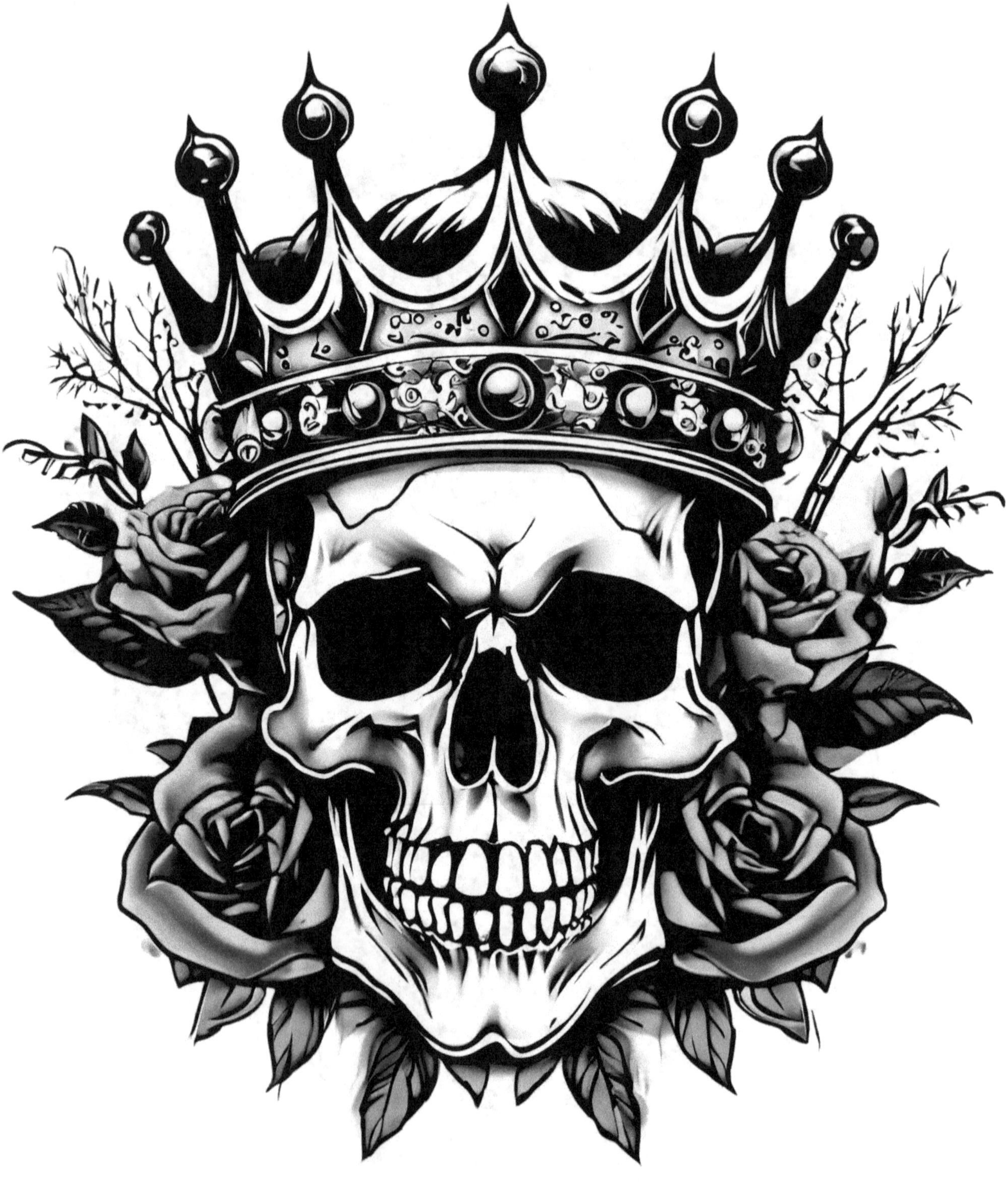

SKULL TATTOOS

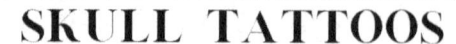

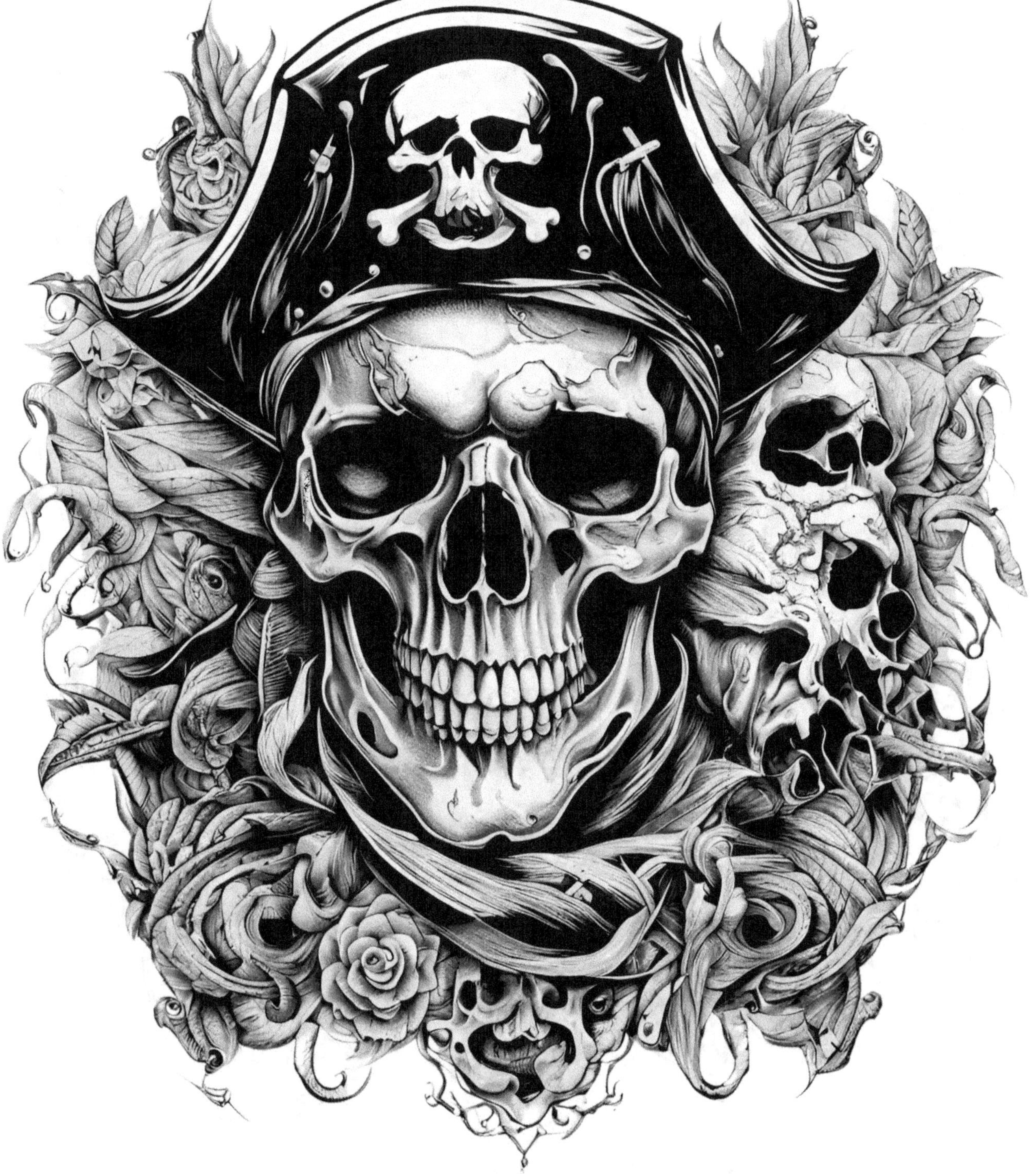

SKULL TATTOOS

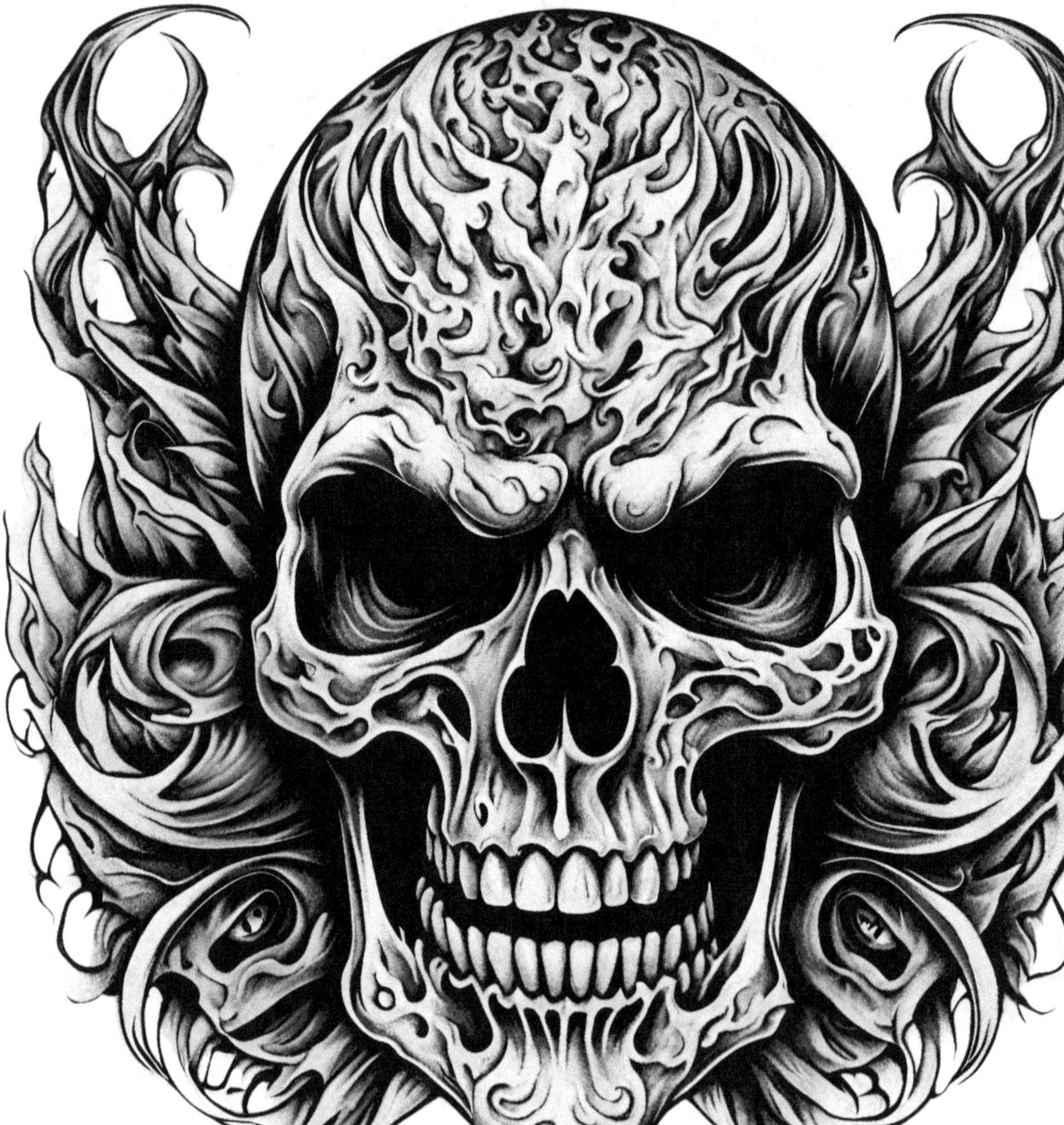

SKULL TATTOOS

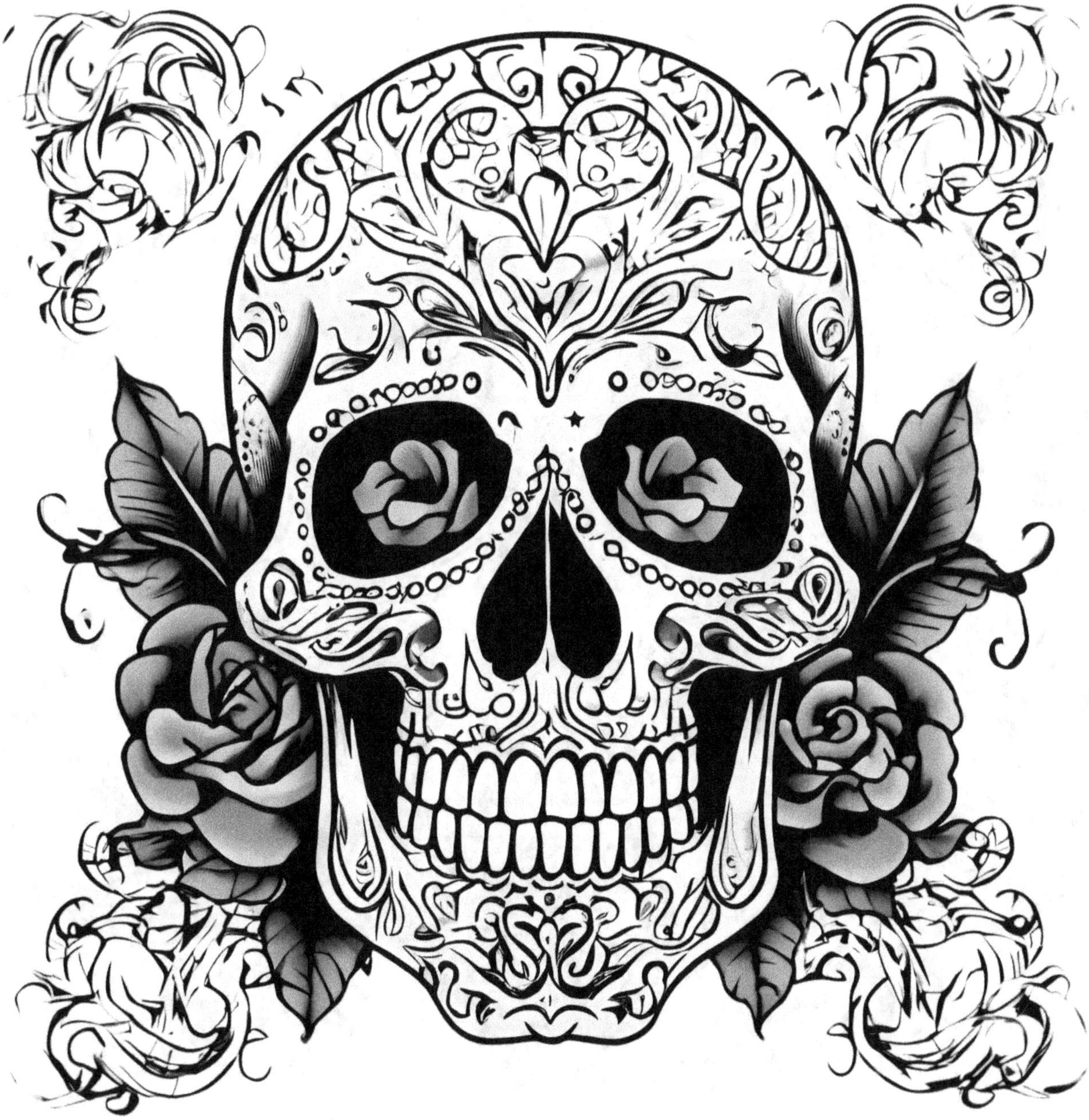

SKULL TATTOOS

PAGE 11

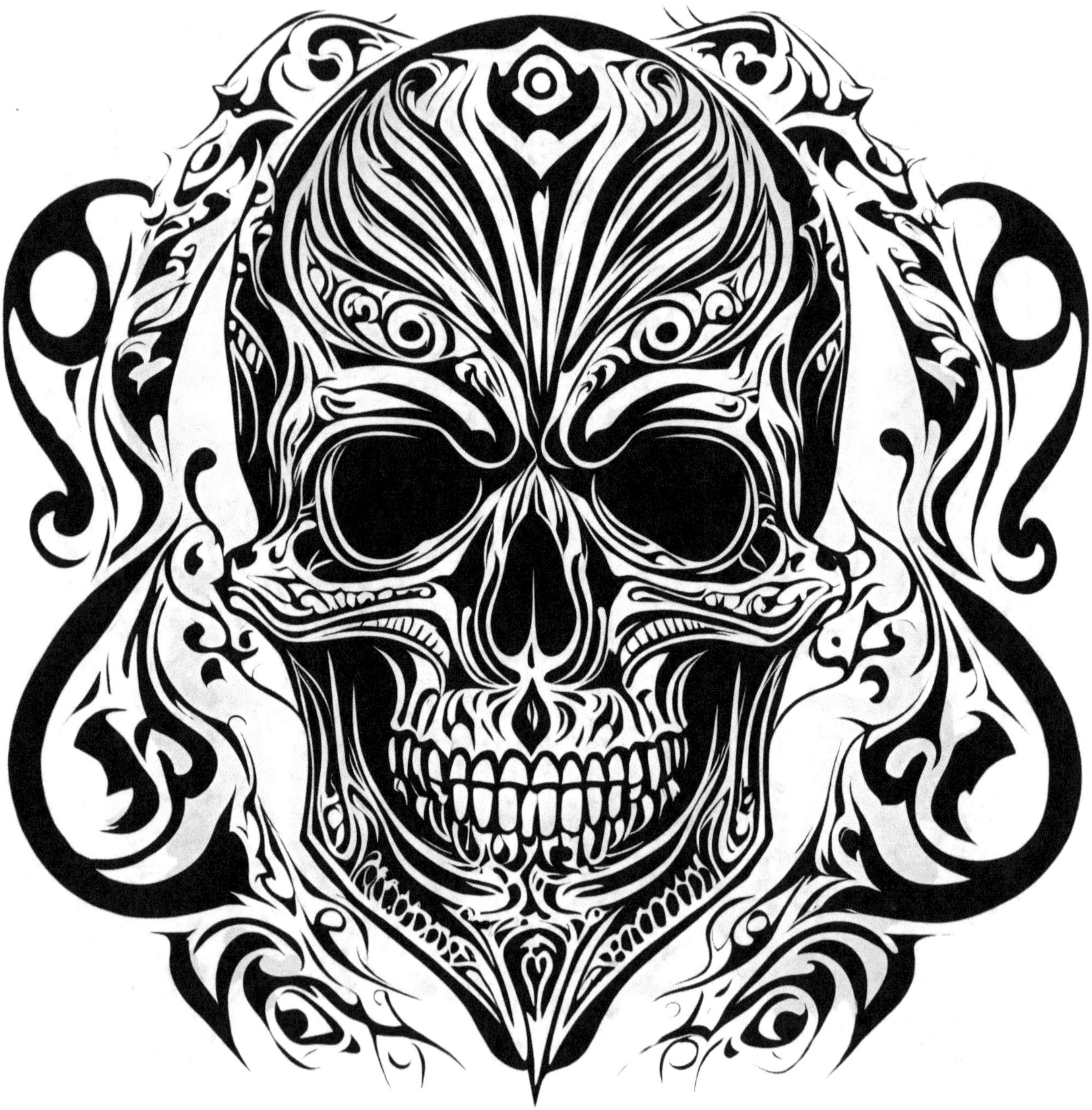

SKULL TATTOOS

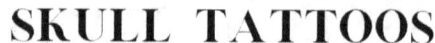

ANIMAL TATTOOS

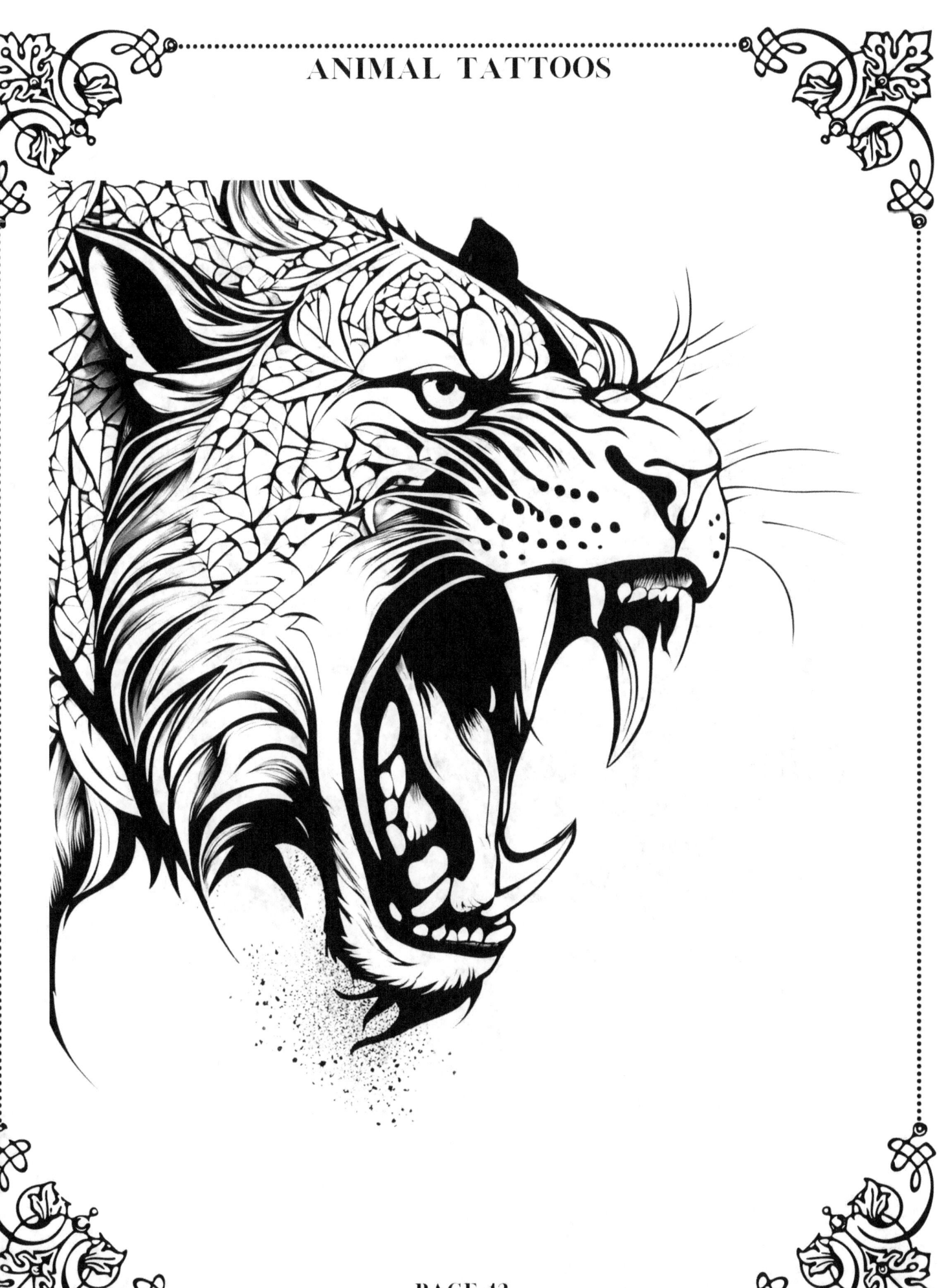

ANIMAL TATTOOS

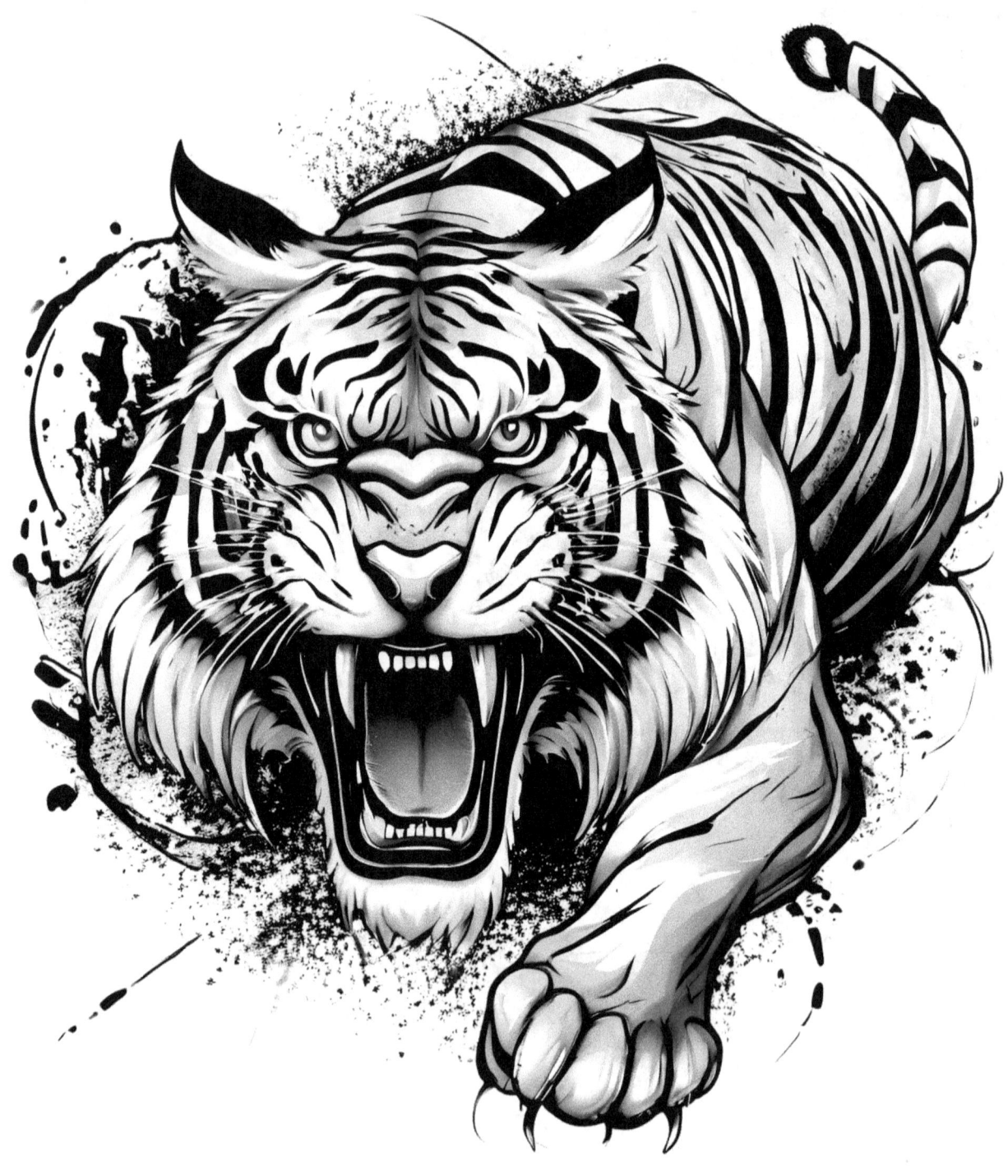

ANIMAL TATTOOS

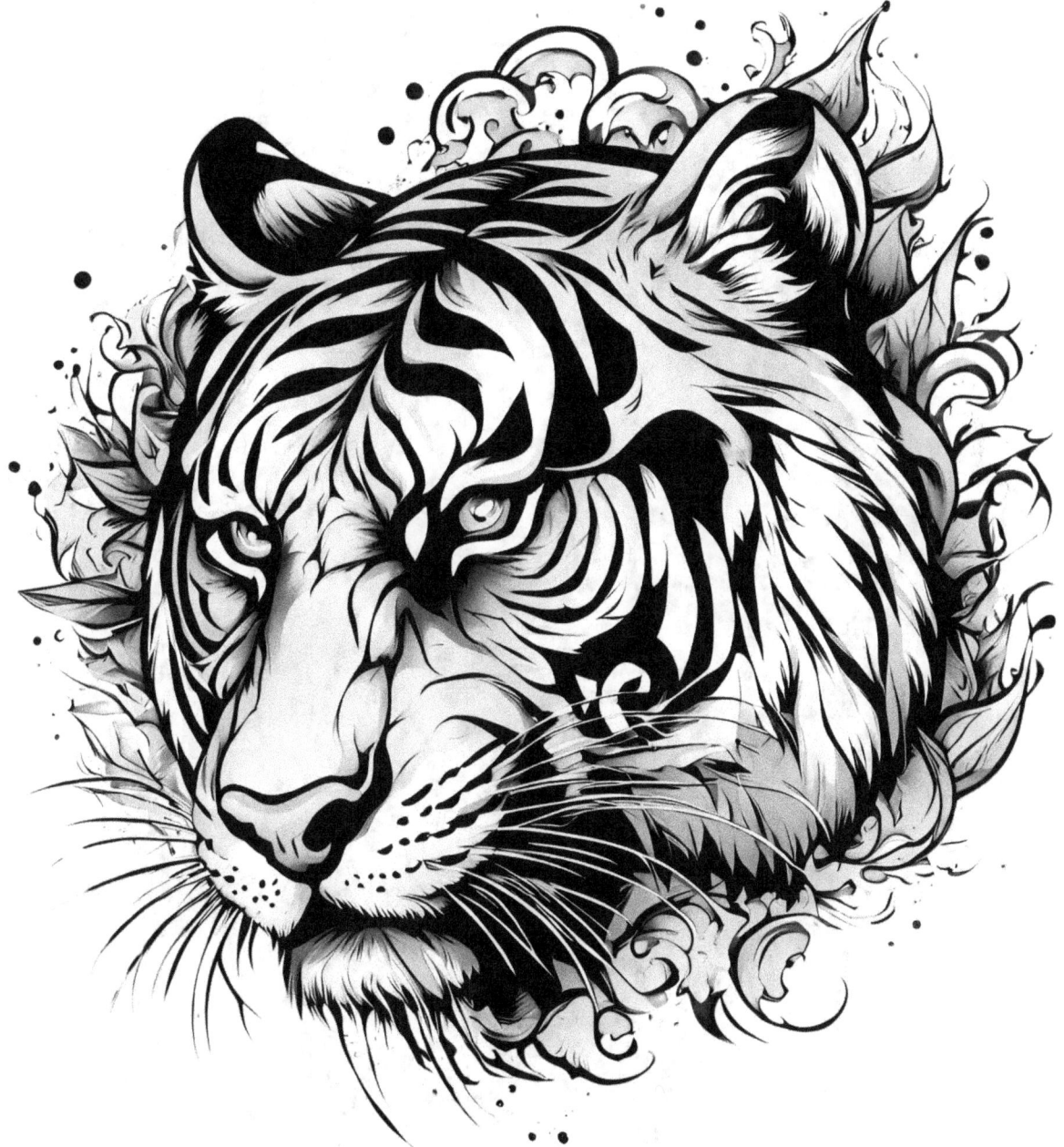

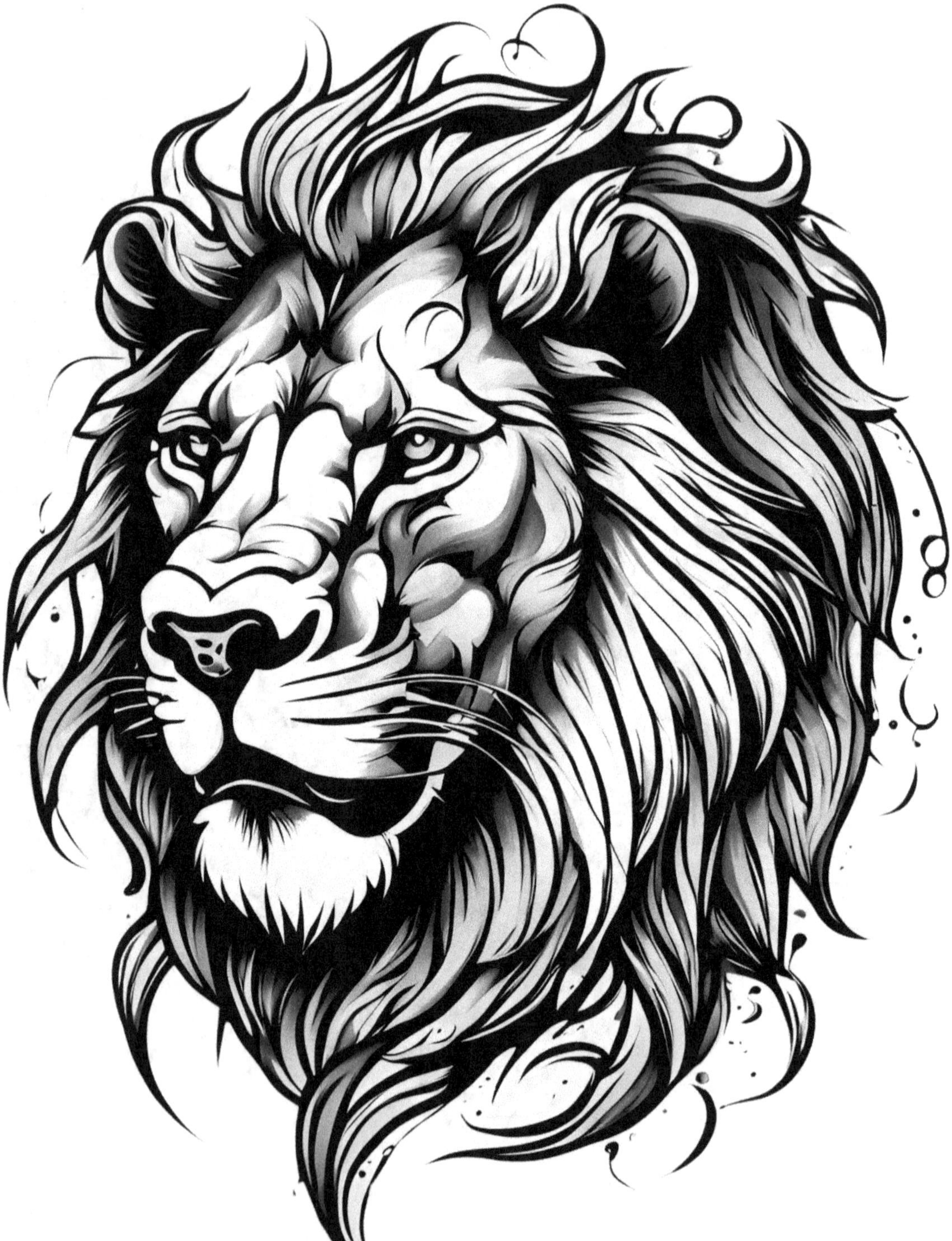

ANIMAL TATTOOS

ANIMAL TATTOOS

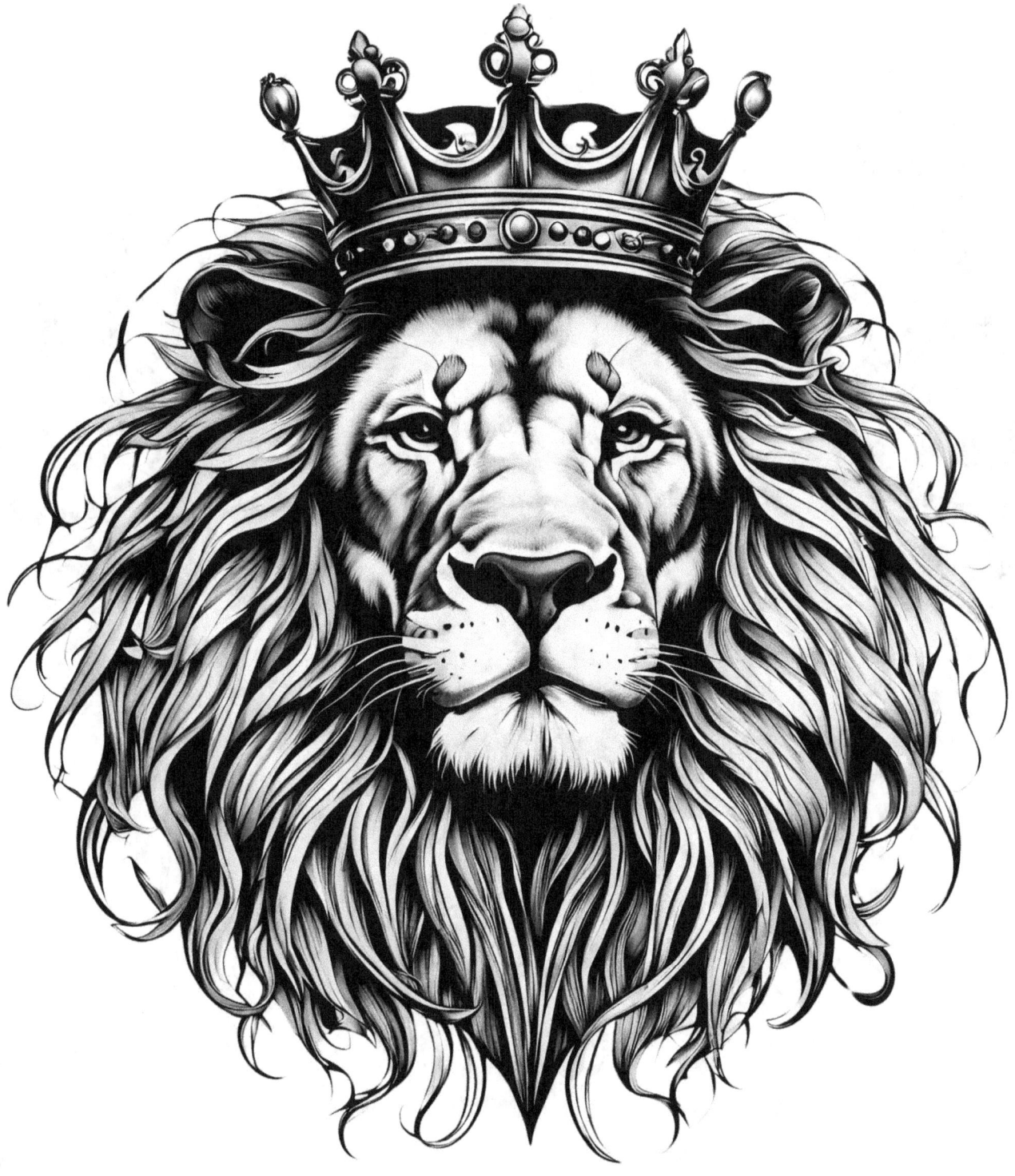

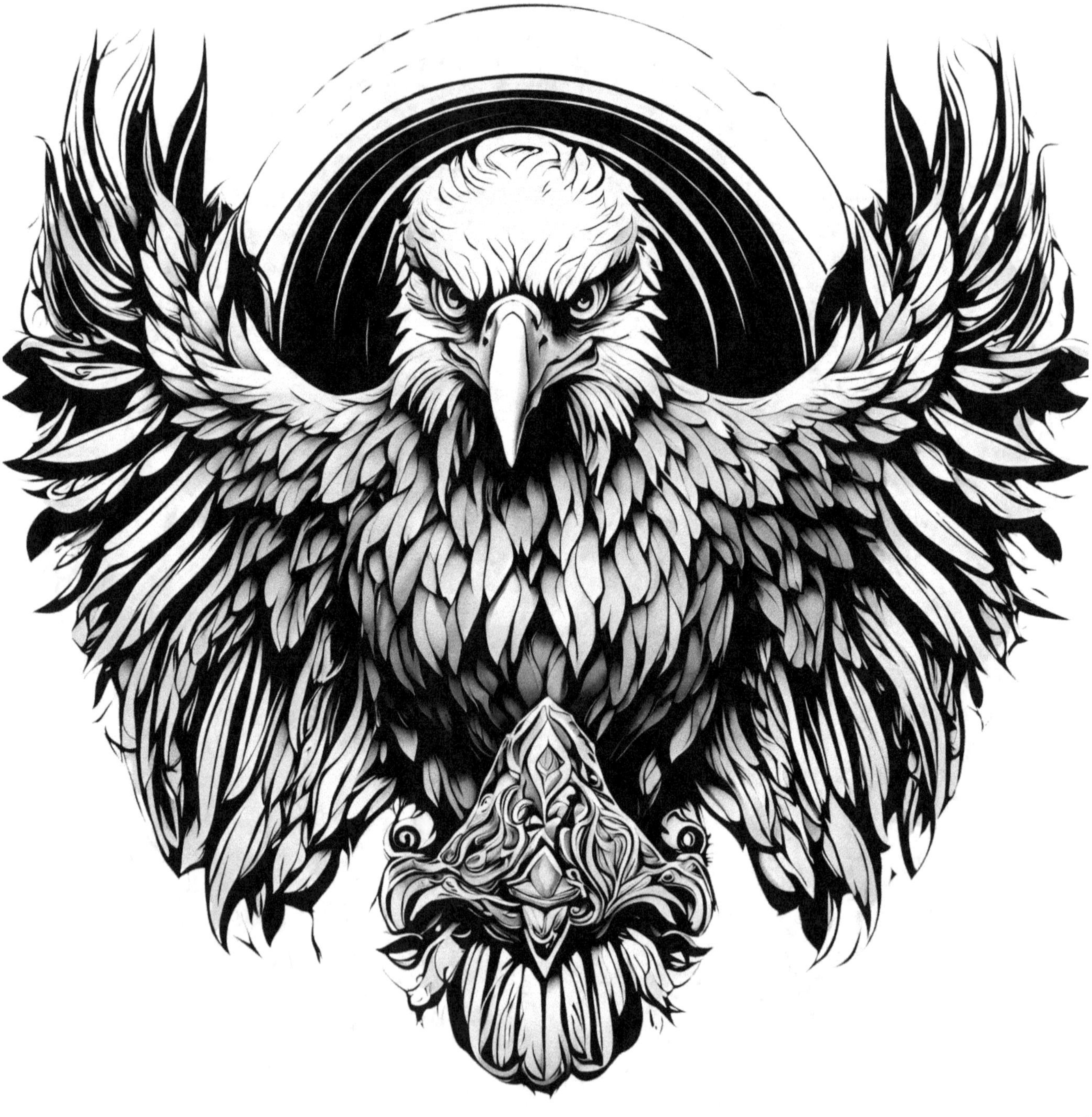

ANIMAL TATTOOS

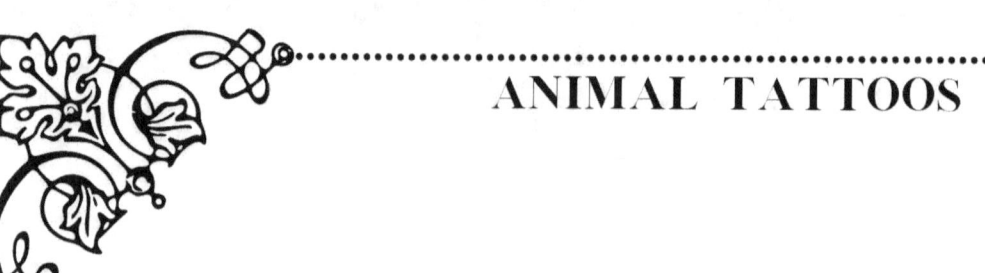

PAGE 18

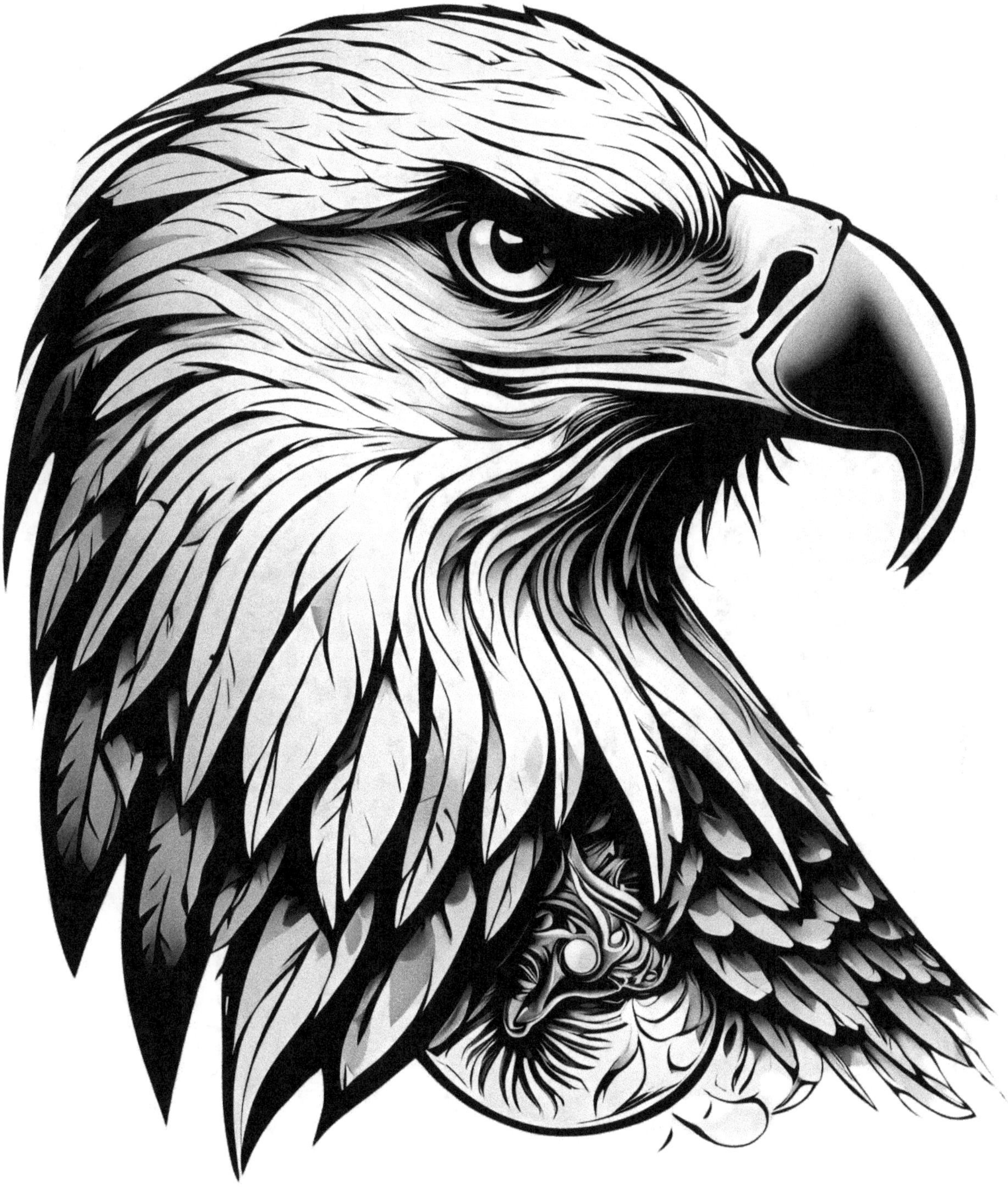

ANIMAL TATTOOS

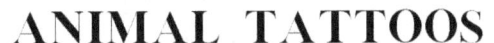

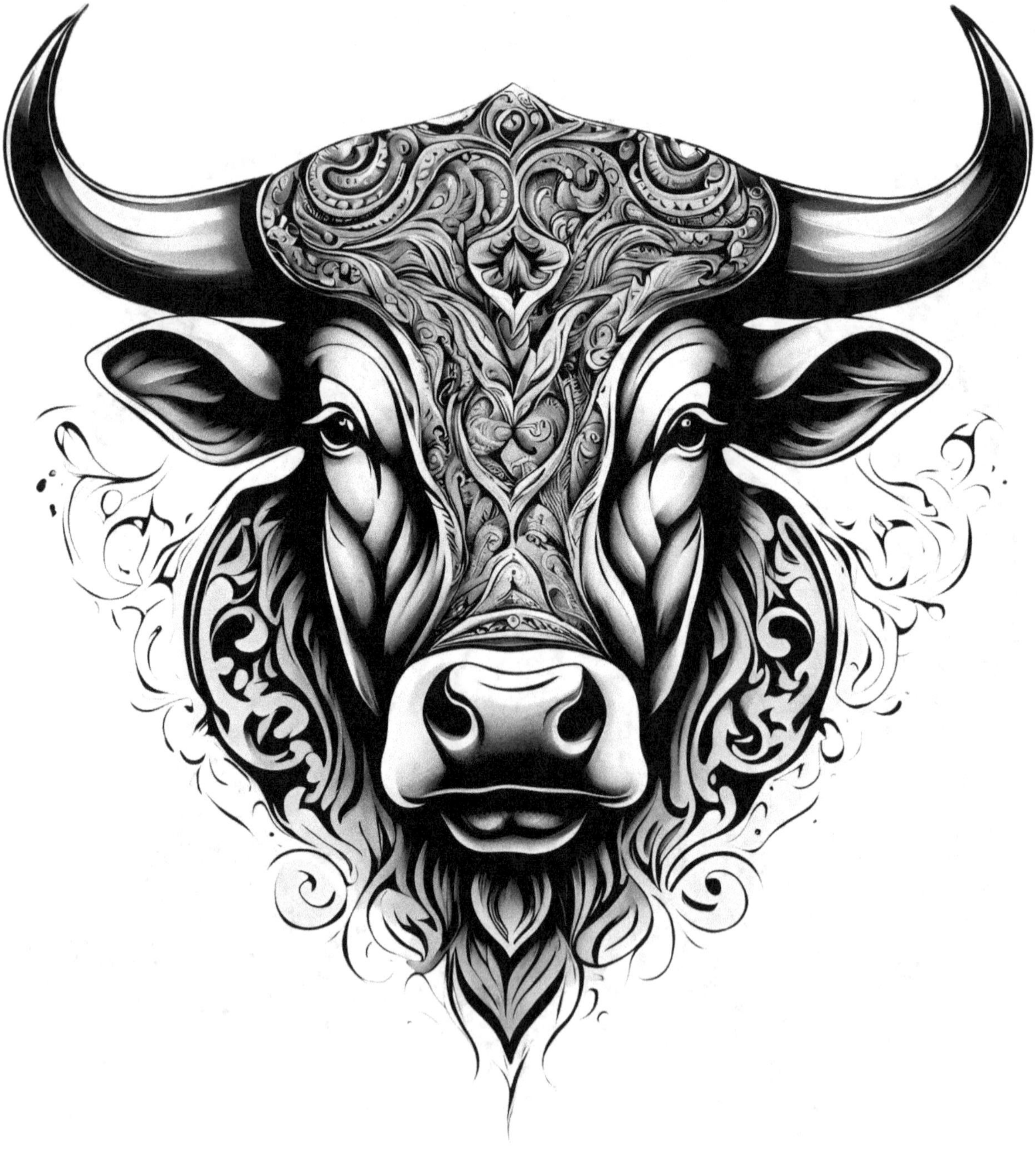

ANIMAL TATTOOS

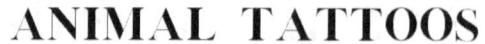

ANIMAL TATTOOS

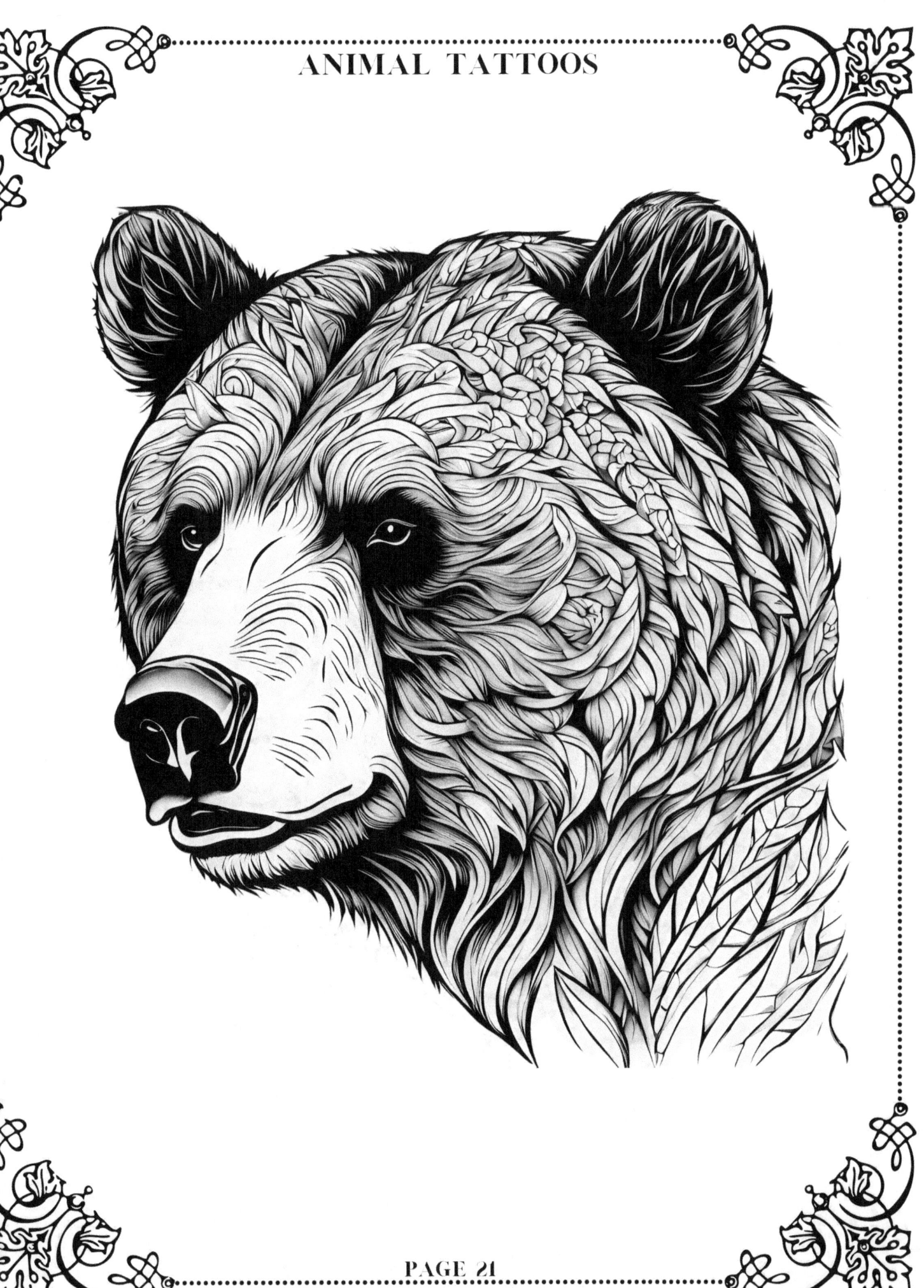

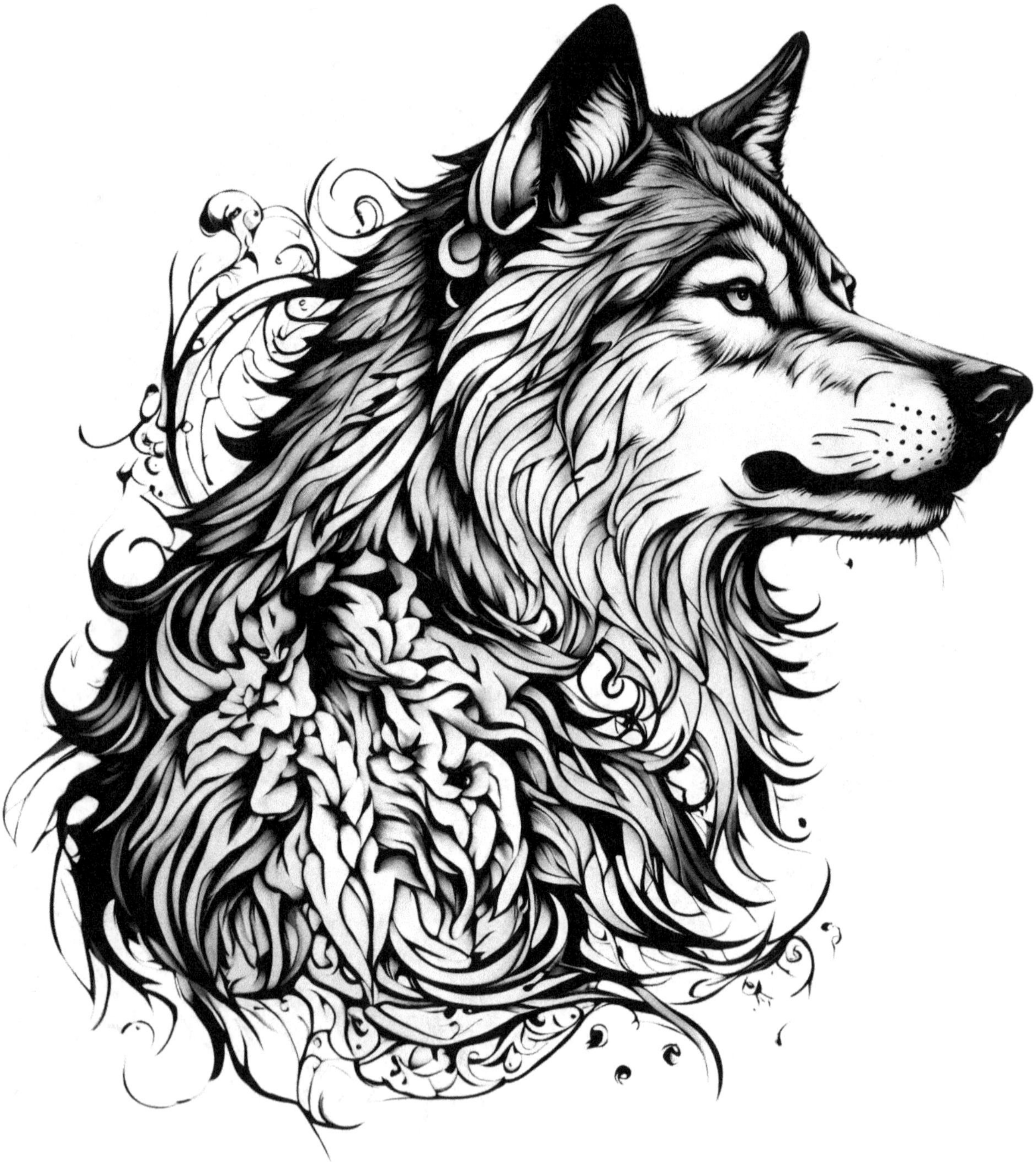

ANIMAL TATTOOS

ANIMAL TATTOOS

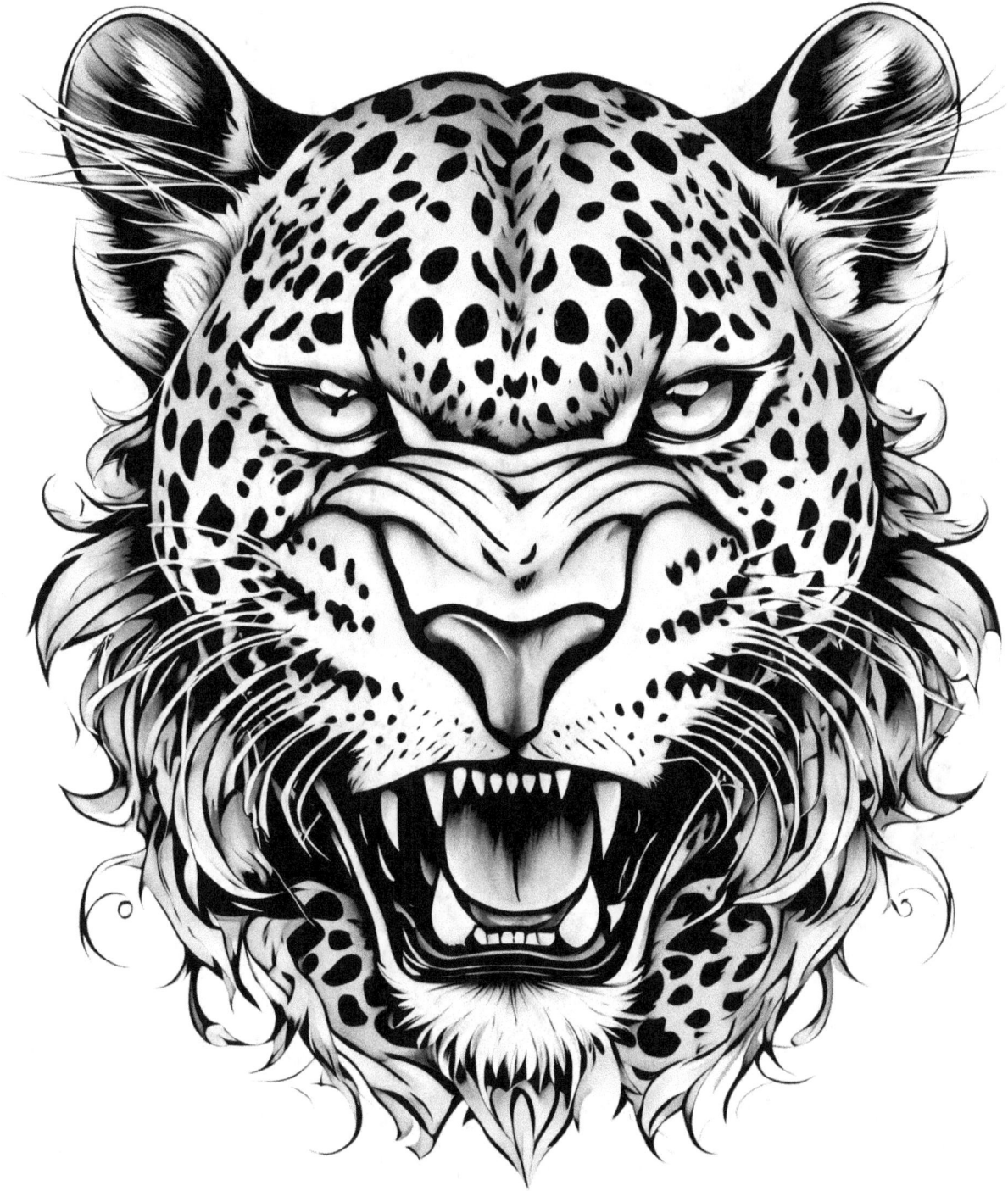

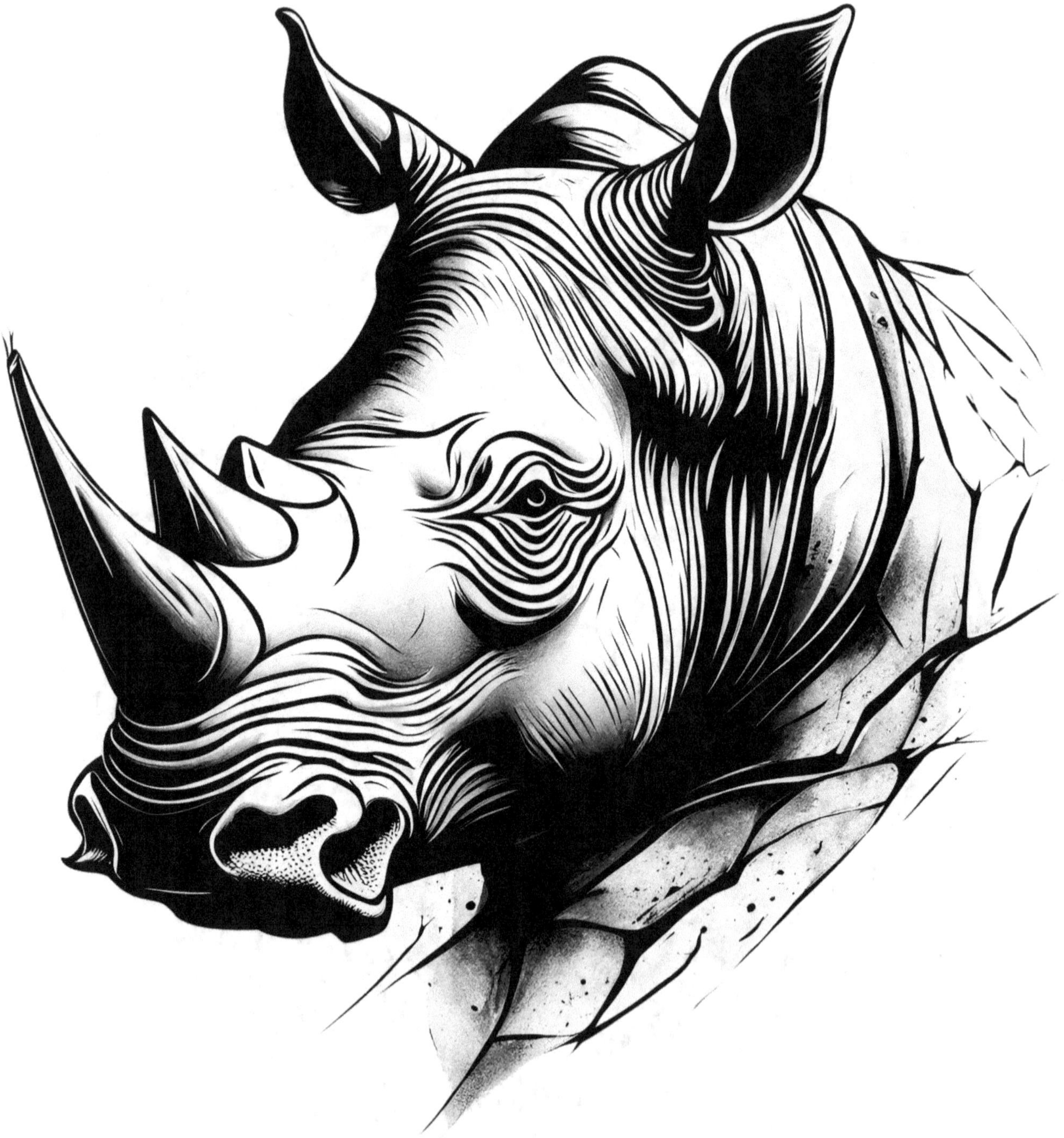

ANIMAL TATTOOS

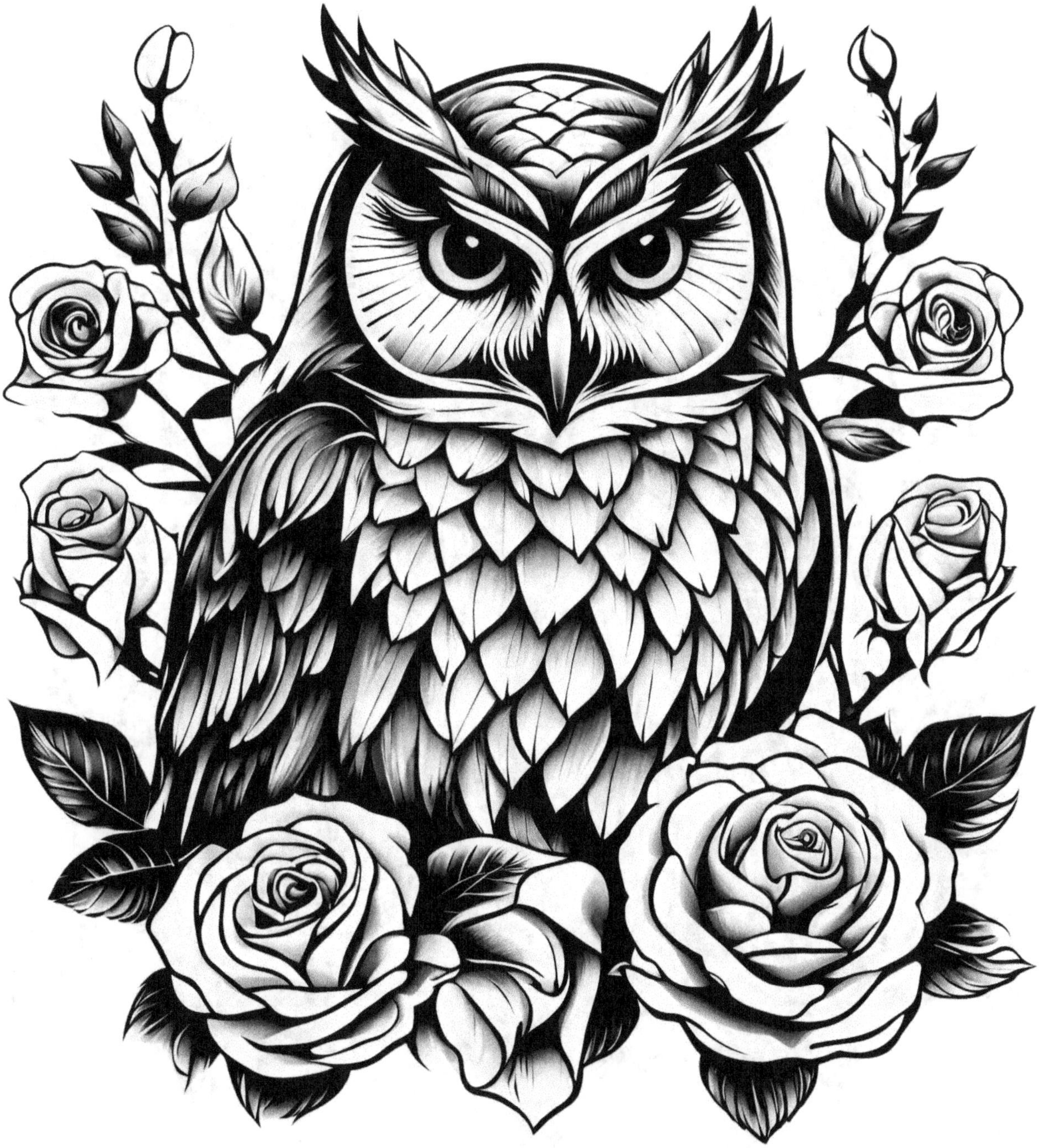

ANIMAL TATTOOS

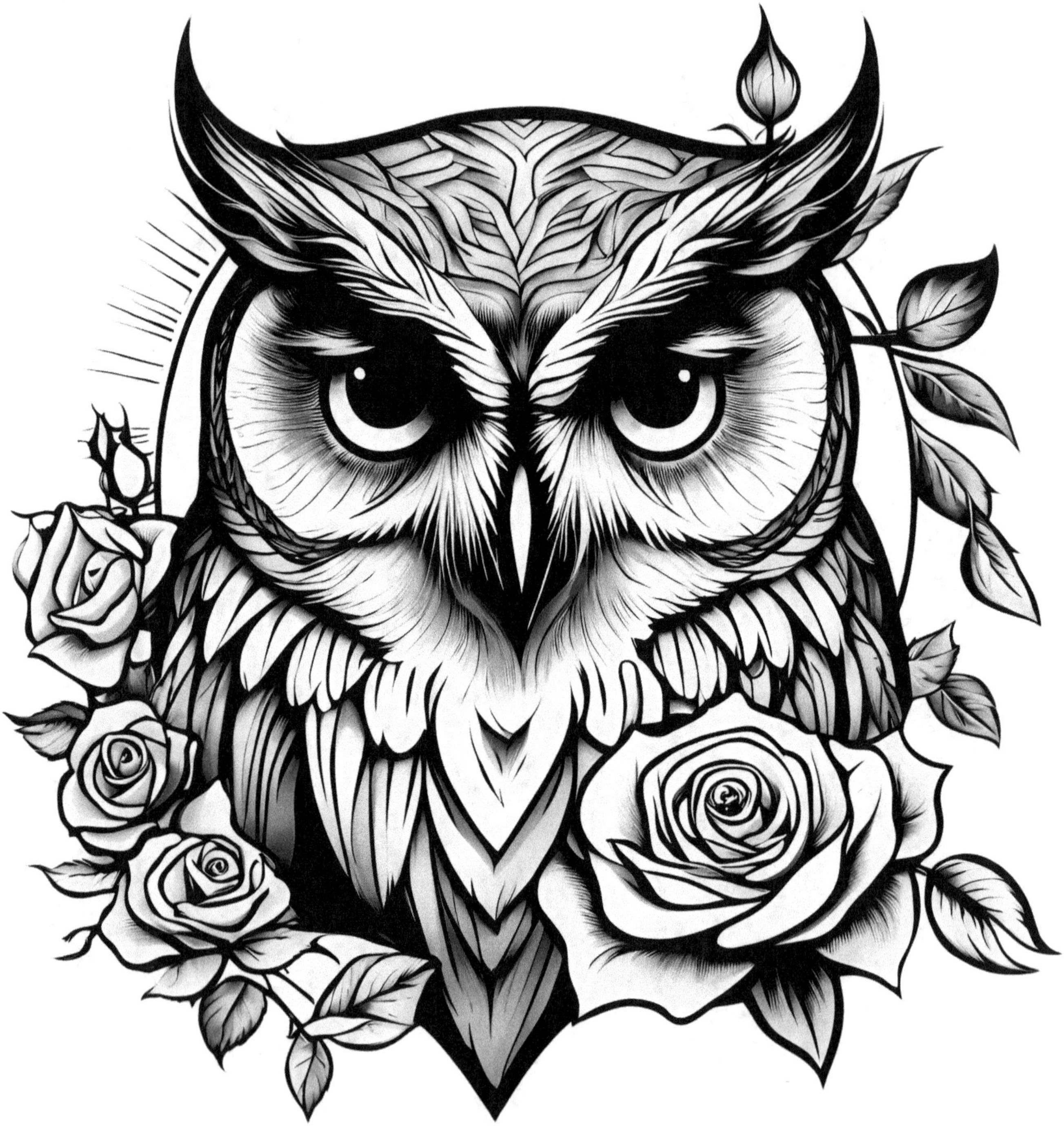

ANIMAL TATTOOS

ANIMAL TATTOOS

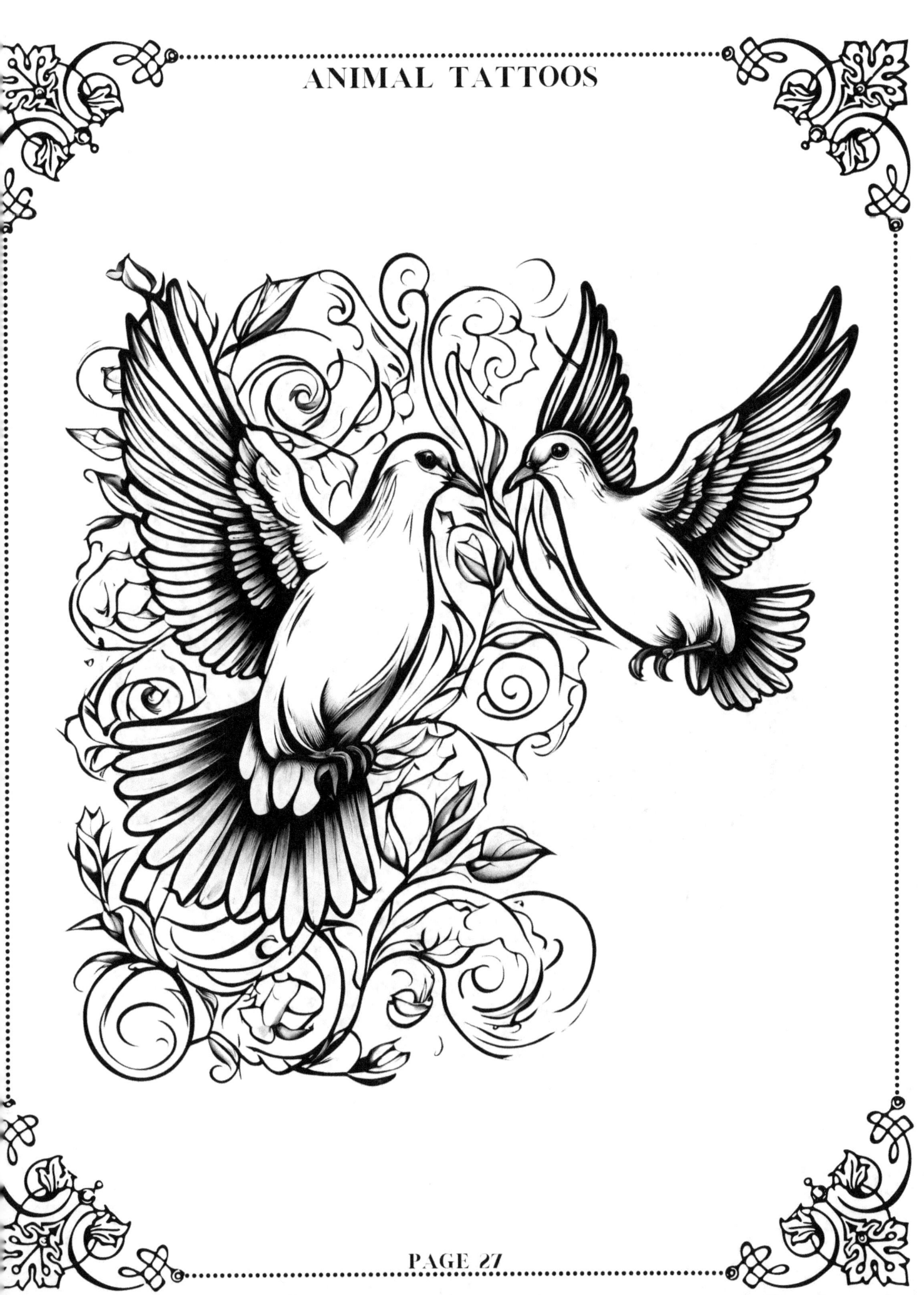

PAGE 27

ANIMAL TATTOOS

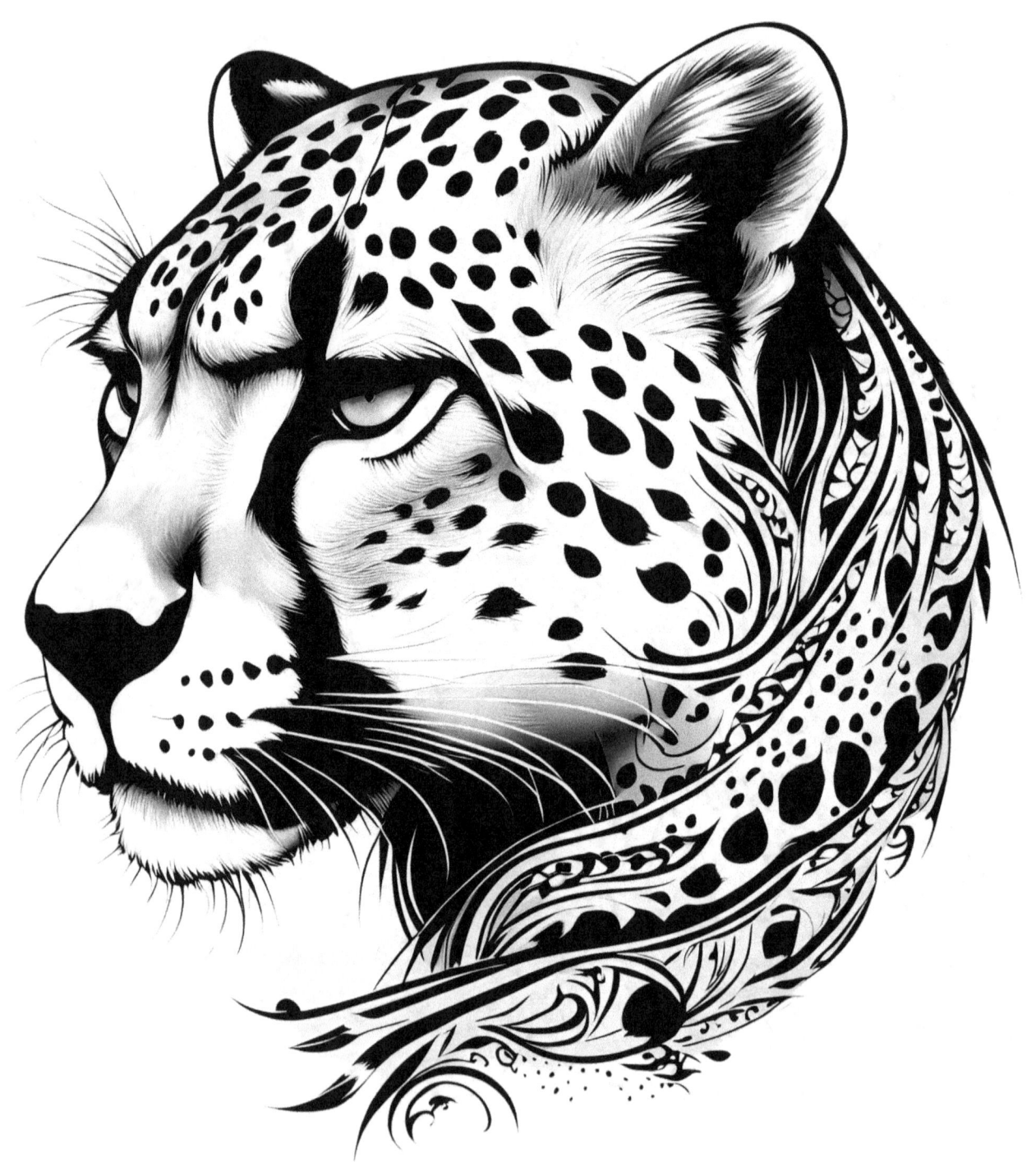

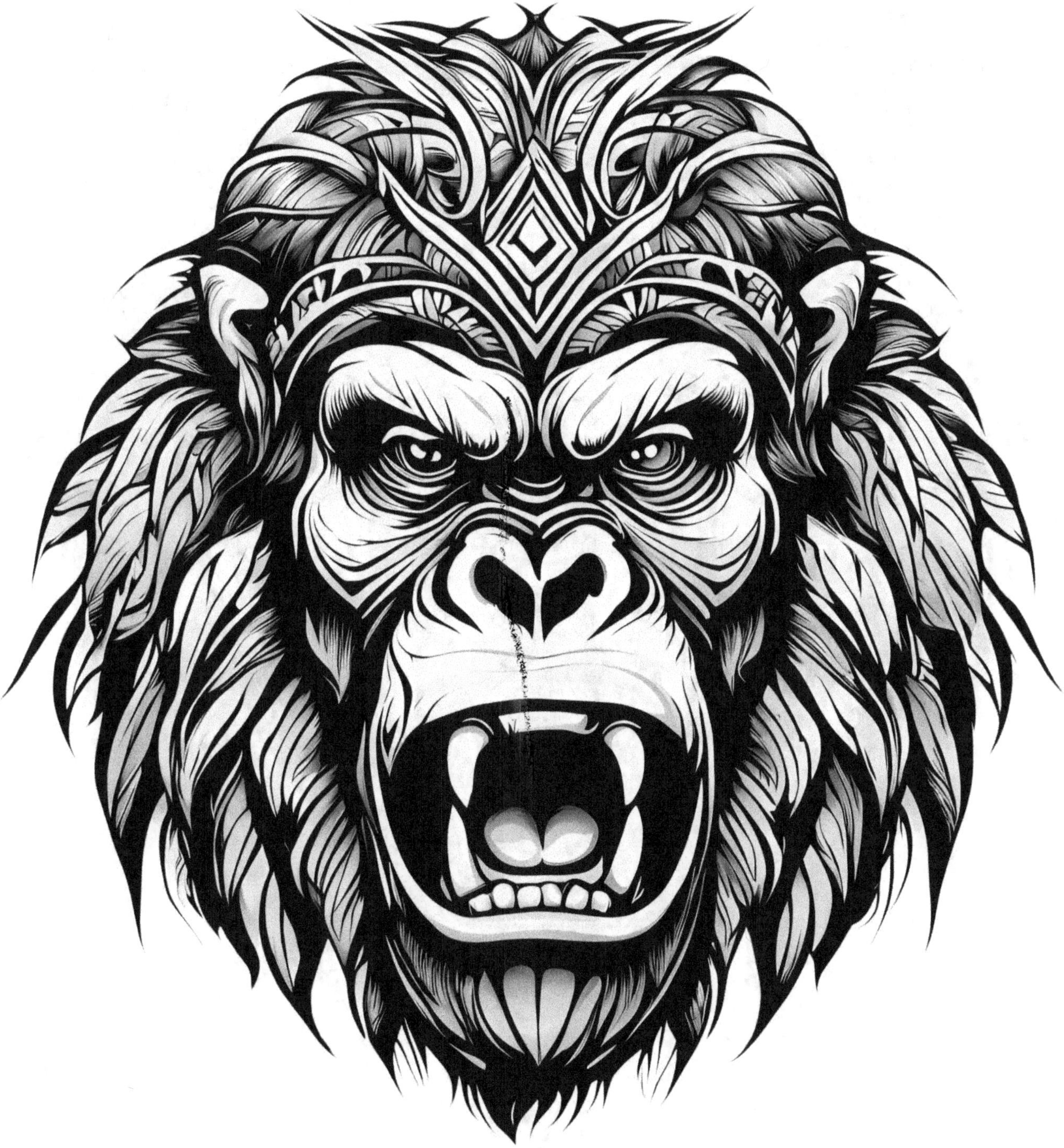

ANIMAL TATTOOS

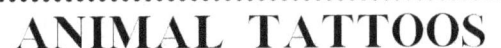

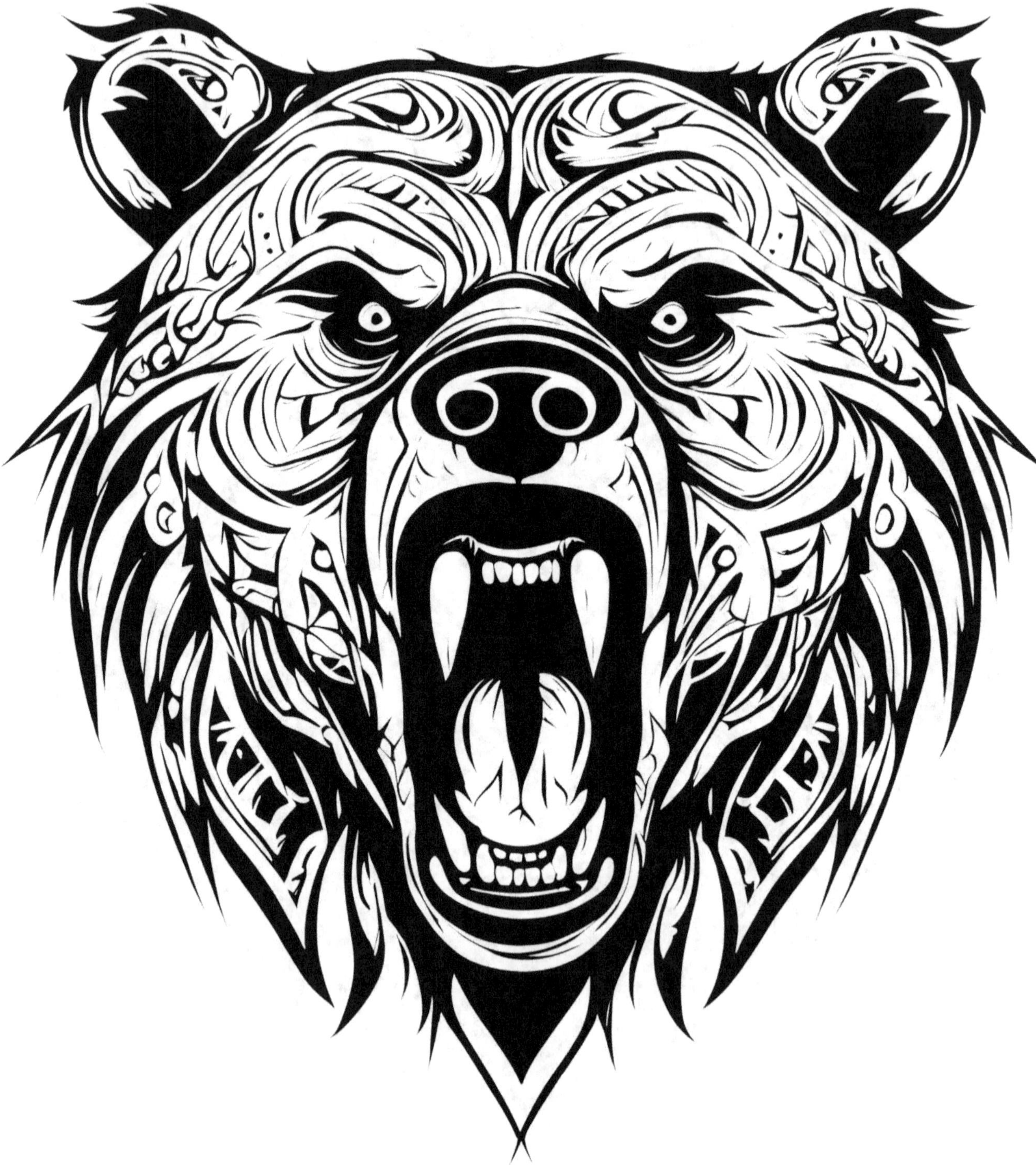

ANIMAL TATTOOS

DRAGON TATTOOS

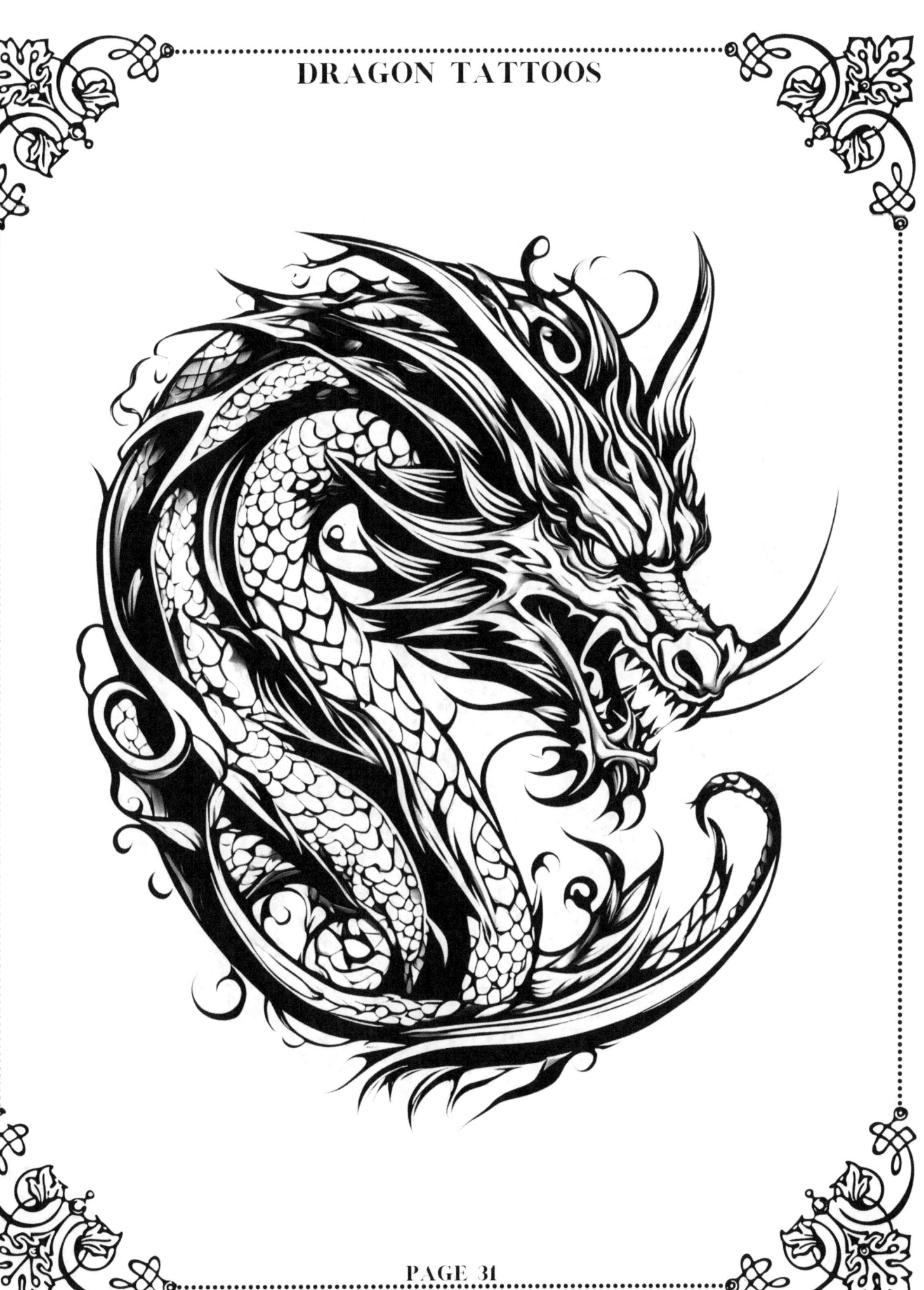

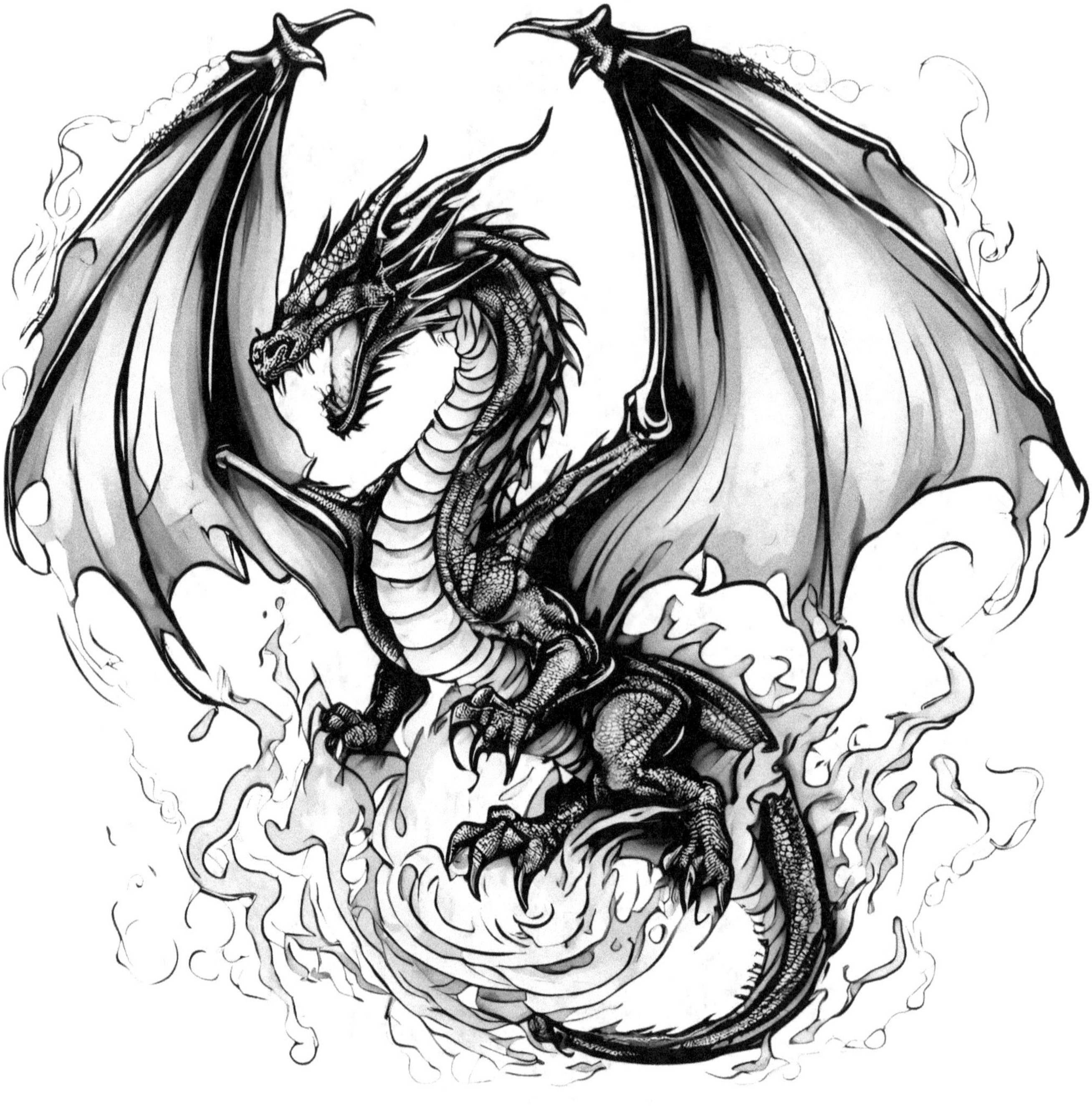

DRAGON TATTOOS

DRAGON TATTOOS

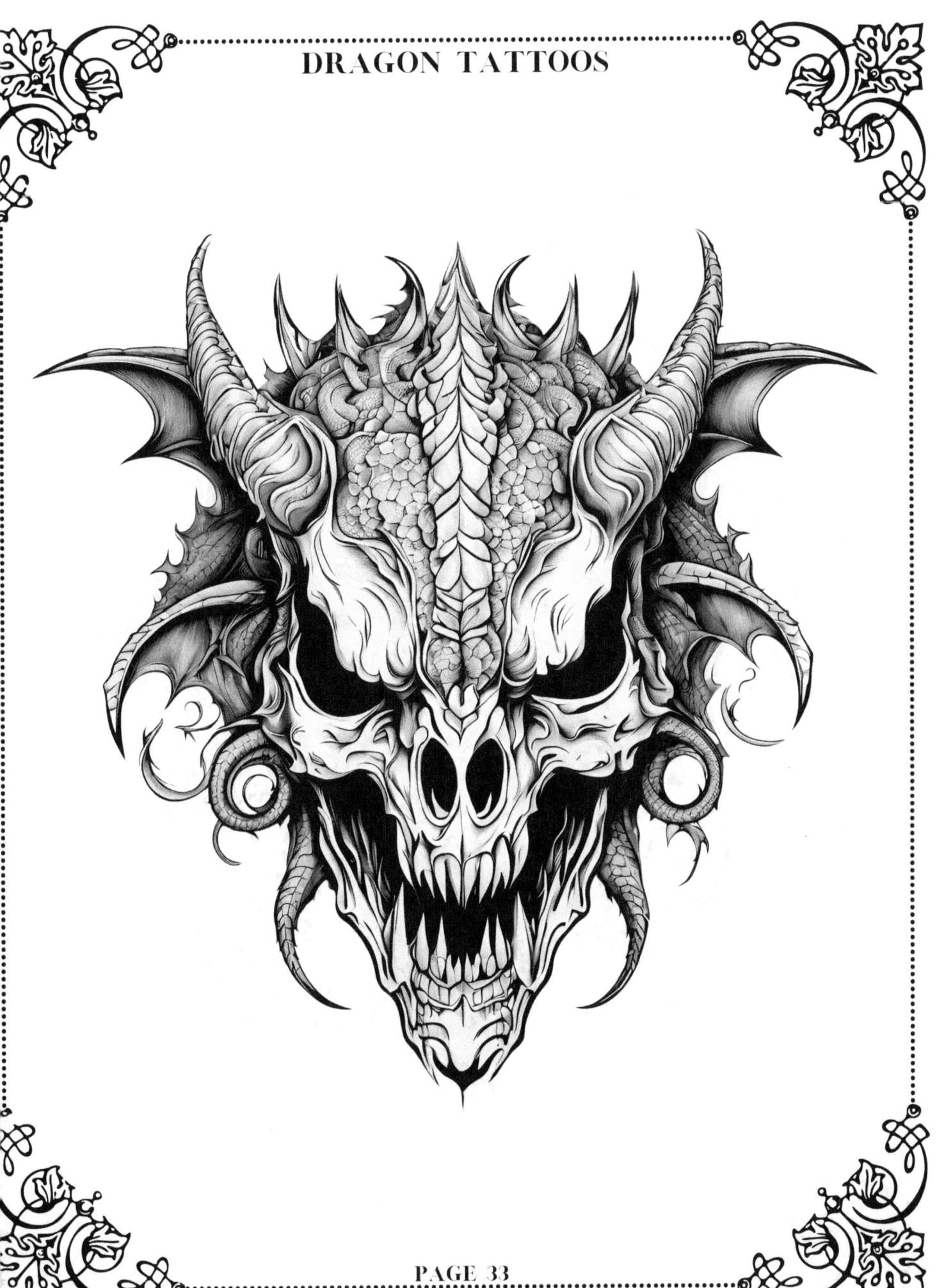

DRAGON TATTOOS

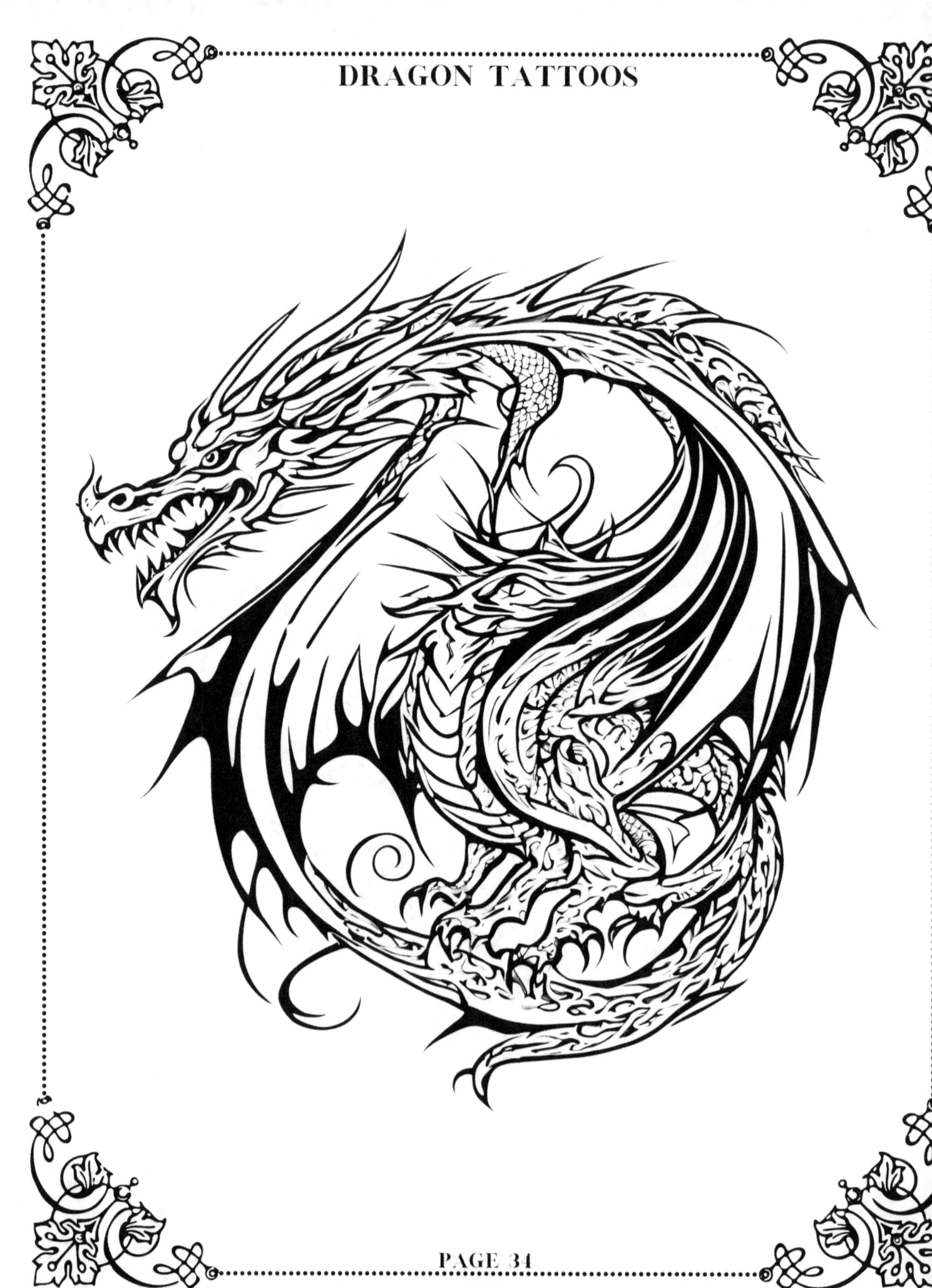

DRAGON TATTOOS

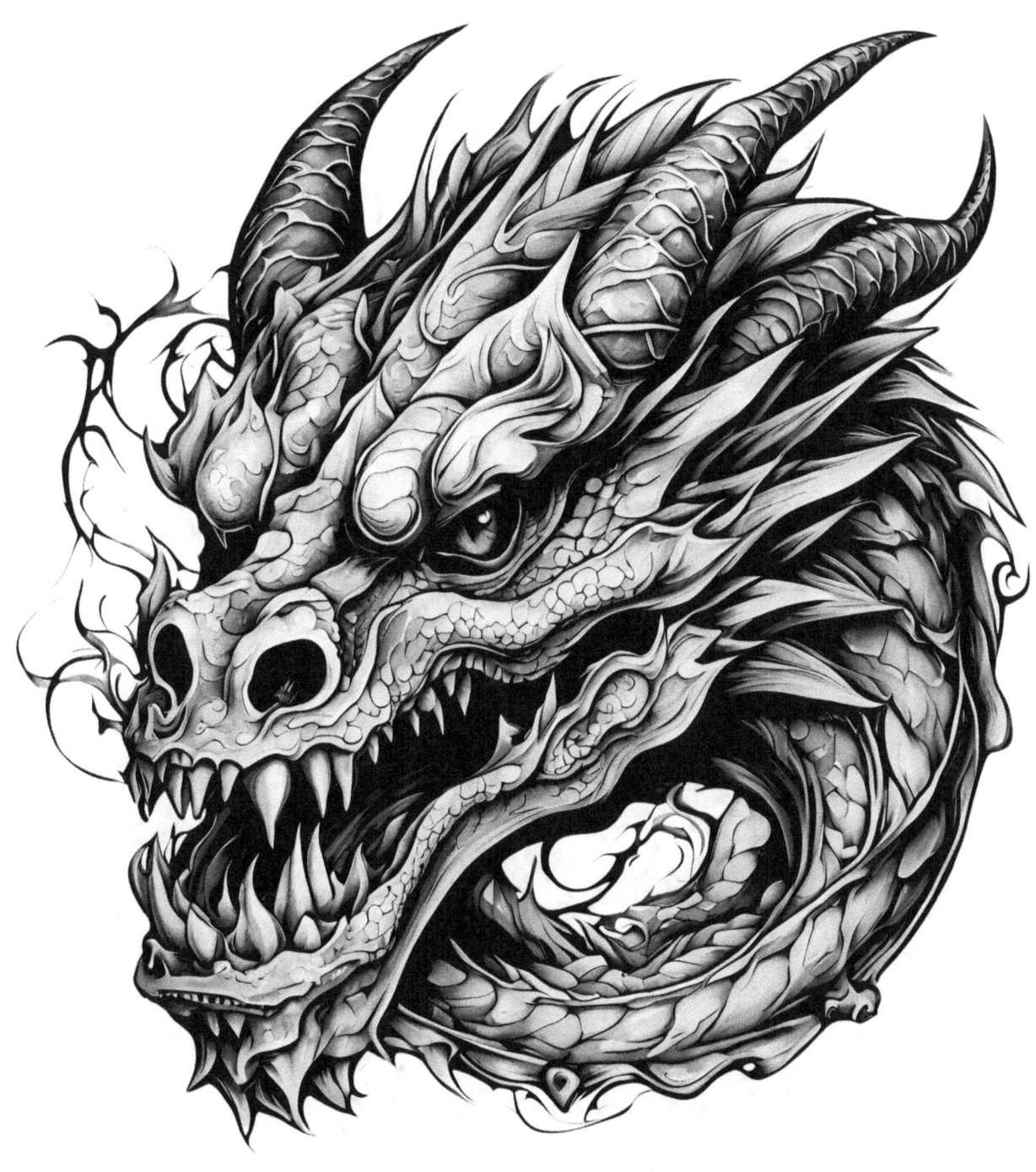

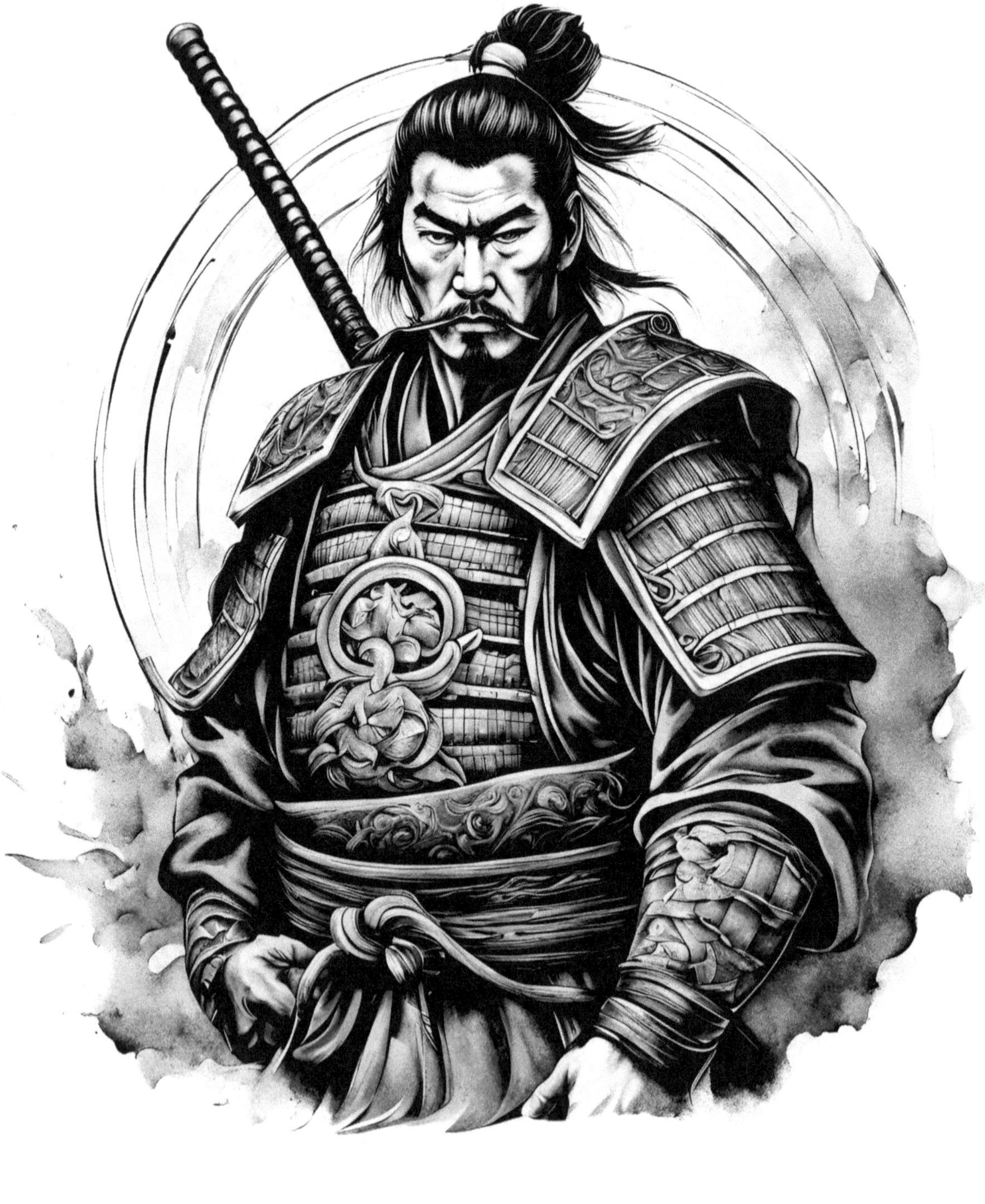

SAMURAI TATTOOS

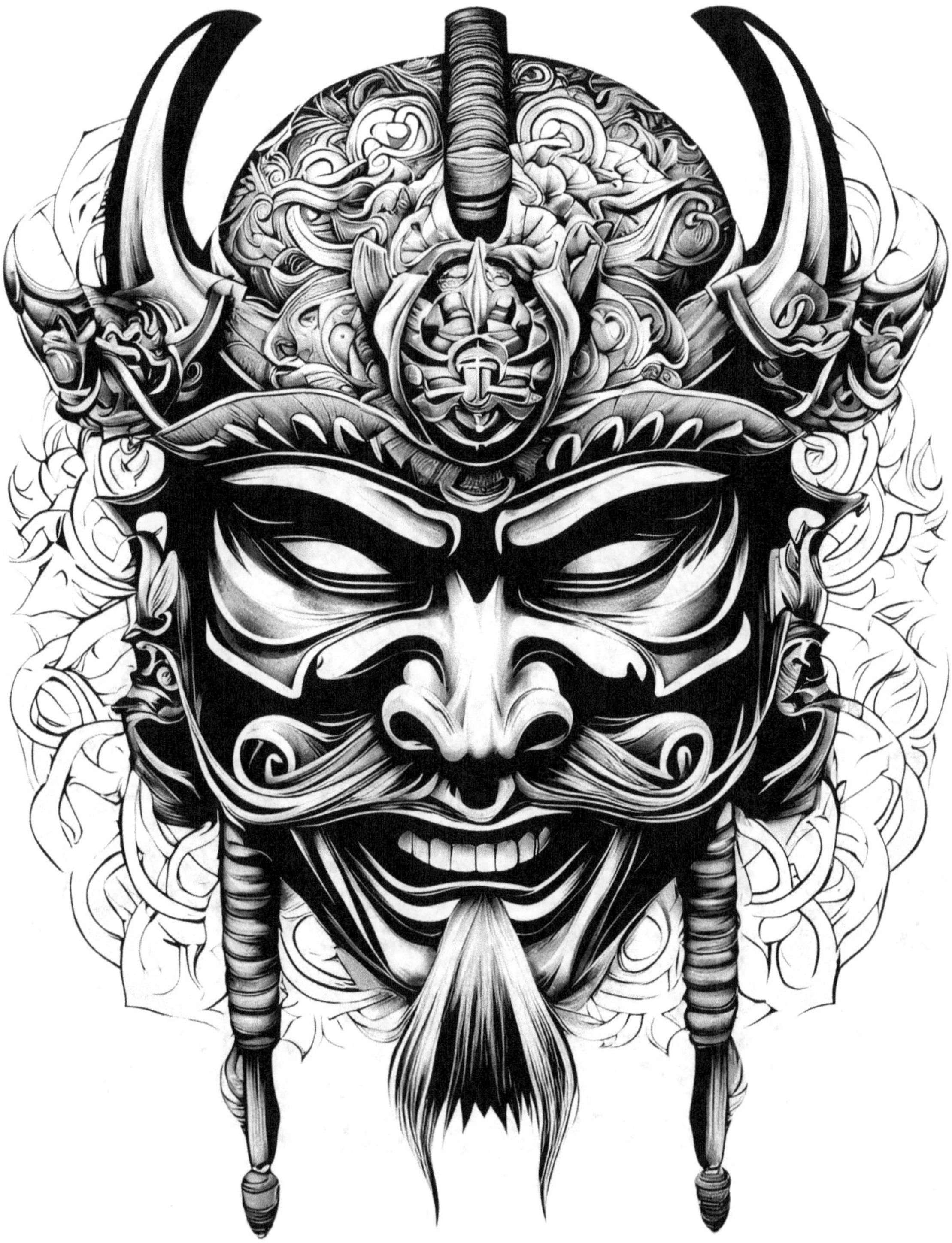

SAMURAI TATTOOS

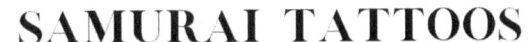

SAMURAI TATTOOS

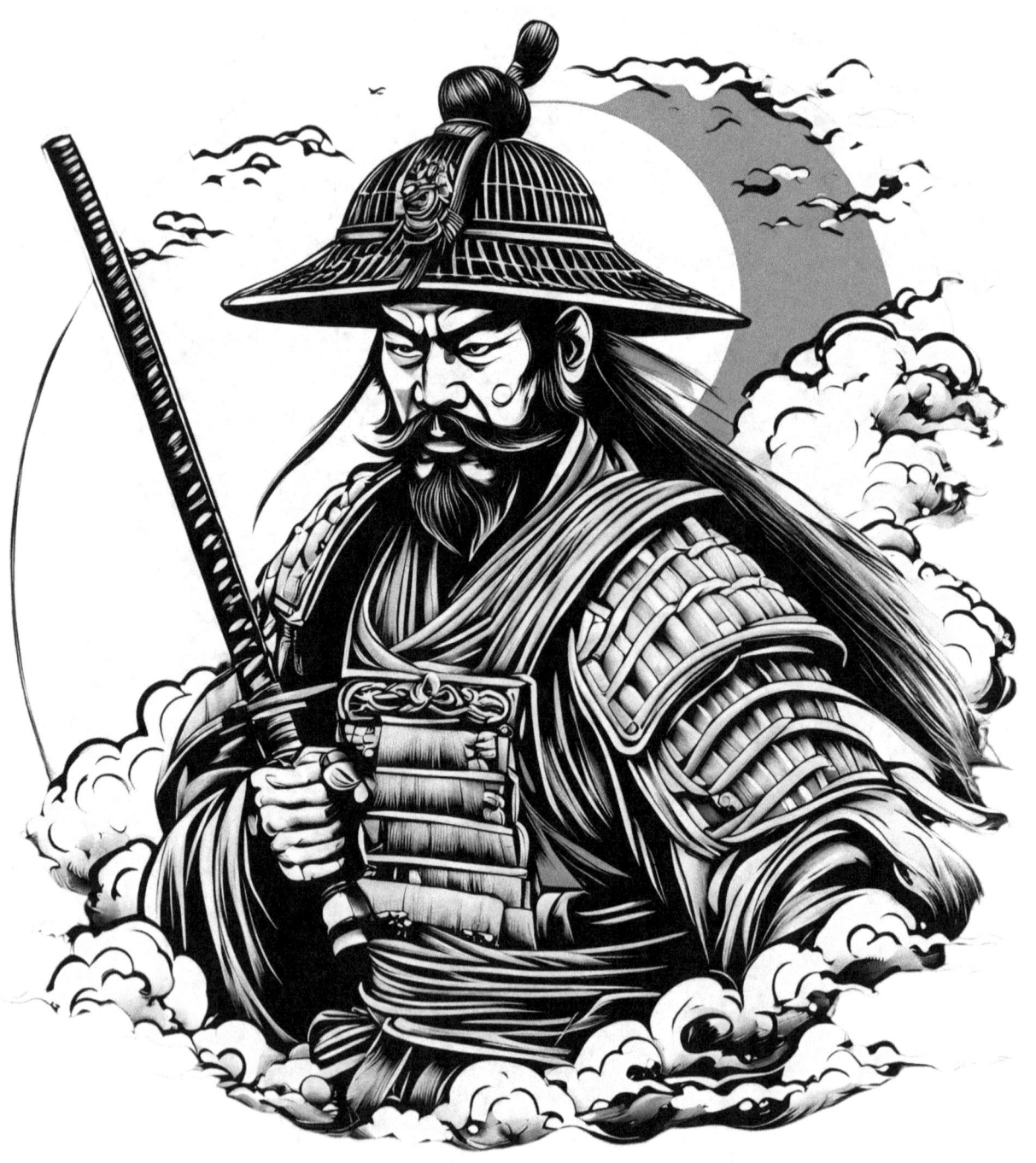

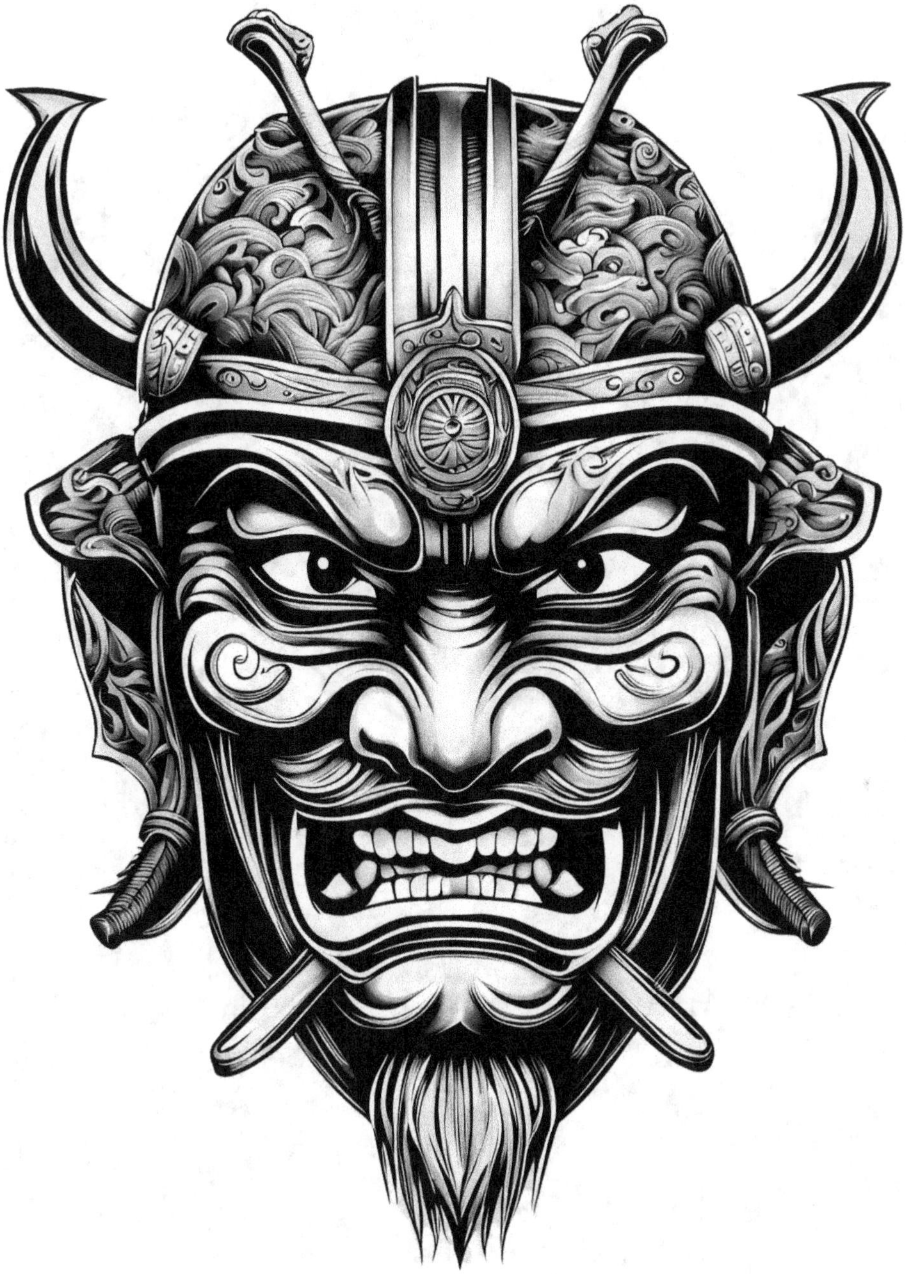

SAMURAI TATTOOS

SAMURAI TATTOOS

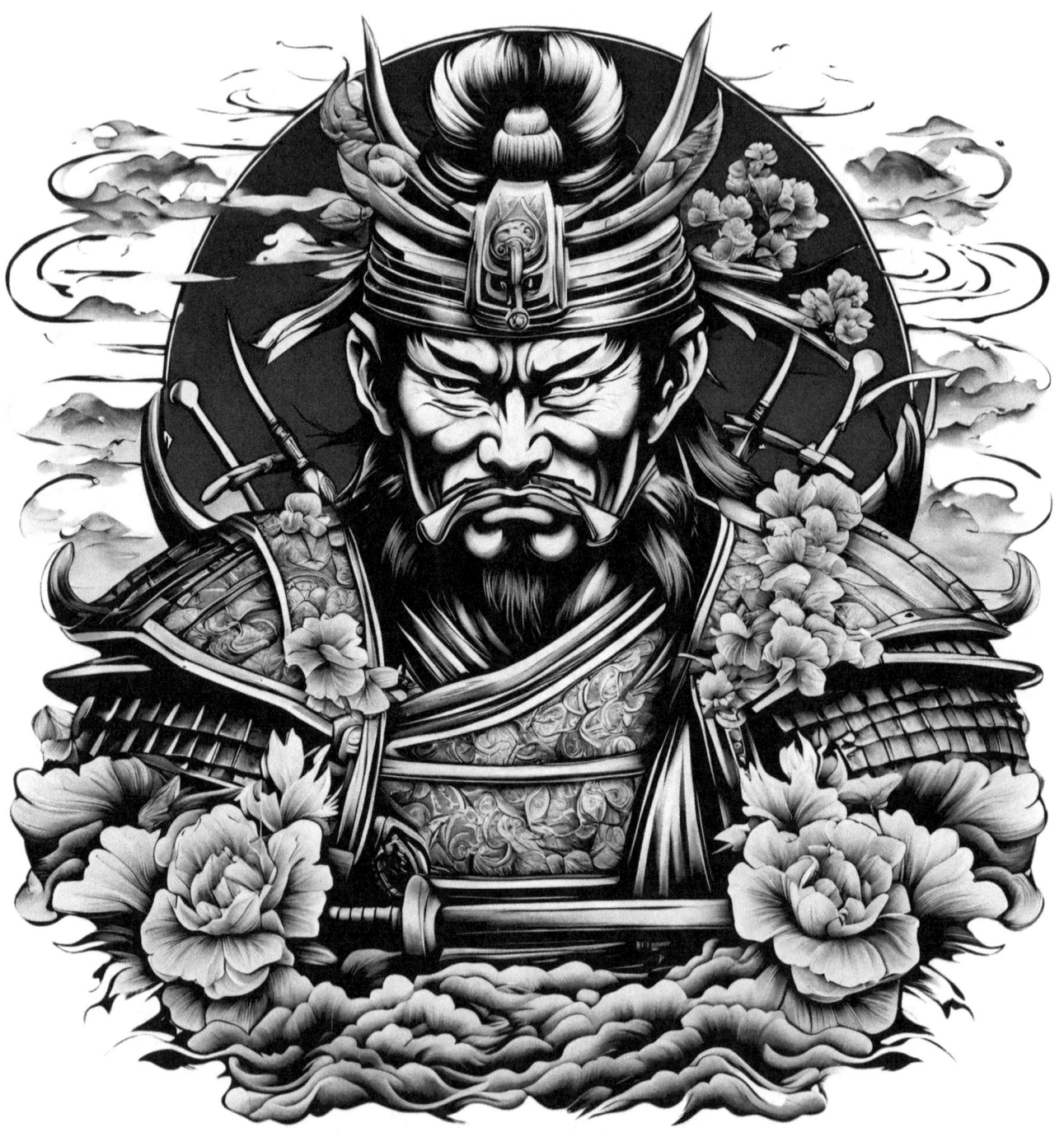

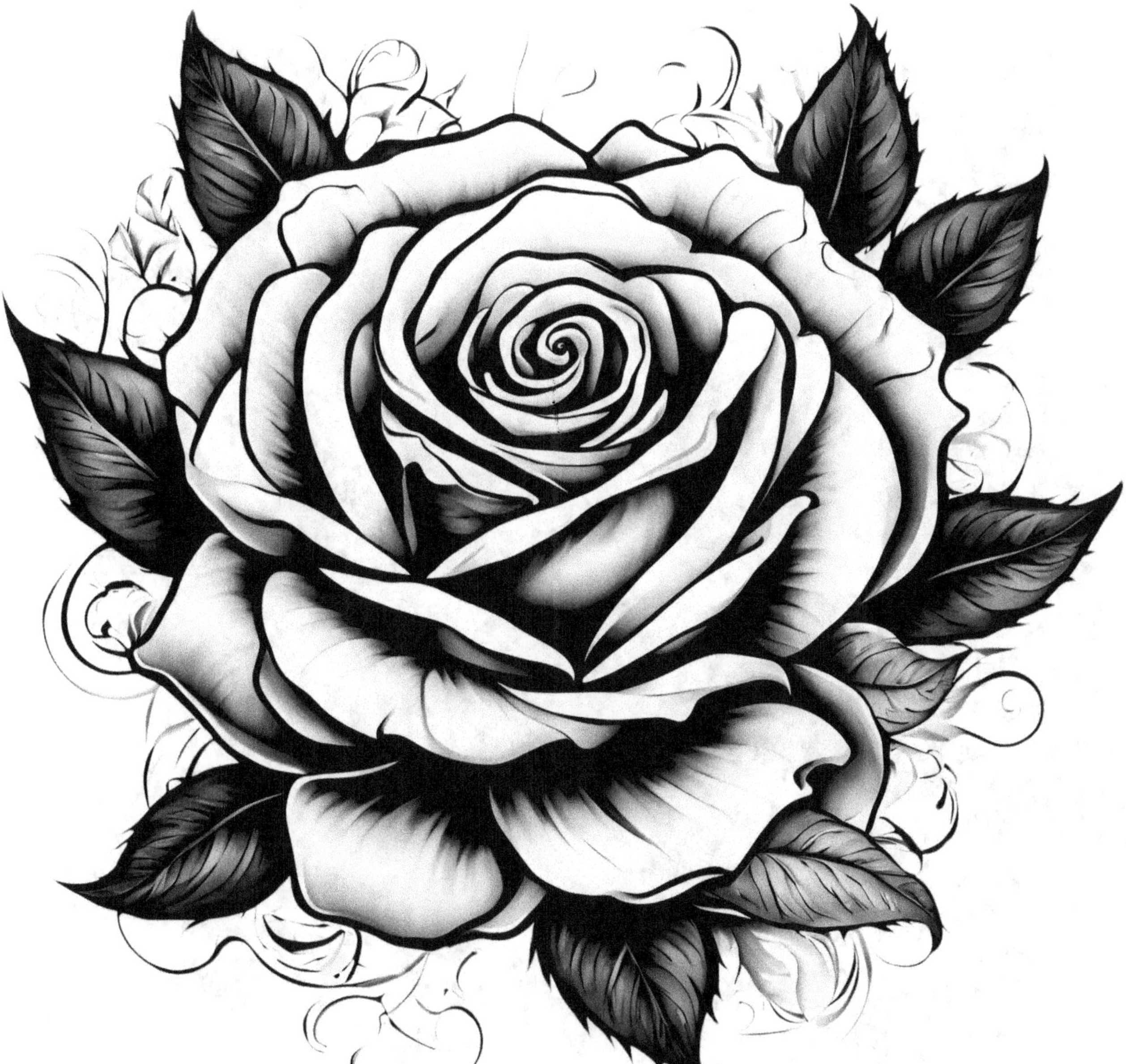

ROSE TATTOOS

ROSE TATTOOS

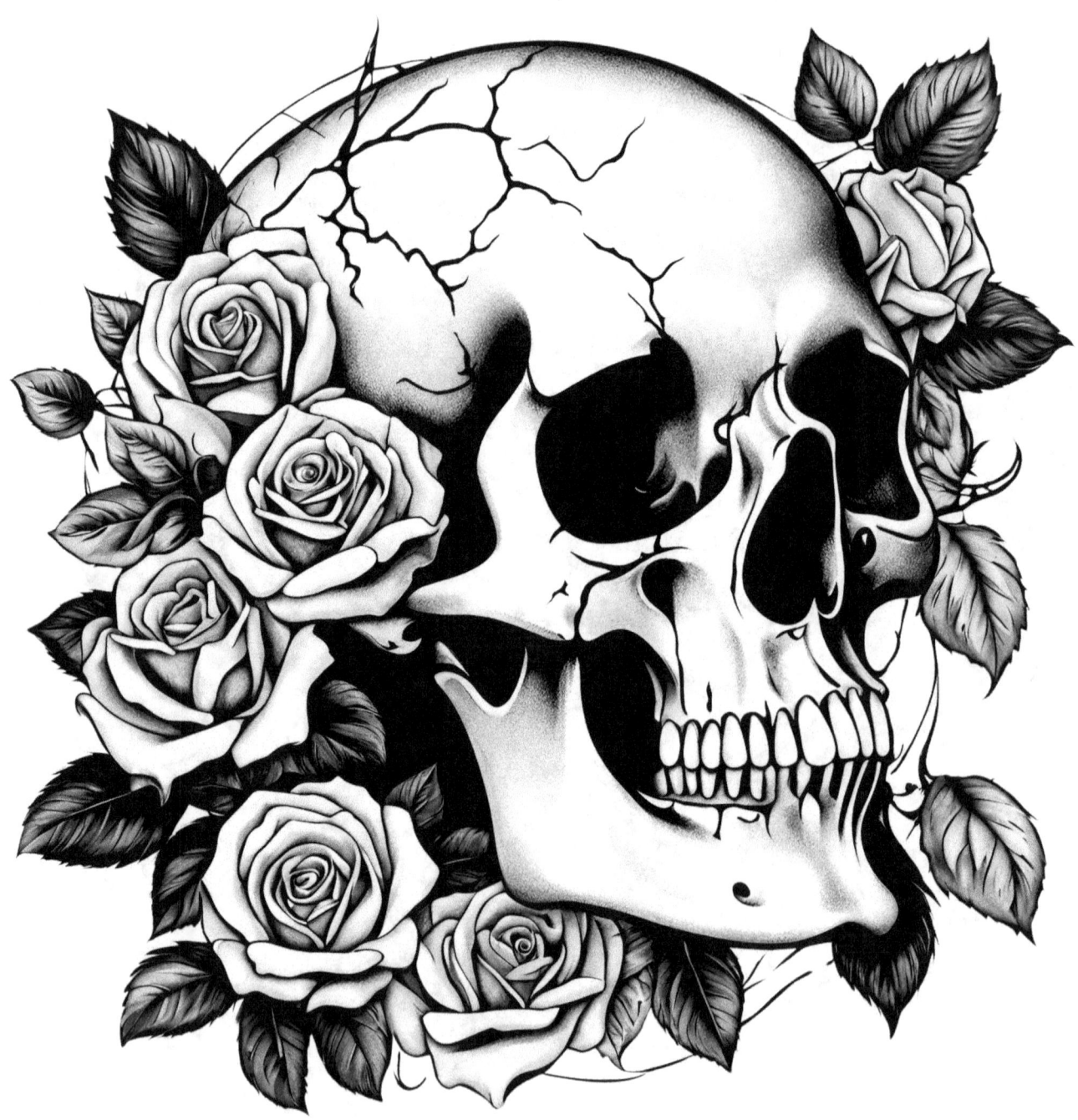

ROSE TATTOOS

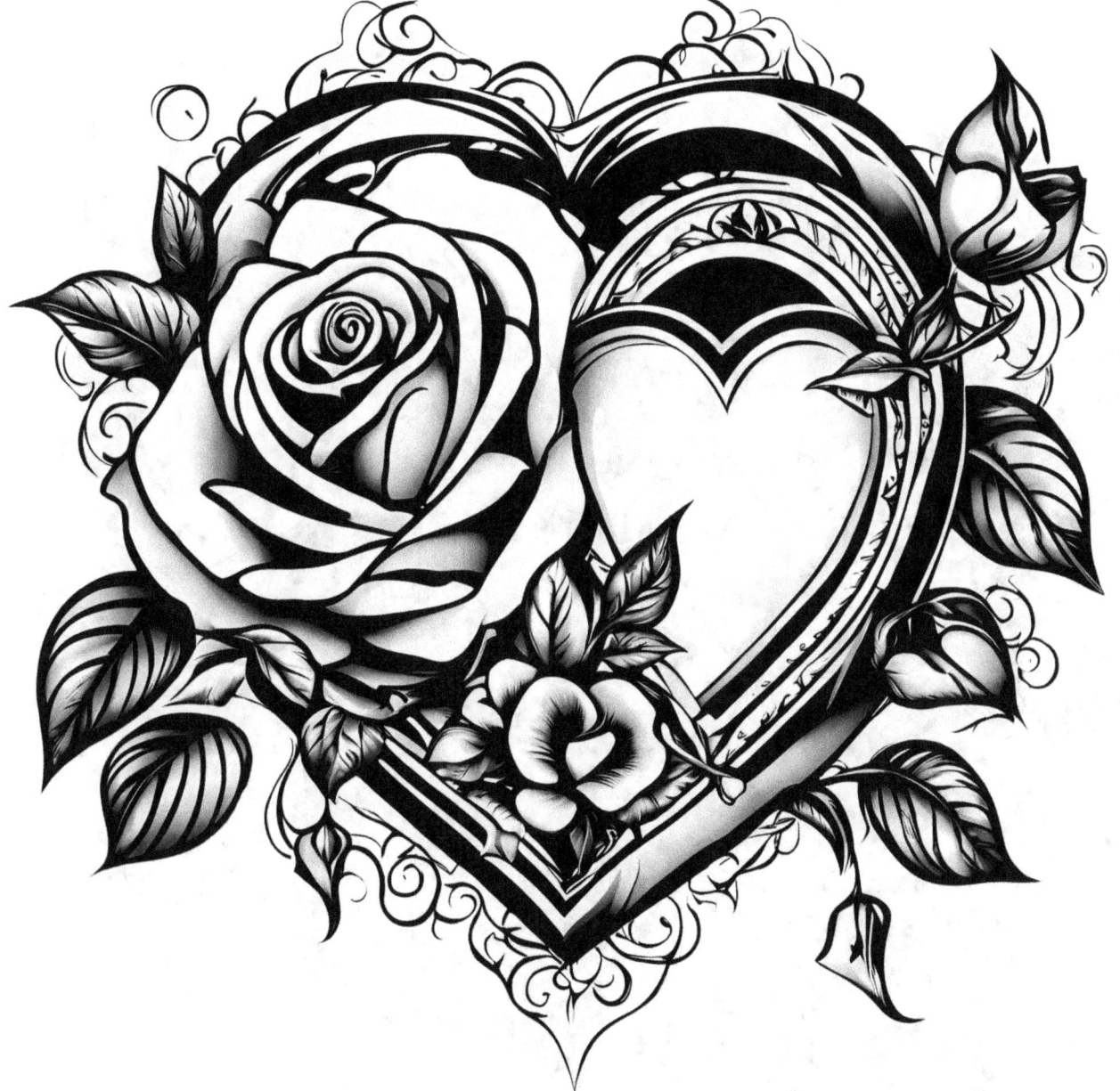

ROSE TATTOOS

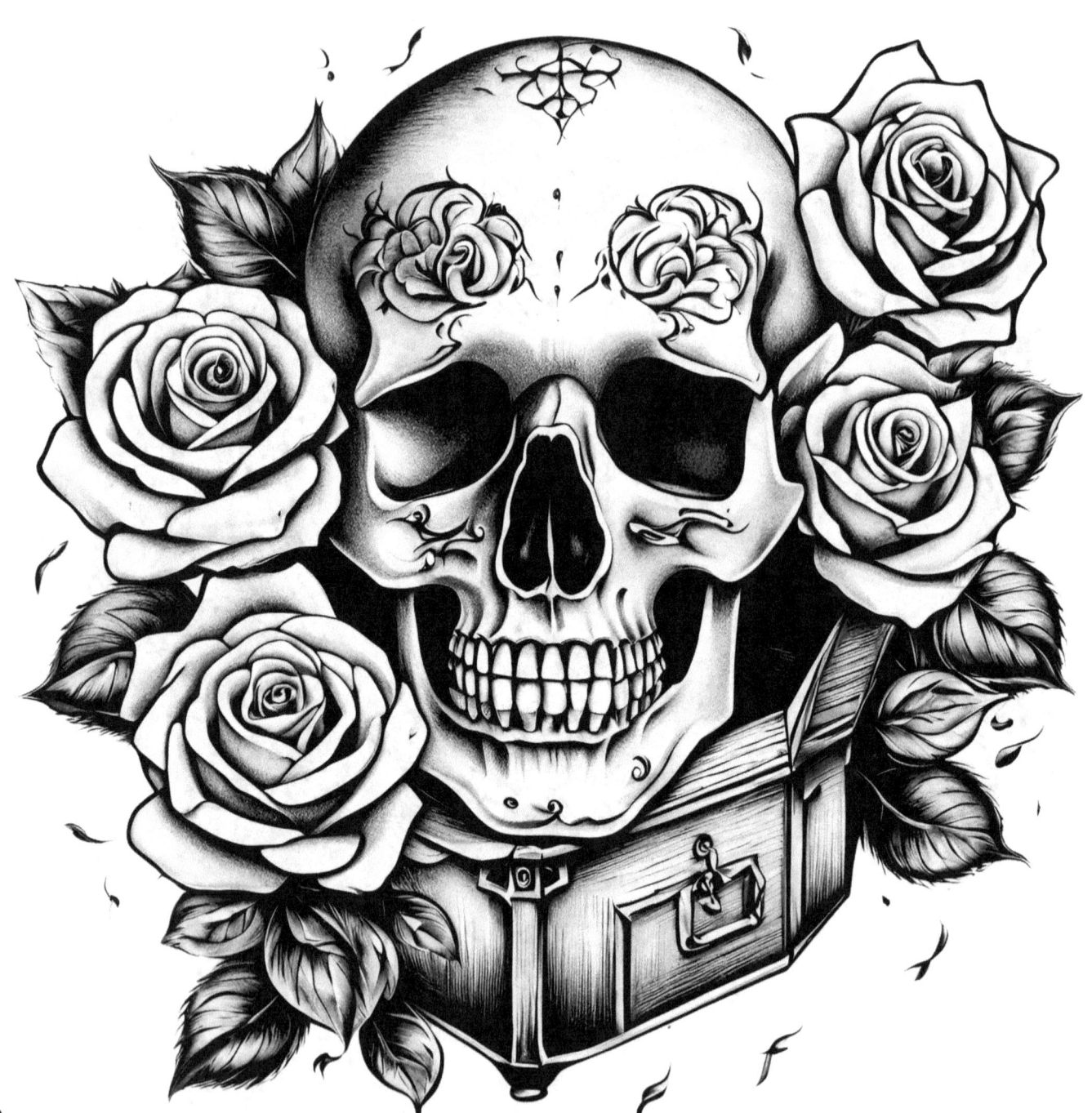

ROSE TATTOOS

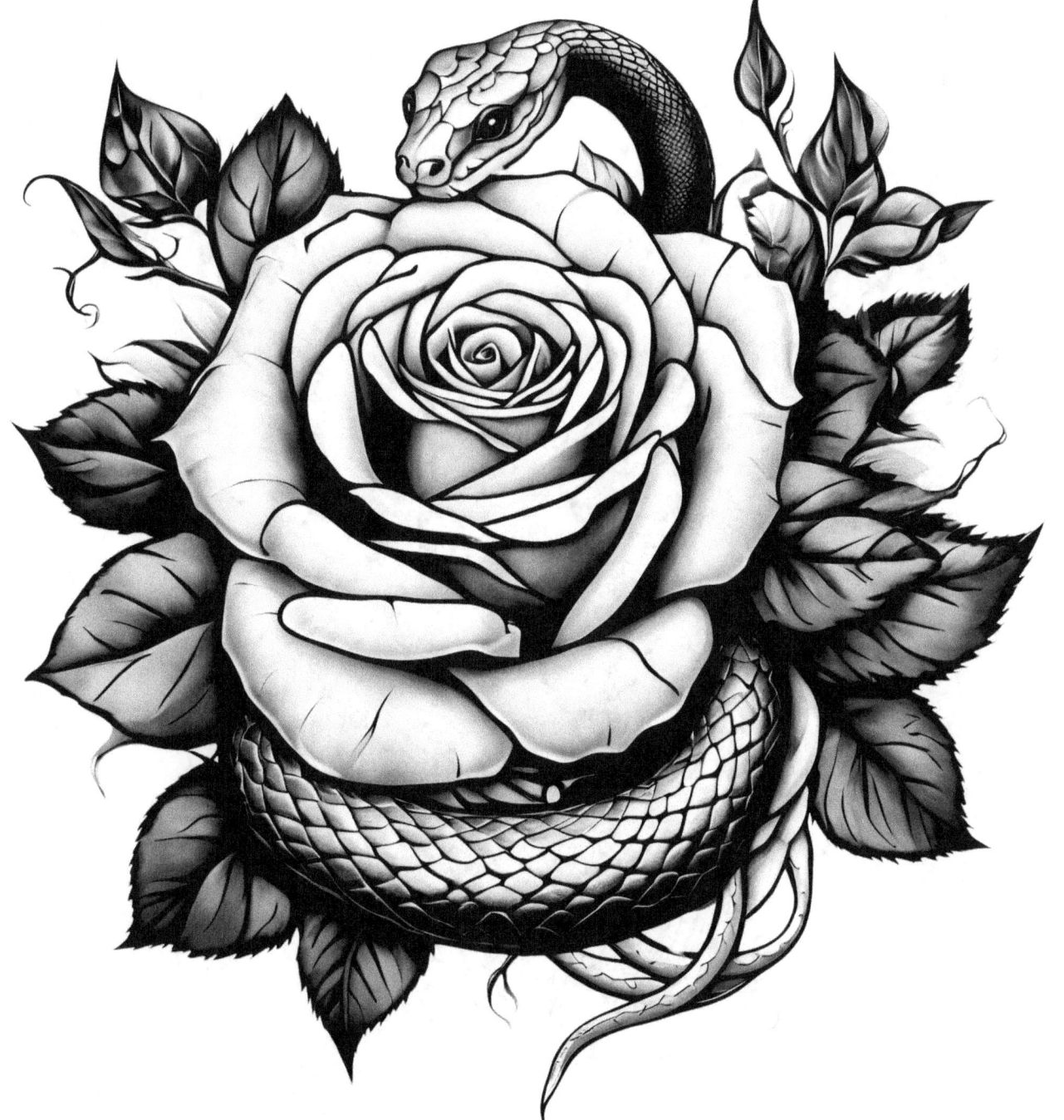

PAGE 43

ANGEL WINGS TATTOOS

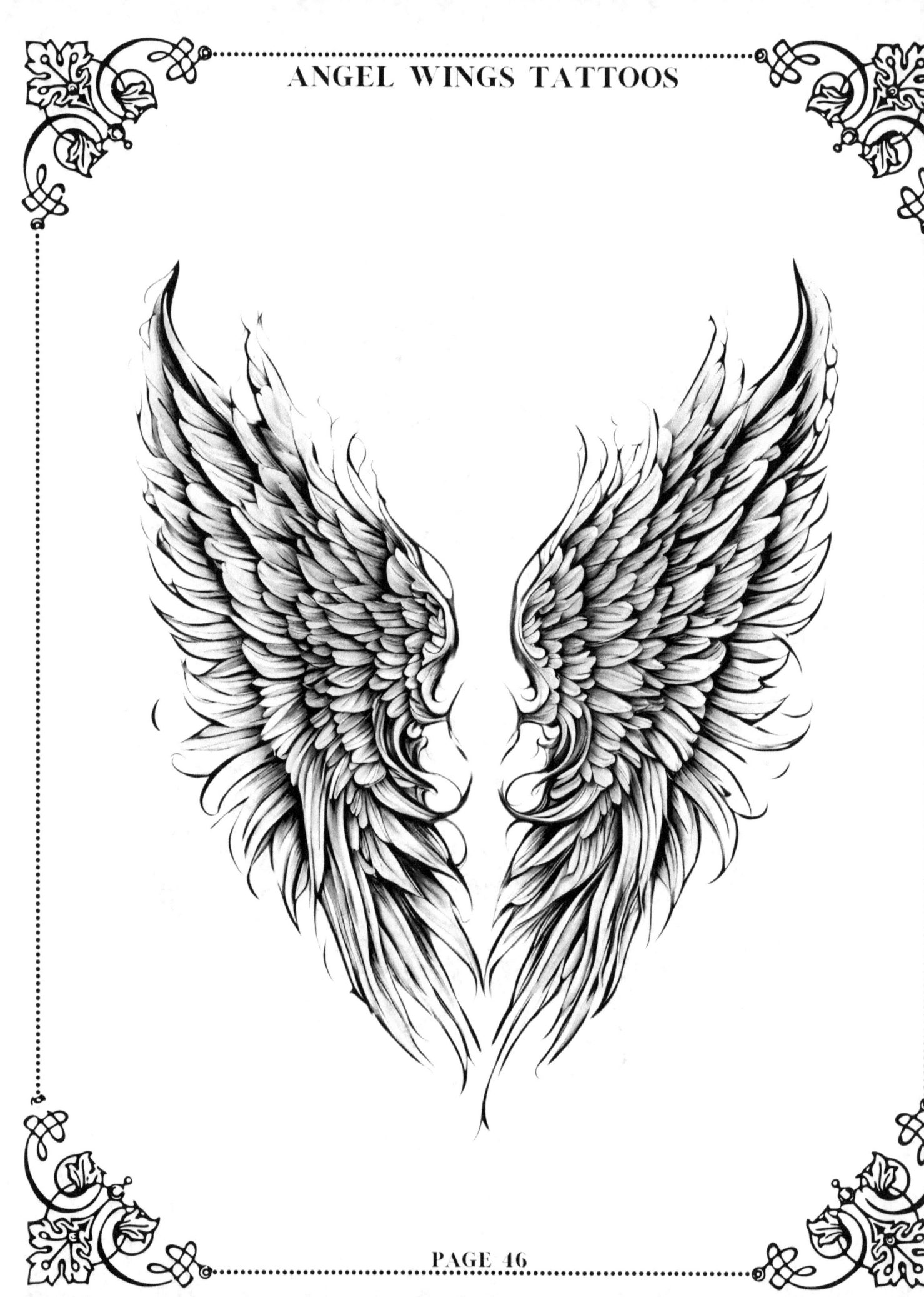

ANGEL WINGS TATTOOS

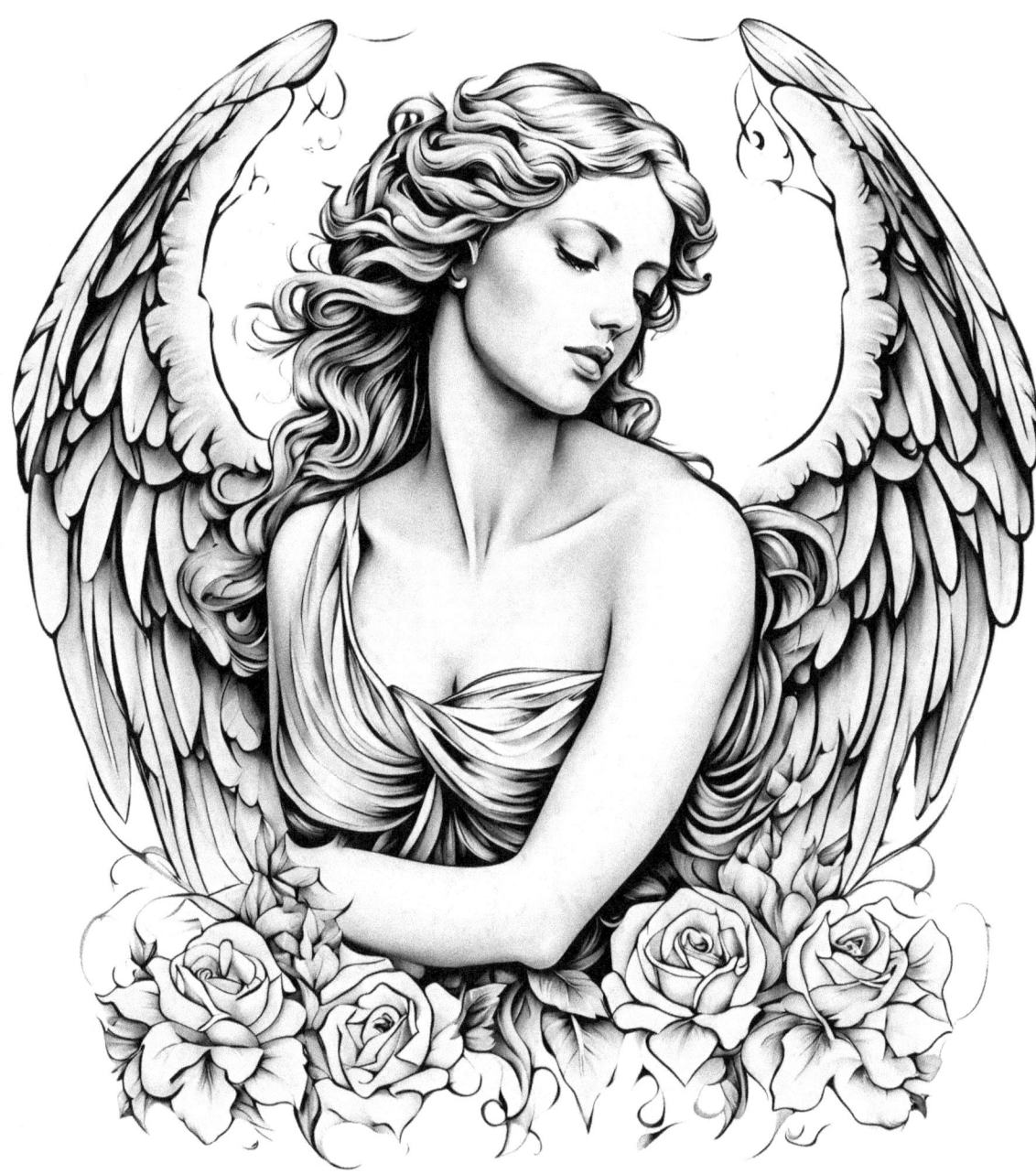

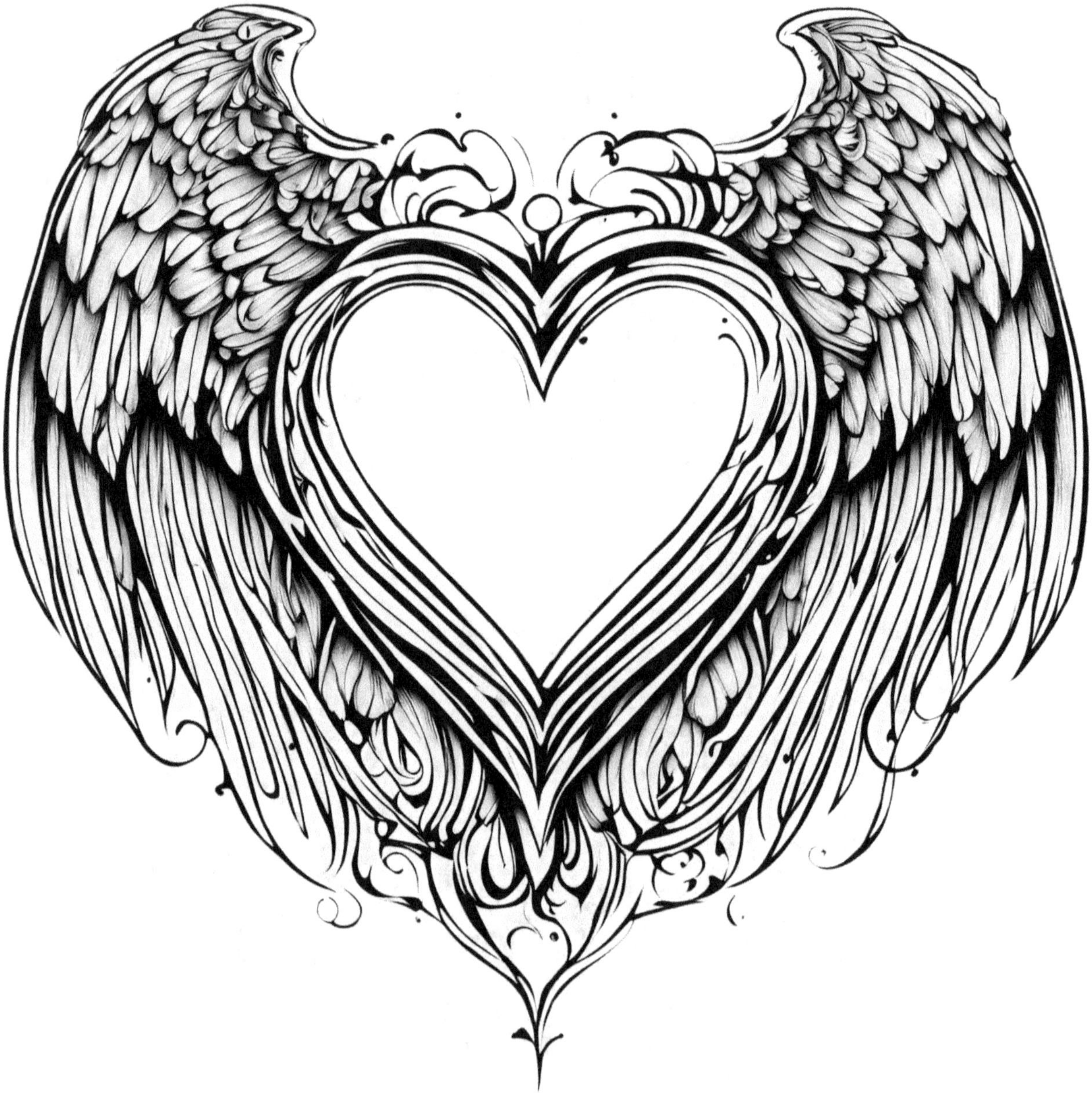

ANGEL WINGS TATTOOS

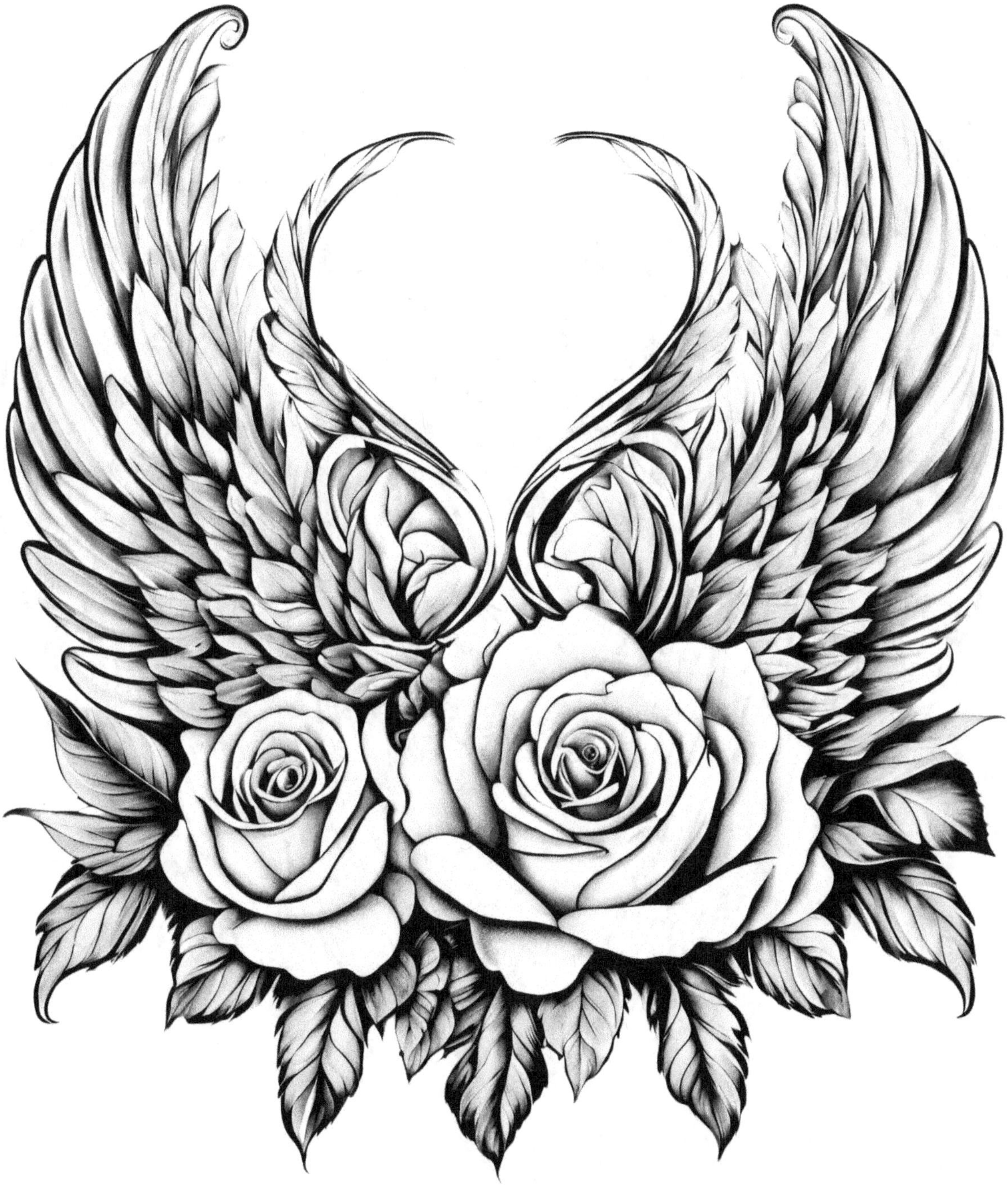

ANGEL WINGS TATTOOS

ANGEL WINGS TATTOOS

LANDSCAPE TATTOOS

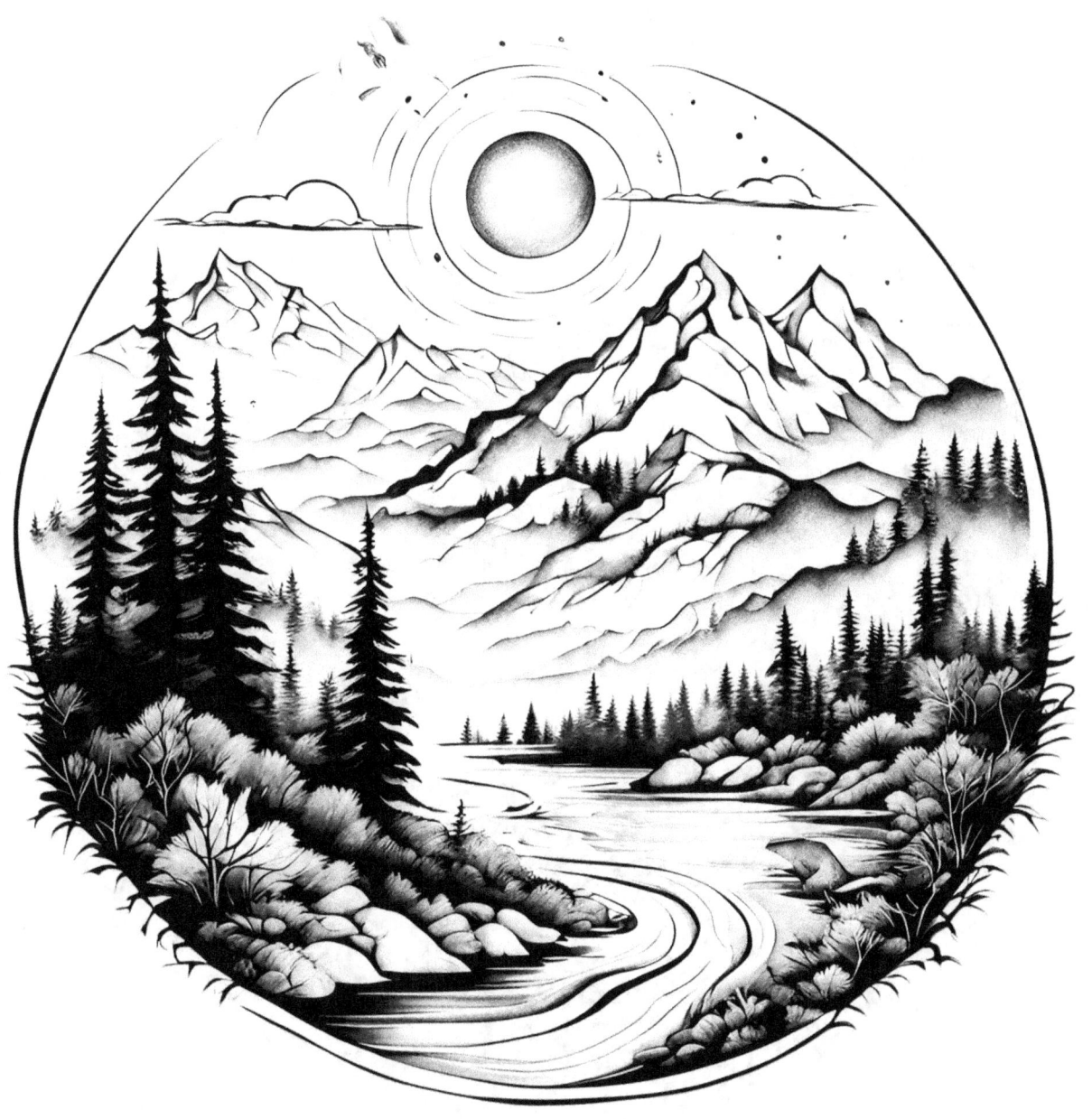

PAGE 51

LANDSCAPE TATTOOS

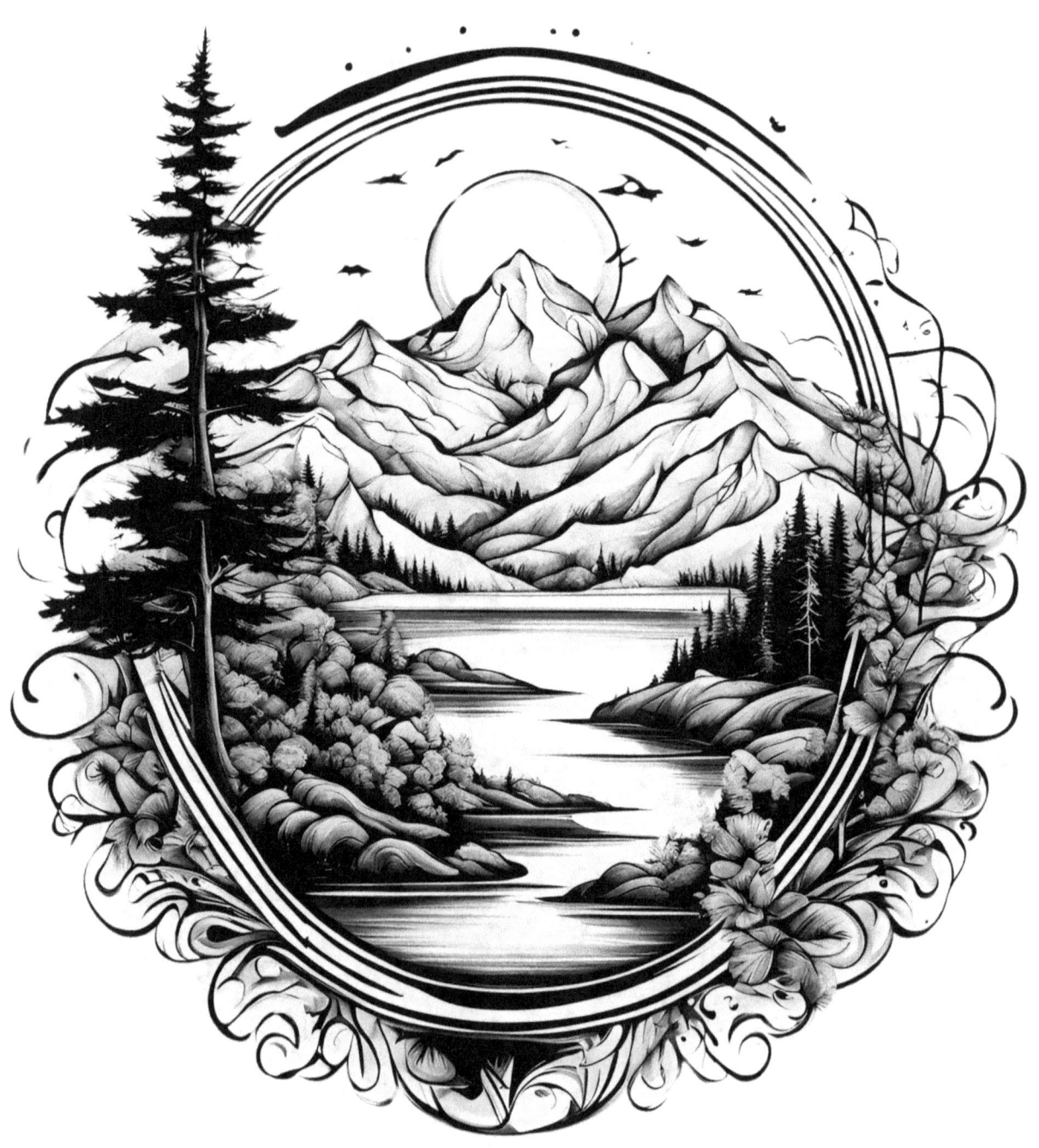

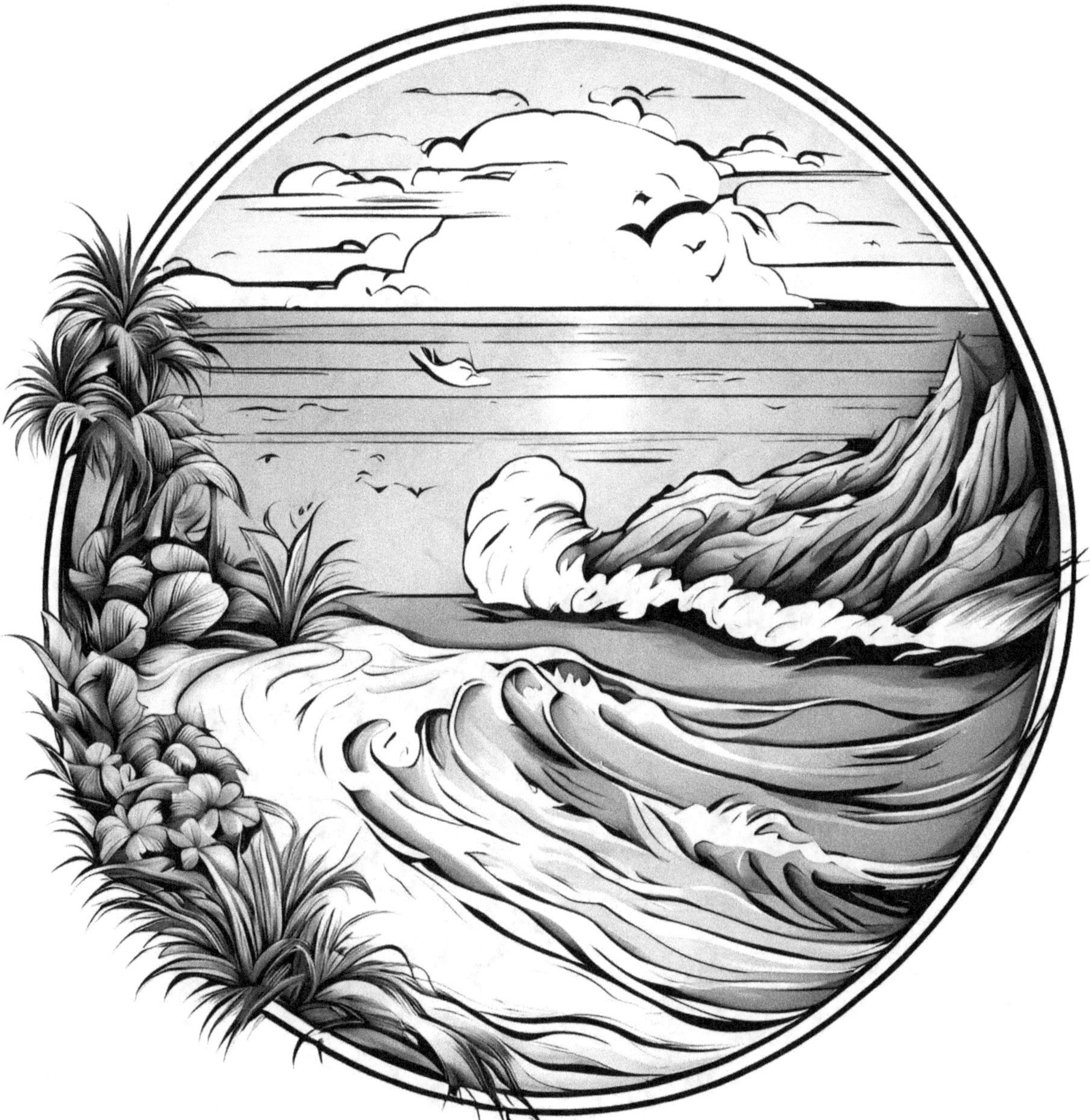

LANDSCAPE TATTOOS

PAGE 53

LANDSCAPE TATTOOS

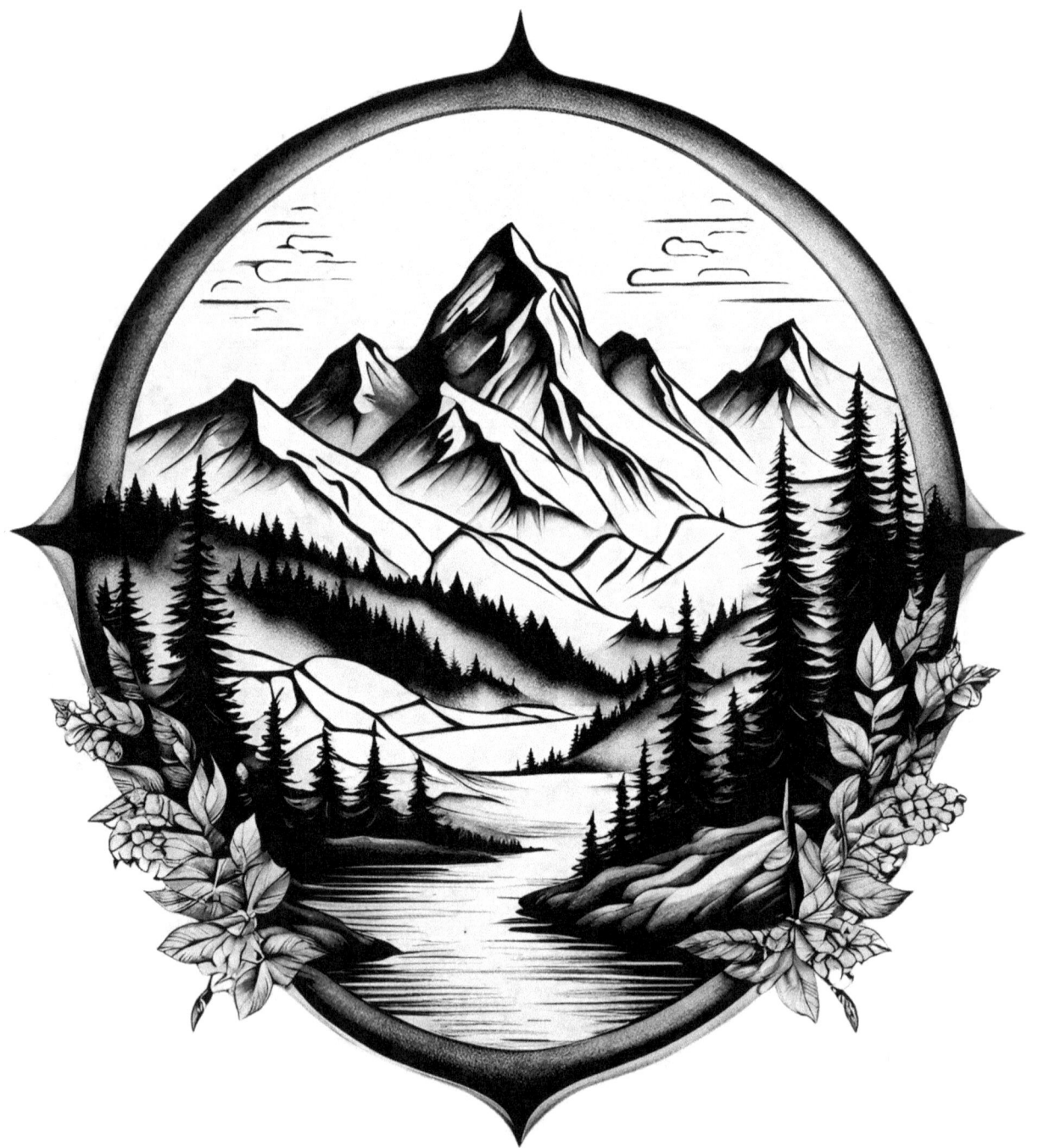

LANDSCAPE TATTOOS

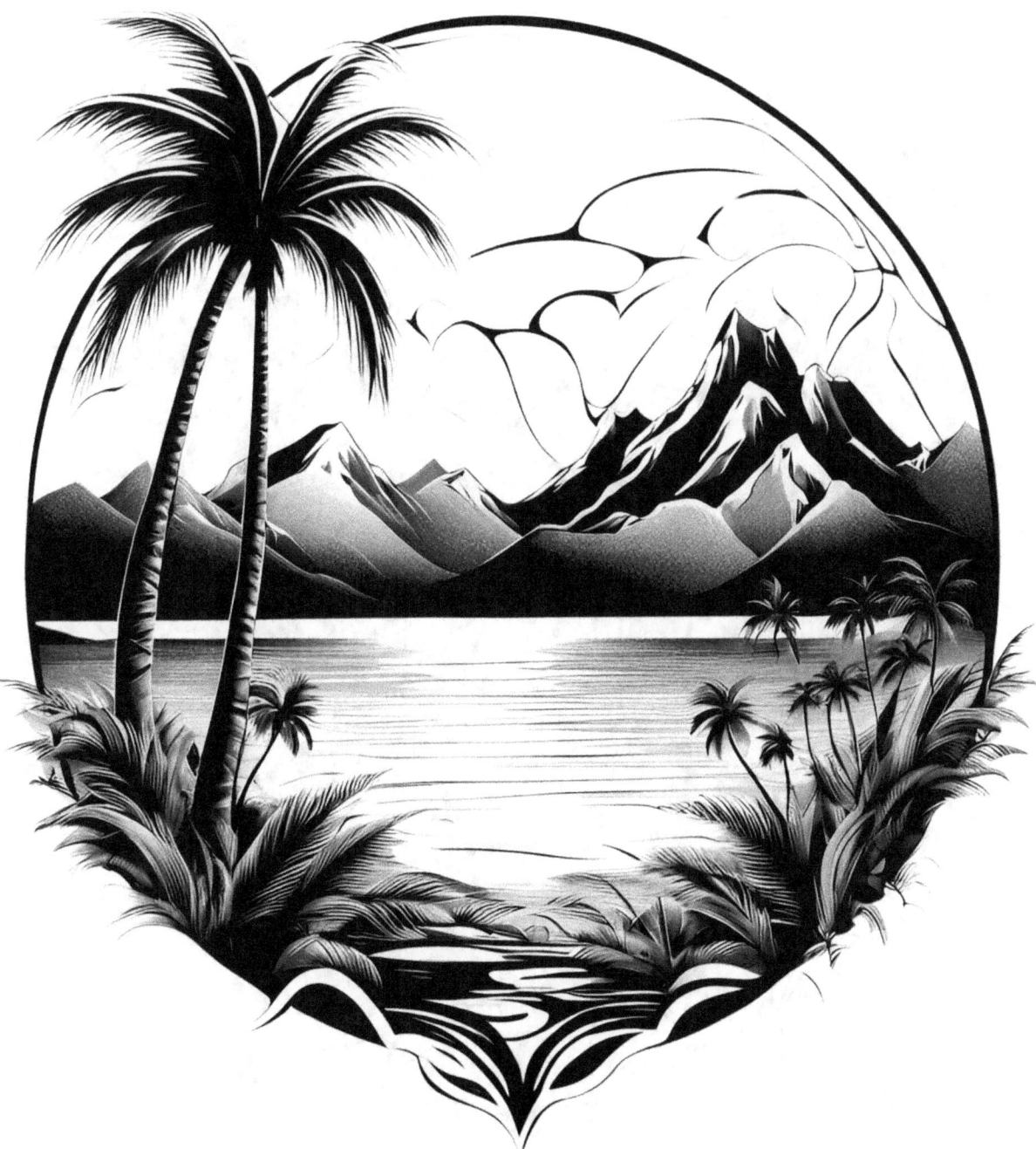

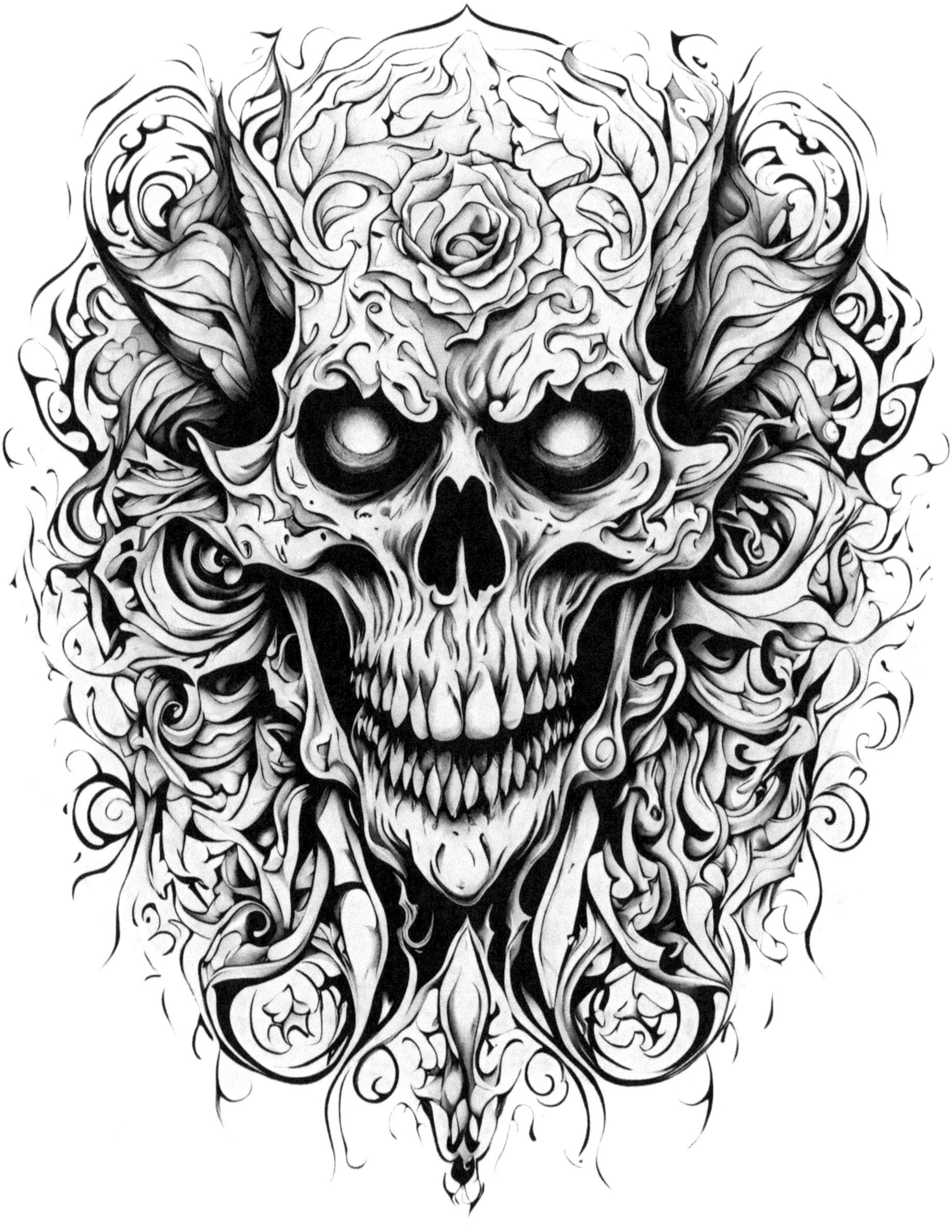

SCARY TATTOOS

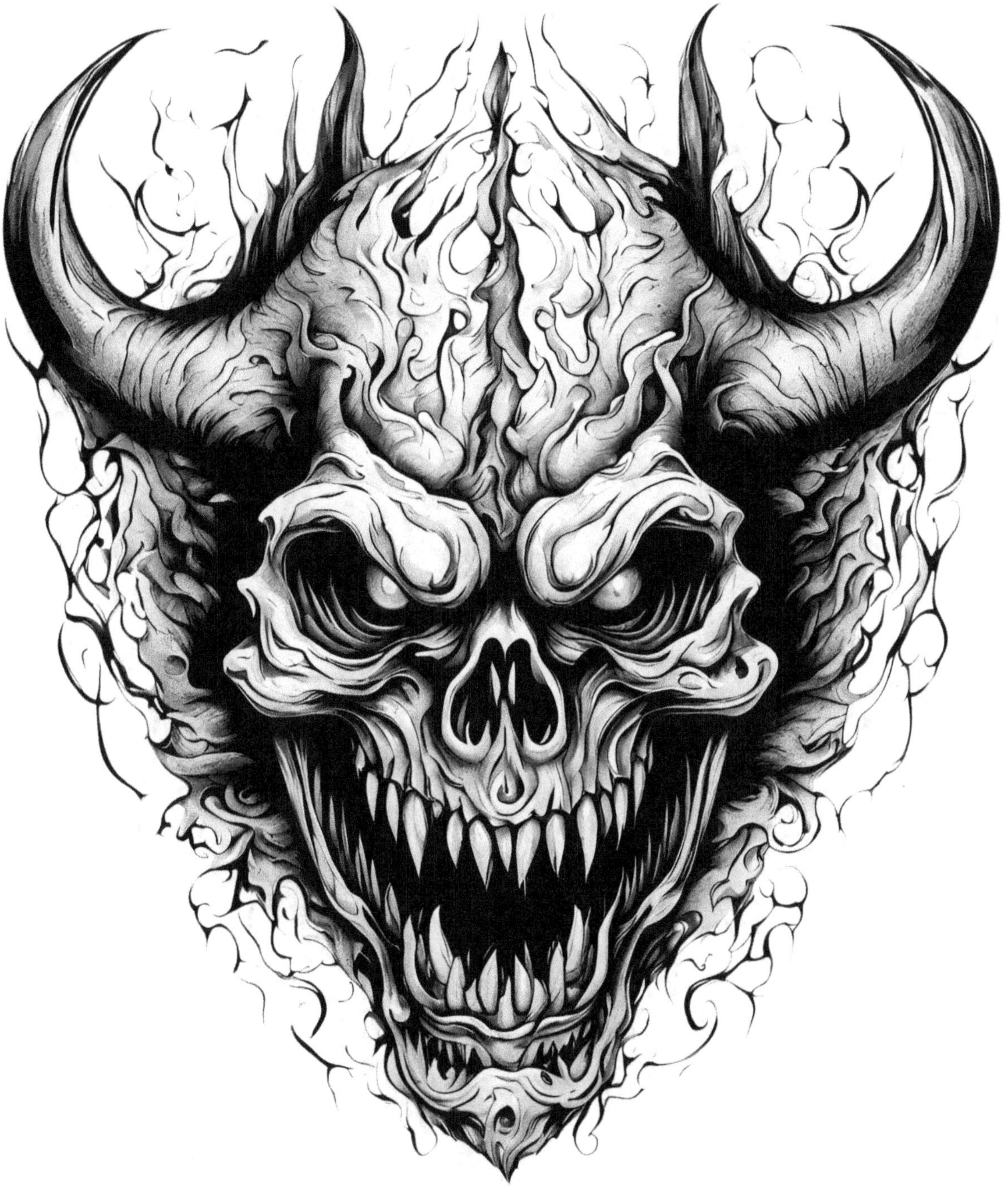

SCARY TATTOOS

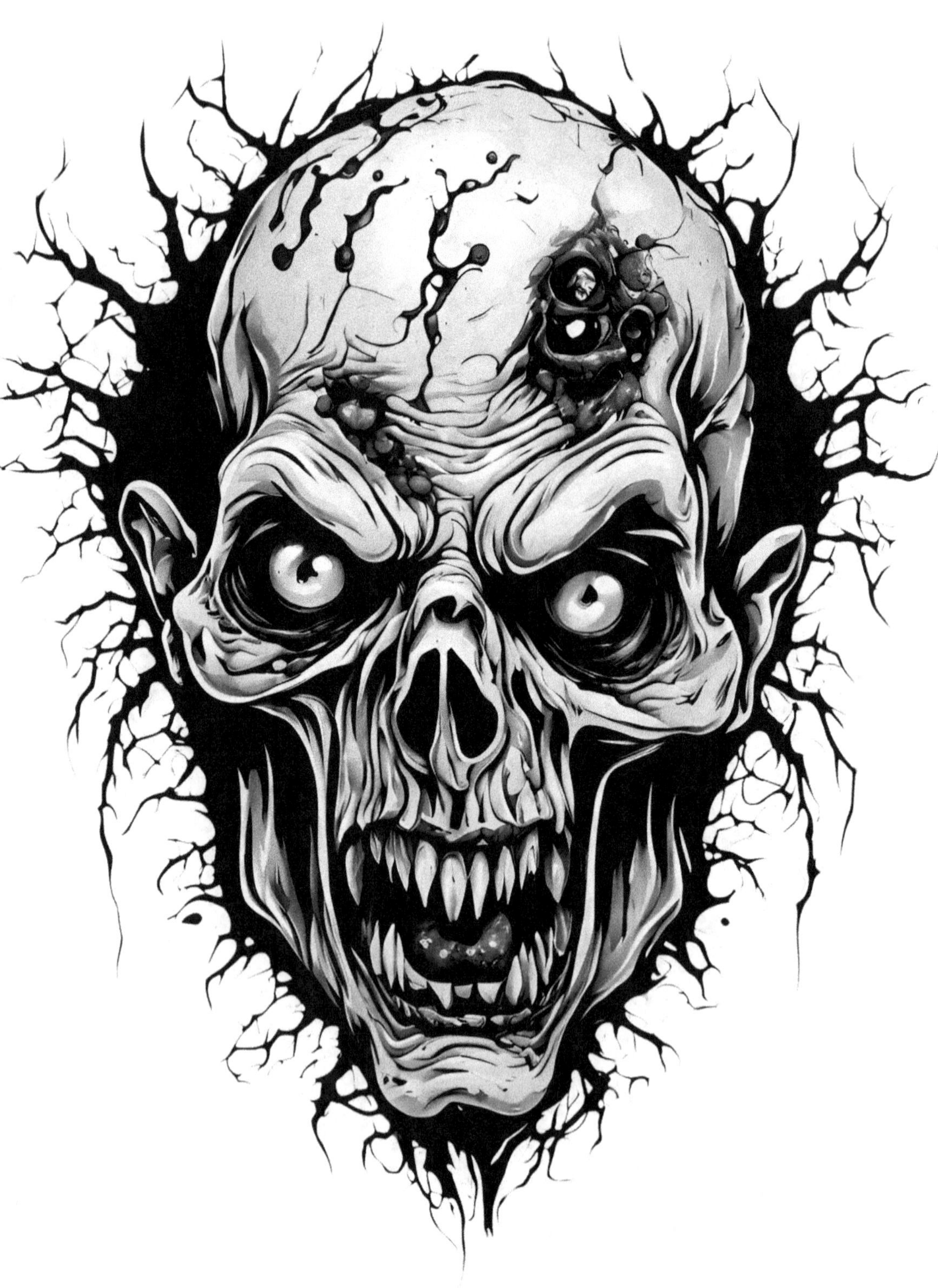

SCARY TATTOOS

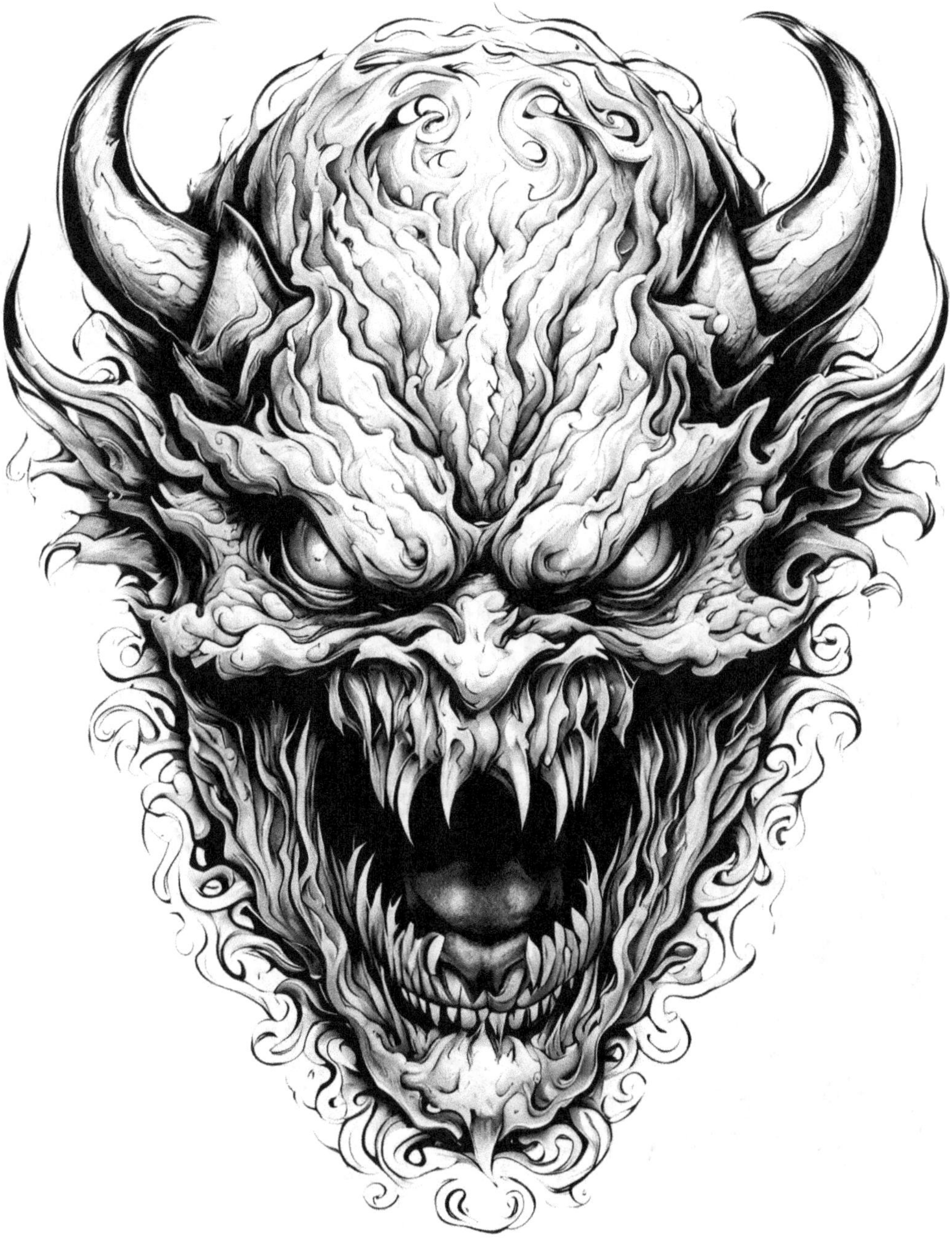

SCARY TATTOOS

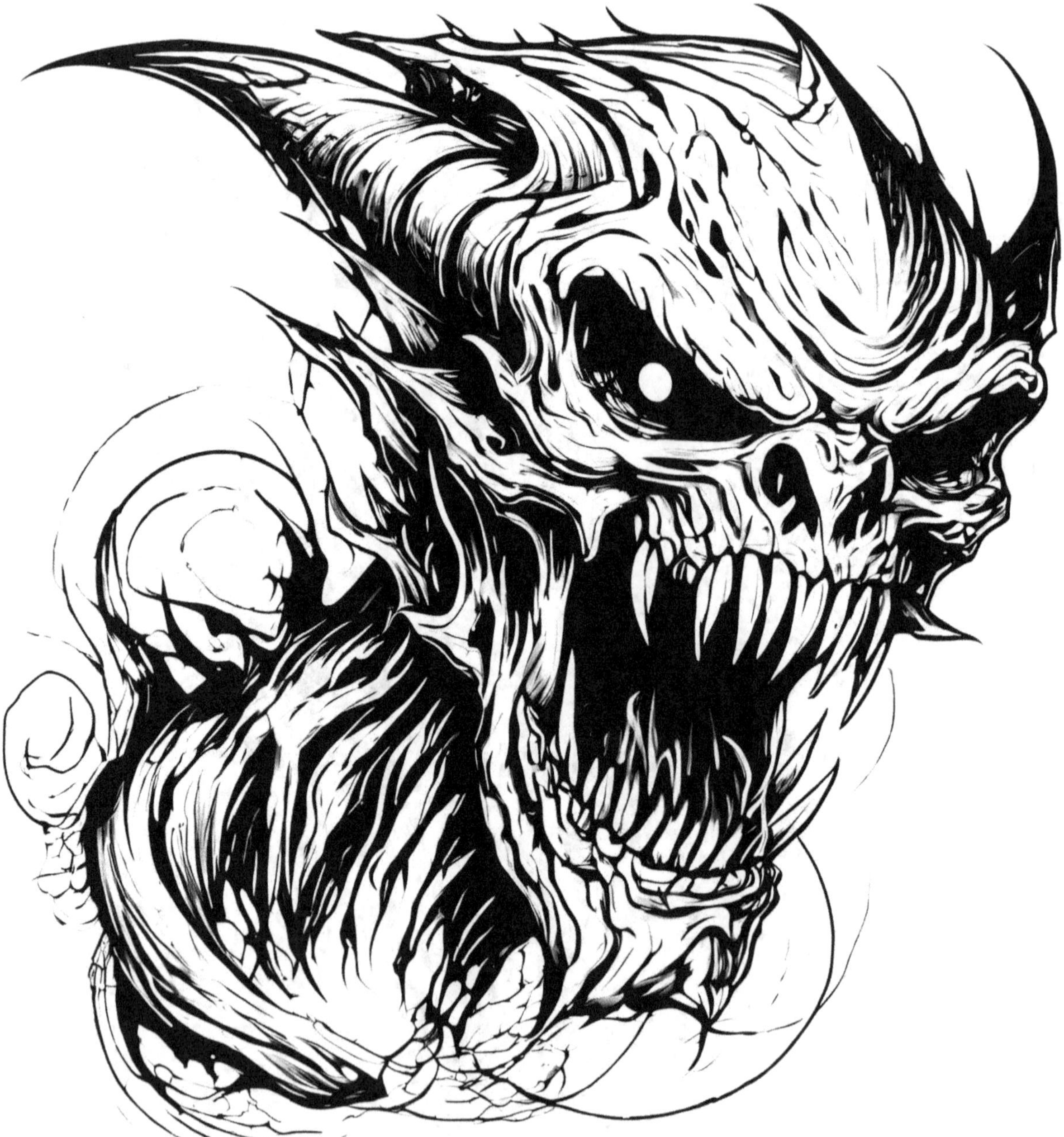

SCARY TATTOOS

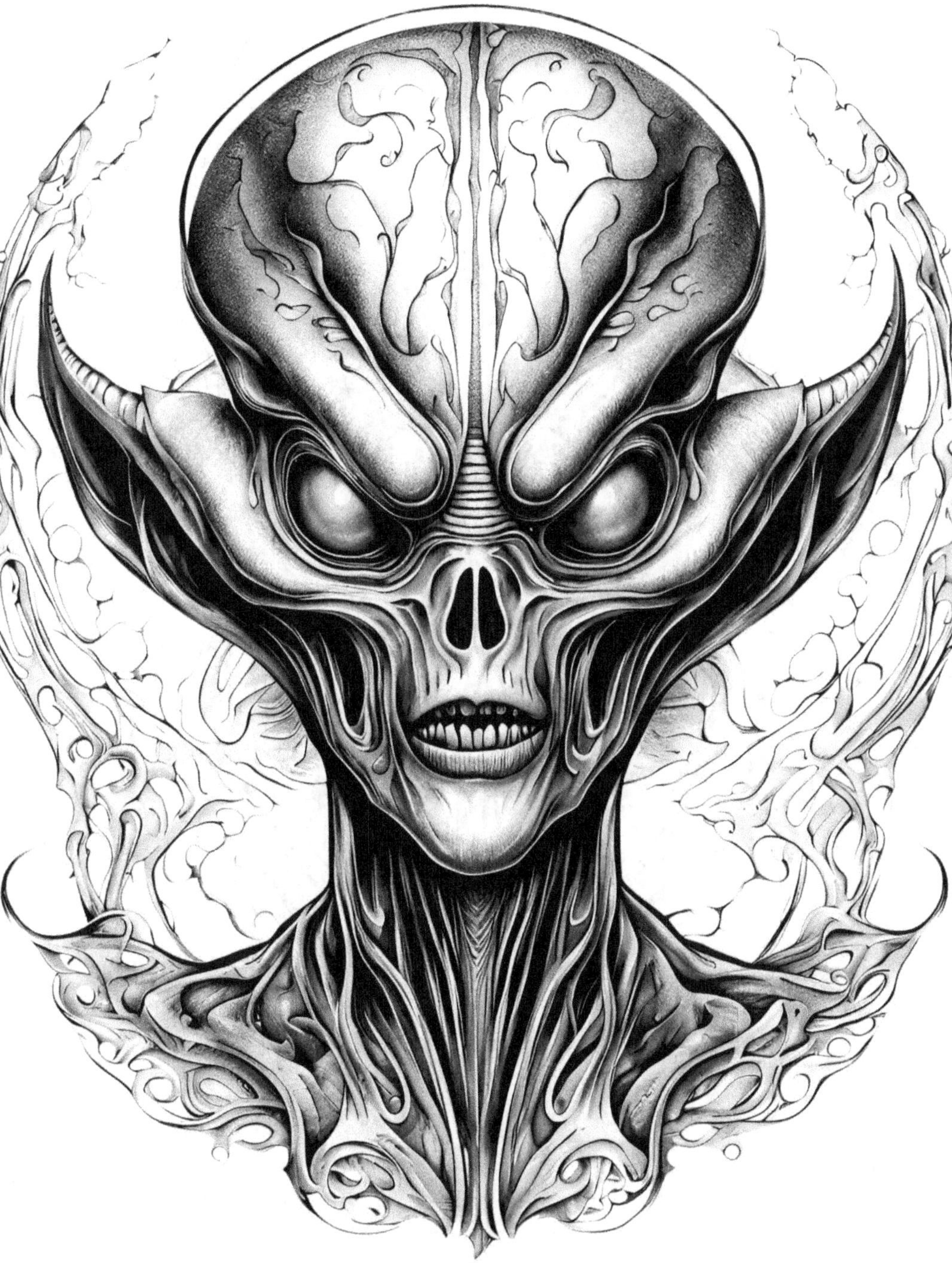

ALIEN TATTOOS

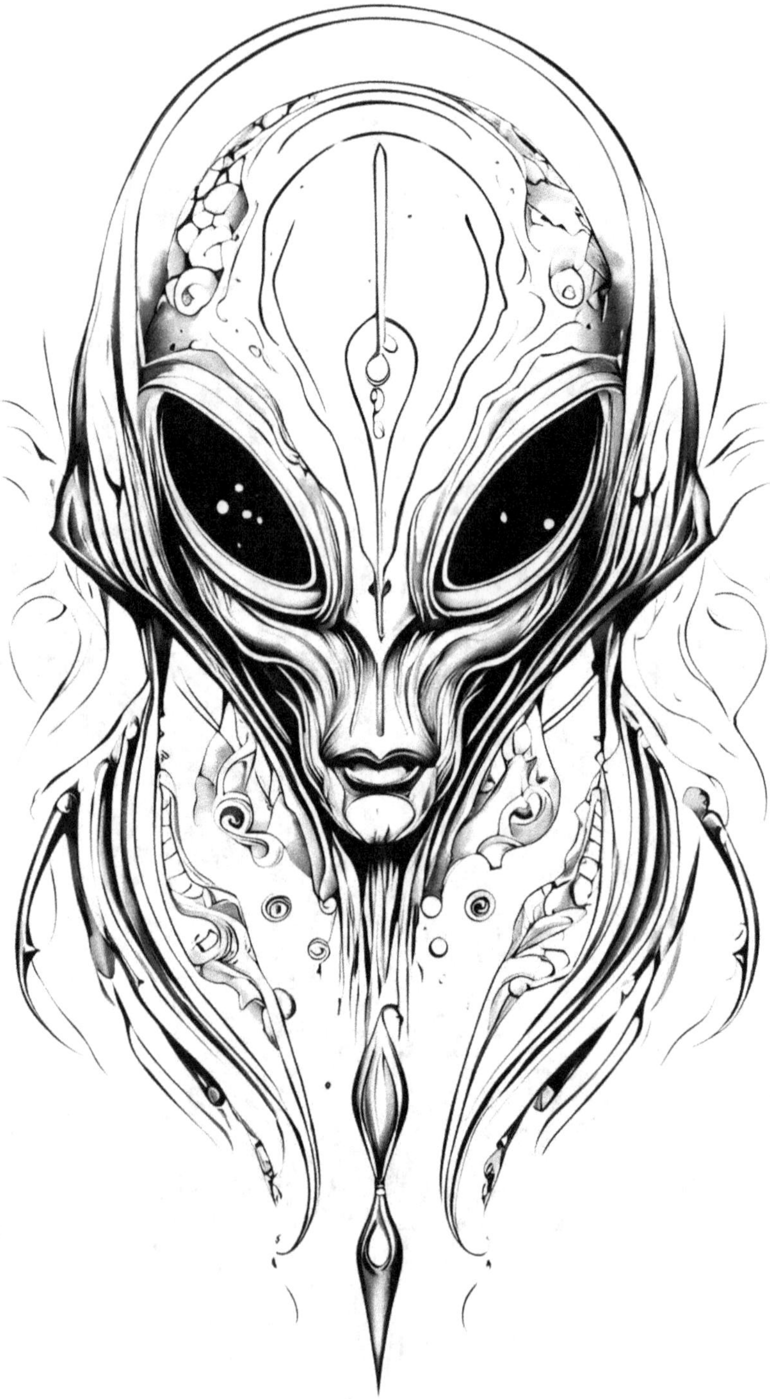

ALIEN TATTOOS

ALIEN TATTOOS

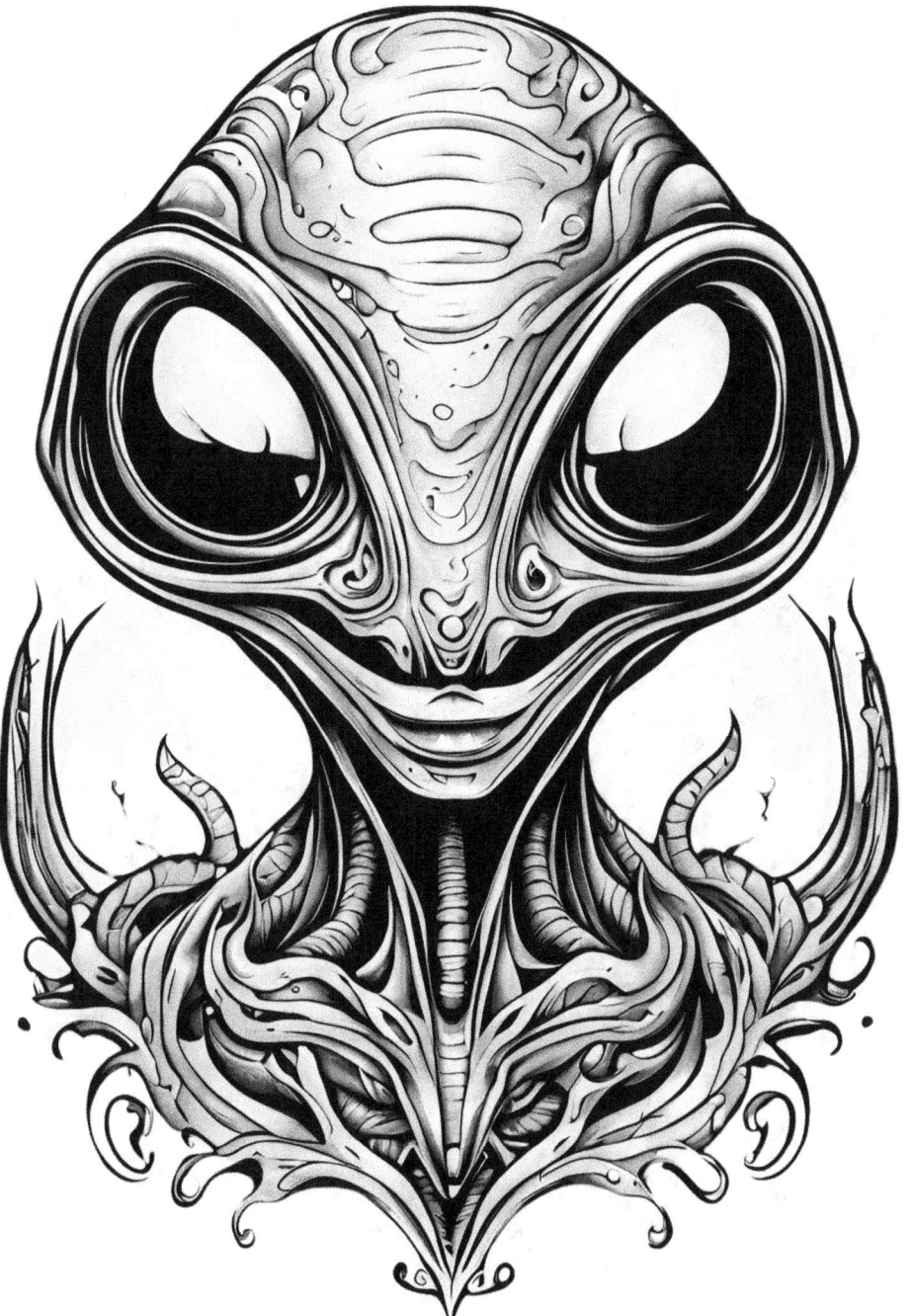

ALIEN TATTOOS

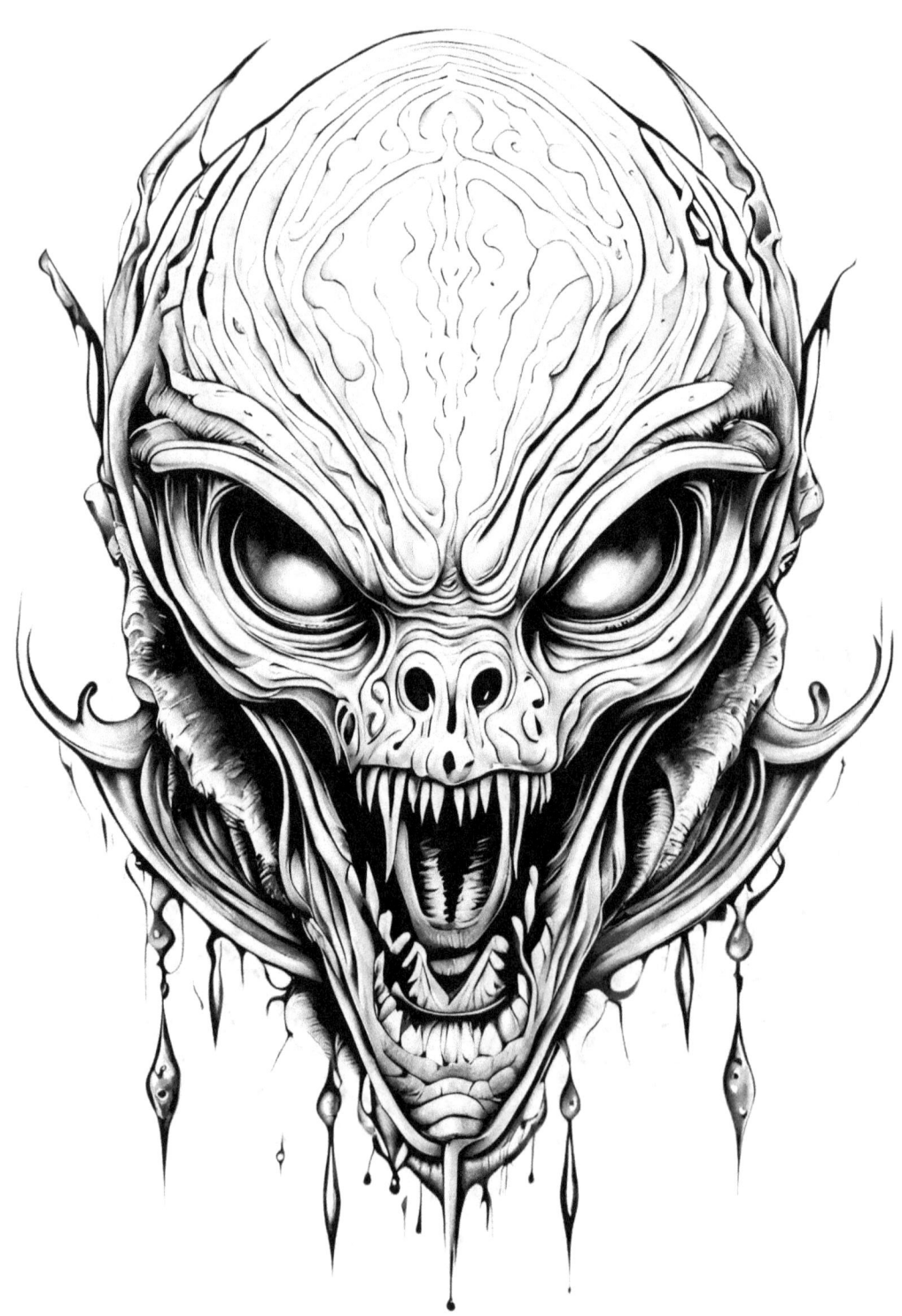

PAGE 64

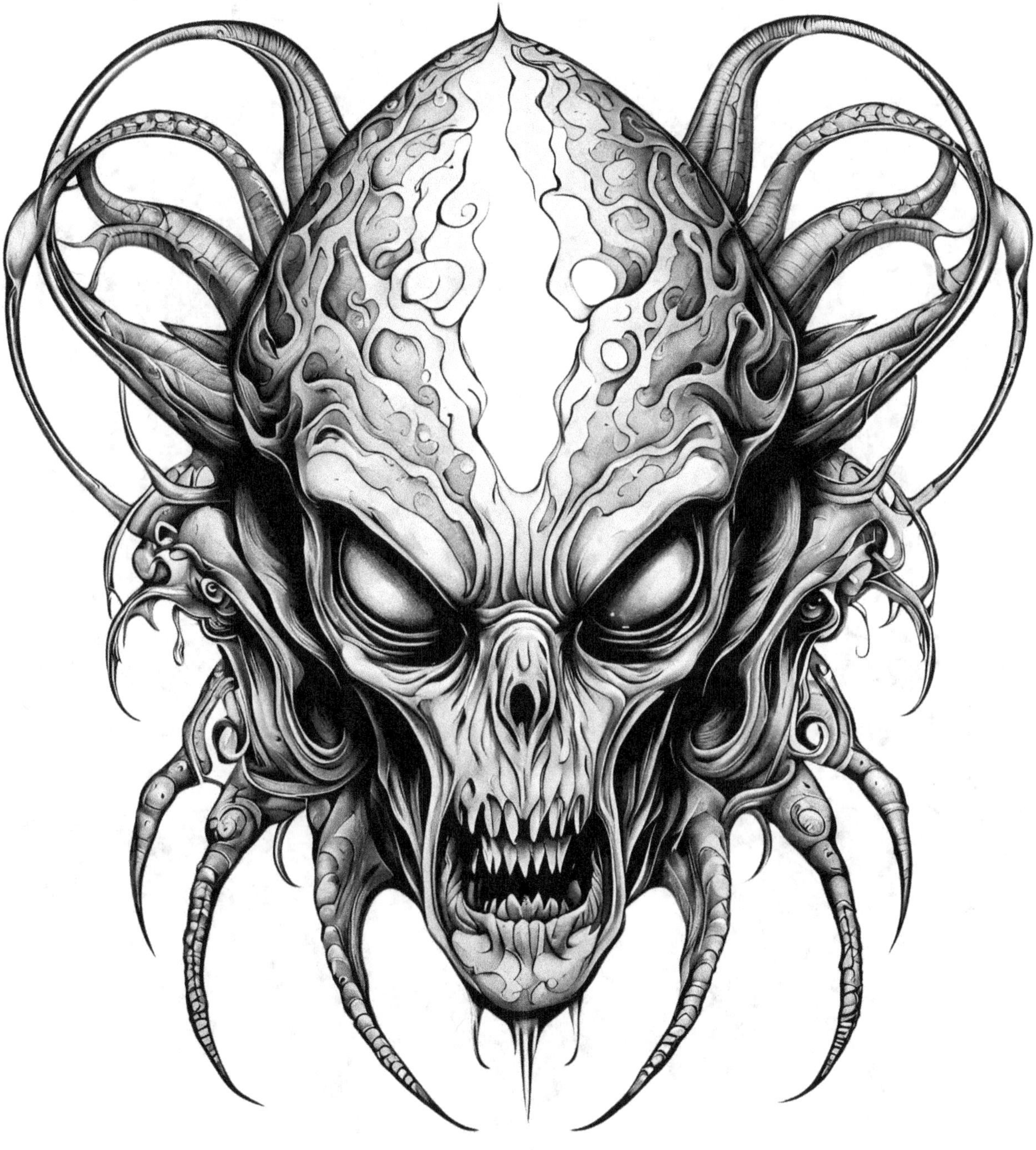

ALIEN TATTOOS

JOKER TATTOOS

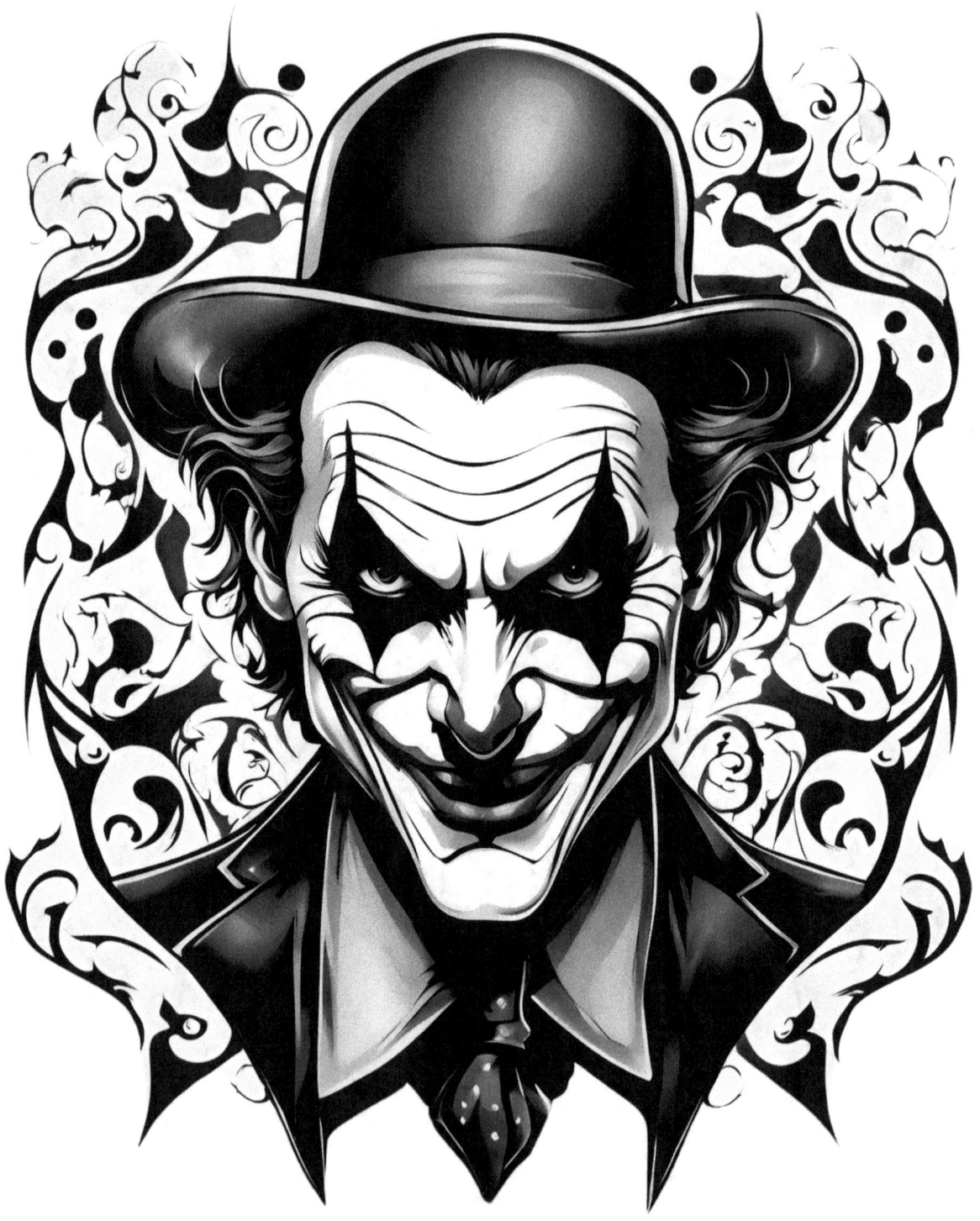

JOKER TATTOOS

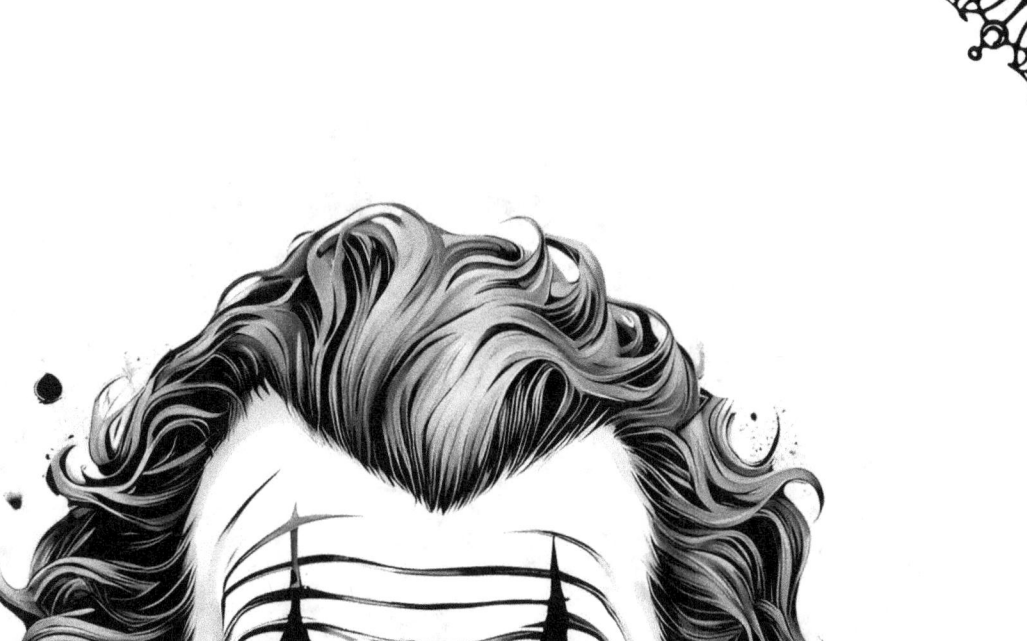

JOKER TATTOOS

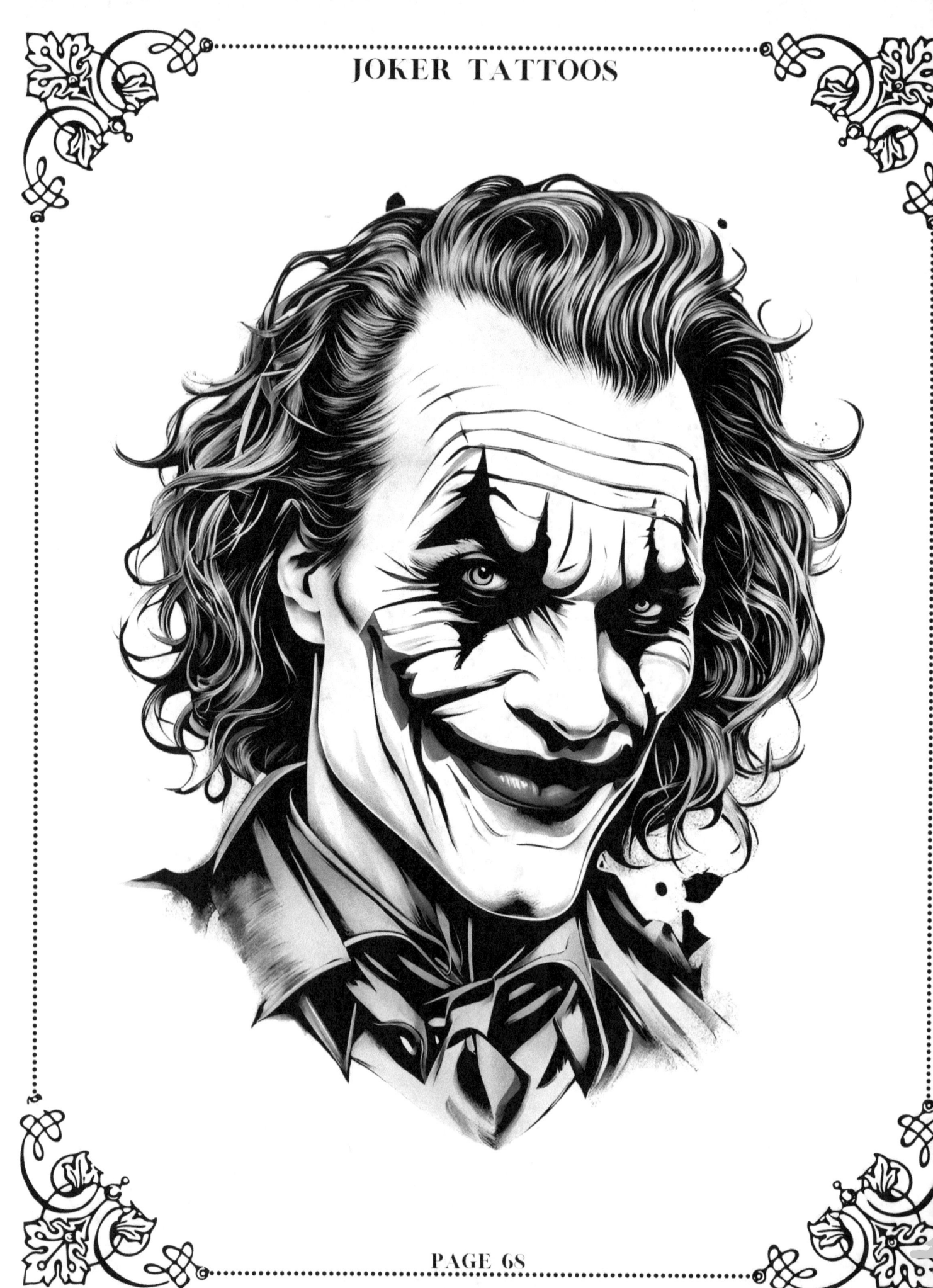

JOKER TATTOOS

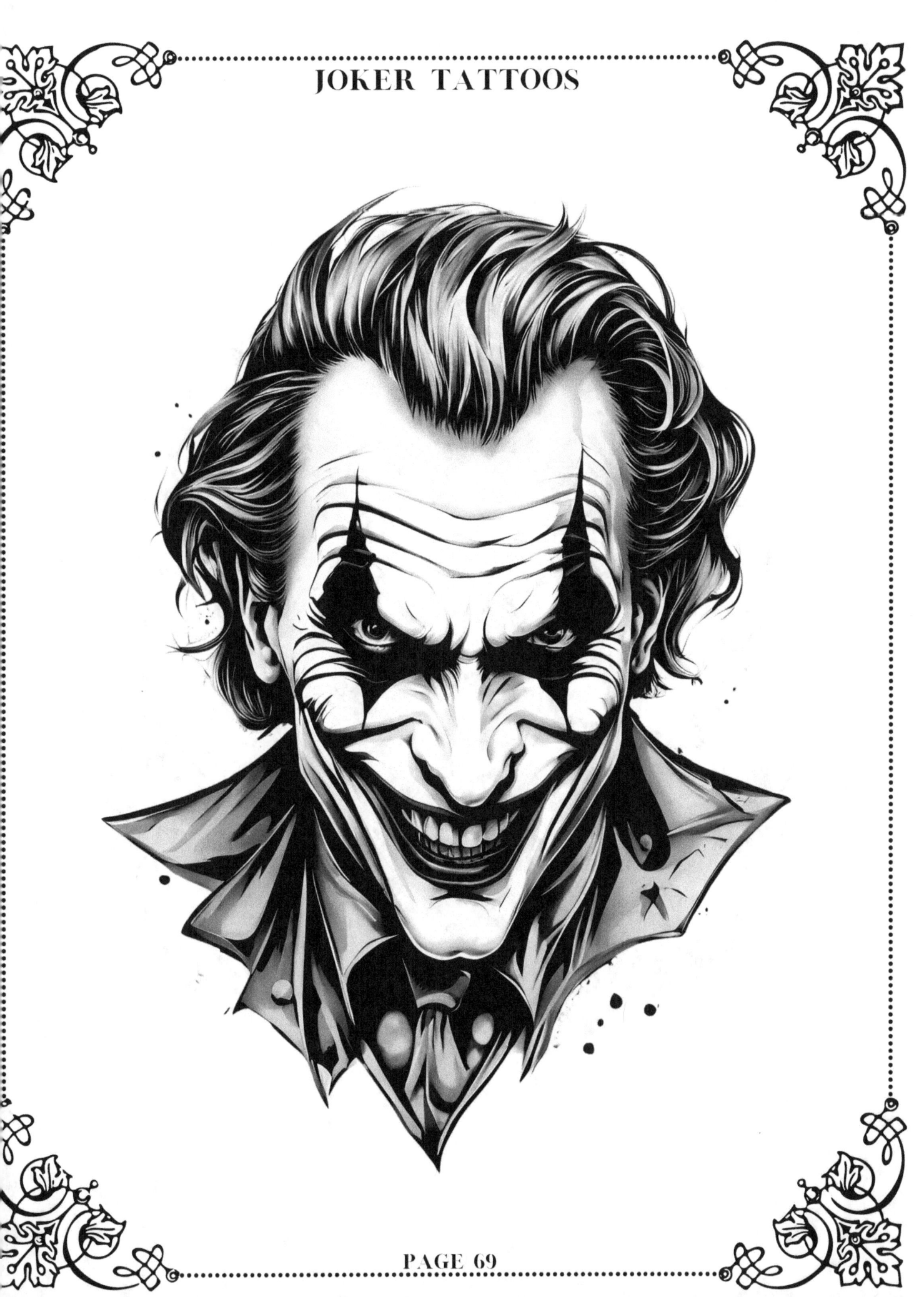

PAGE 69

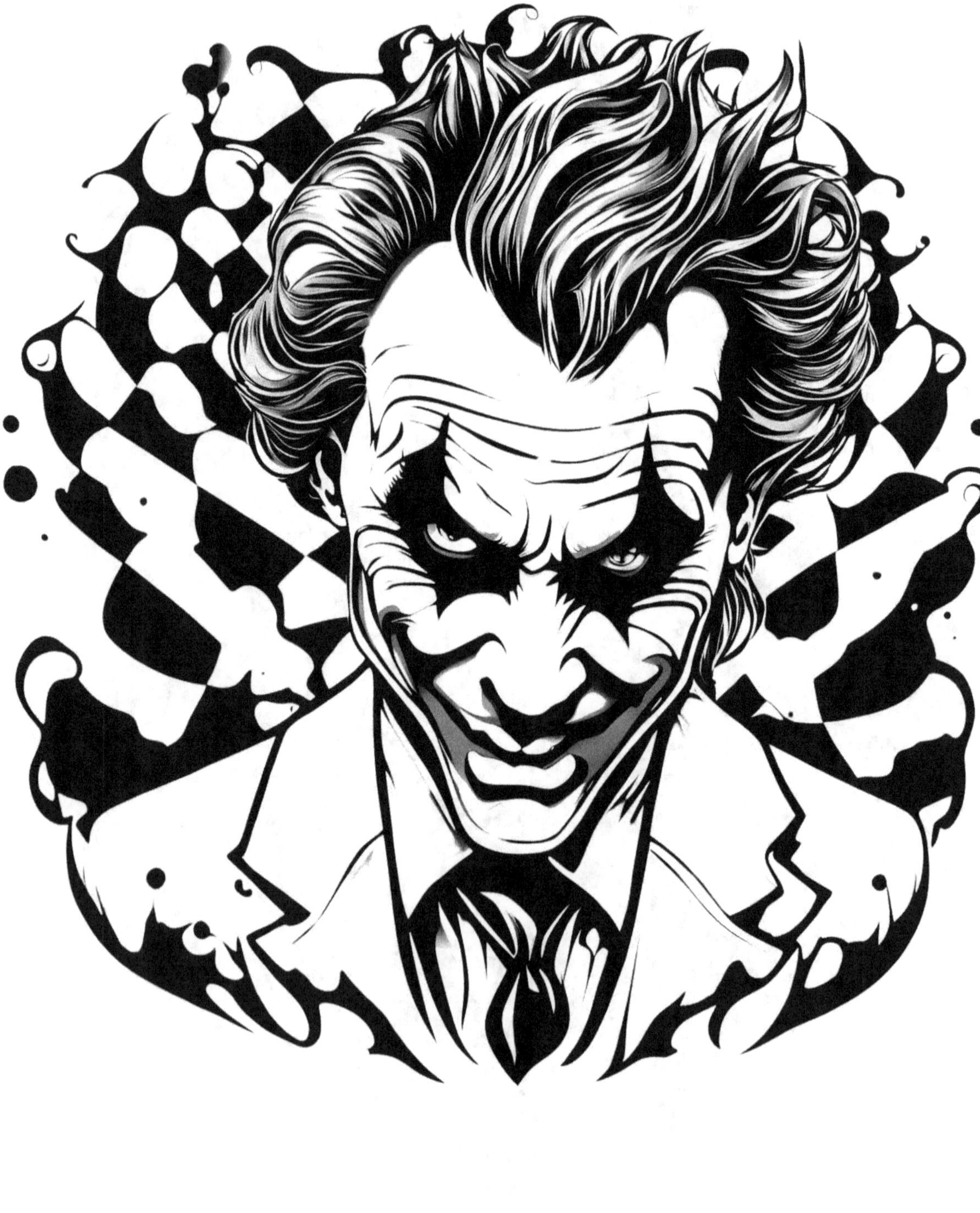

JOKER TATTOOS

DIAMOND TATTOOS

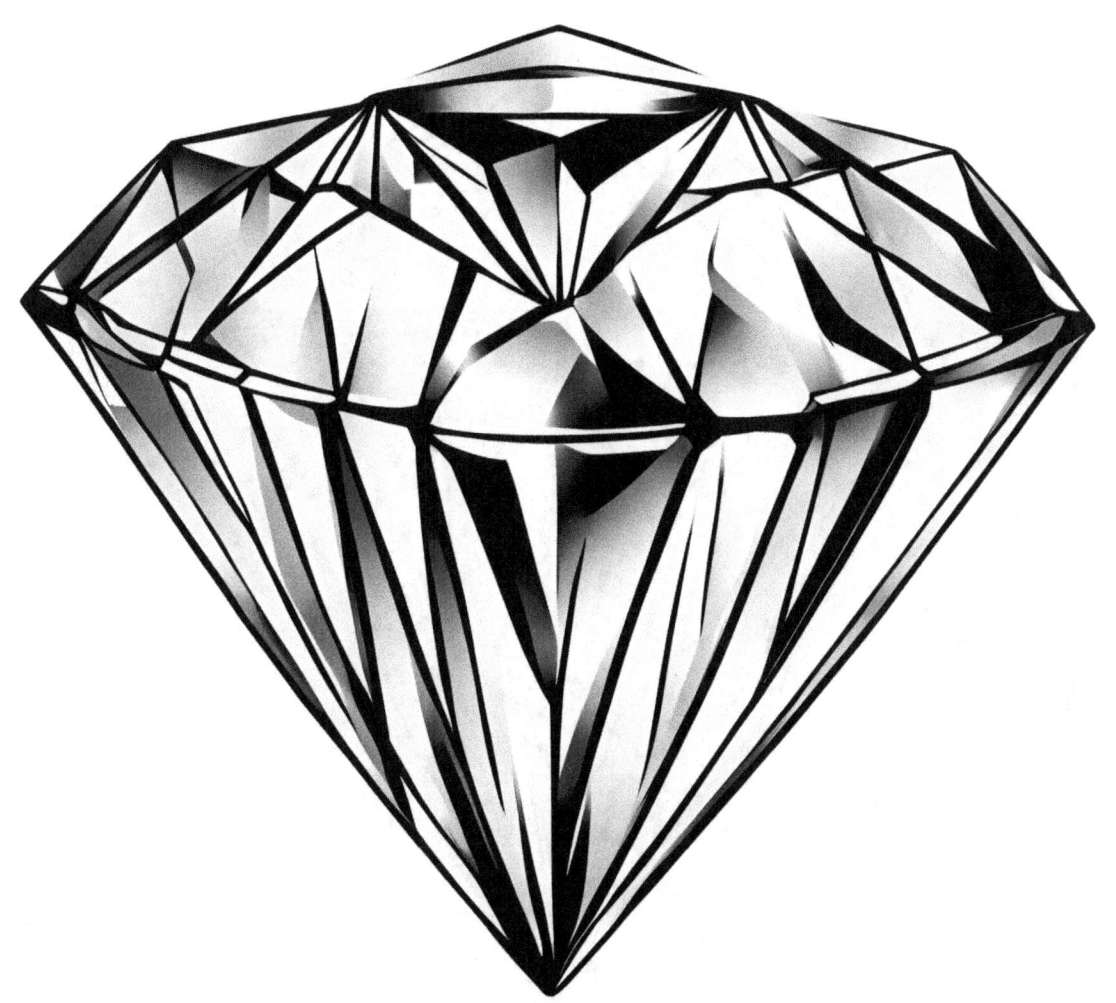

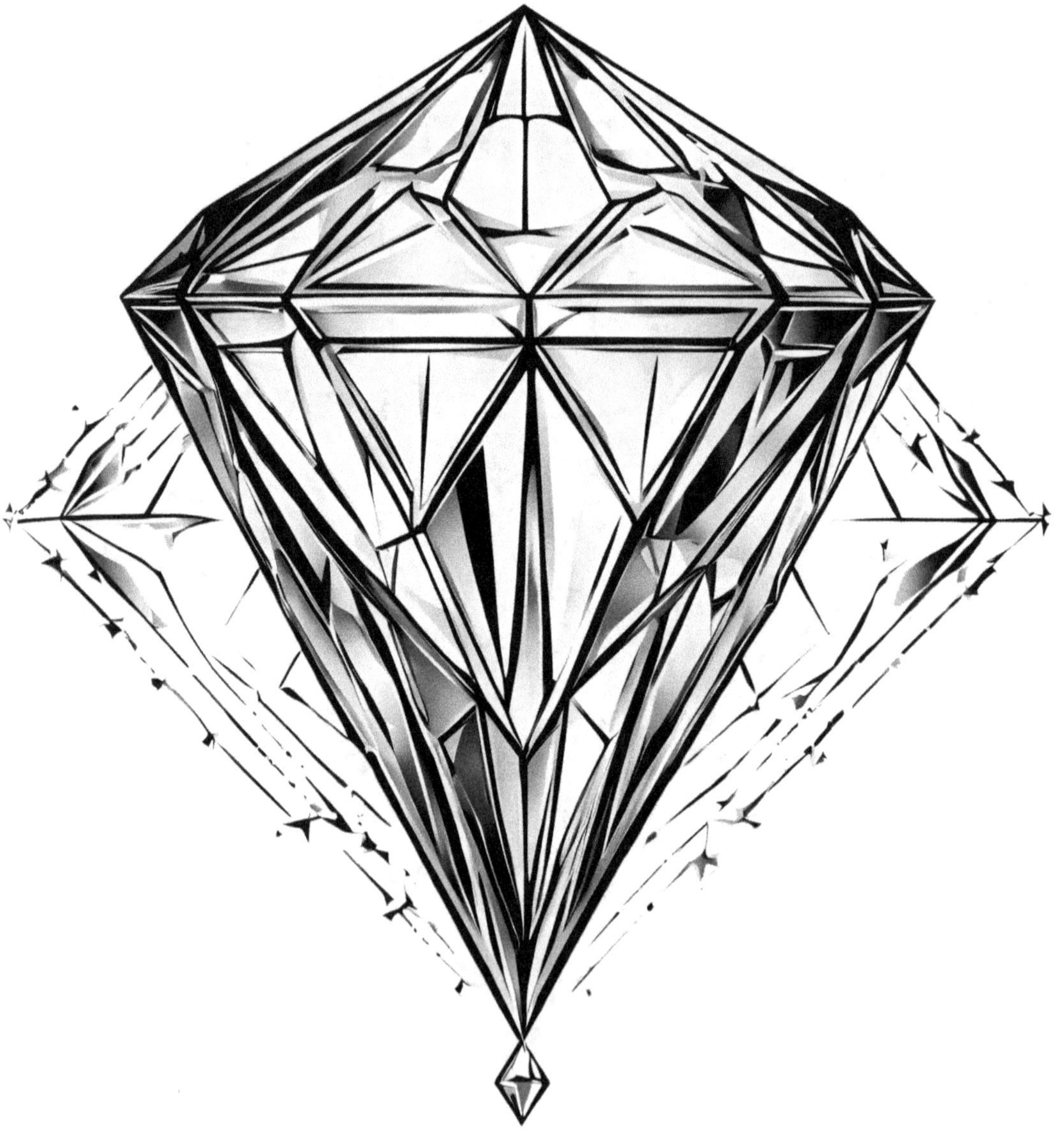

DIAMOND TATTOOS

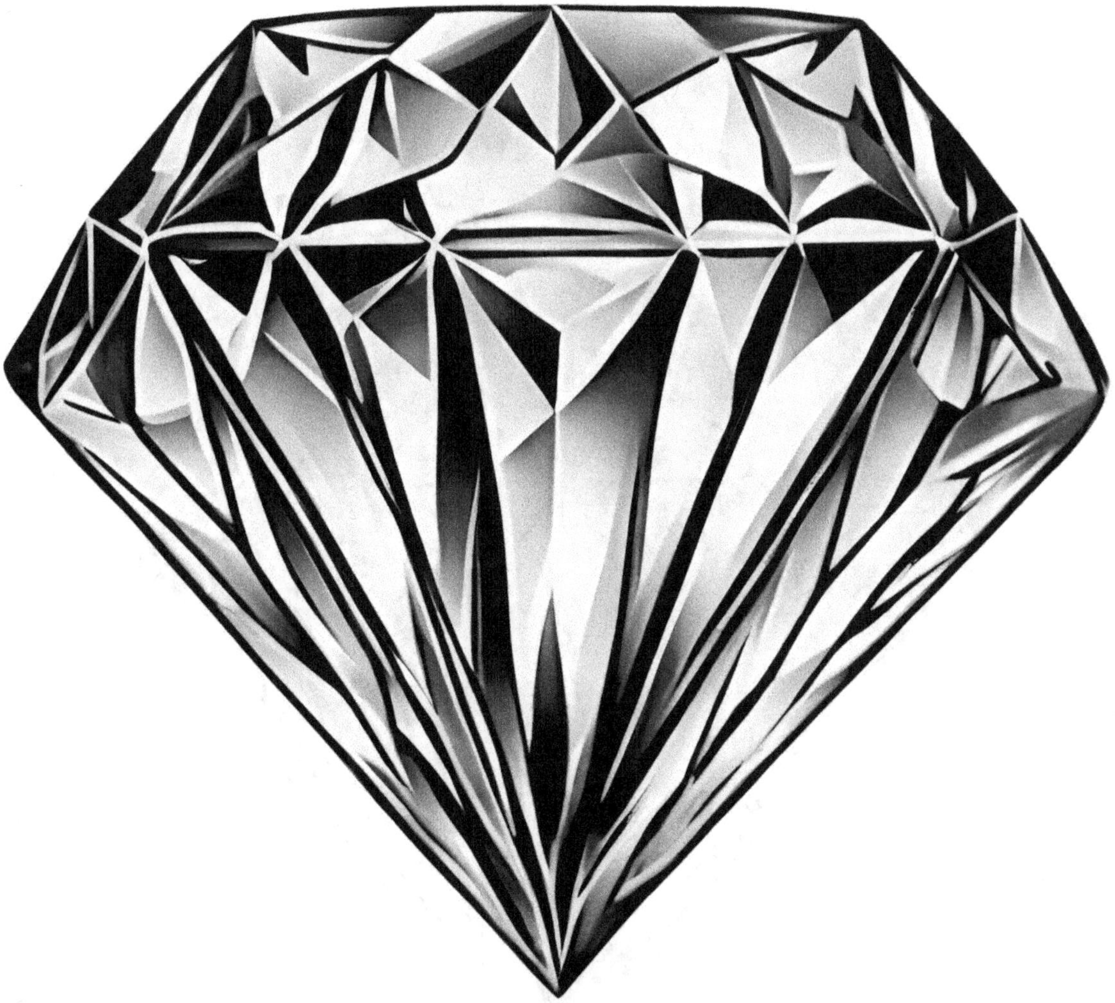

DIAMOND TATTOOS

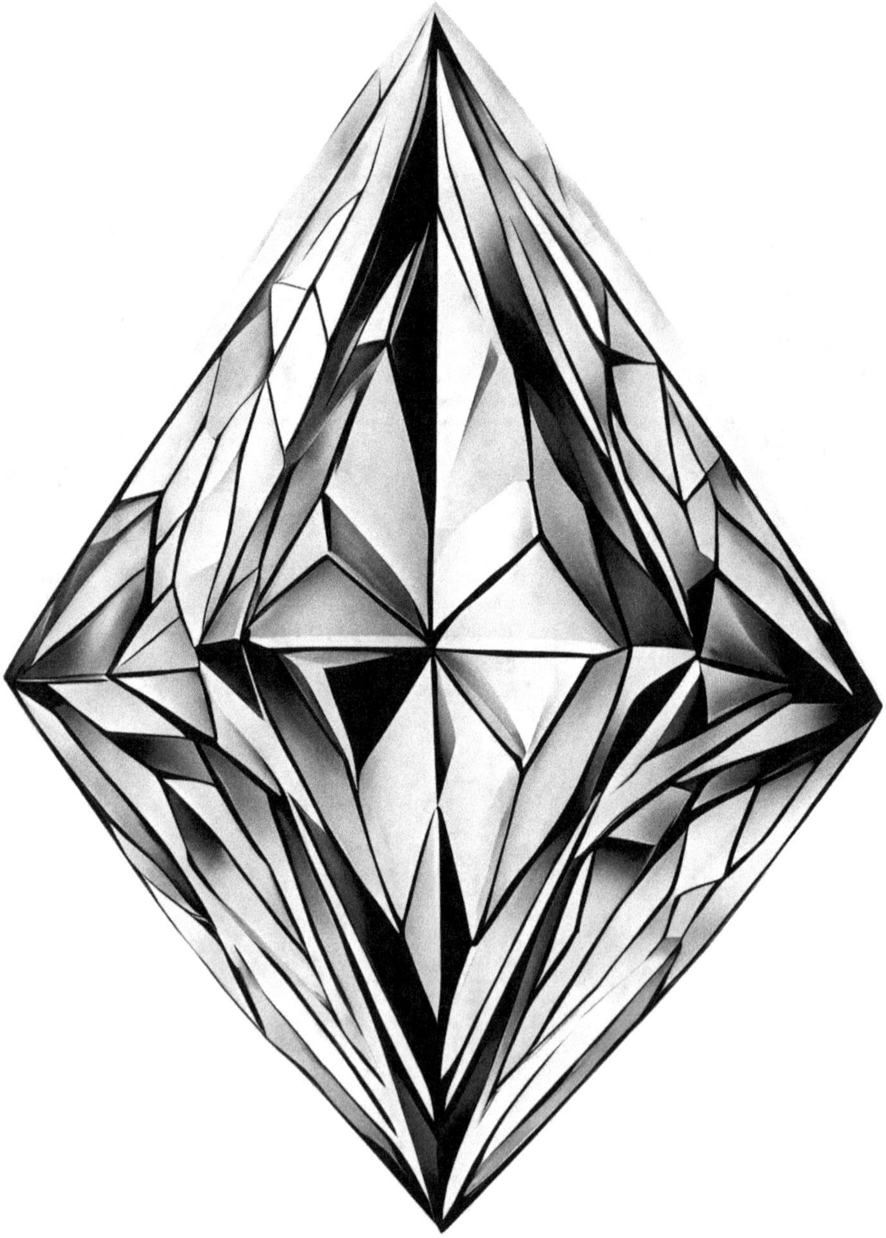

DIAMOND TATTOOS

DIAMOND TATTOOS

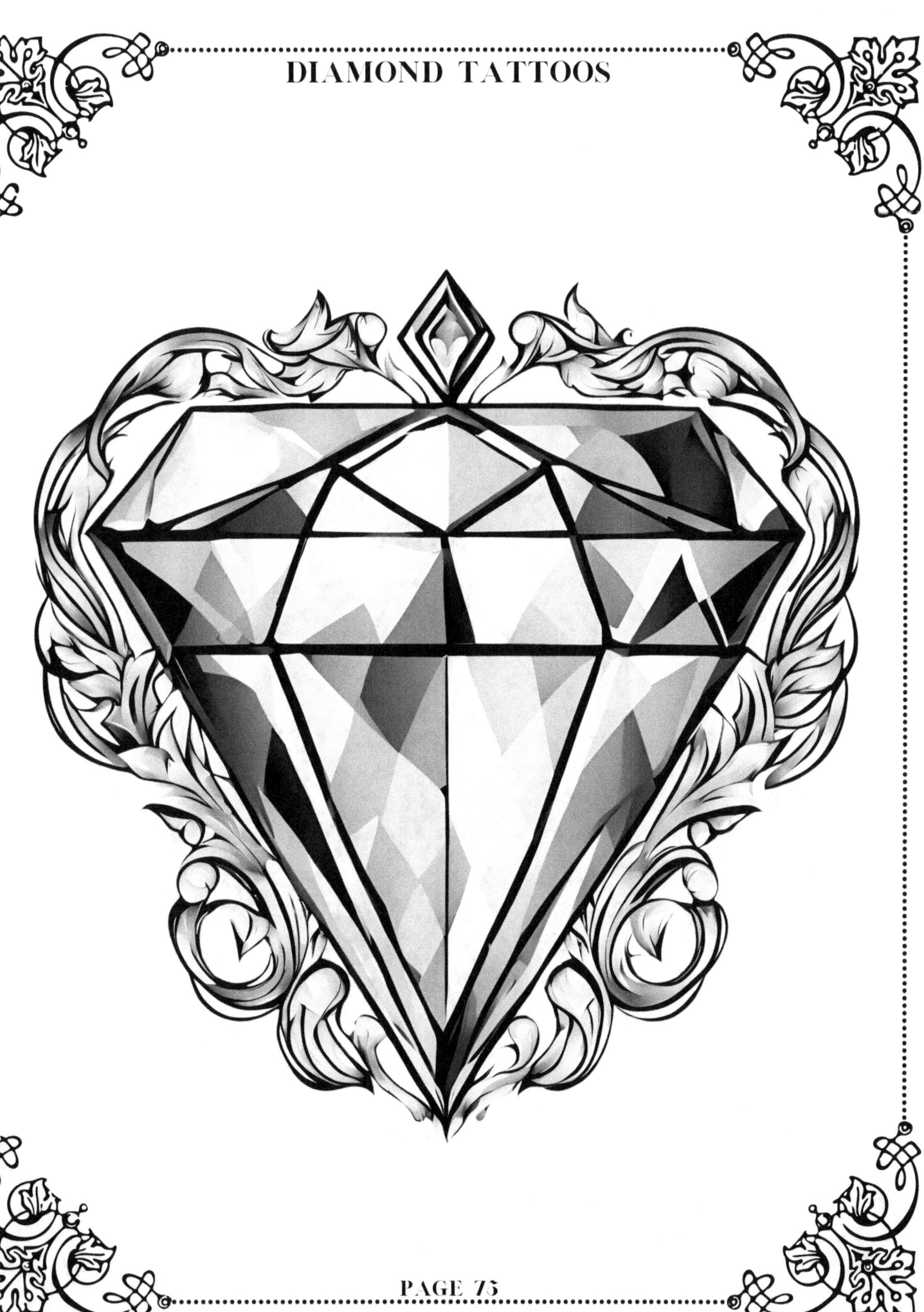

ANCHOR TATTOOS

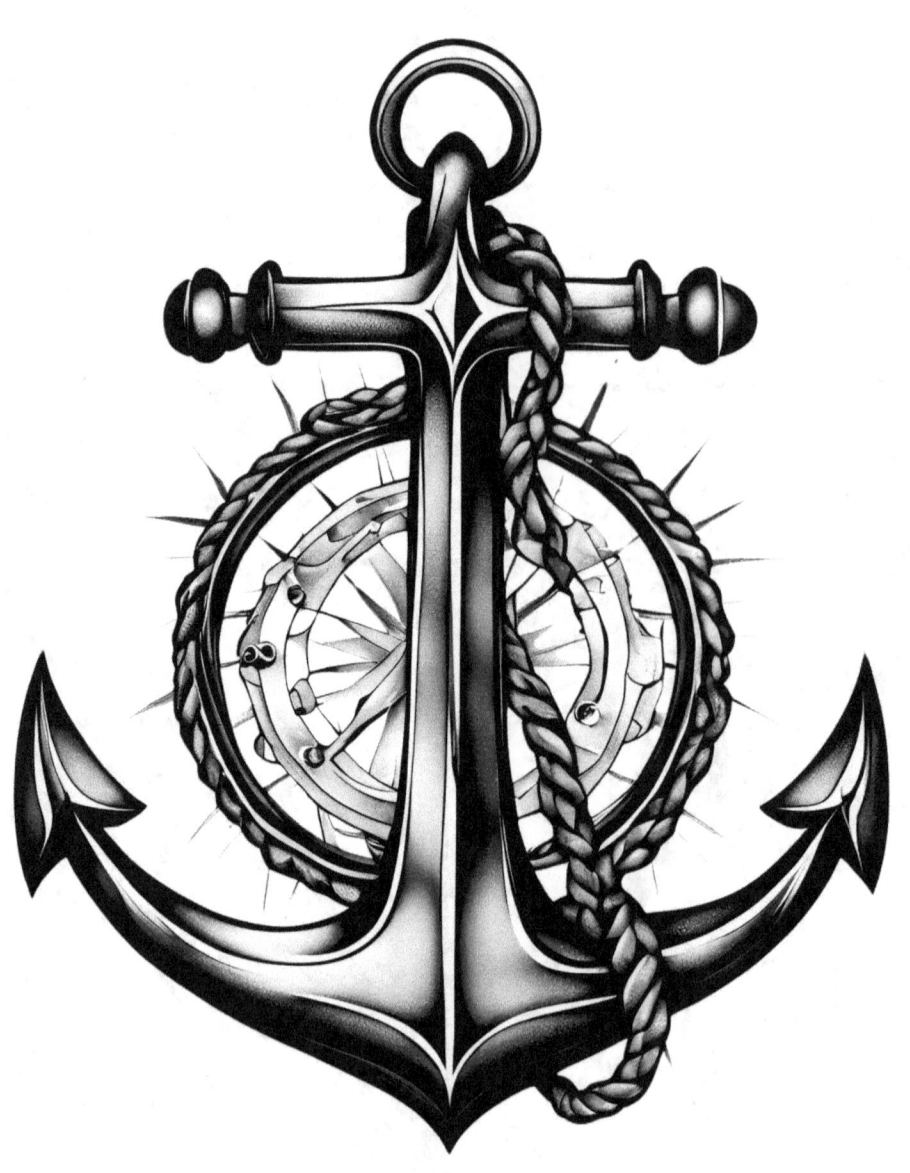

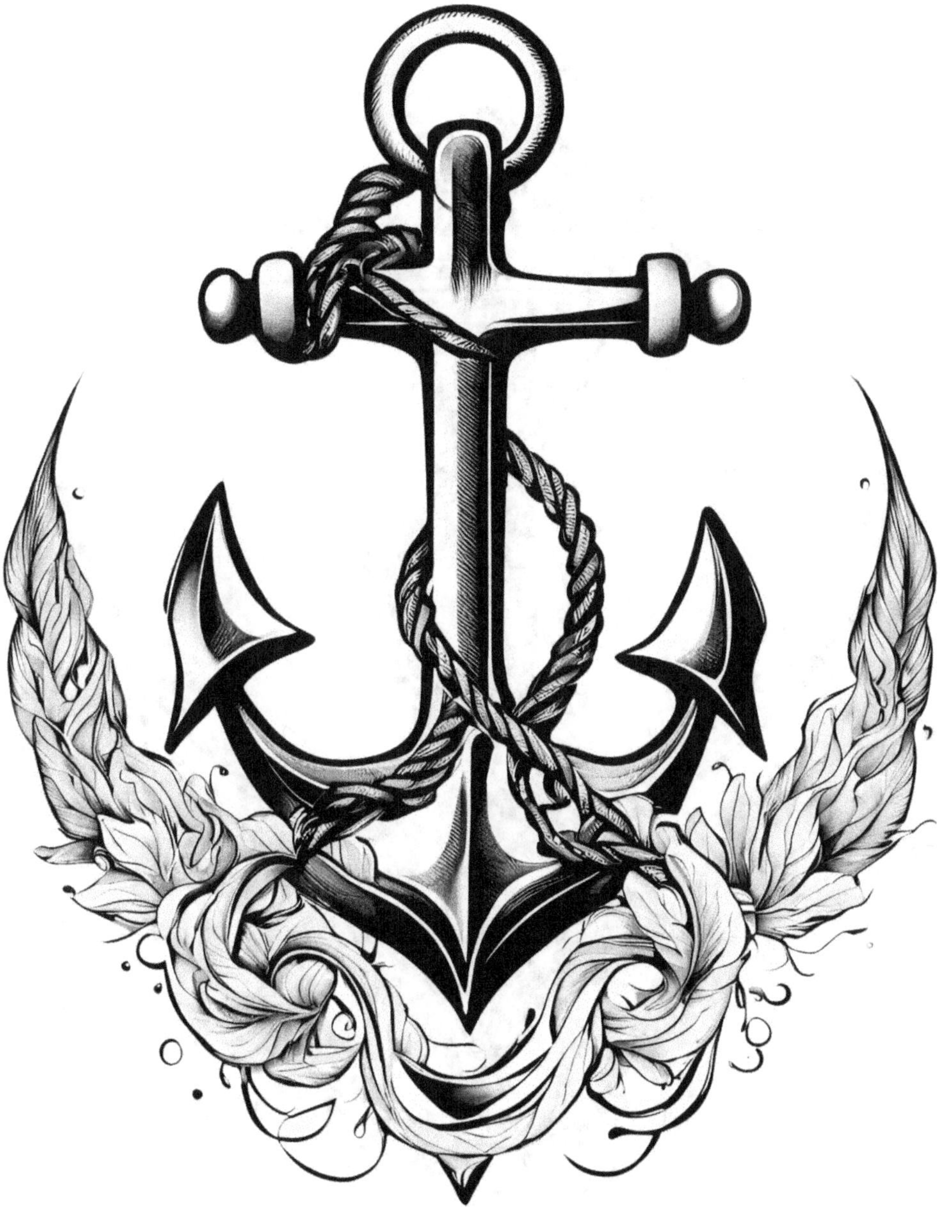

ANCHOR TATTOOS

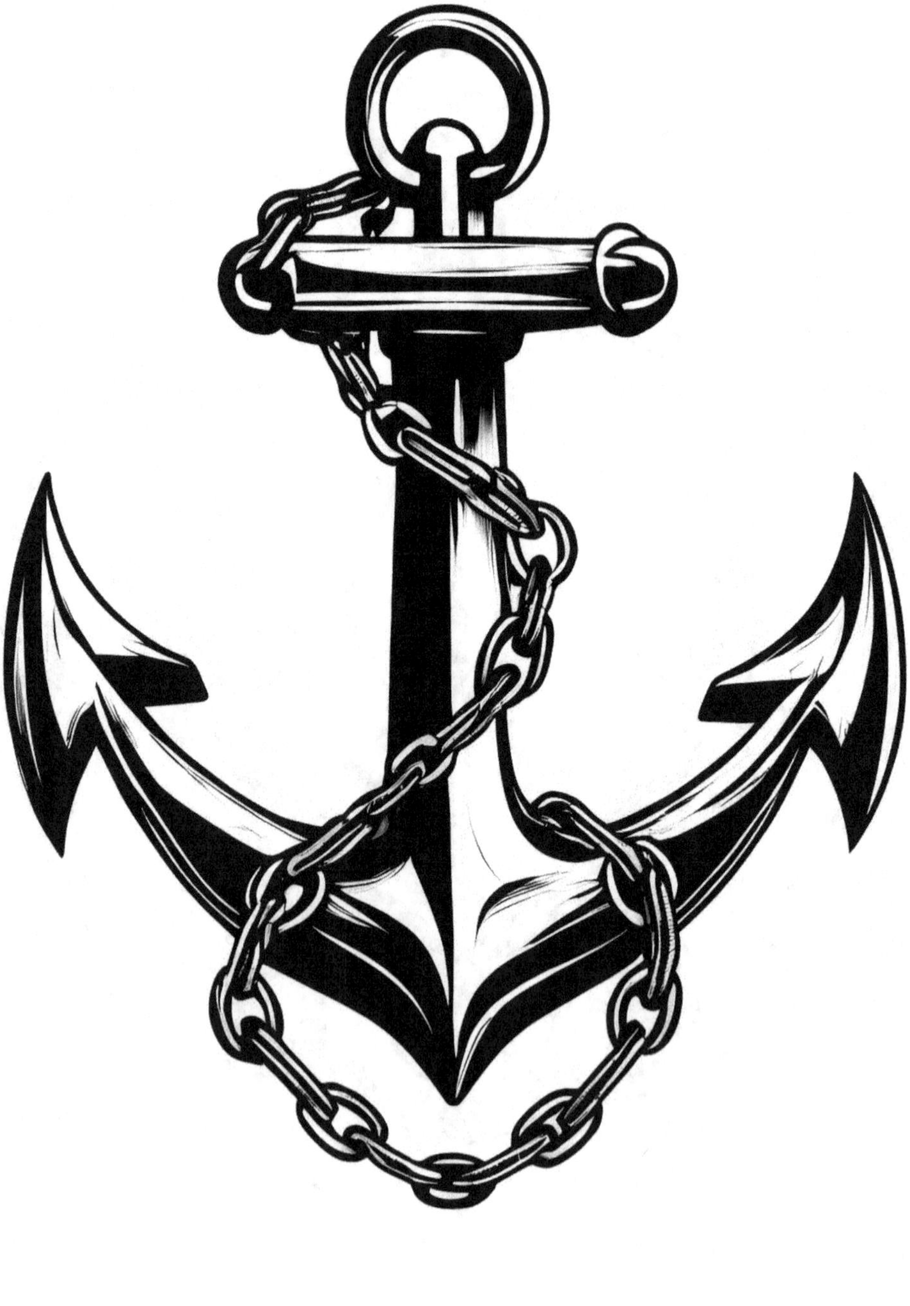

ANCHOR TATTOOS

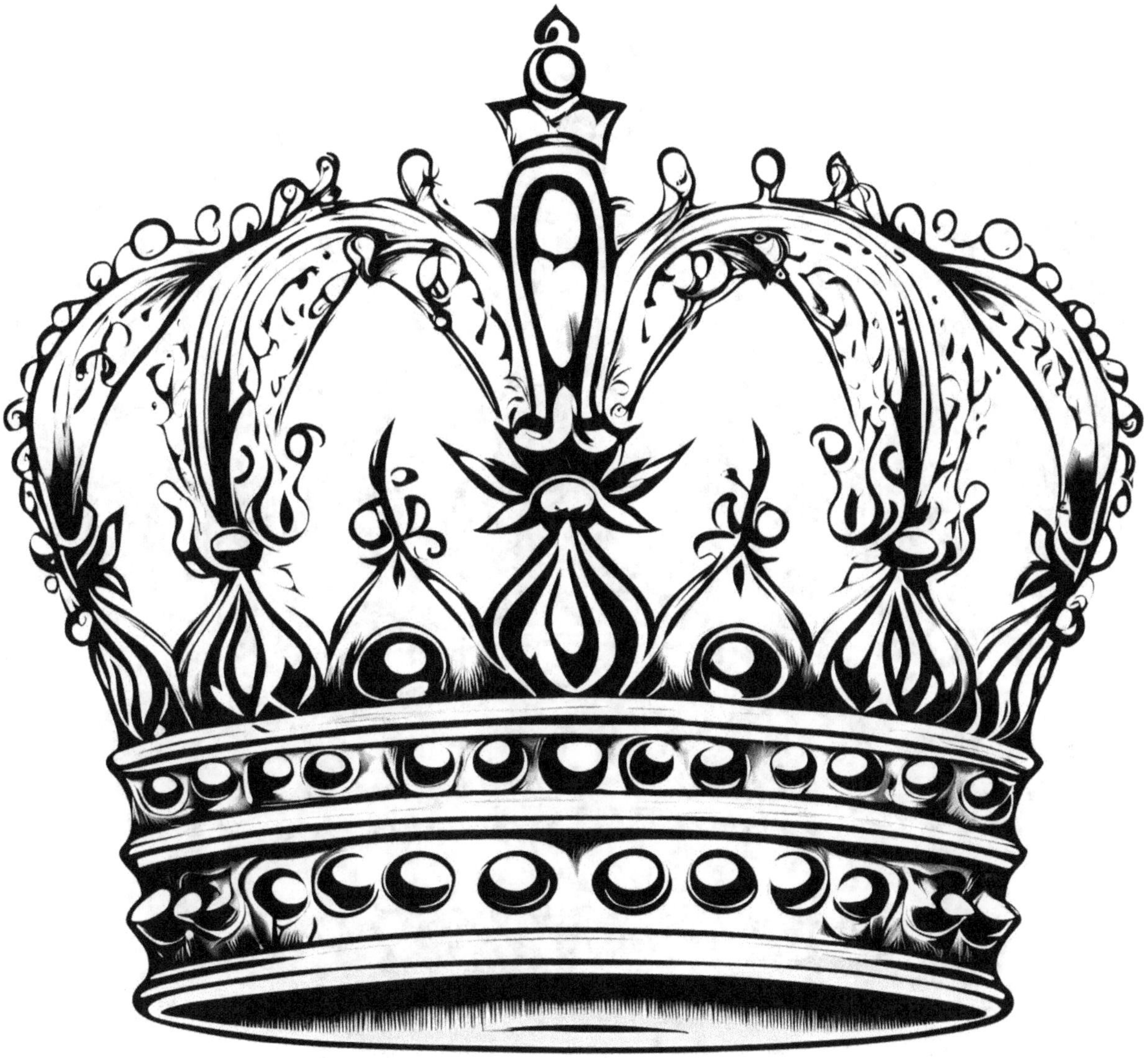

CROWN TATTOOS

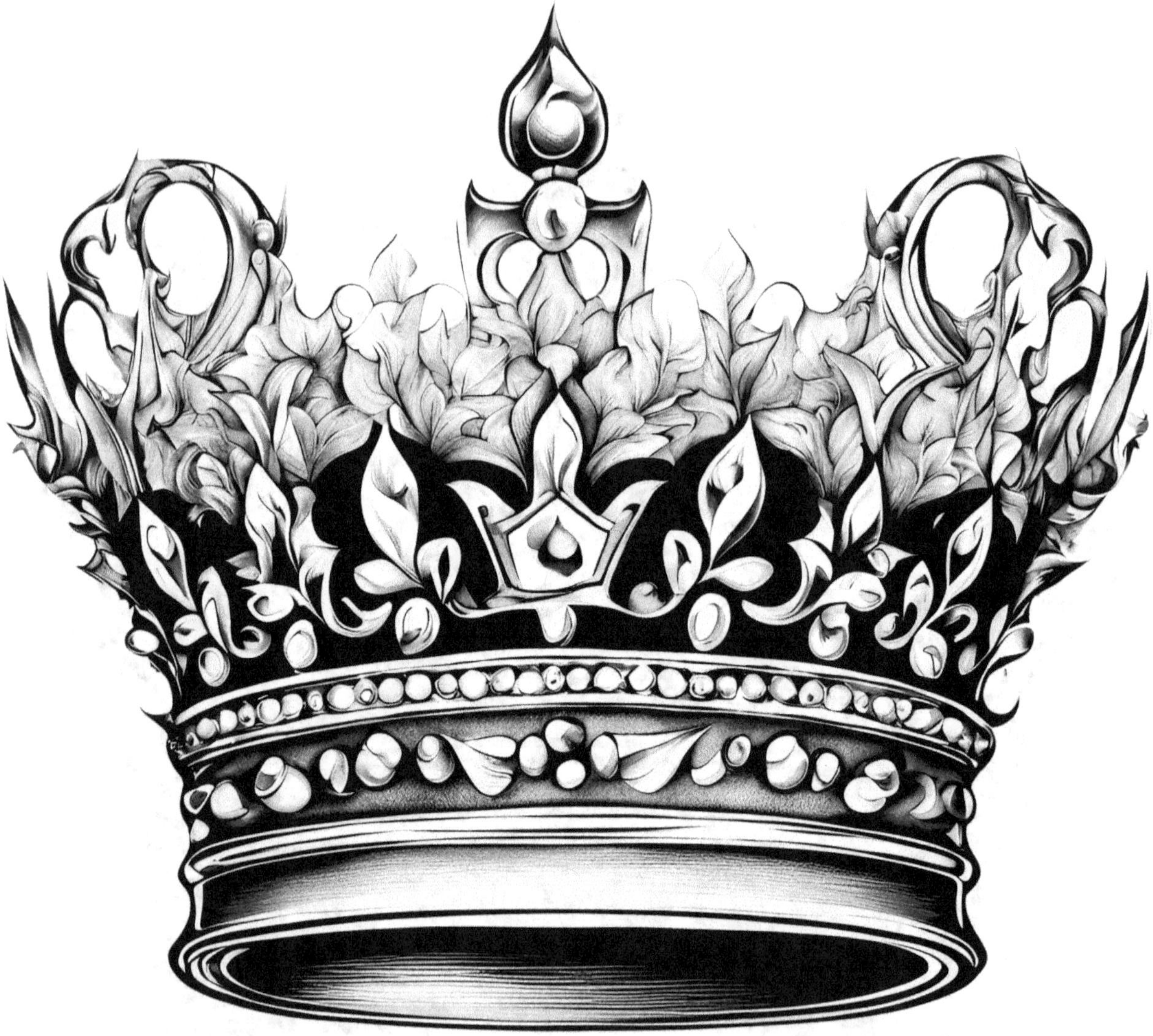

CROWN TATTOOS

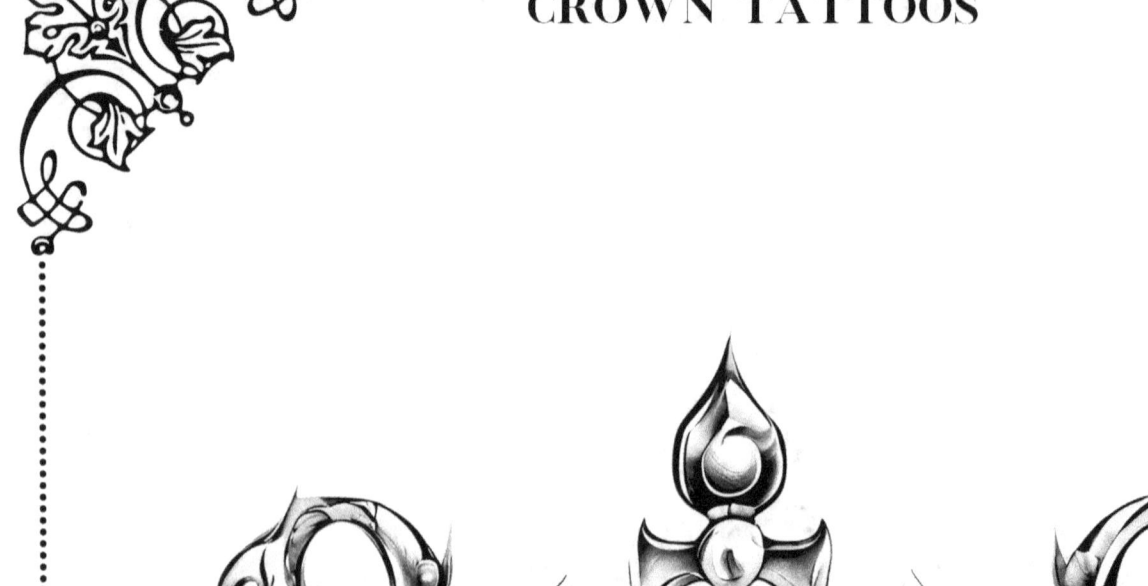

PAGE 80

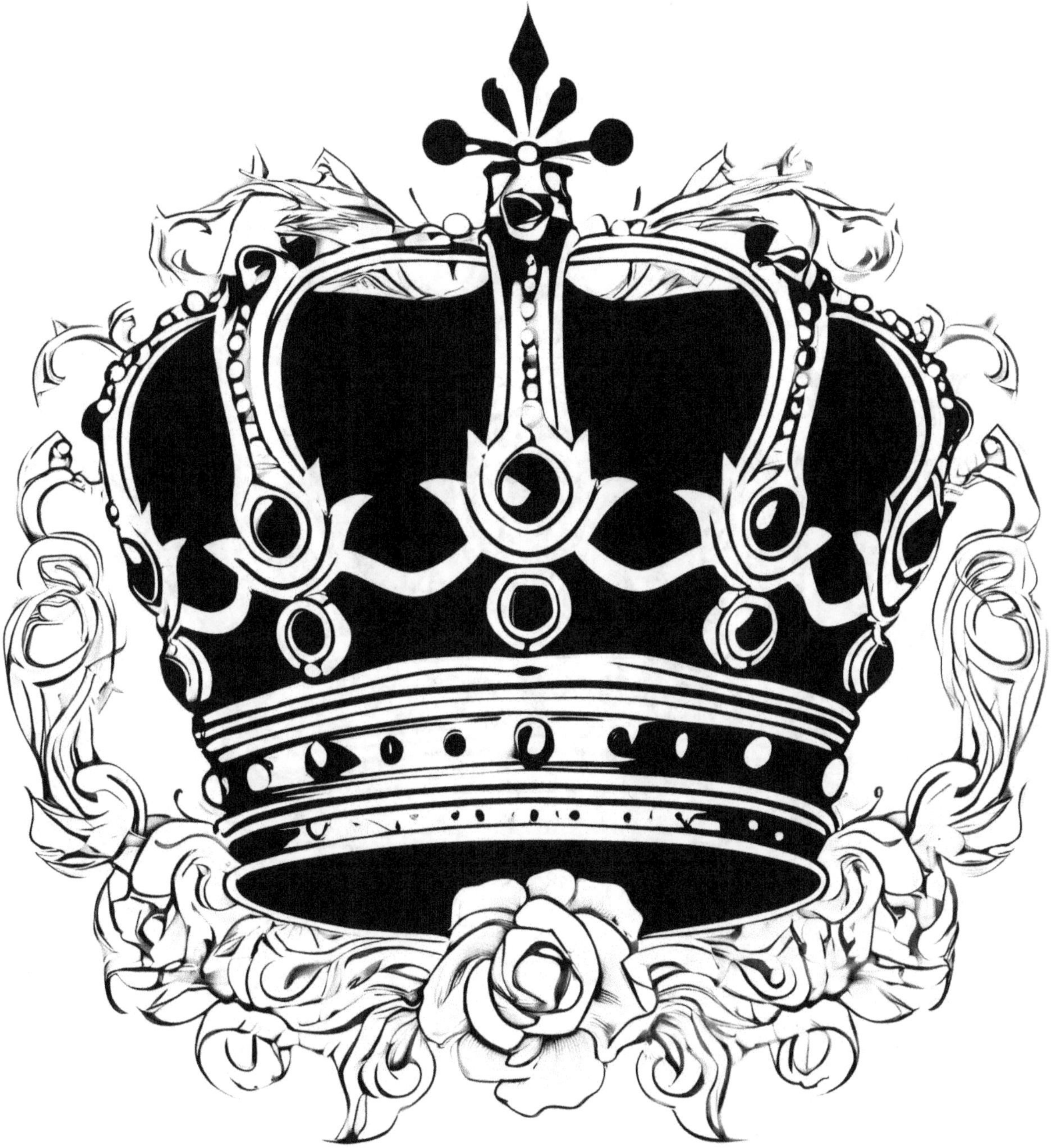

CROWN TATTOOS

CROWN TATTOOS

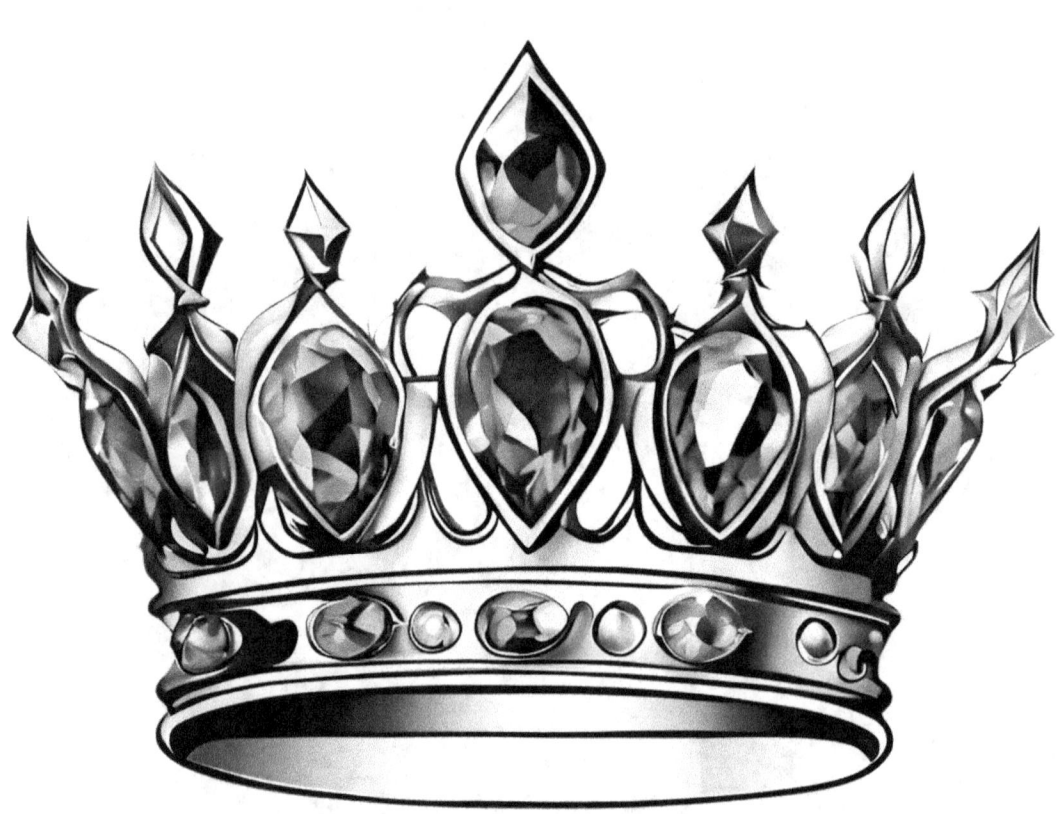

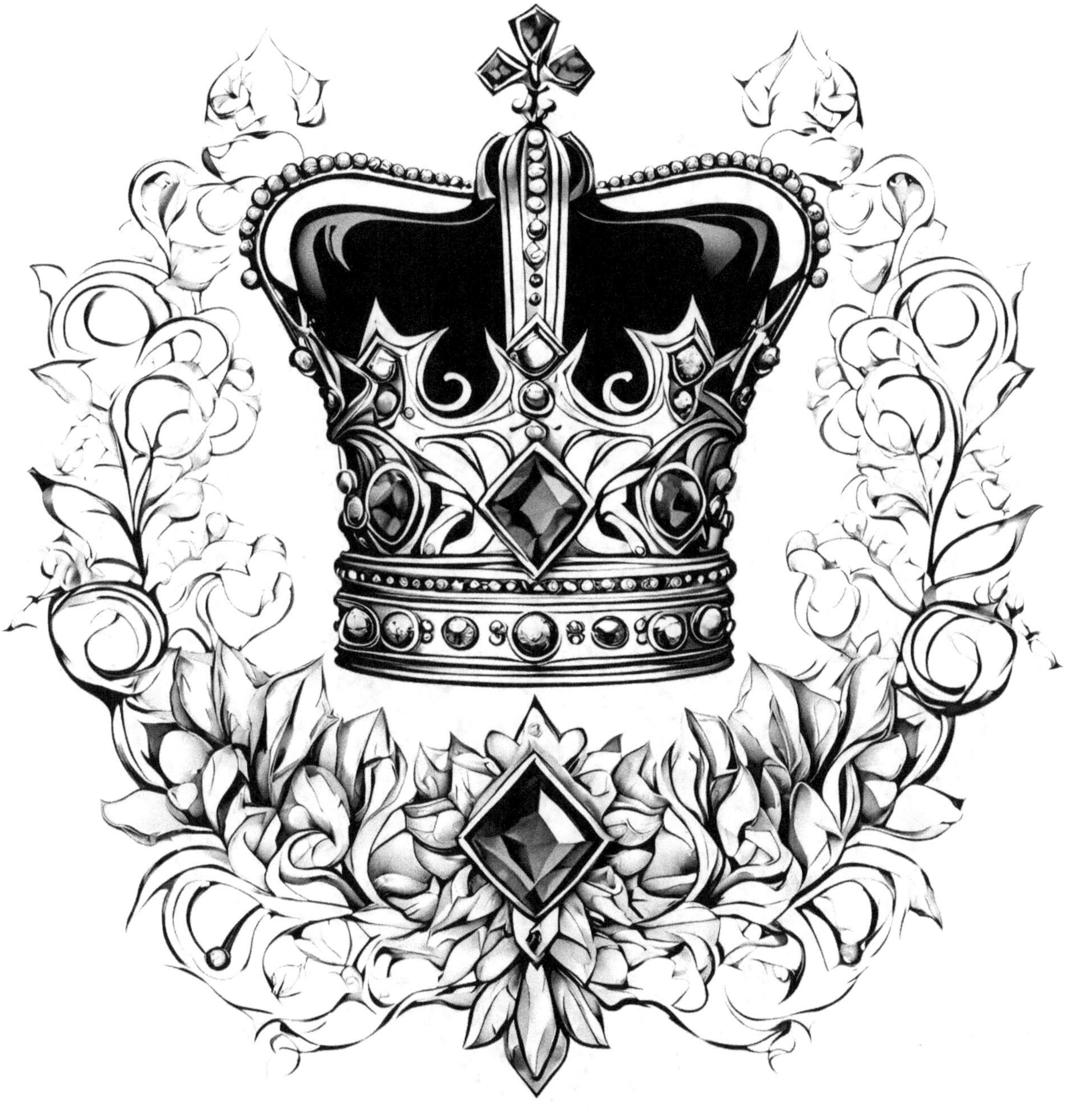

CROWN TATTOOS

PAGE 83

SNAKE TATTOOS

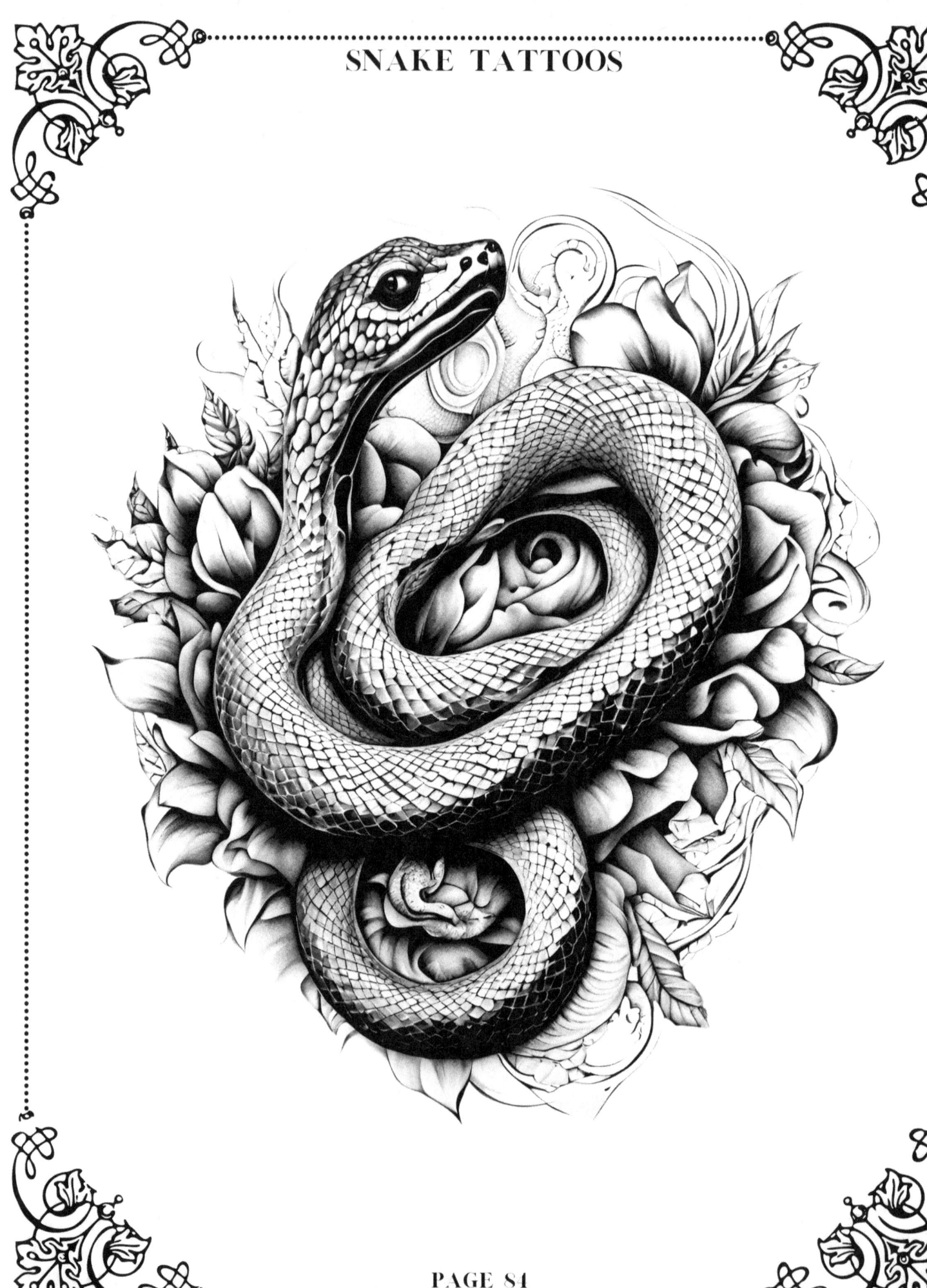

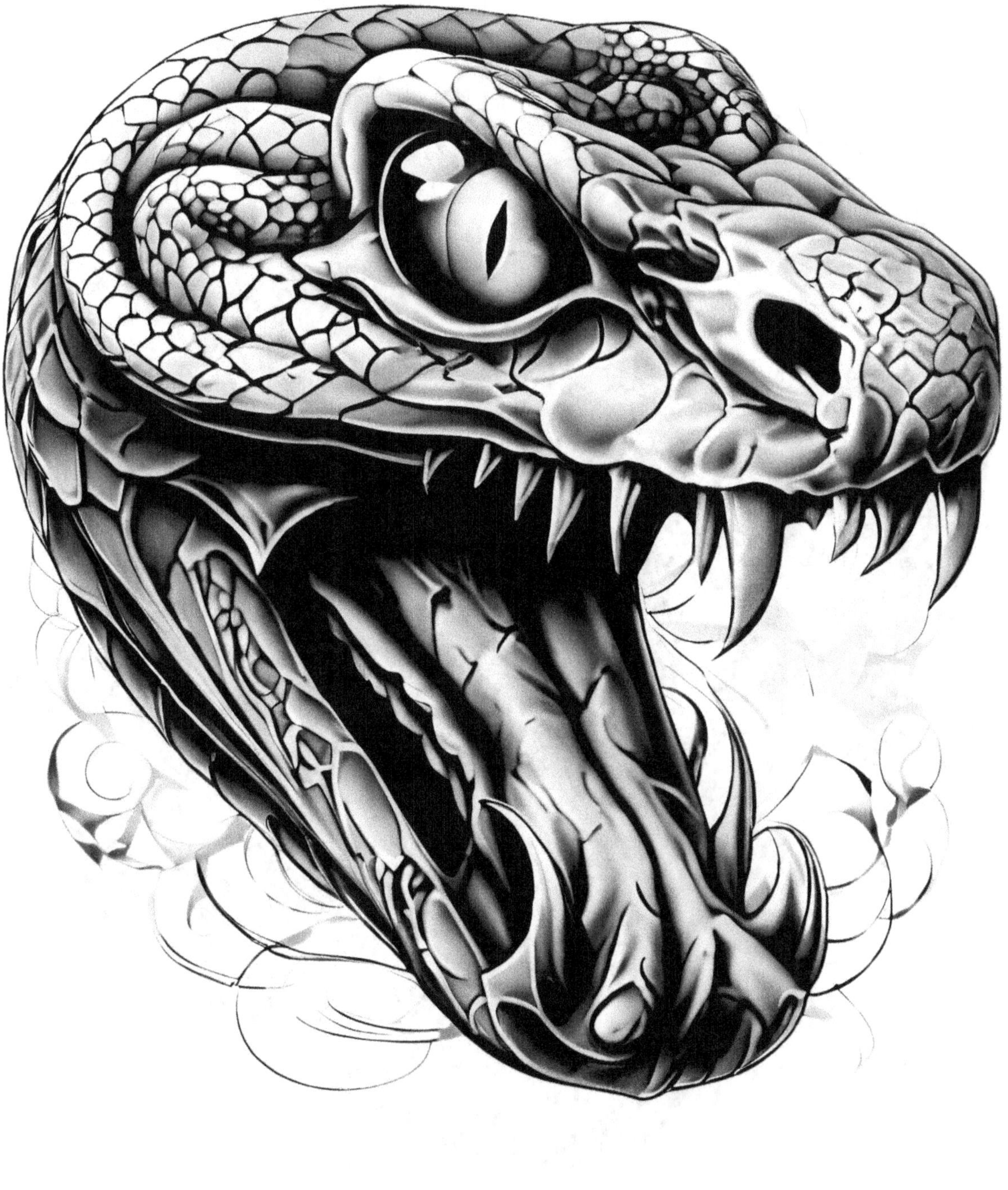

SNAKE TATTOOS

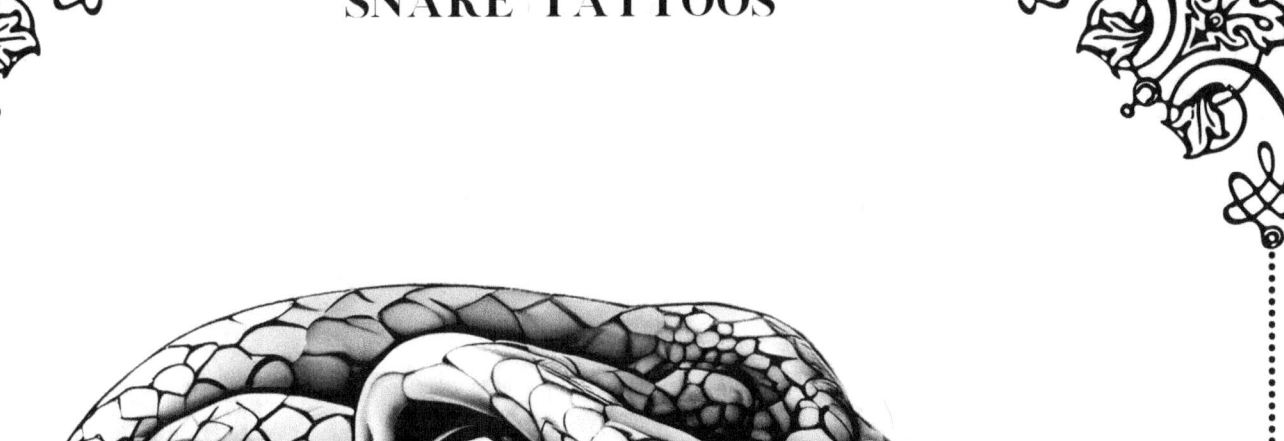

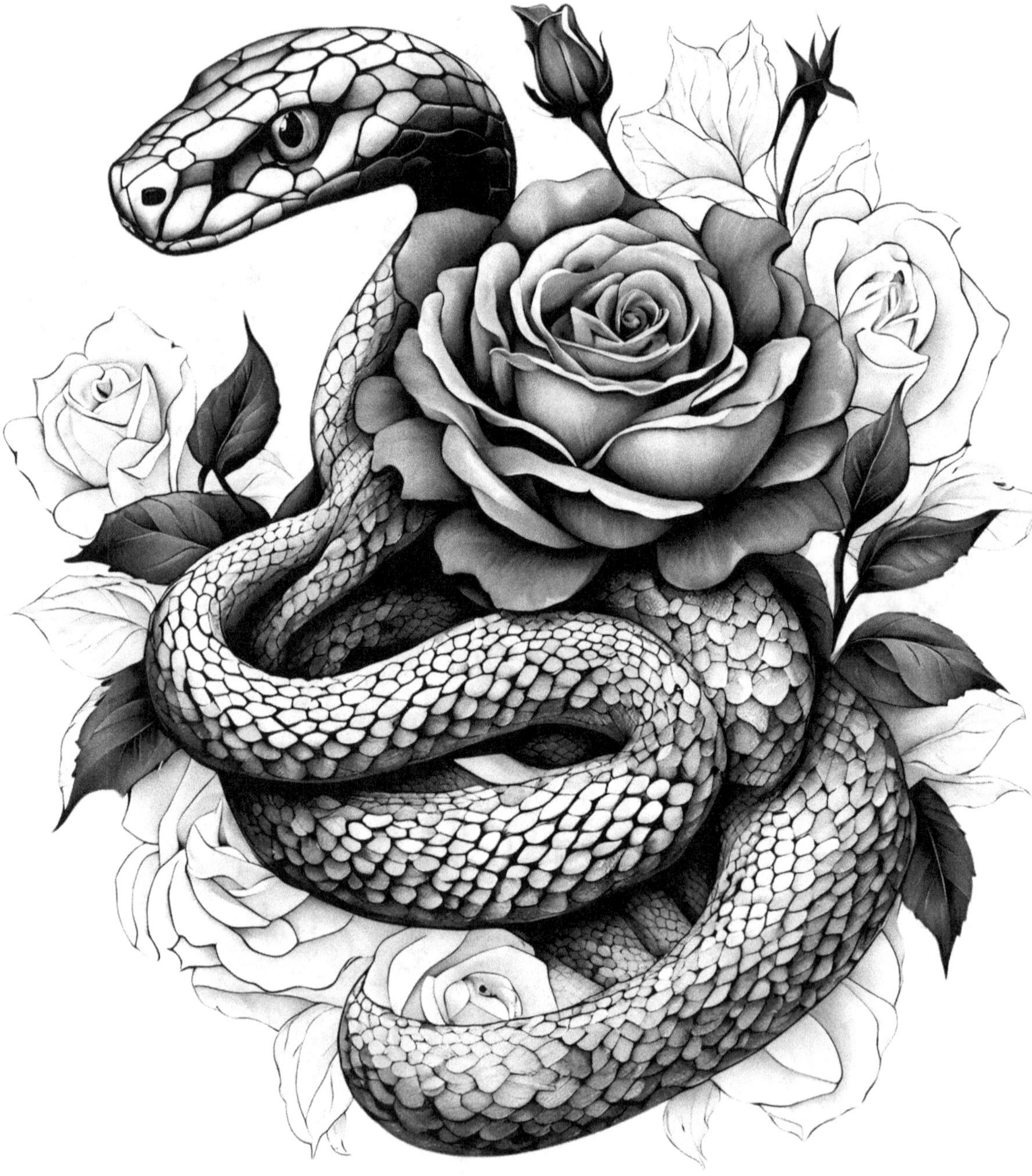

SNAKE TATTOOS

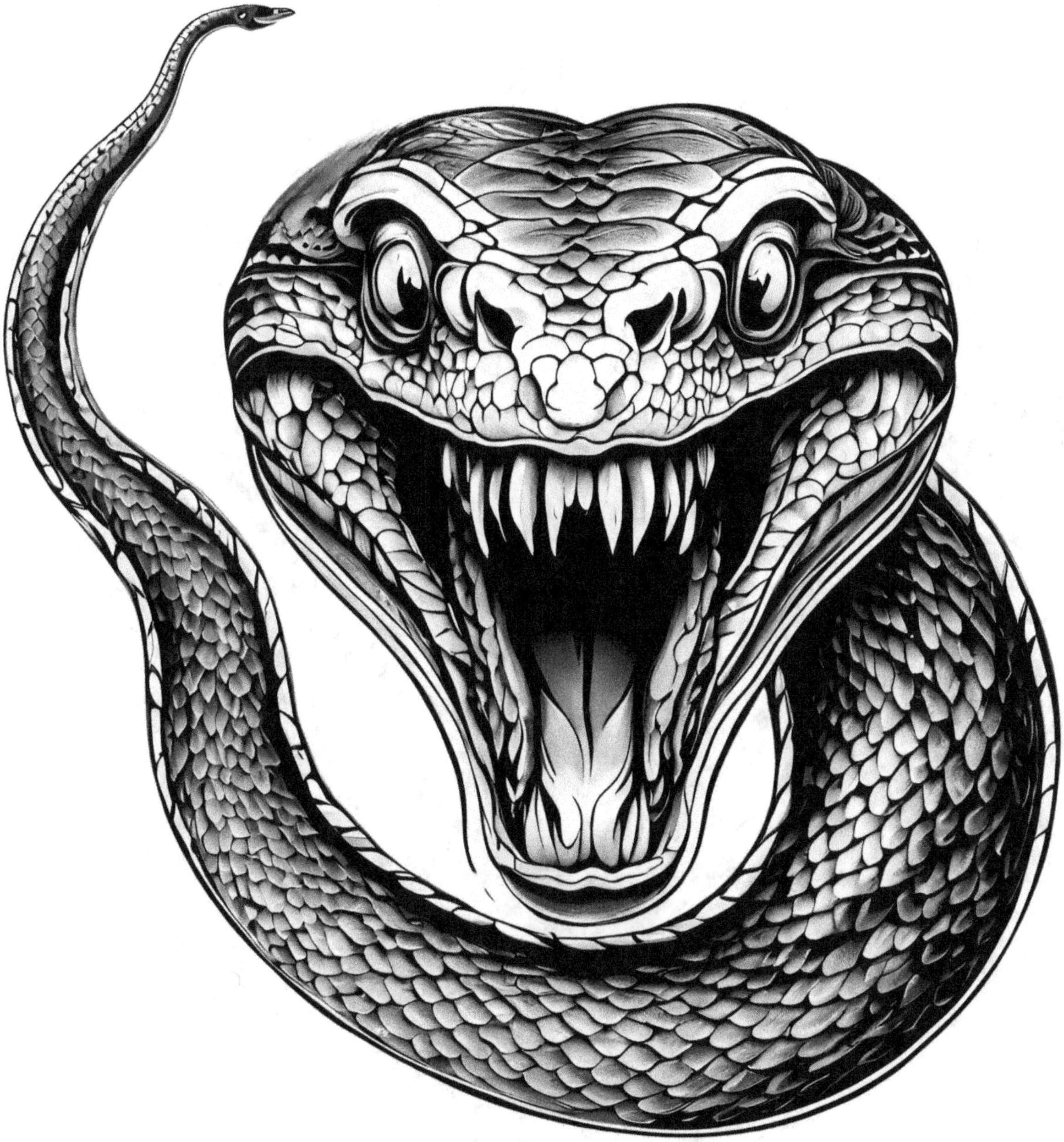

SNAKE TATTOOS

MUSICAL TATTOOS

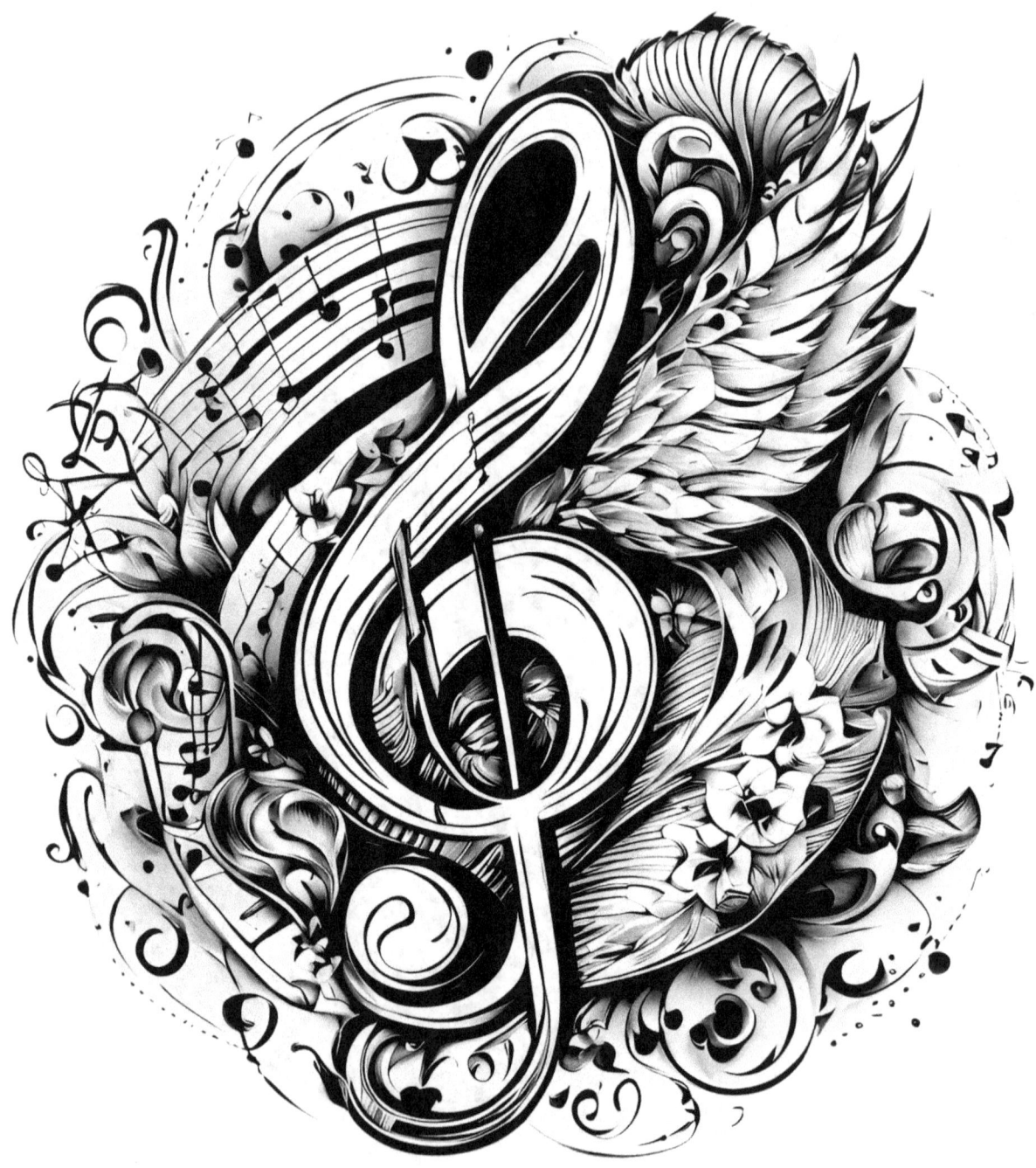

MUSICAL TATTOOS

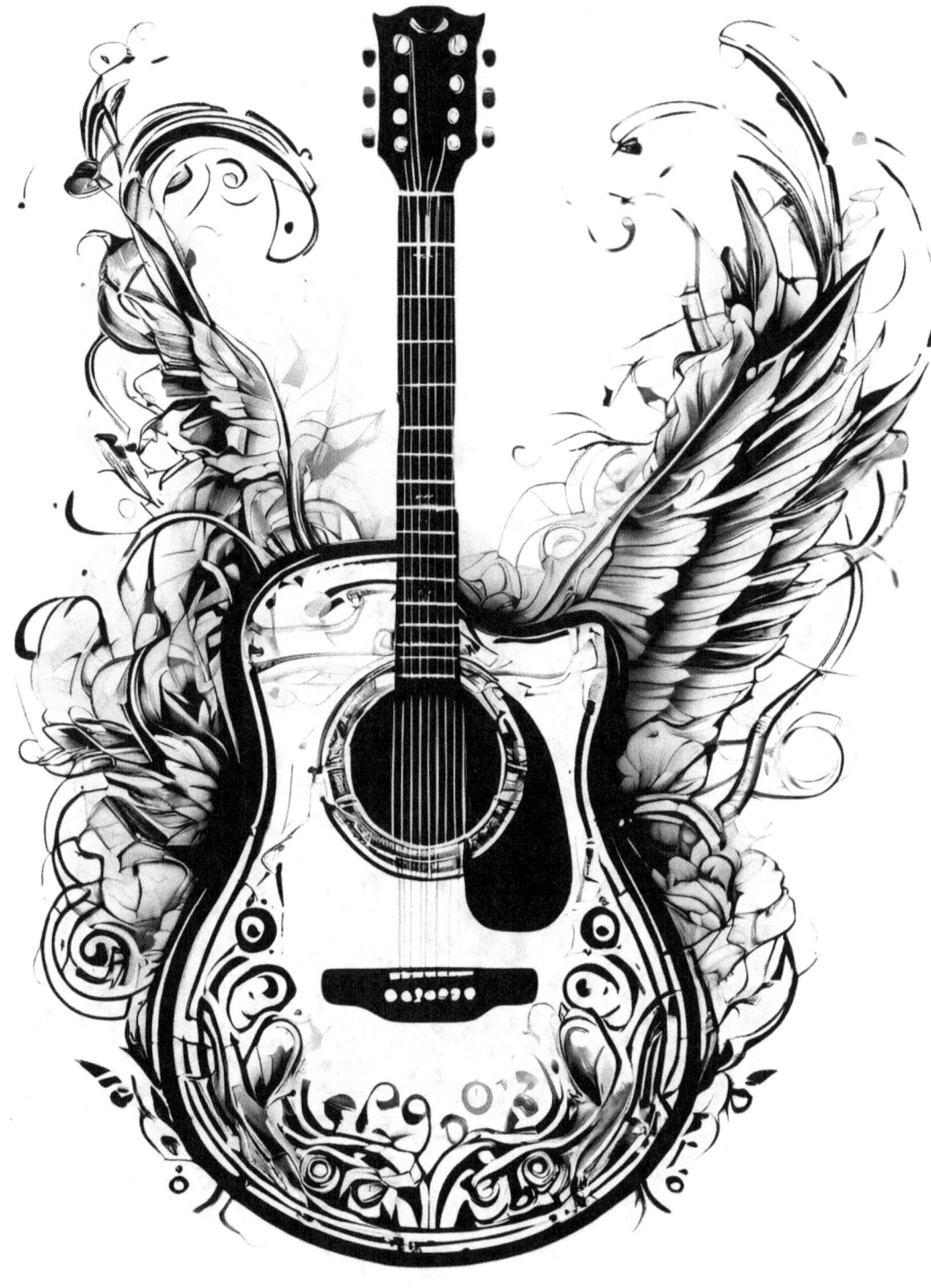

MUSICAL TATTOOS

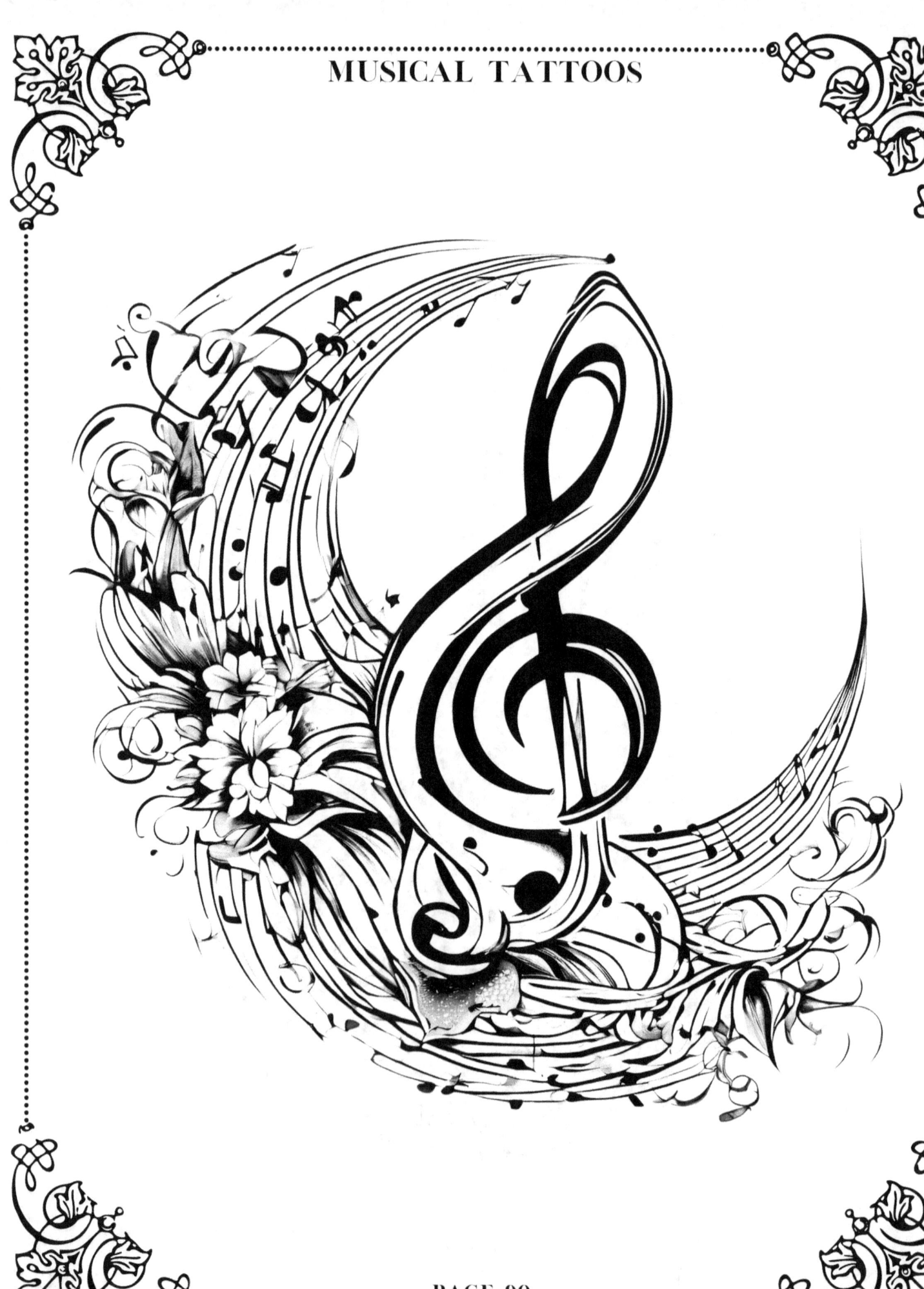

MUSICAL TATTOOS

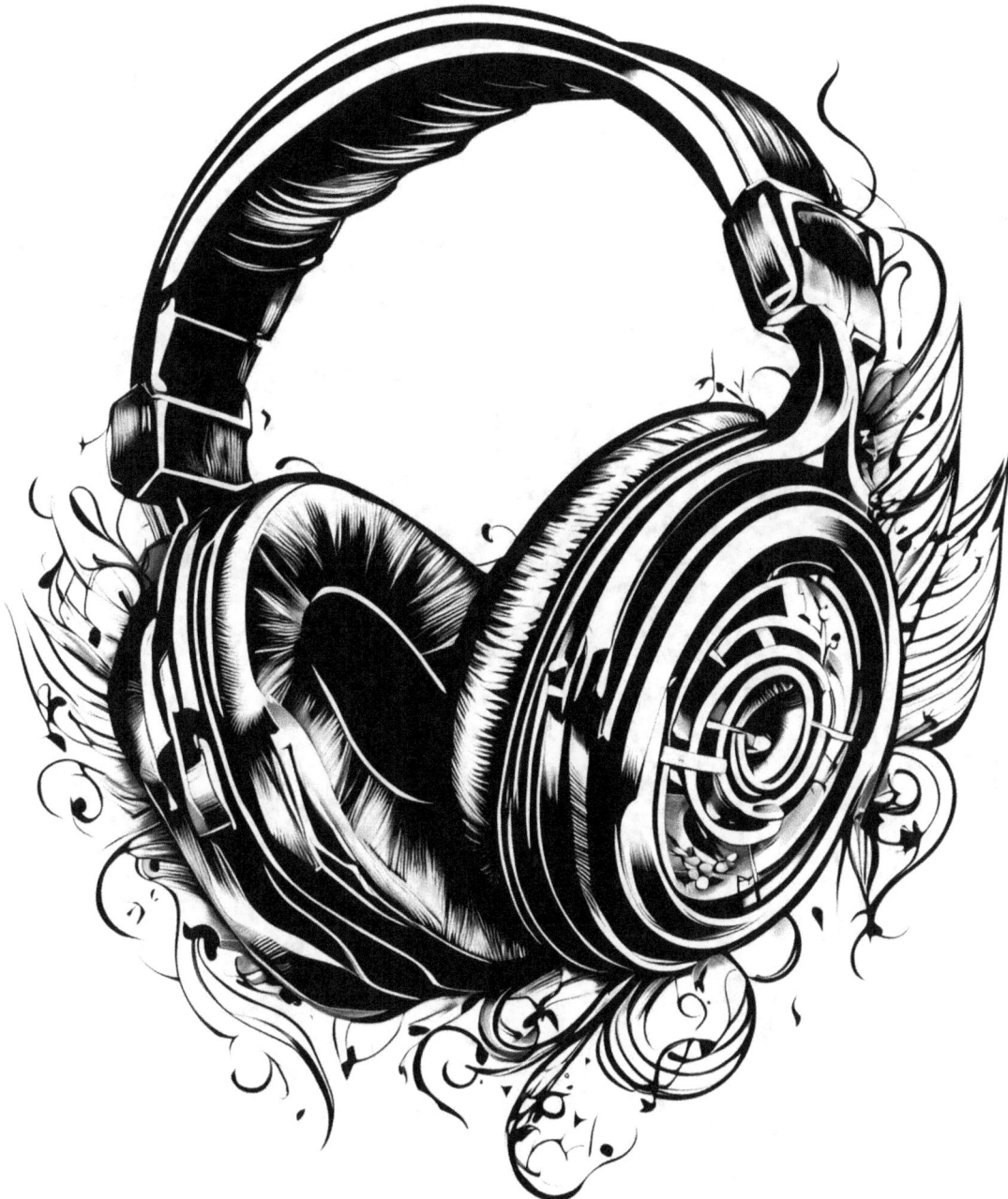

BUTTERFLY TATTOOS

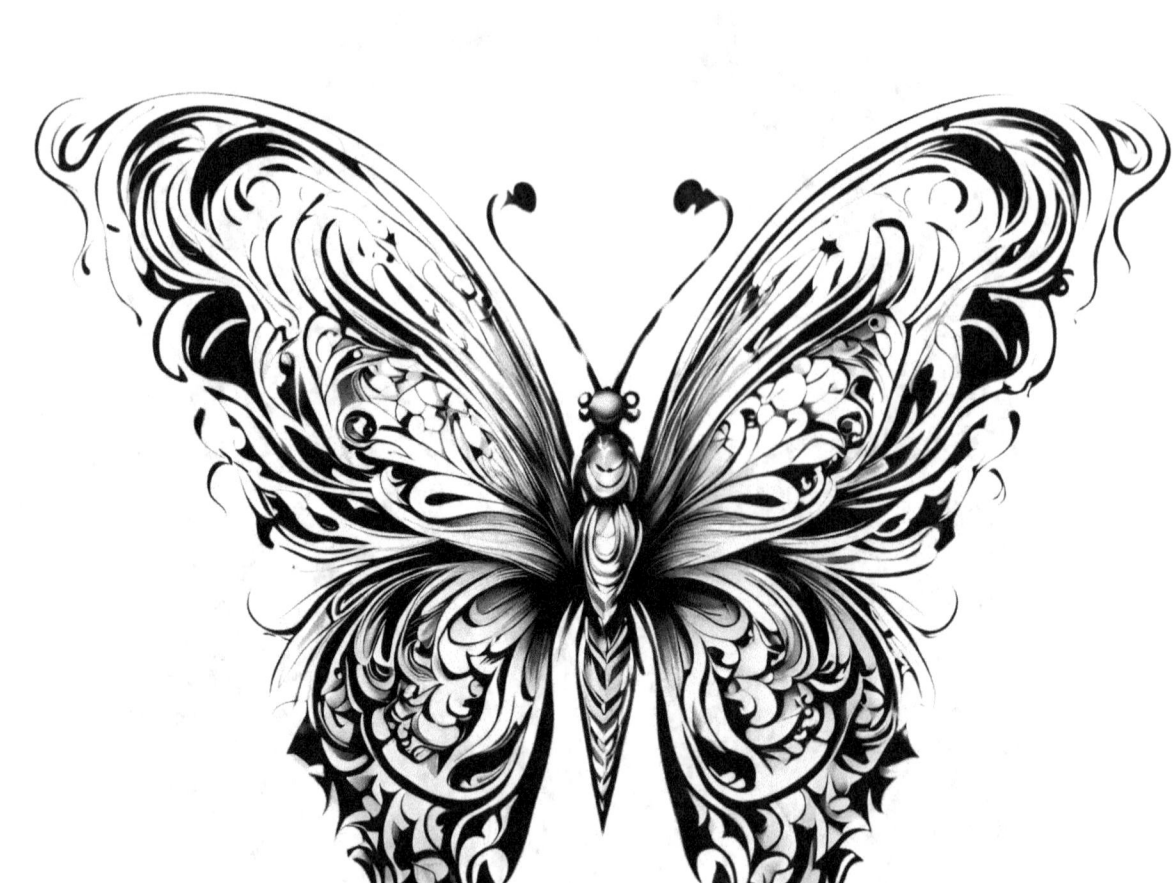

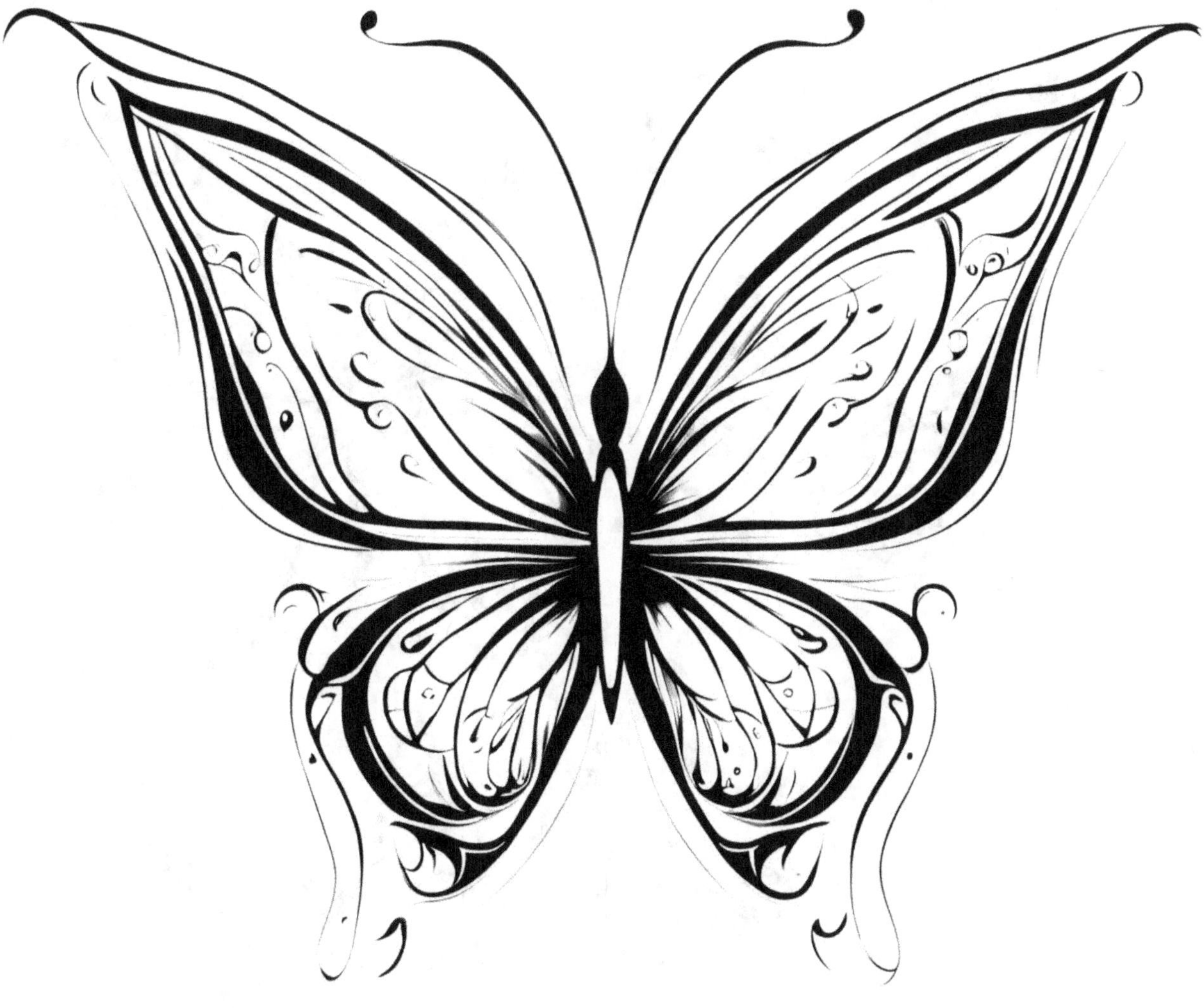

BUTTERFLY TATTOOS

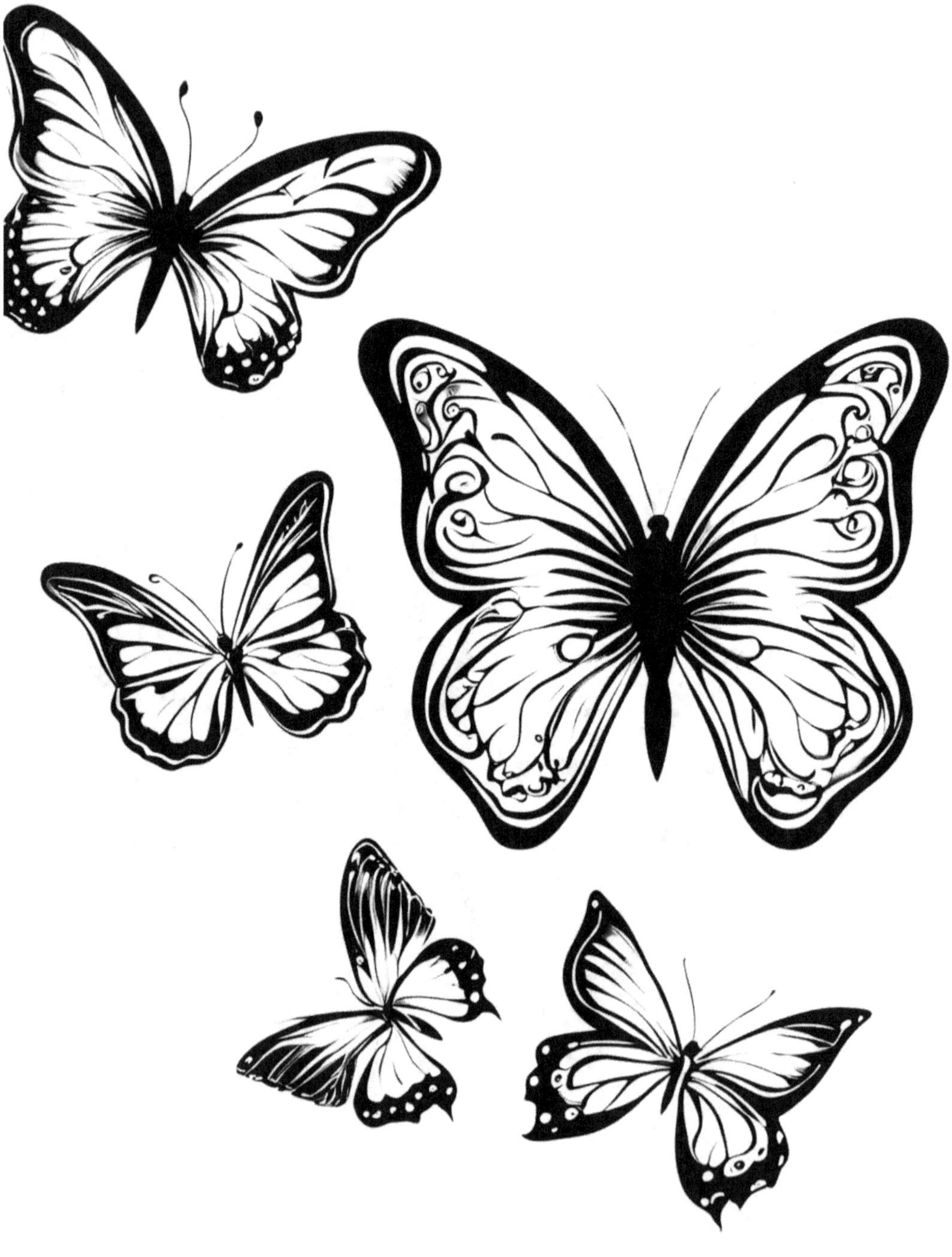

BUTTERFLY TATTOOS

VIKING TATTOOS

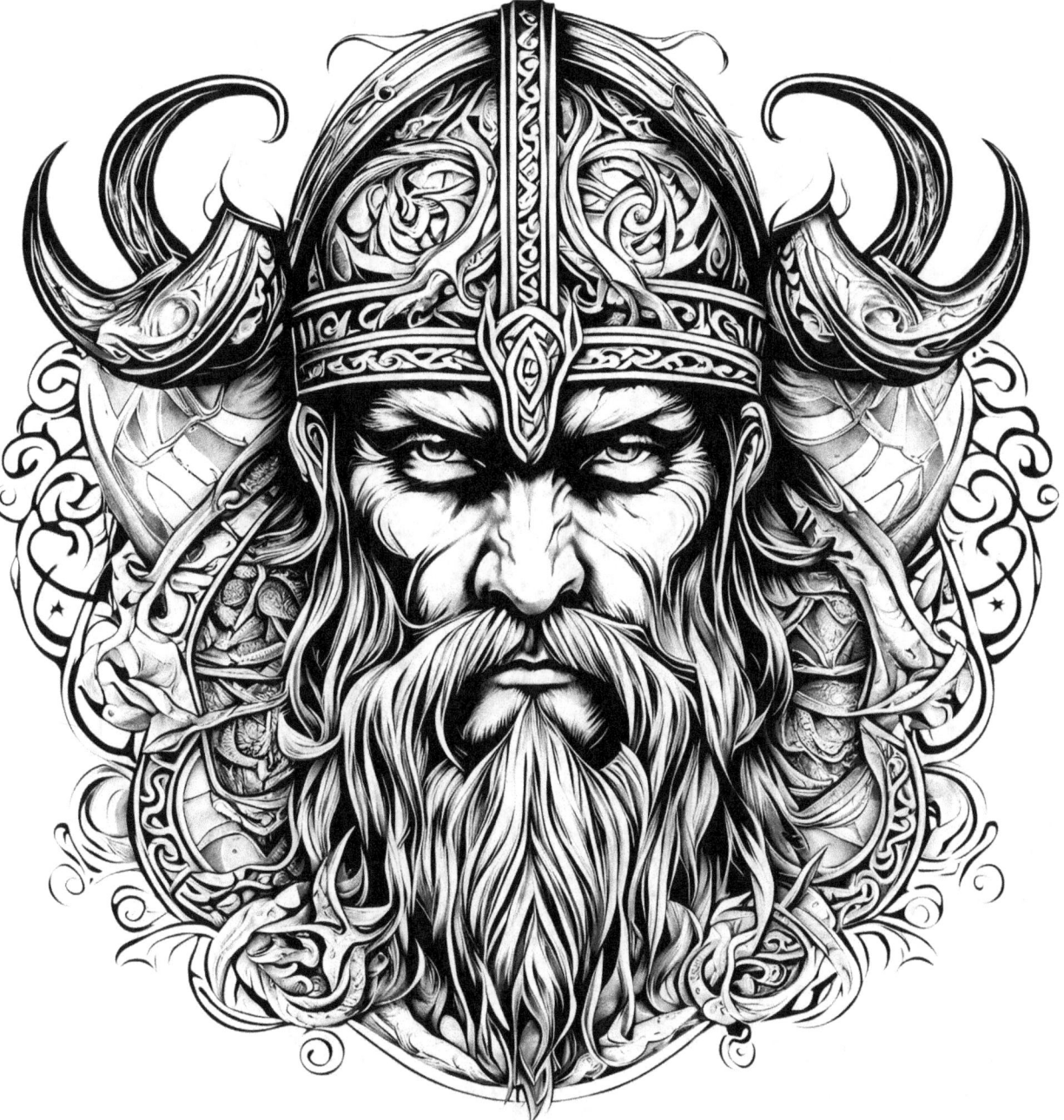

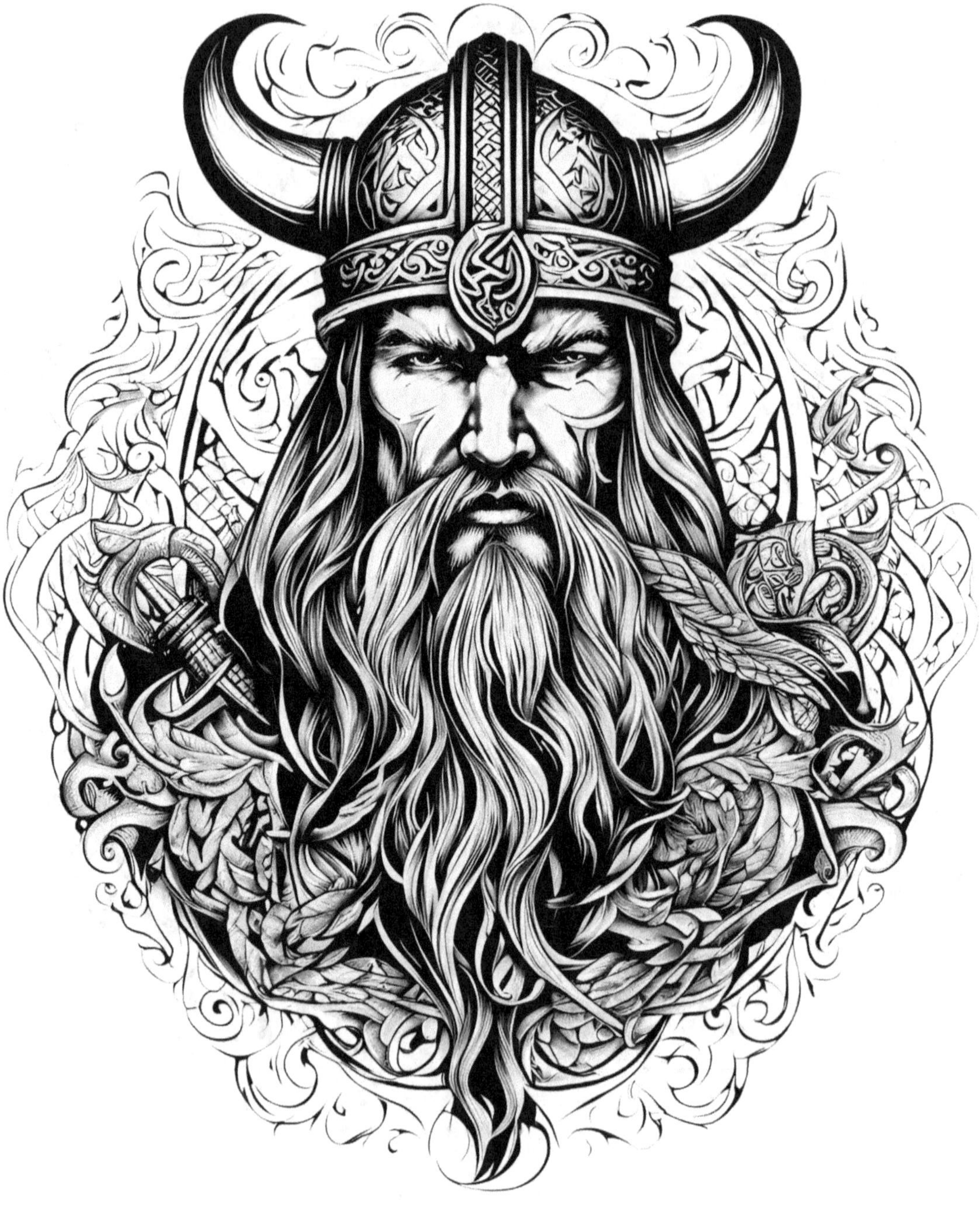

VIKING TATTOOS

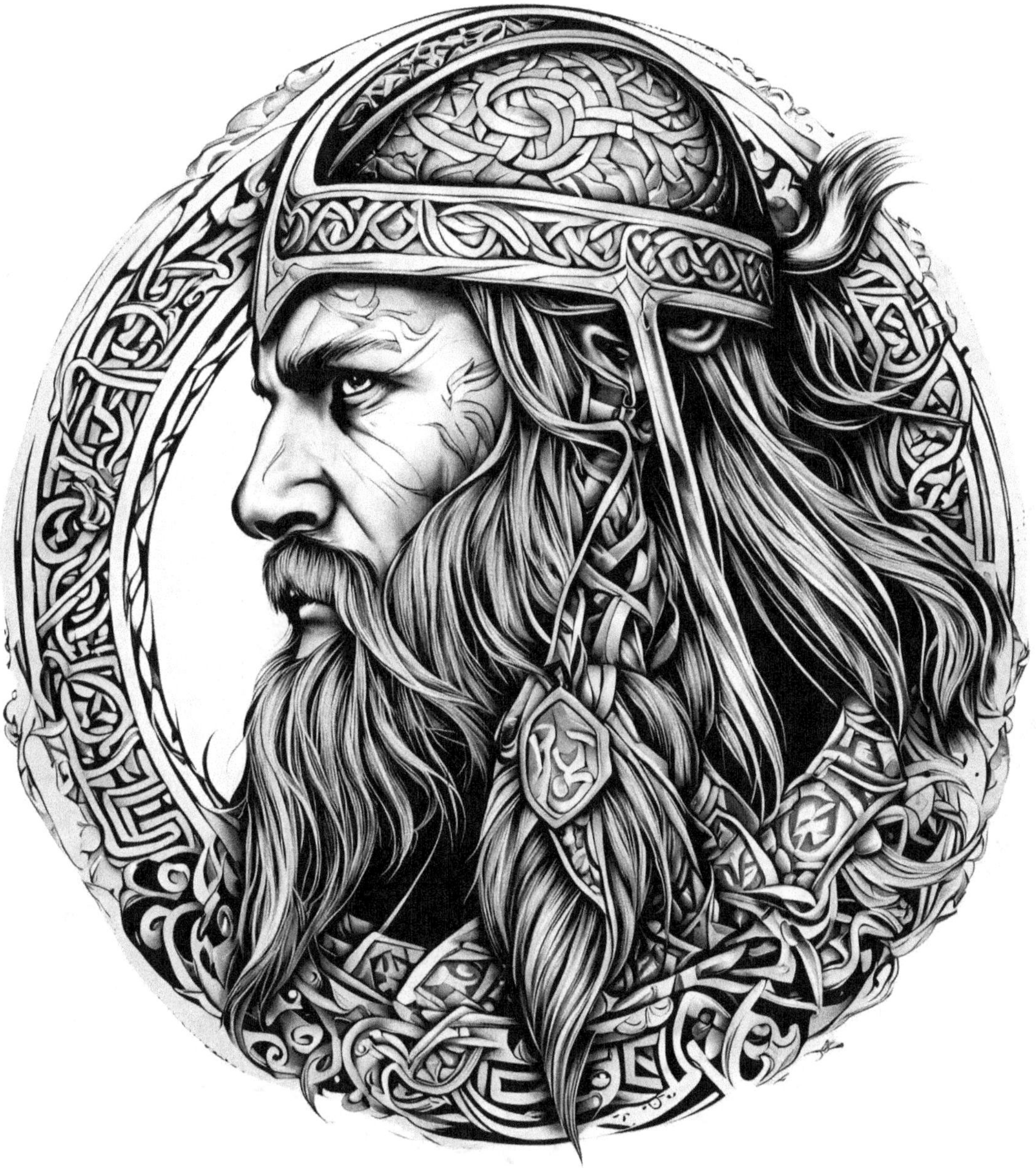

VIKING TATTOOS

PAGE 97

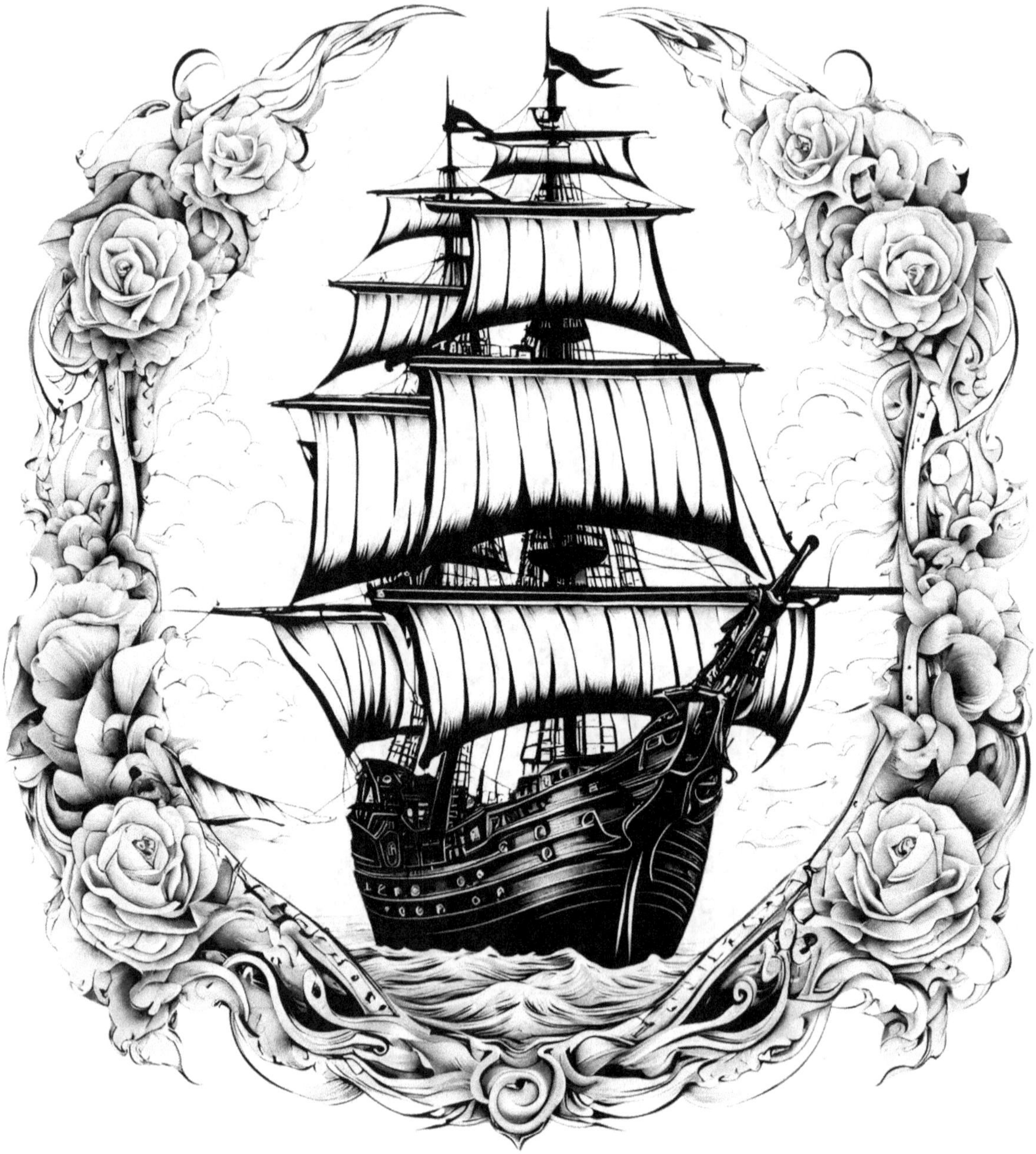

PIRATE SHIP TATTOOS

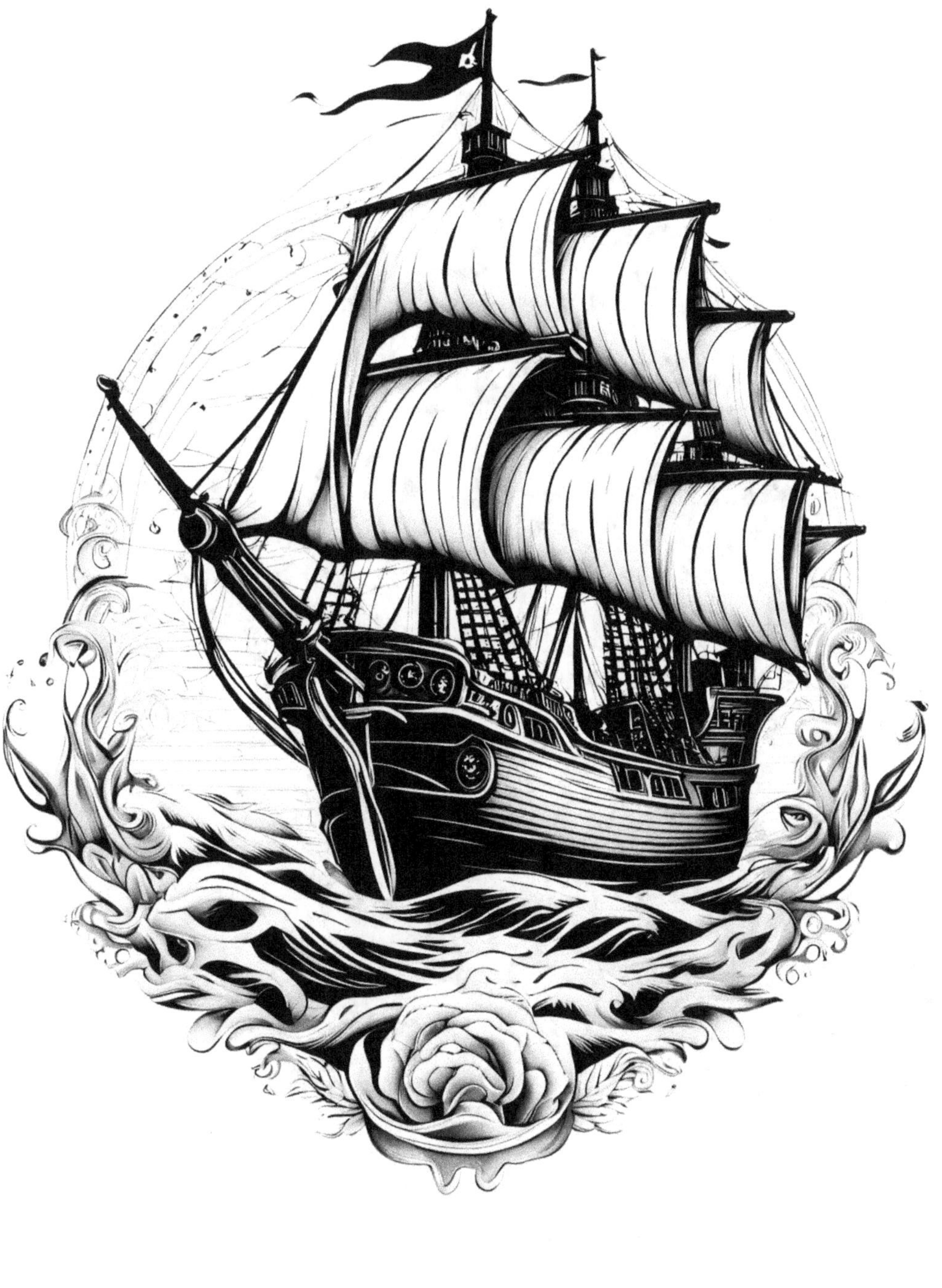

PIRATE SHIP TATTOOS

PIRATE SHIP TATTOOS

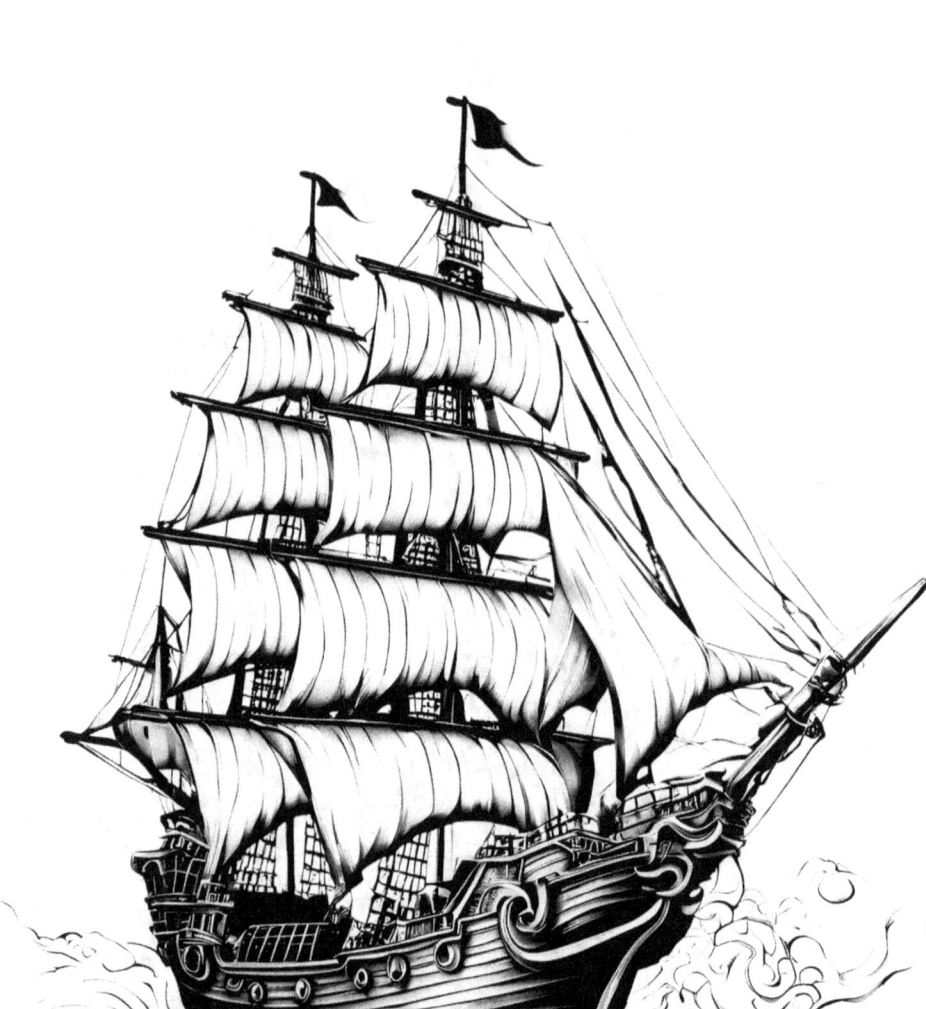

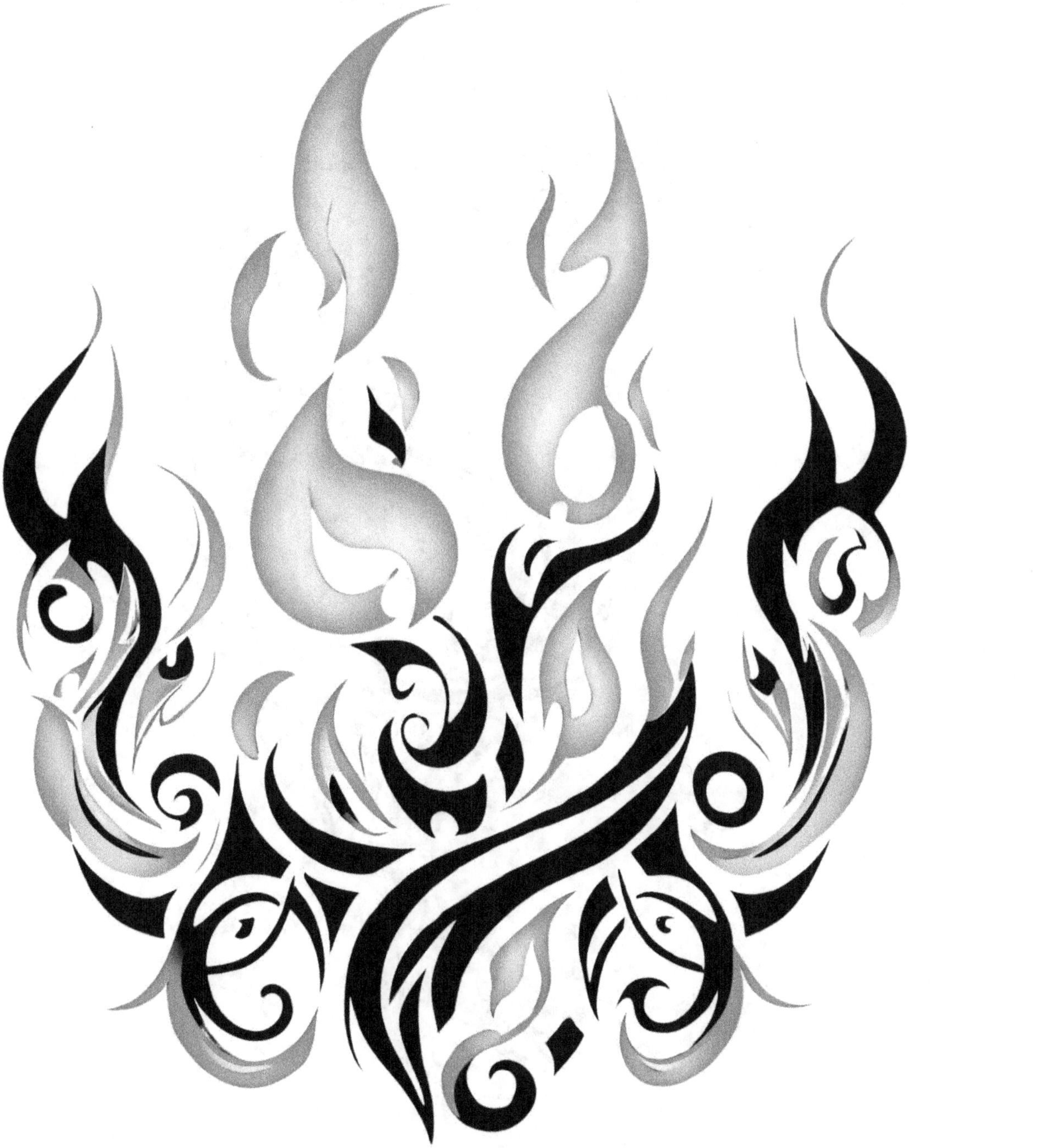

TRIBAL TATTOOS

TRIBAL TATTOOS

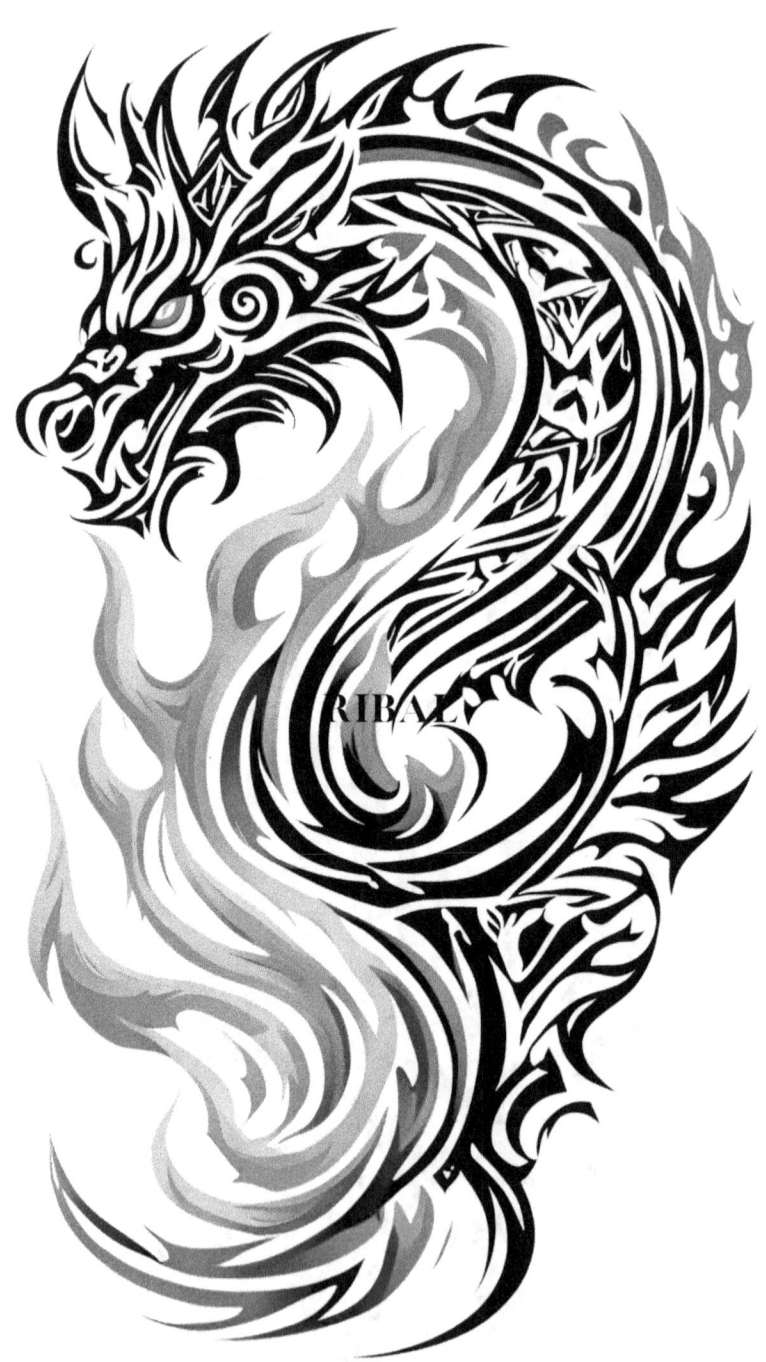

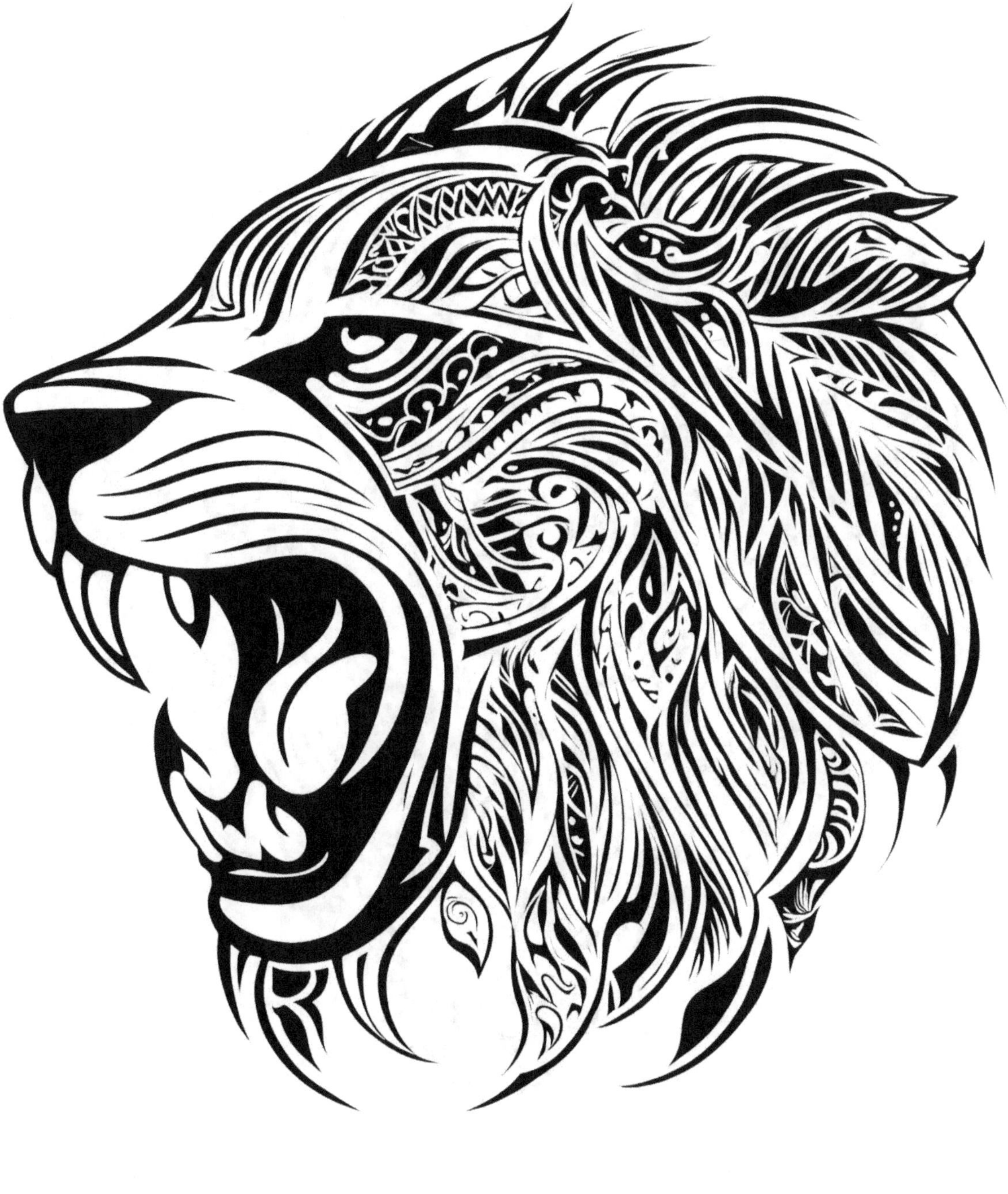

TRIBAL TATTOOS

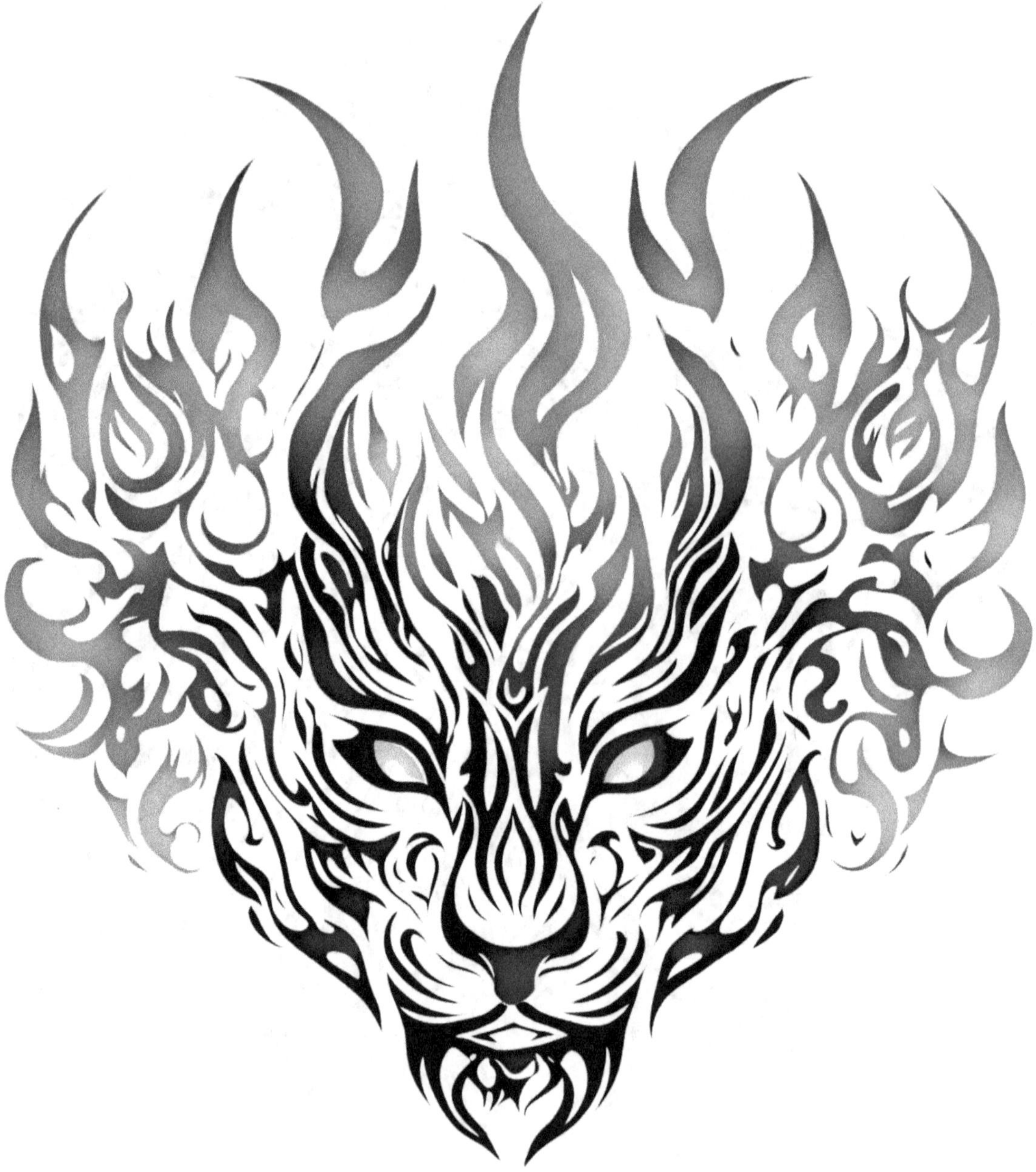

TRIBAL TATTOOS

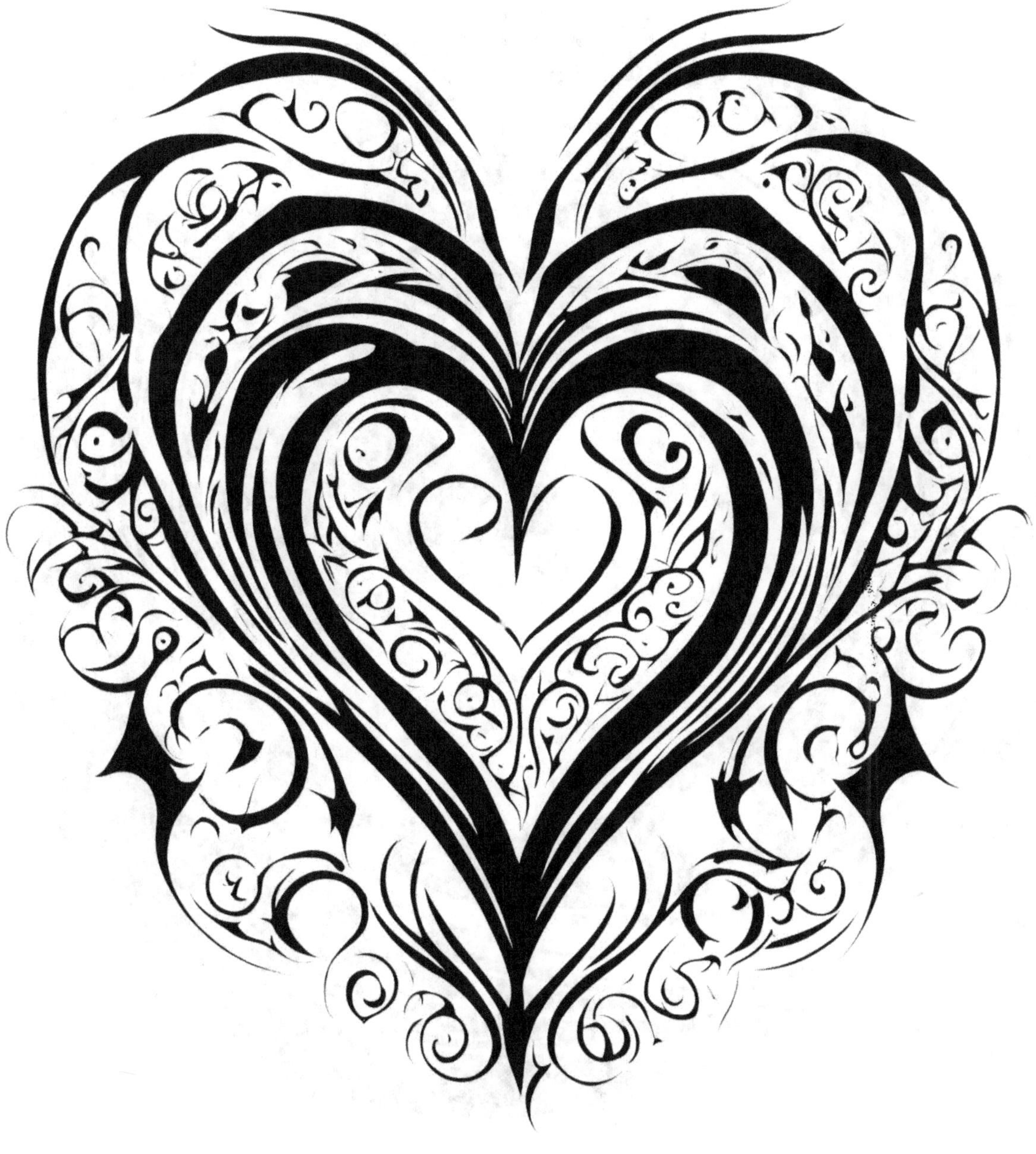

TRIBAL TATTOOS

SPACE THEMED TATTOOS

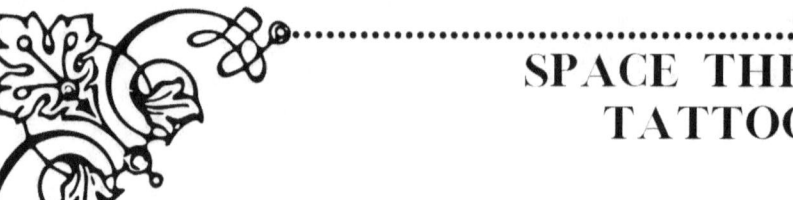

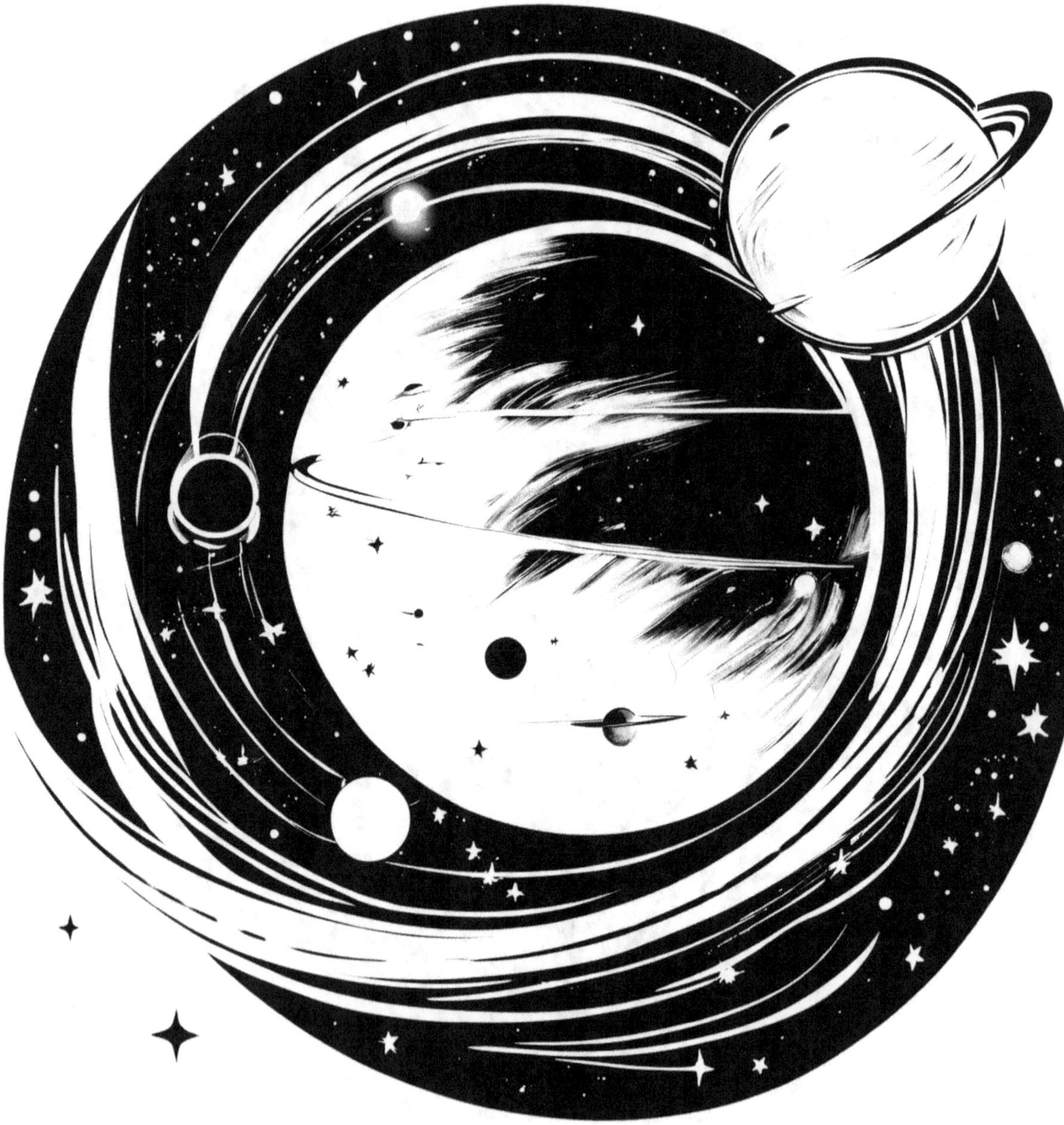

SPACE THEMED TATTOOS

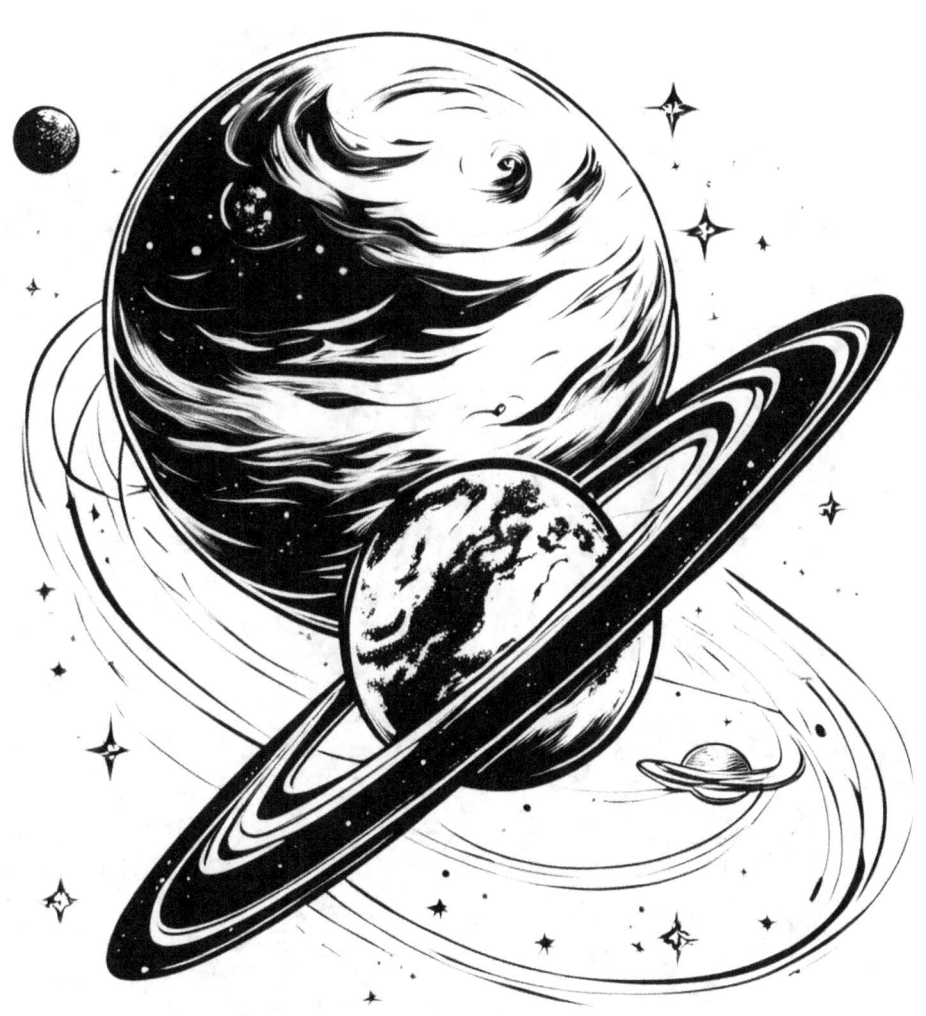

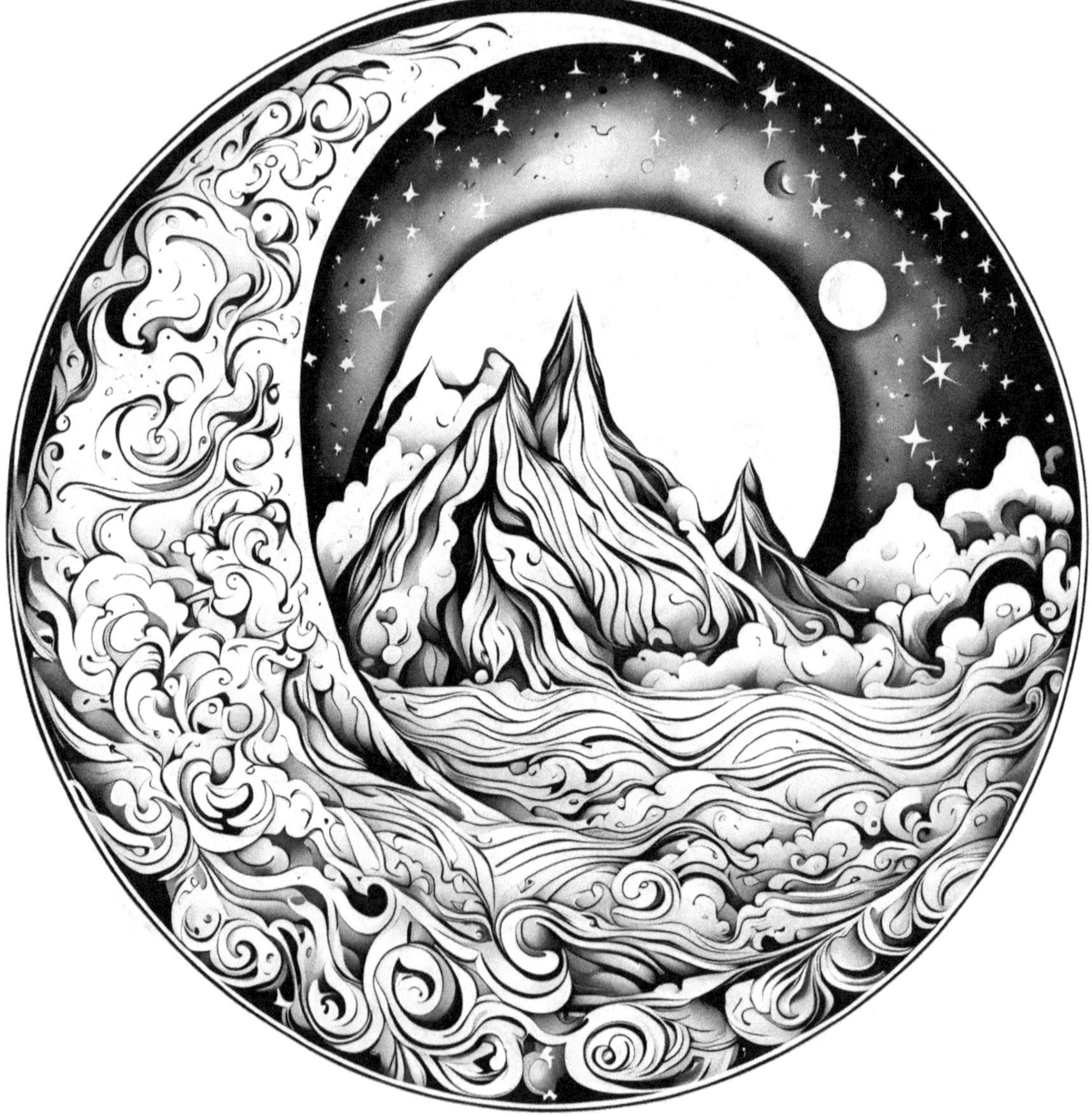

SPACE THEMED TATTOOS

SPACE THEMED TATTOOS

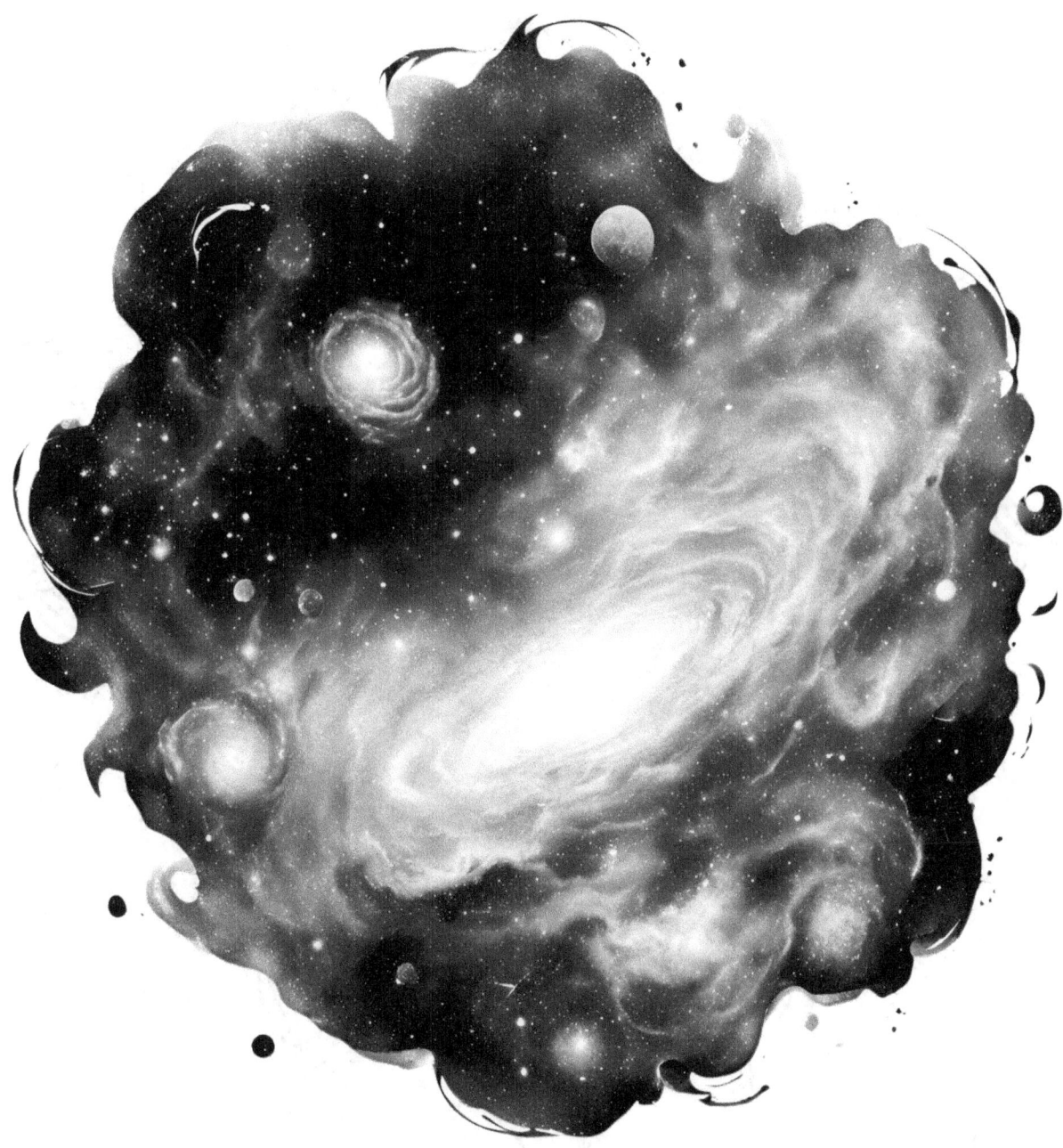

SPACE THEMED TATTOOS

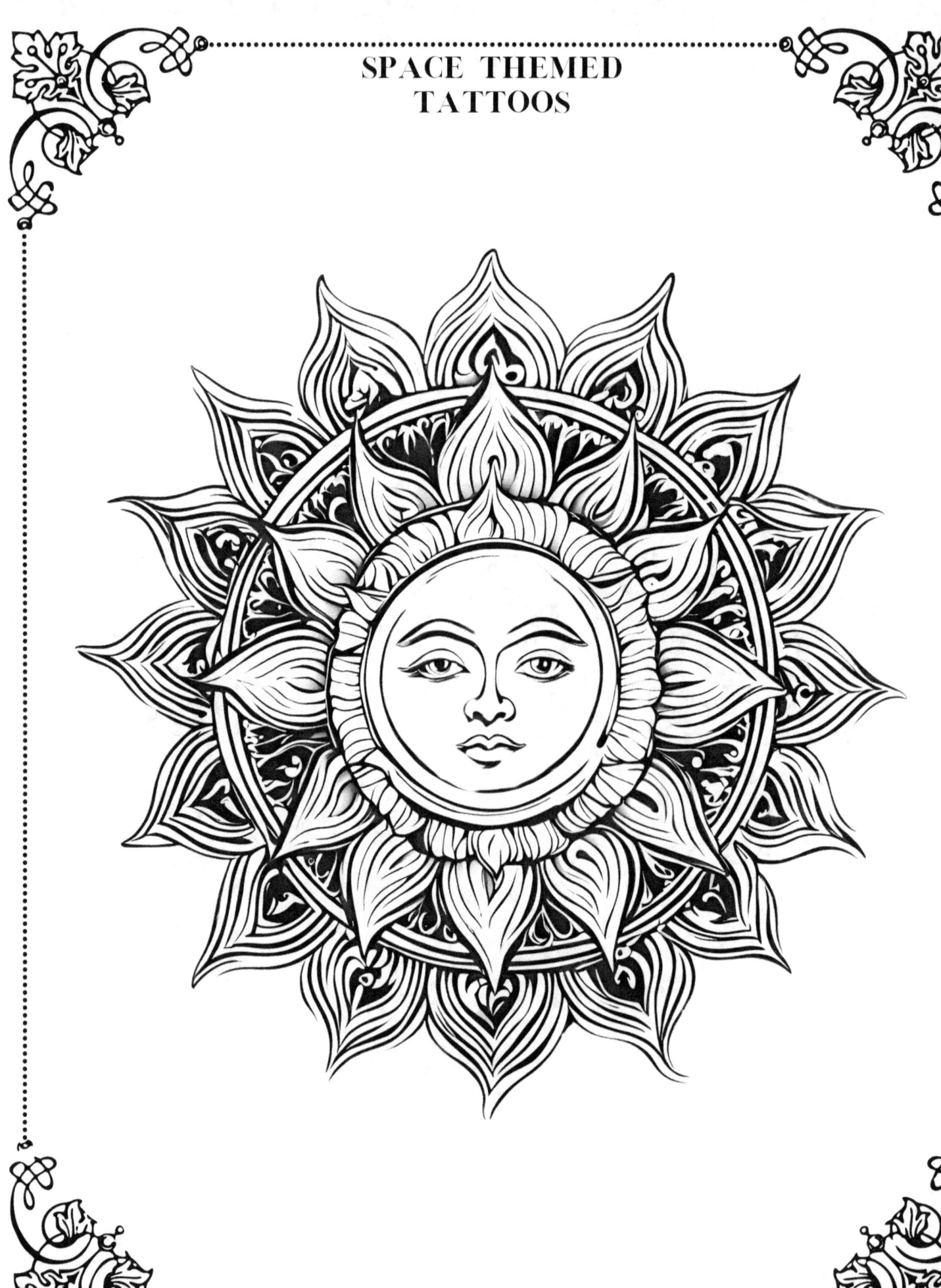

SPACESHIP TATTOOS

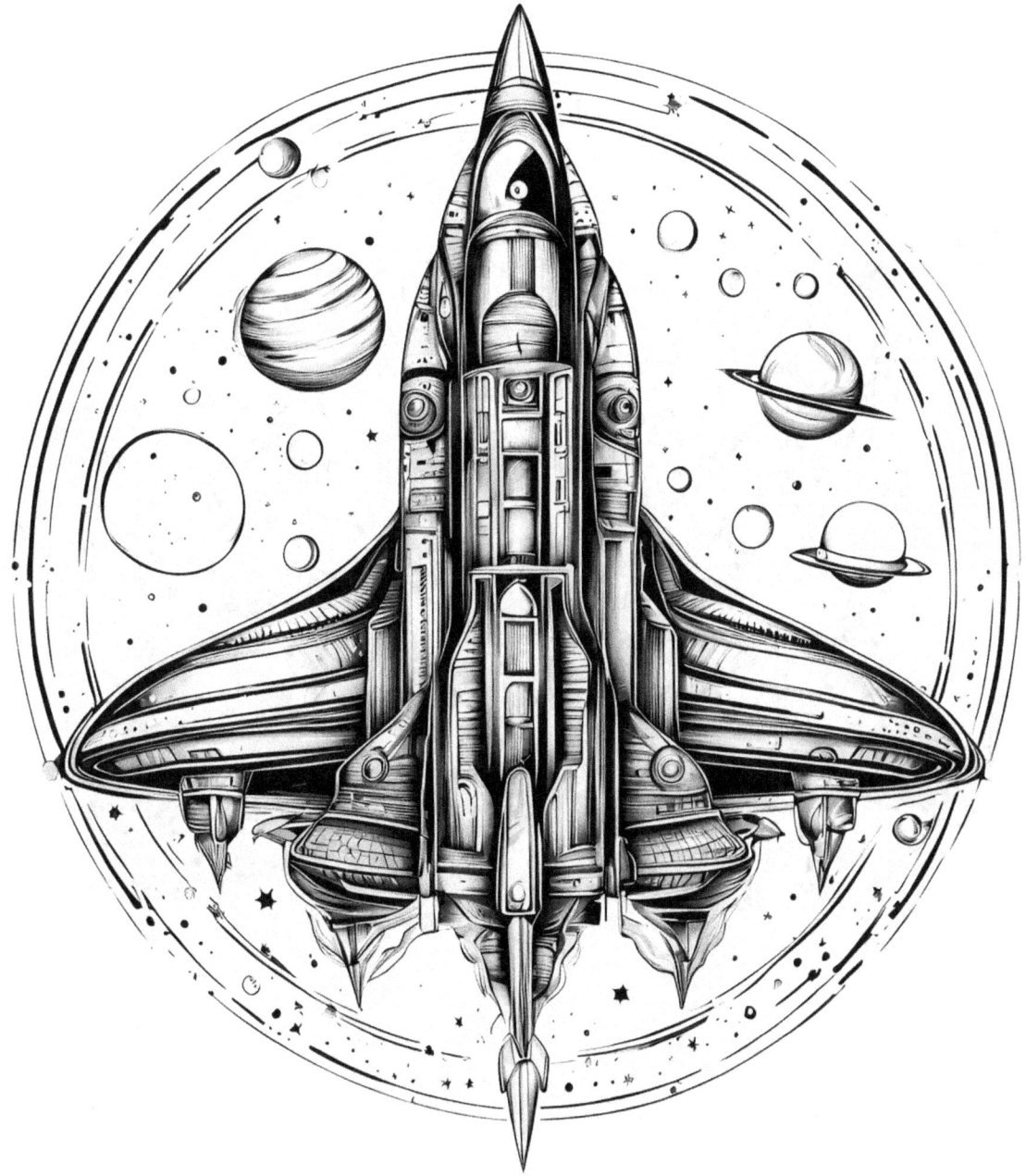

PAGE 111

SPACESHIP TATTOOS

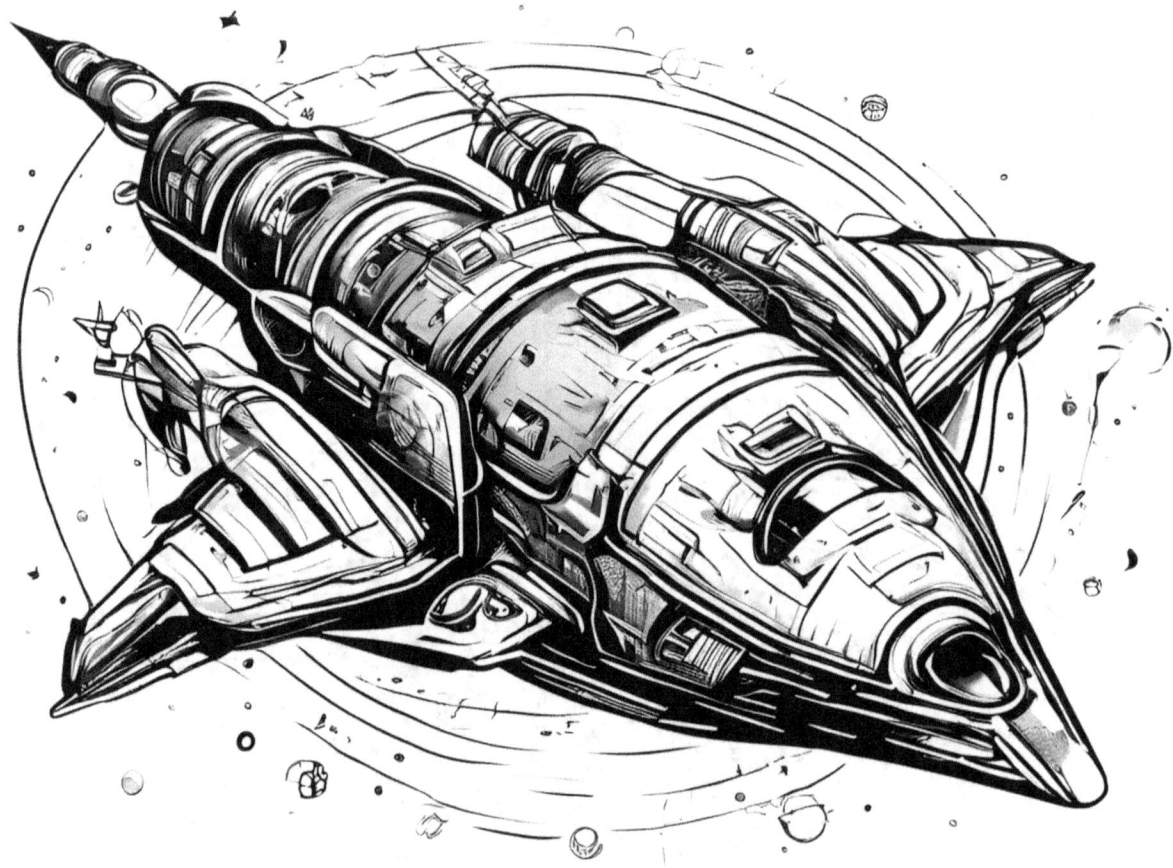

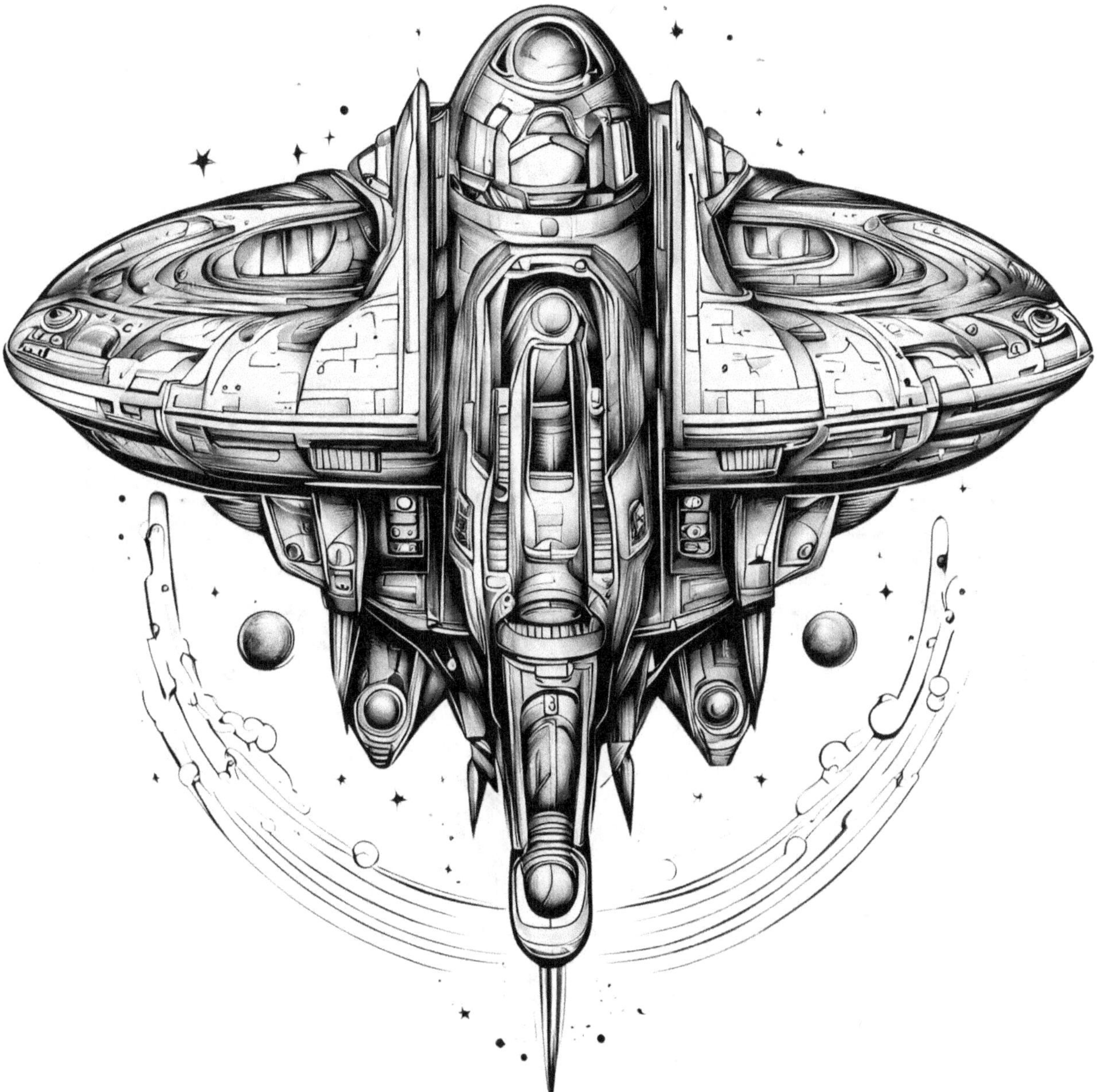

SPACESHIP TATTOOS

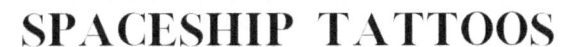

PAGE 113

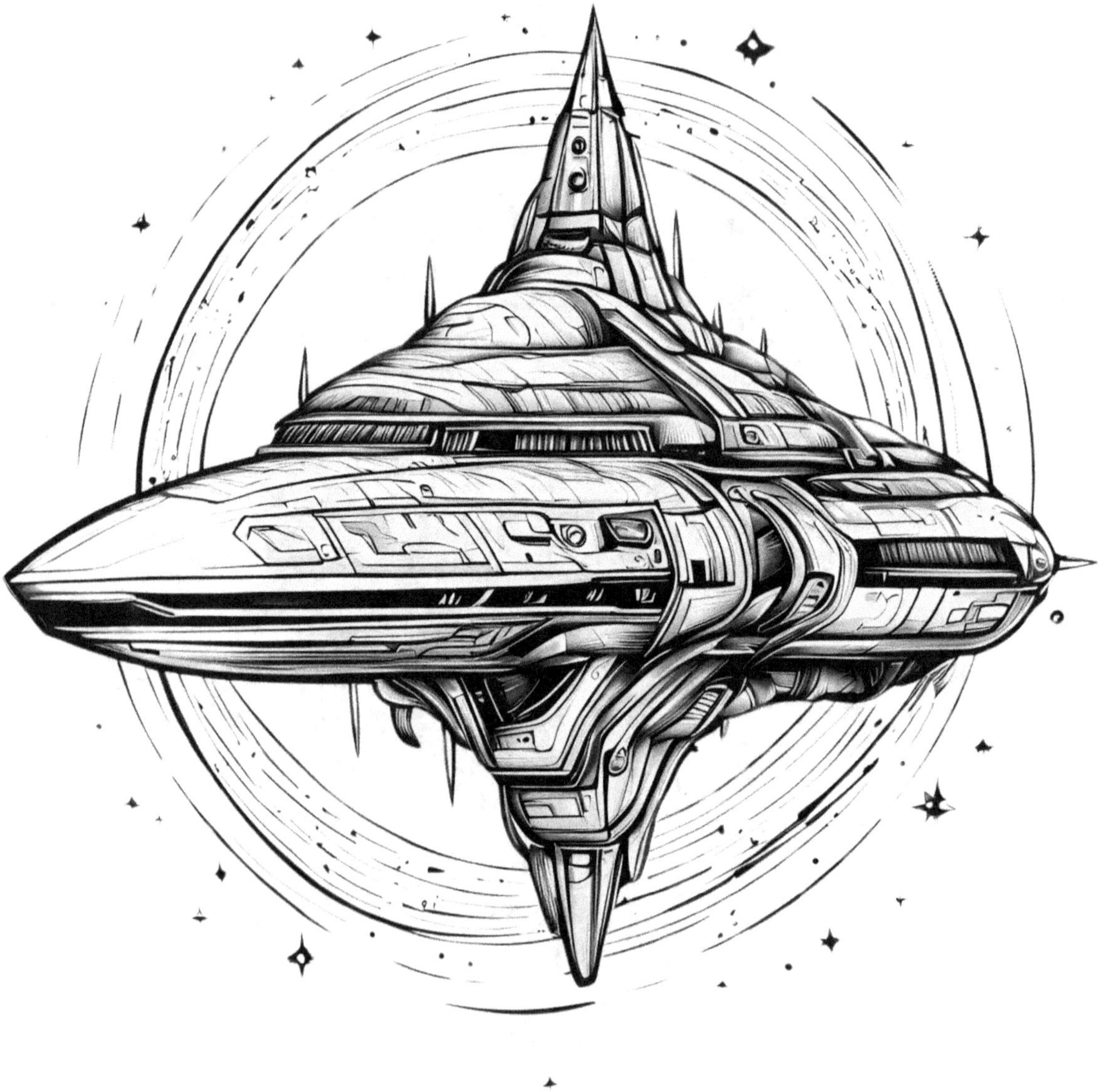

SPACESHIP TATTOOS

PAGE 114

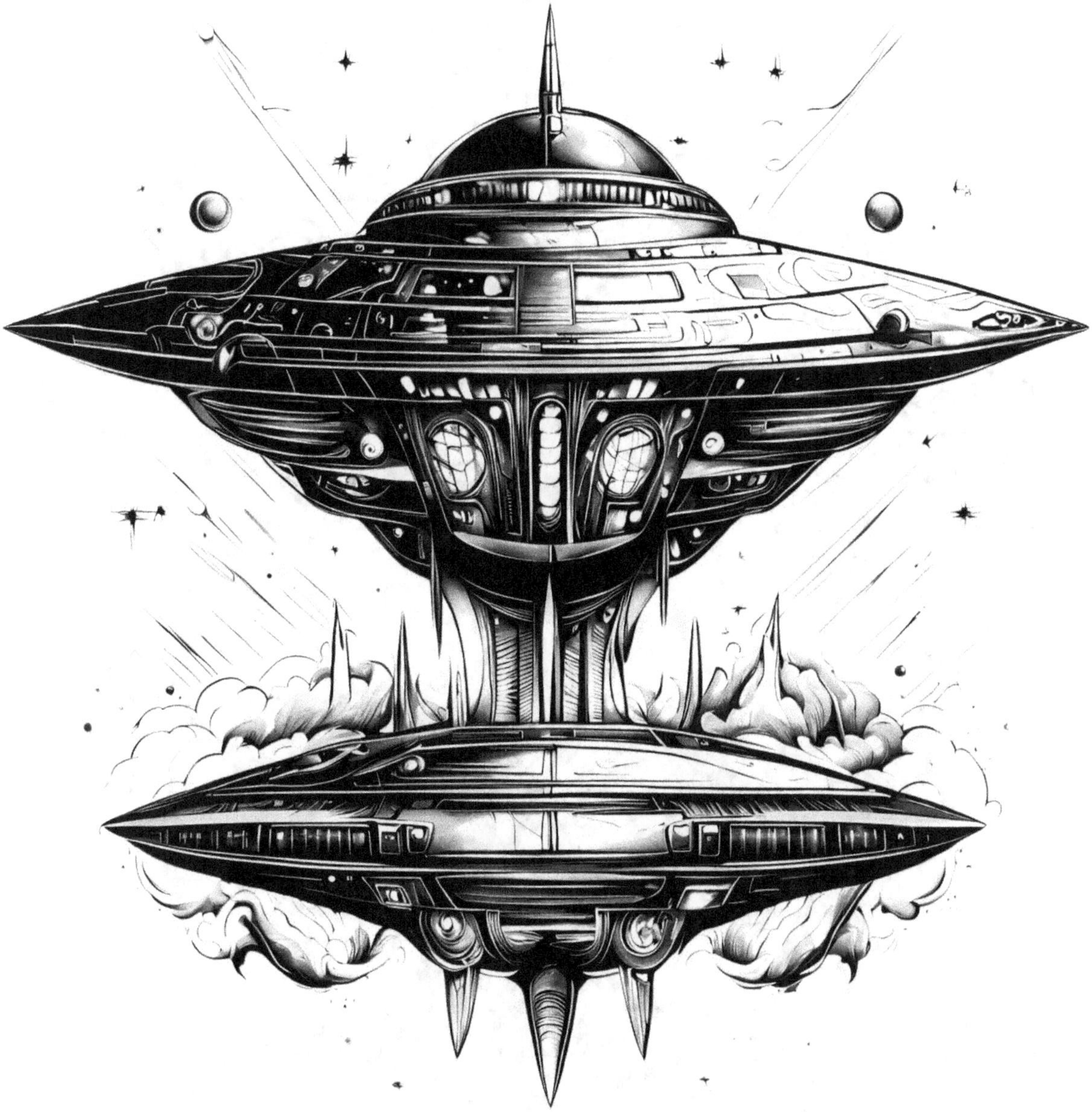

SPACESHIP TATTOOS

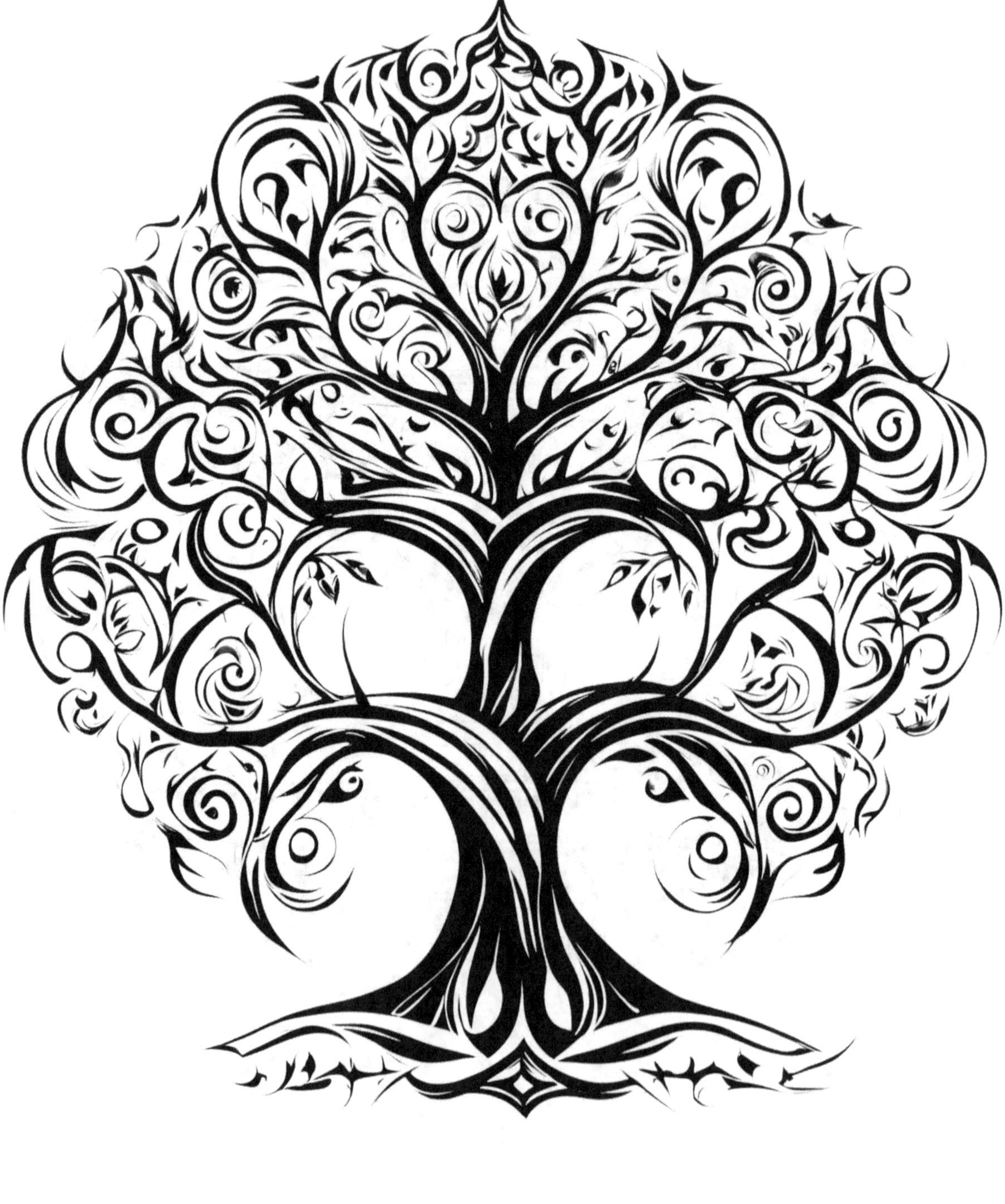

TREE TATTOOS

TREE TATTOOS

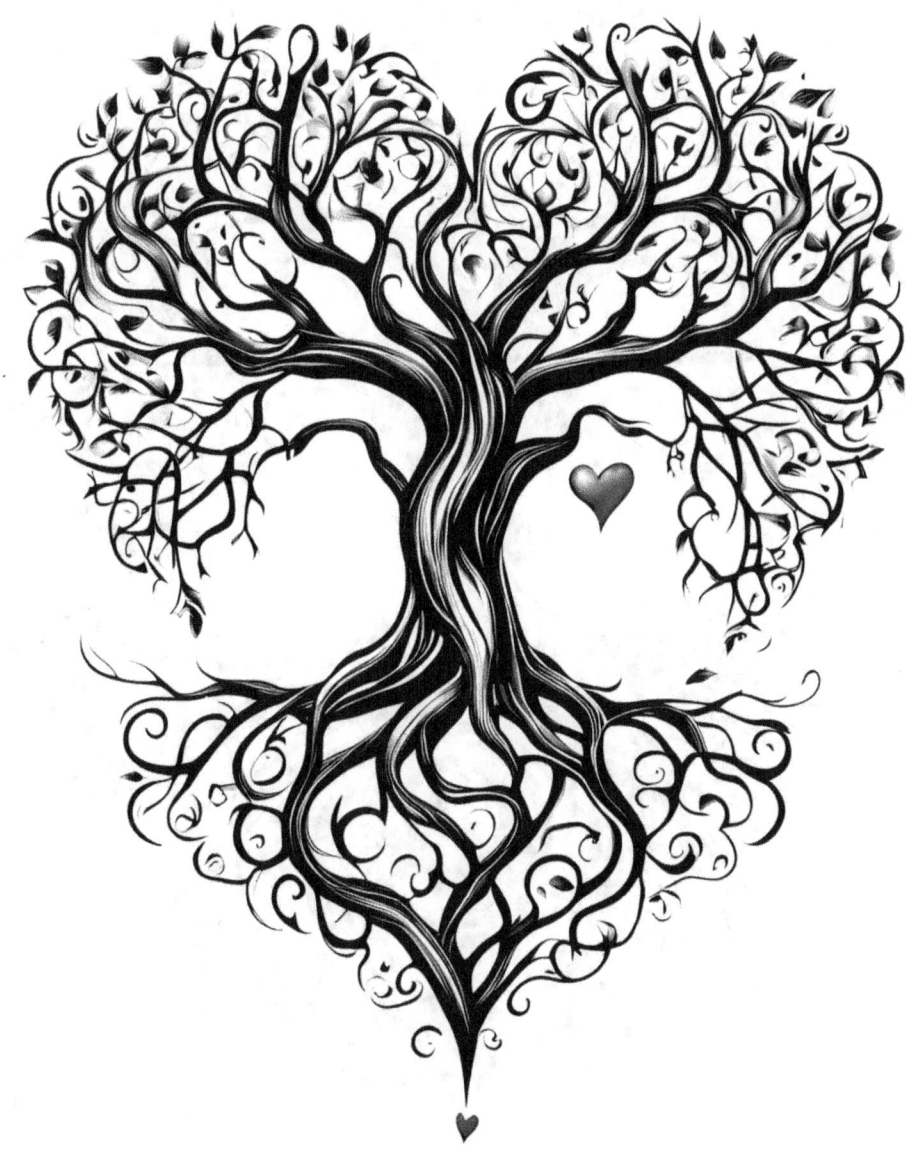

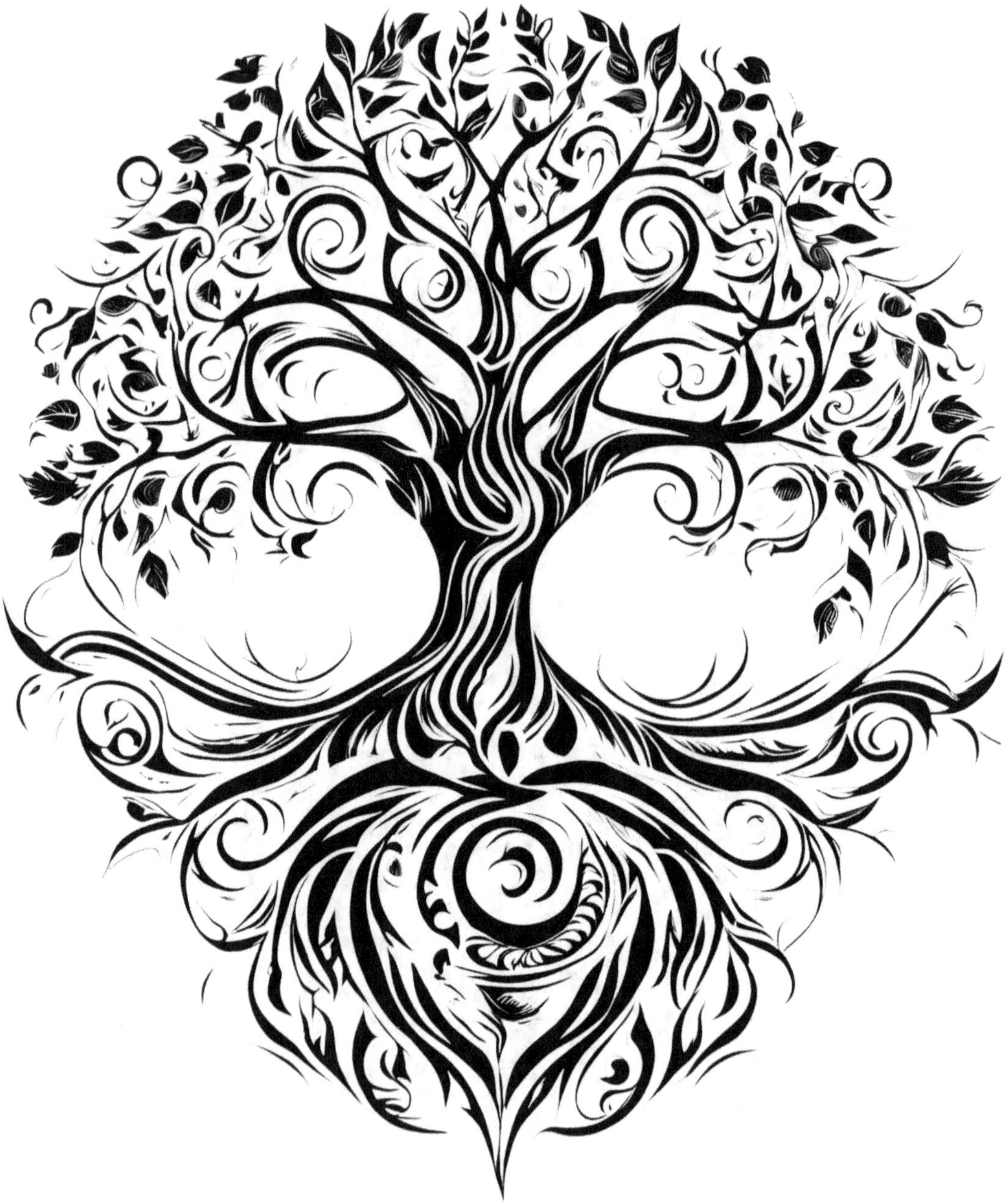

TREE TATTOOS

TREE TATTOOS

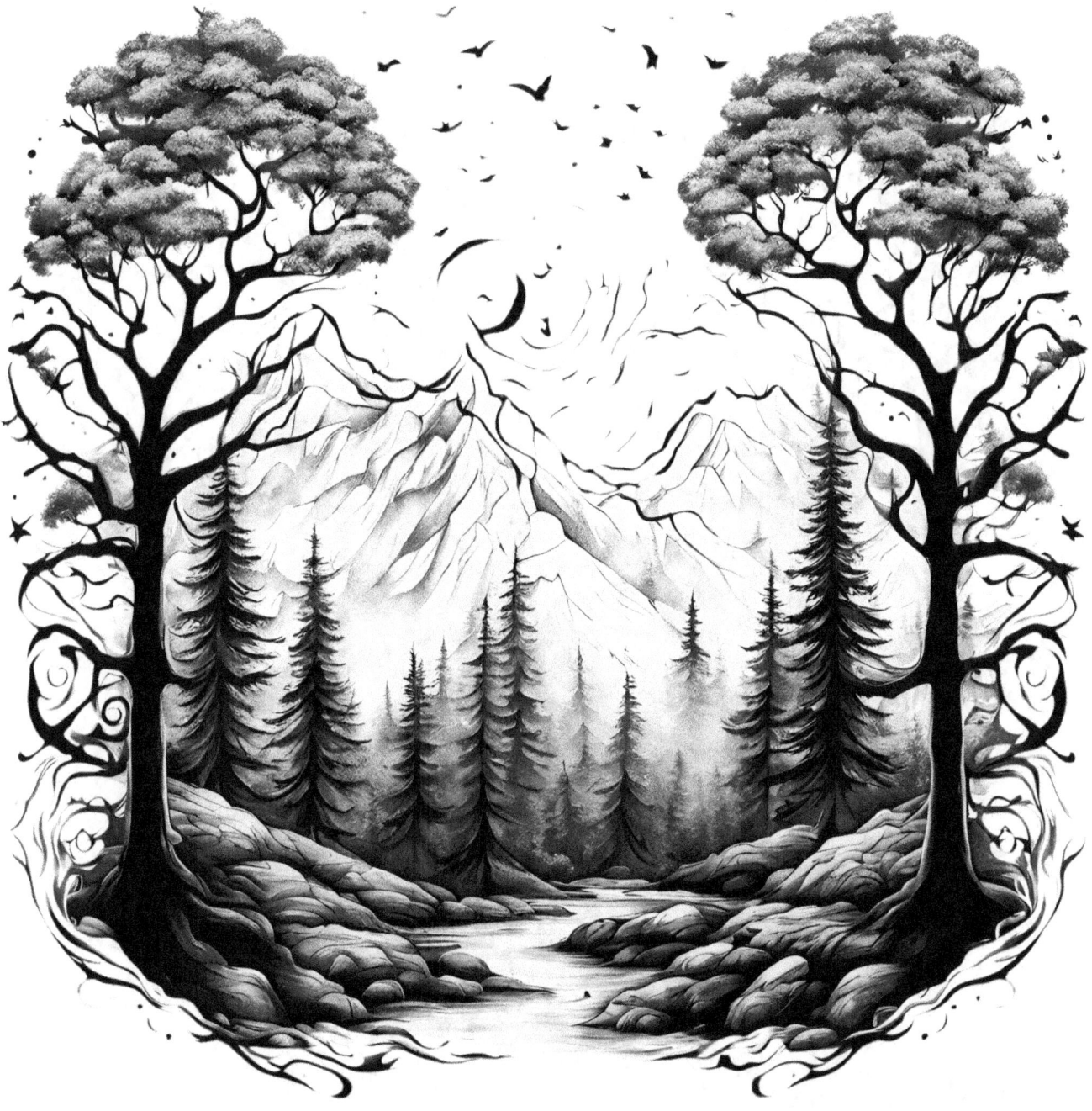

TREE TATTOOS

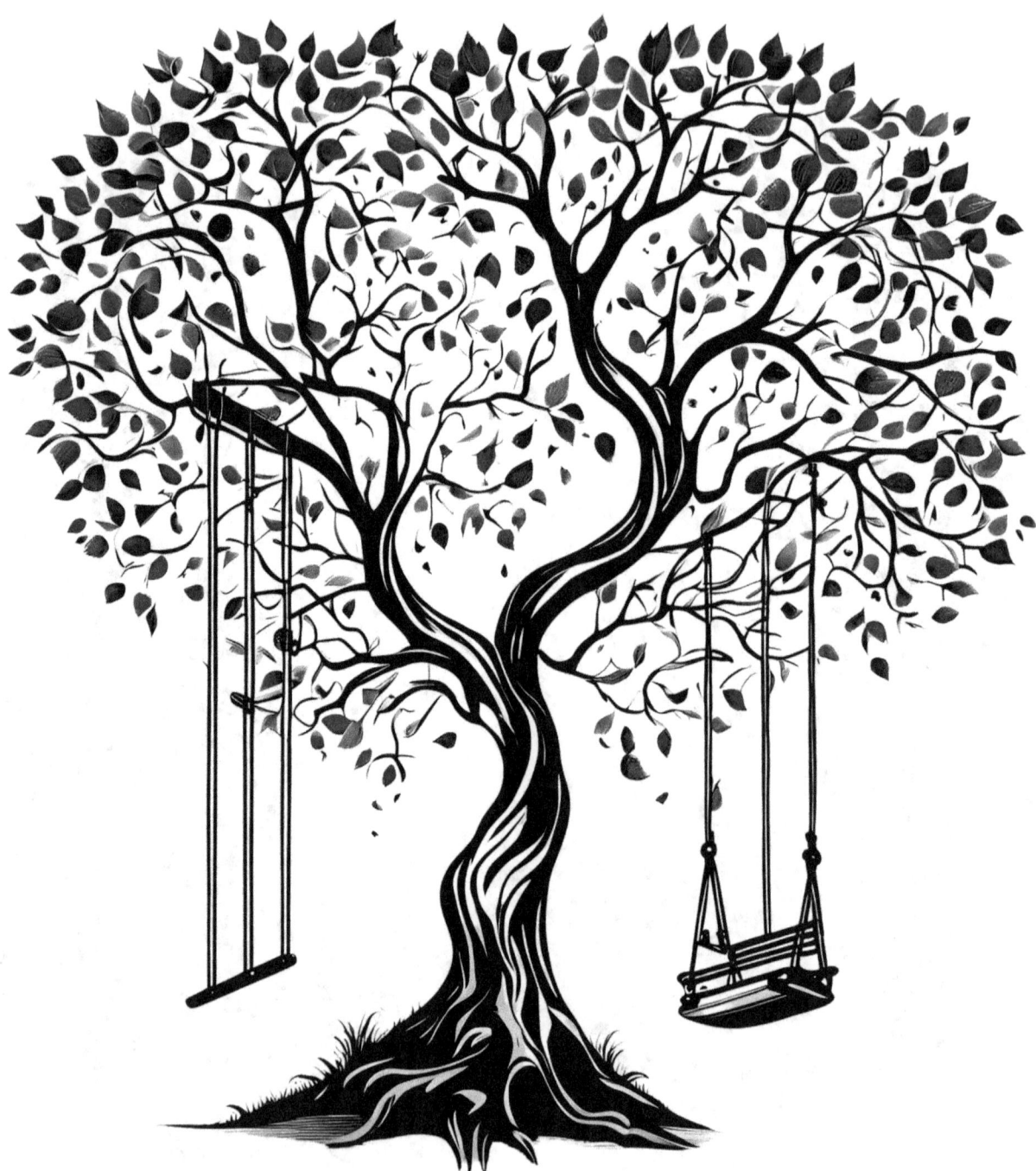

STAR TATTOOS

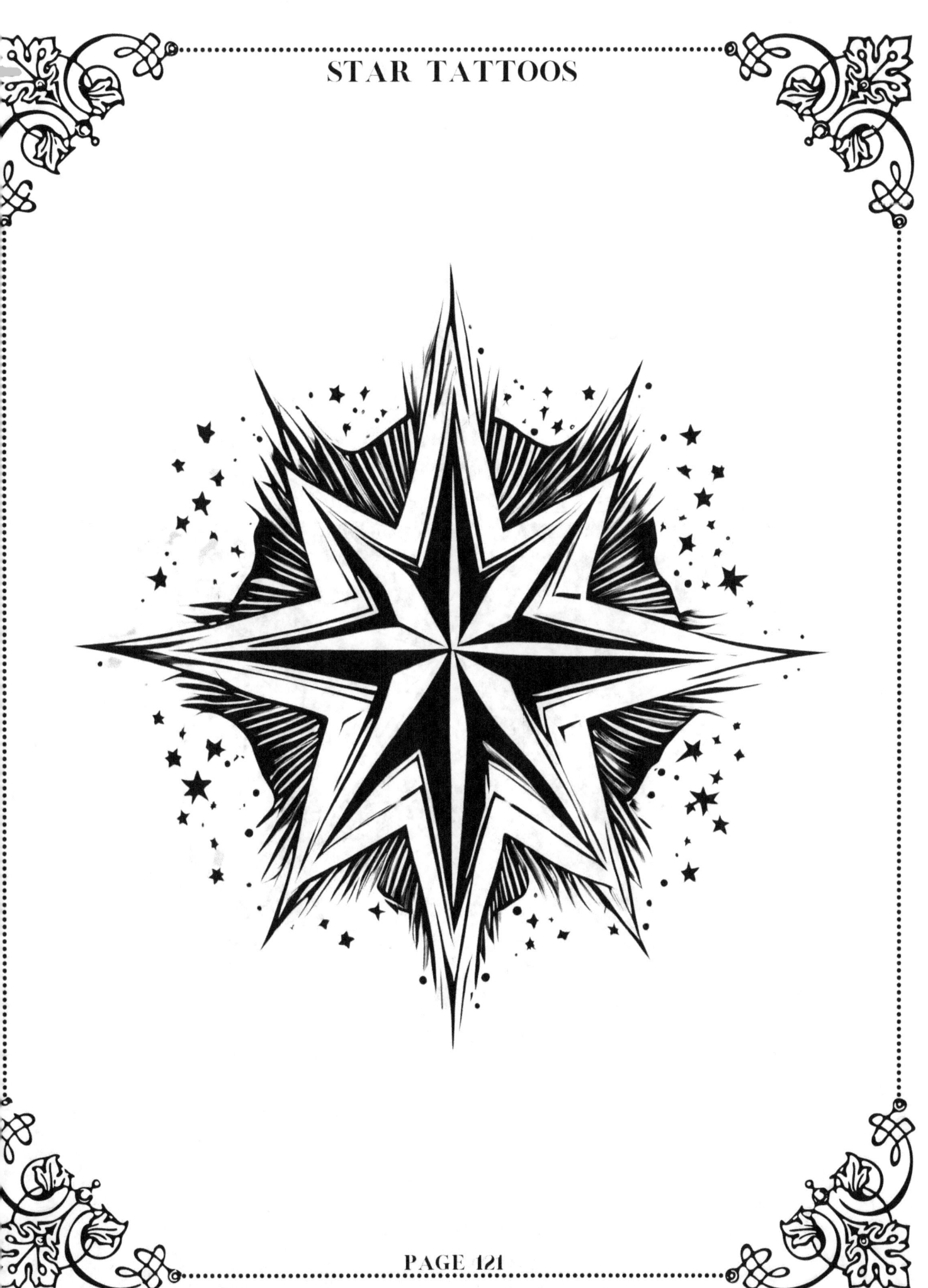

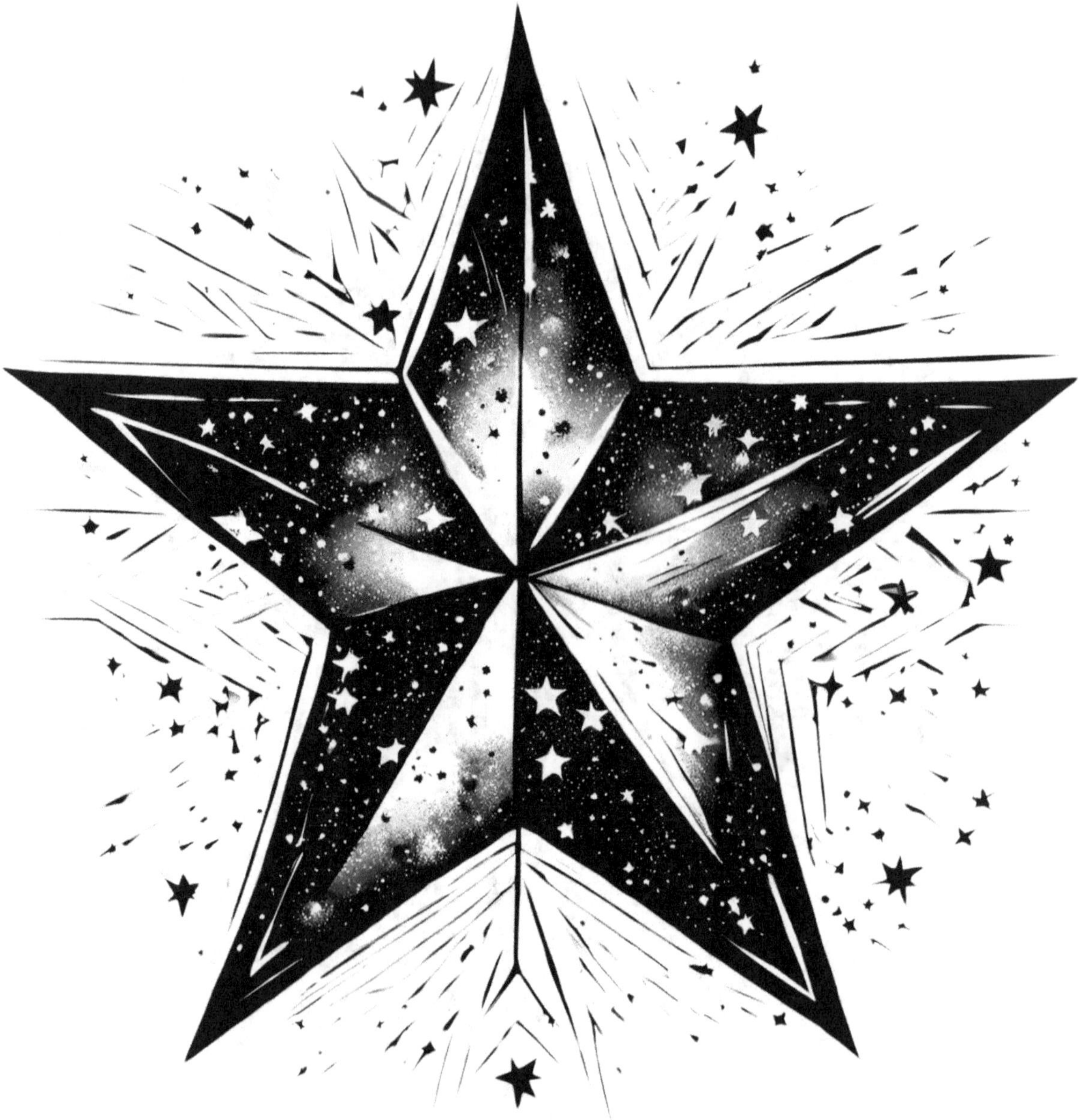

STAR TATTOOS

STAR TATTOOS

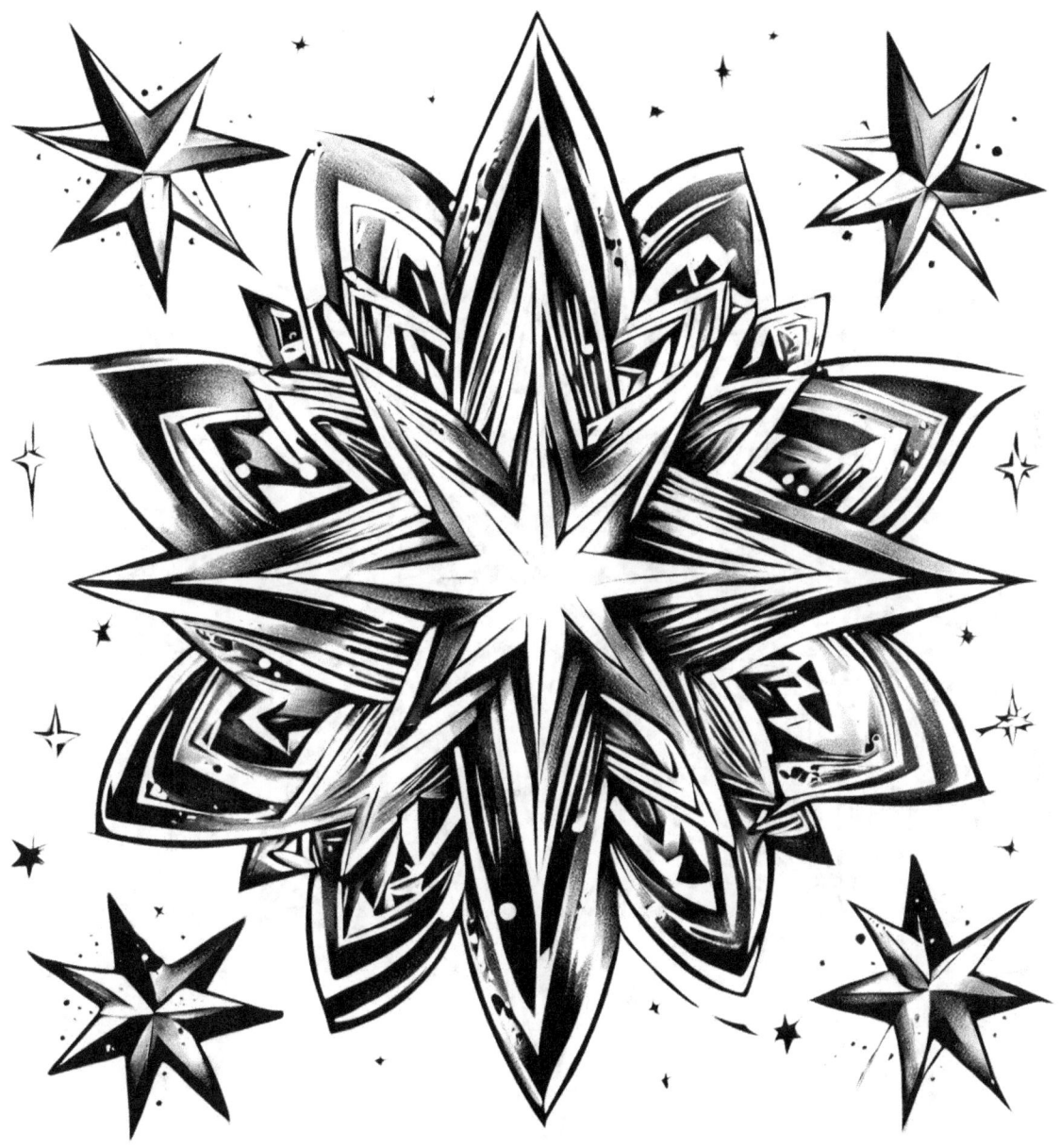

STAR TATTOOS

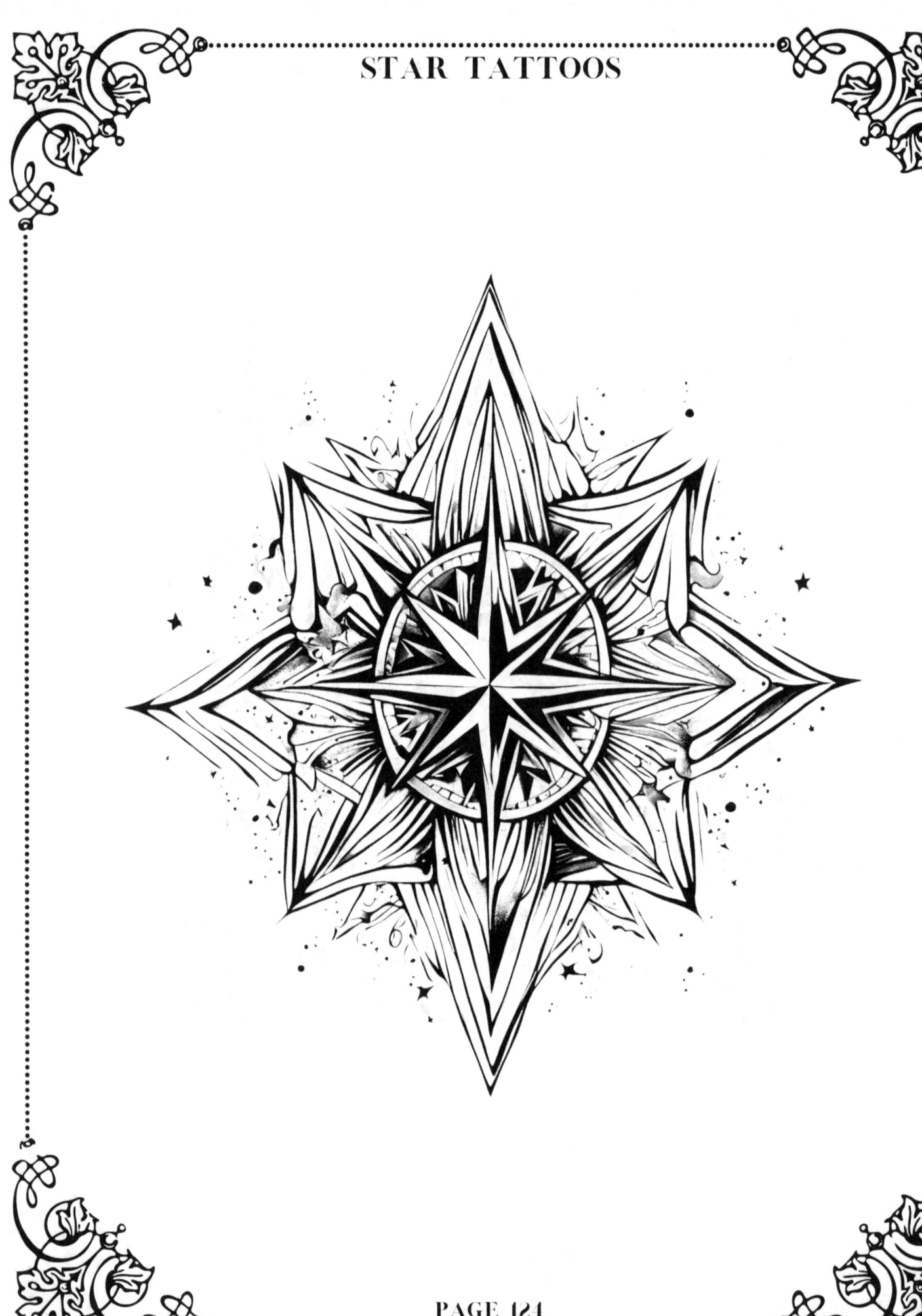

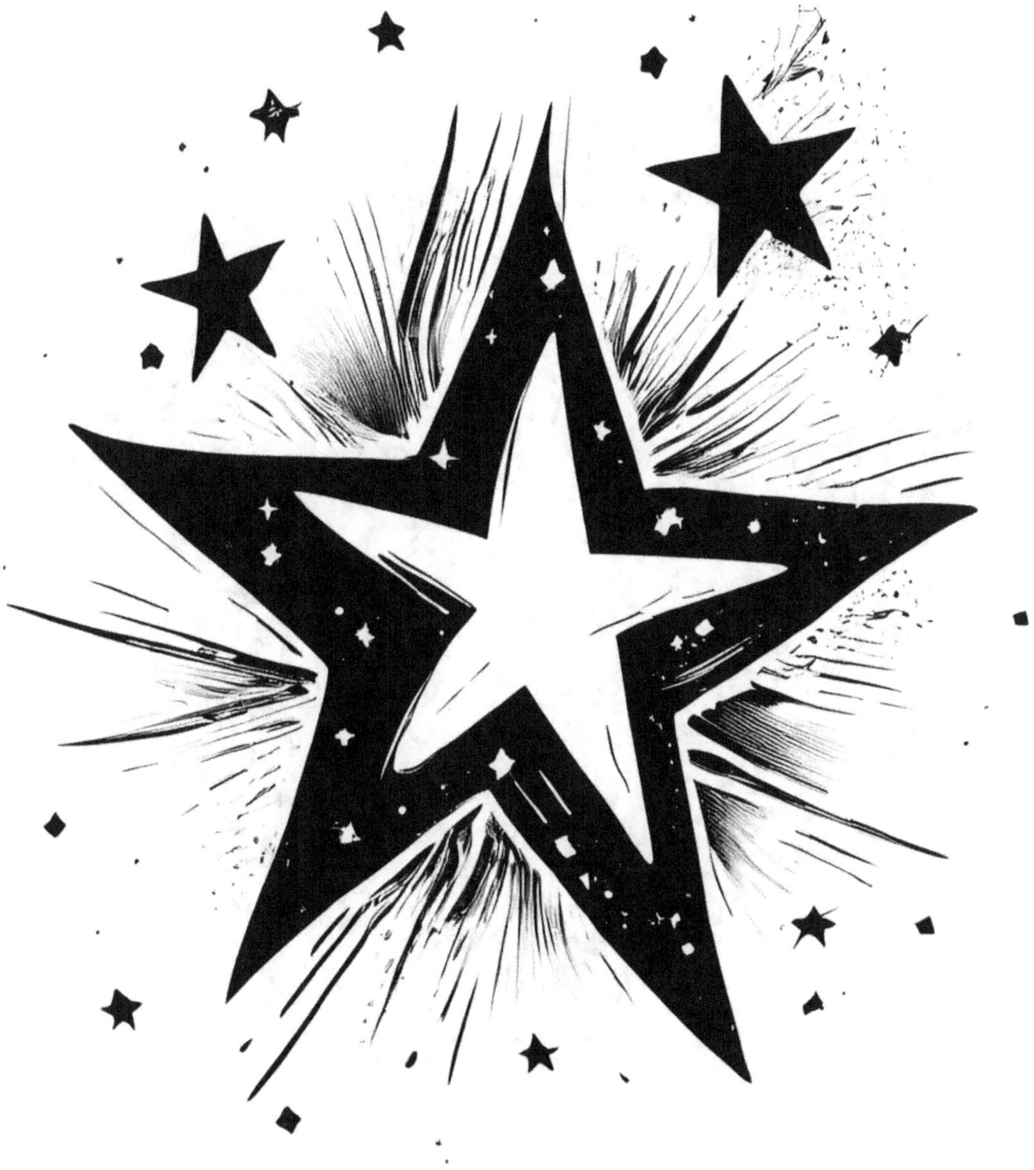

STAR TATTOOS

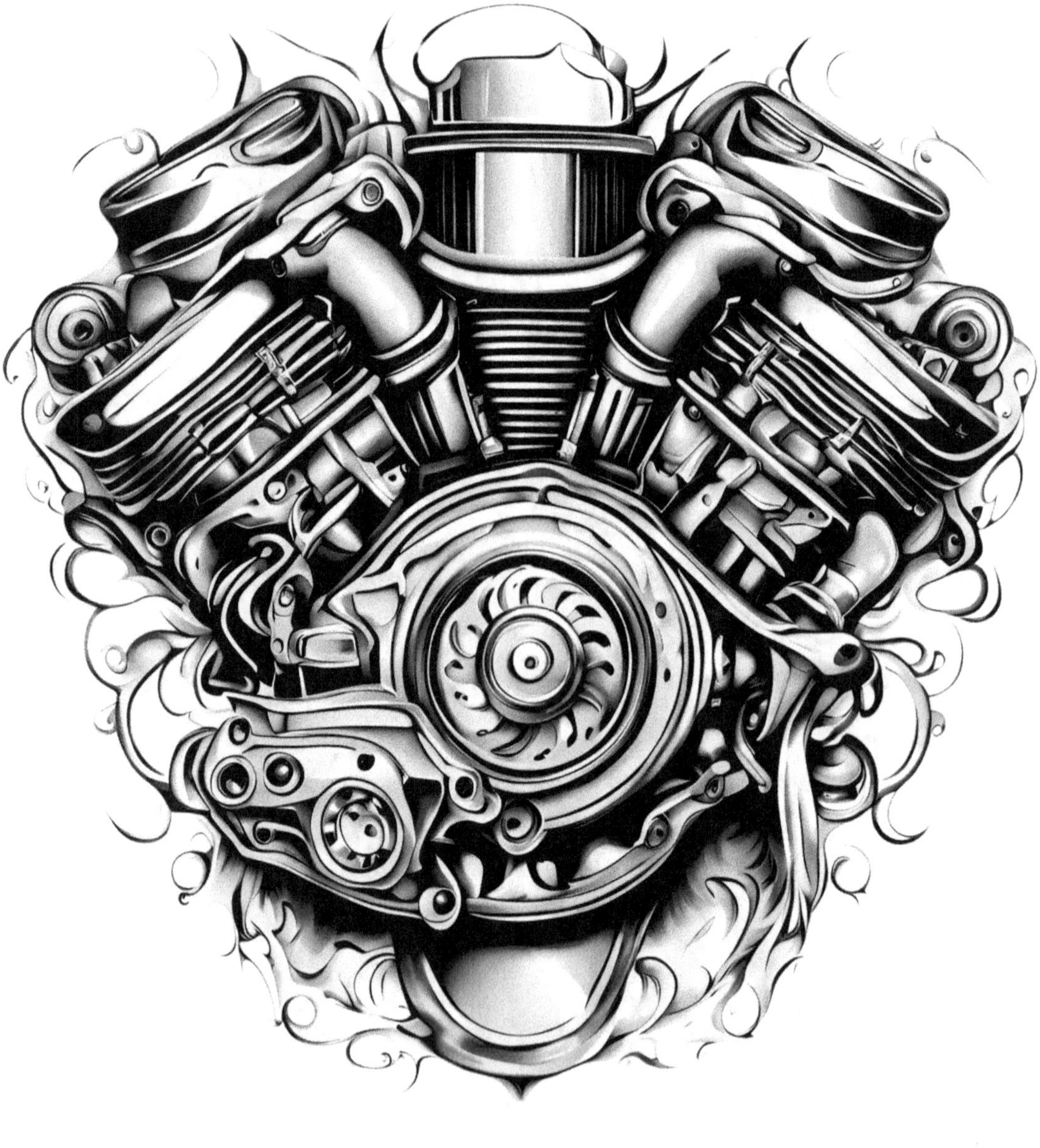

ENGINE TATTOOS

ENGINE TATTOOS

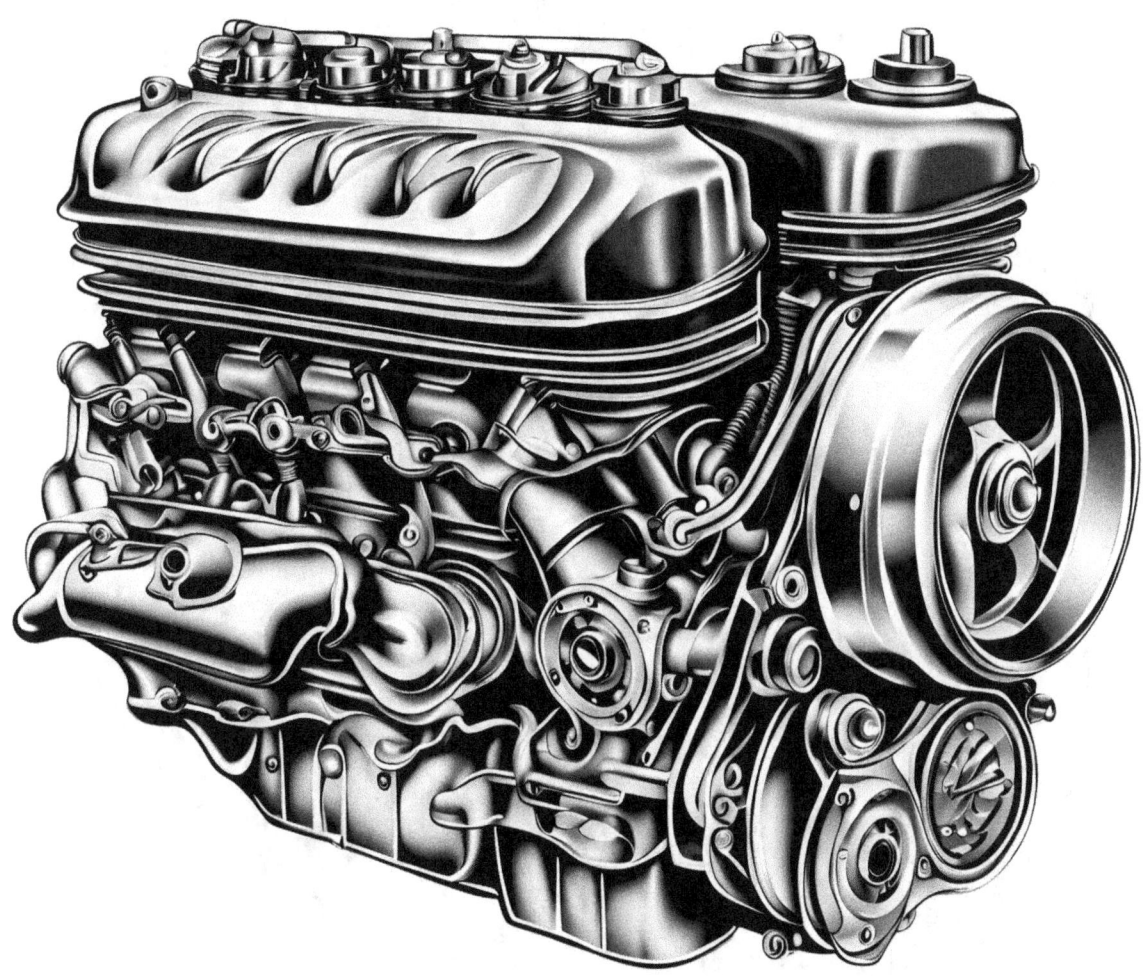

PAGE 127

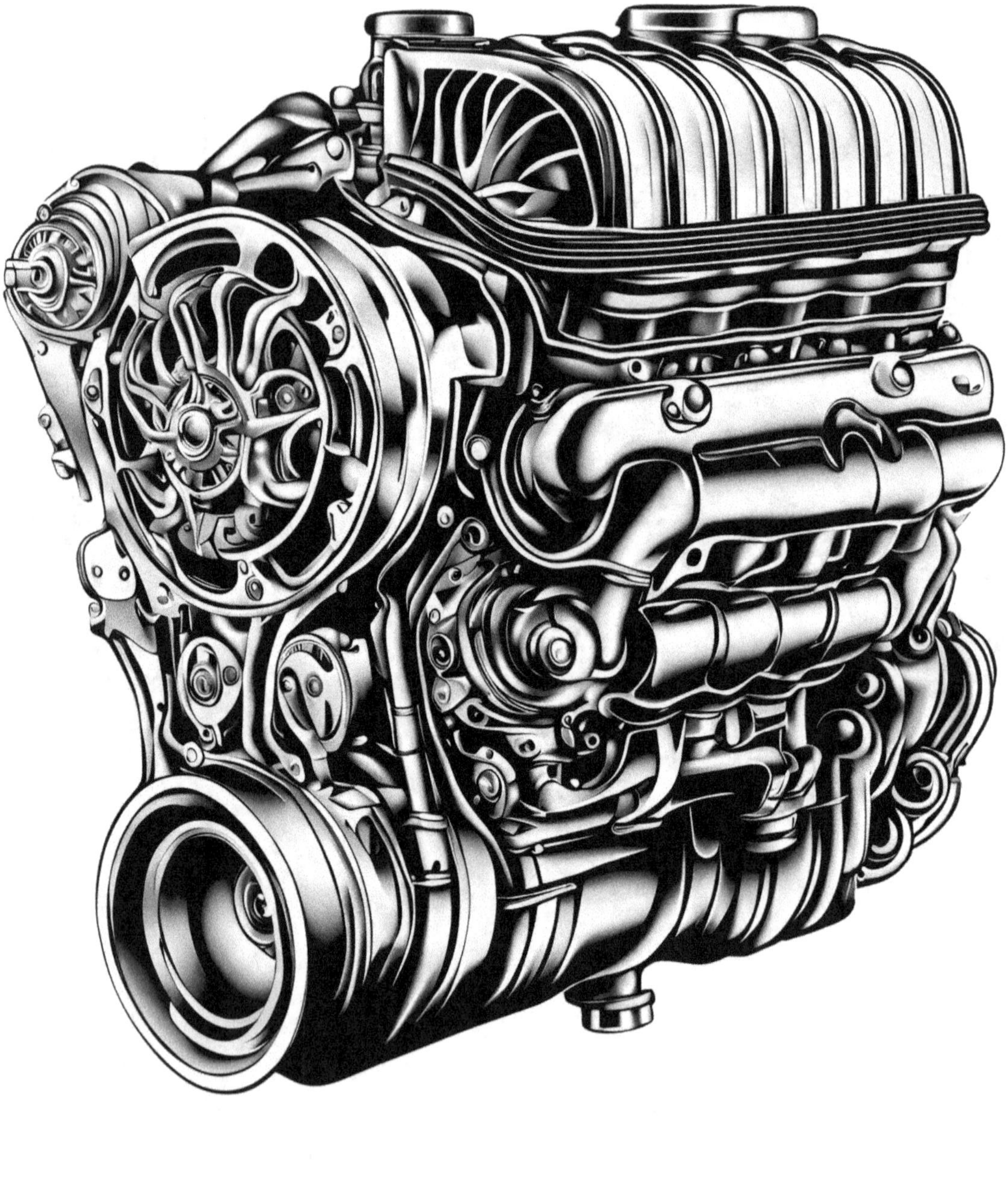

ENGINE TATTOOS

PAGE 128

ENGINE TATTOOS

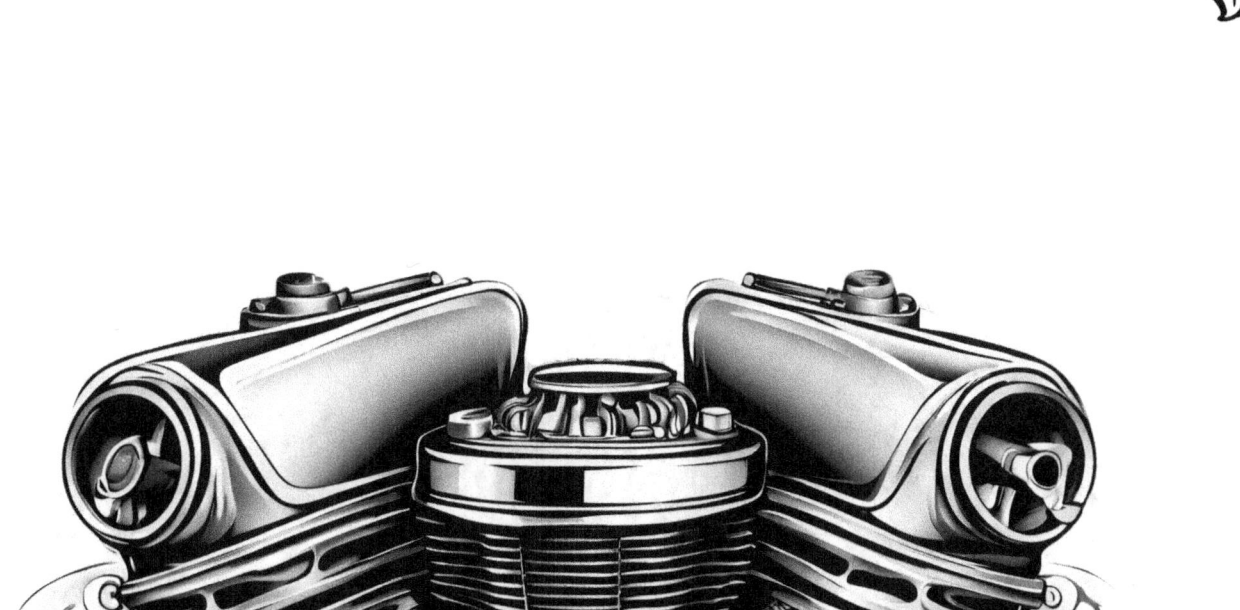

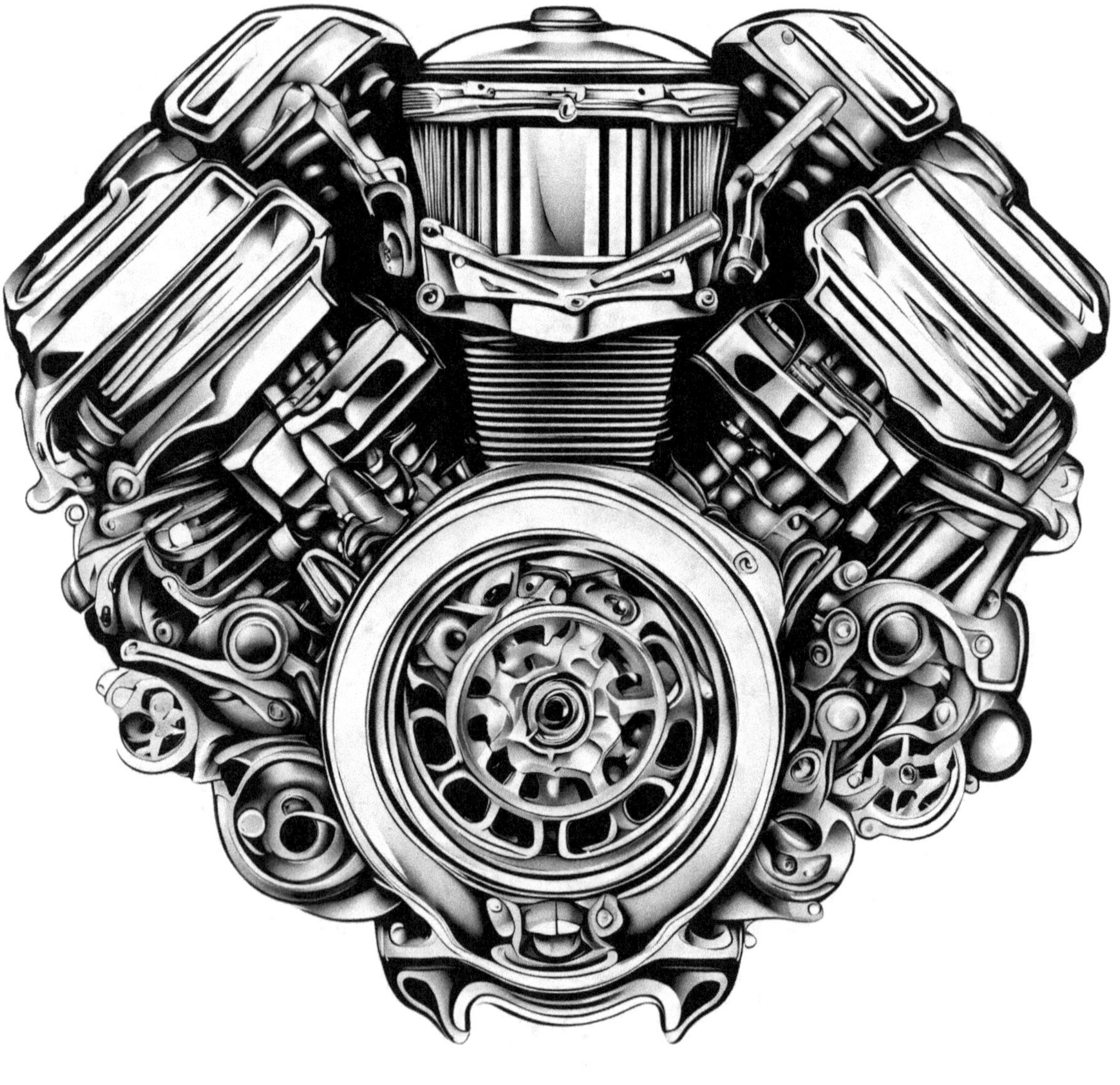

ENGINE TATTOOS

ALCOHOL TATTOOS

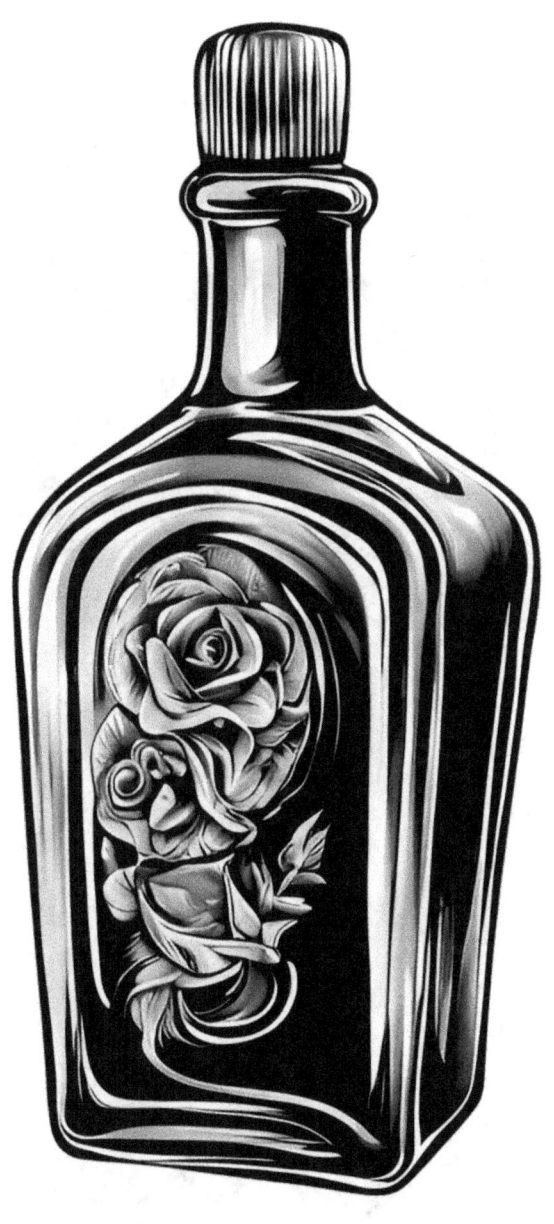

ALCOHOL TATTOOS

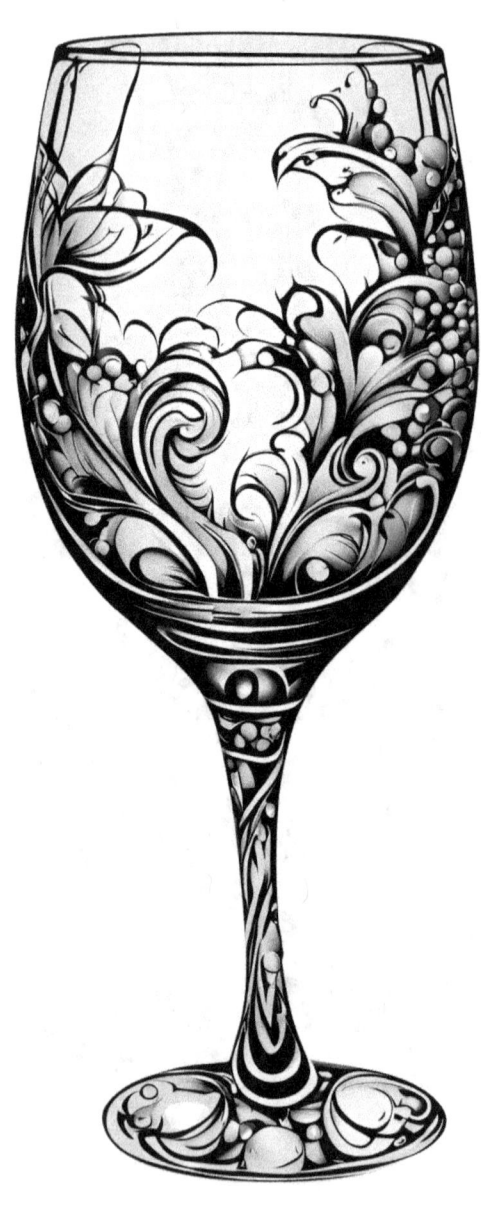

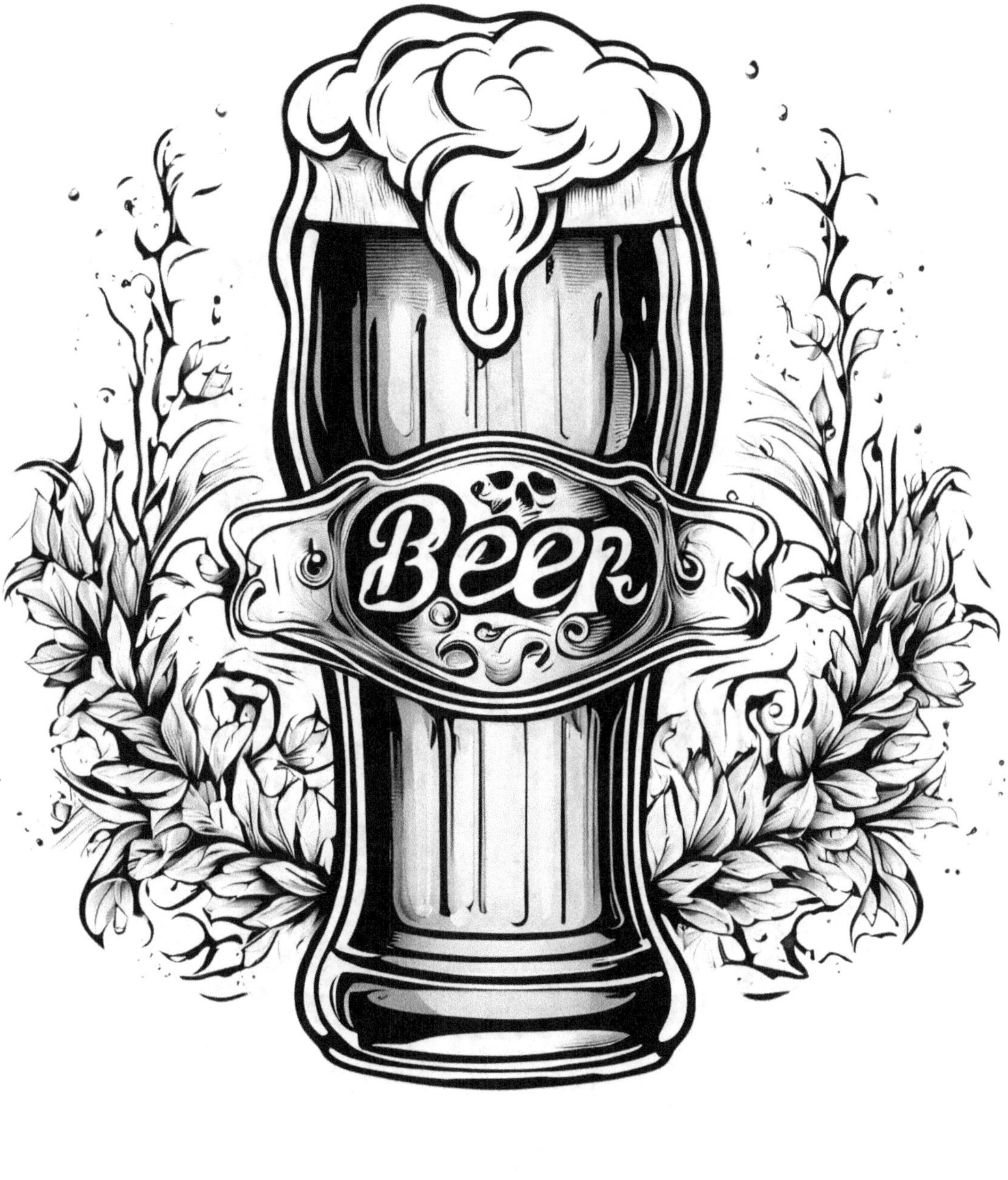

ALCOHOL TATTOOS

ALCOHOL TATTOOS

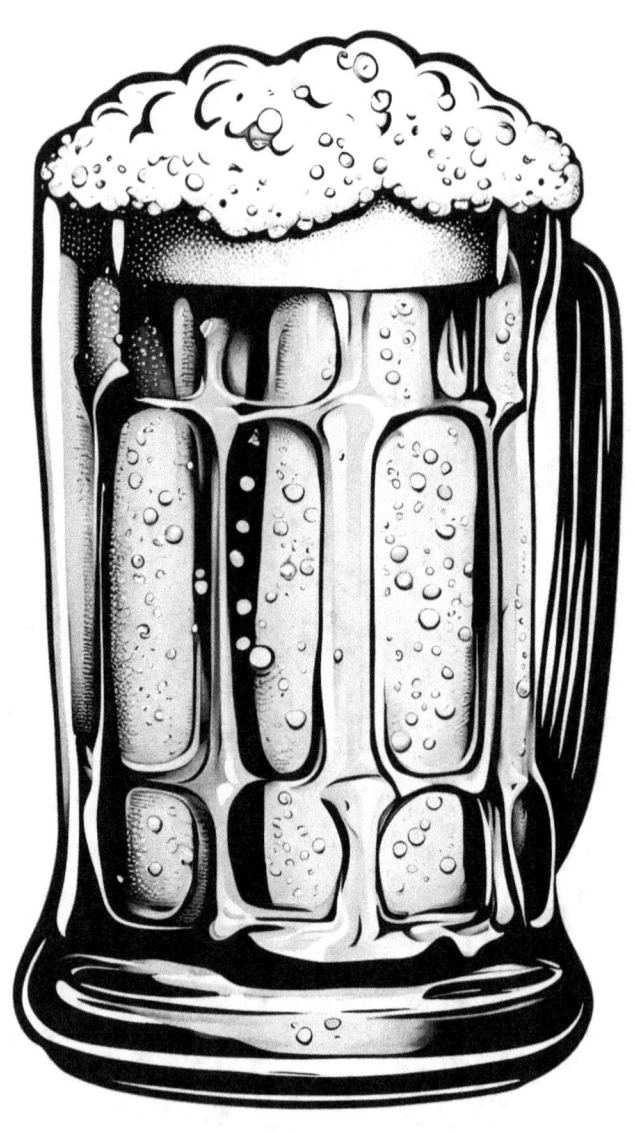

ALCOHOL TATTOOS

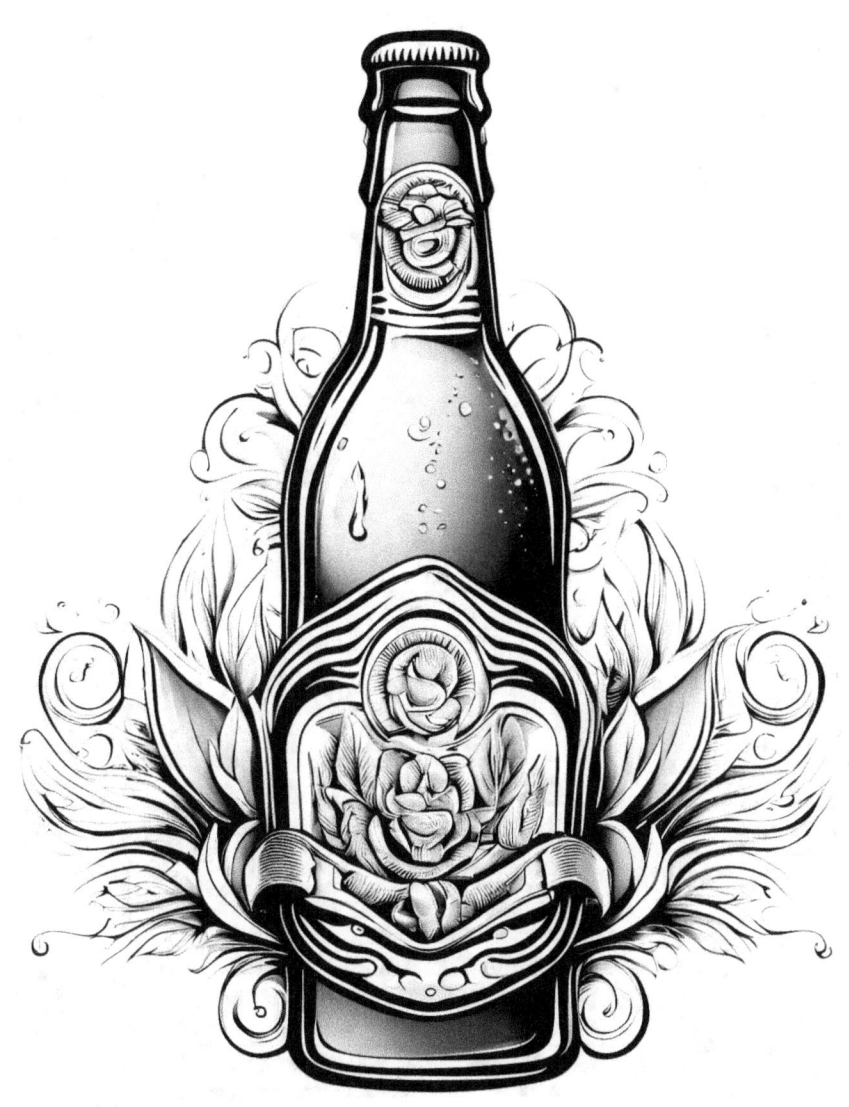

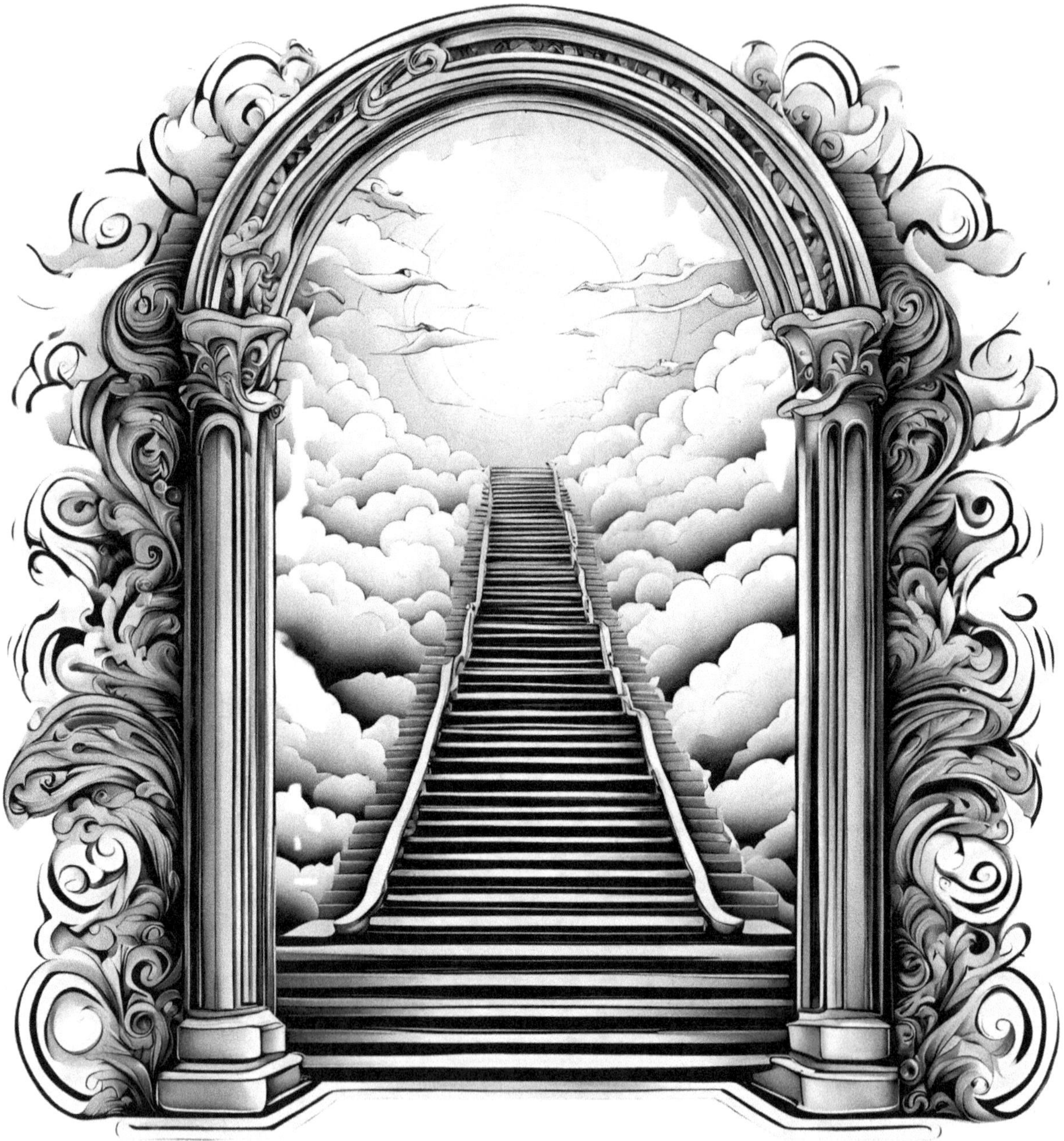

STAIRWAY TATTOOS

STAIRWAY TATTOOS

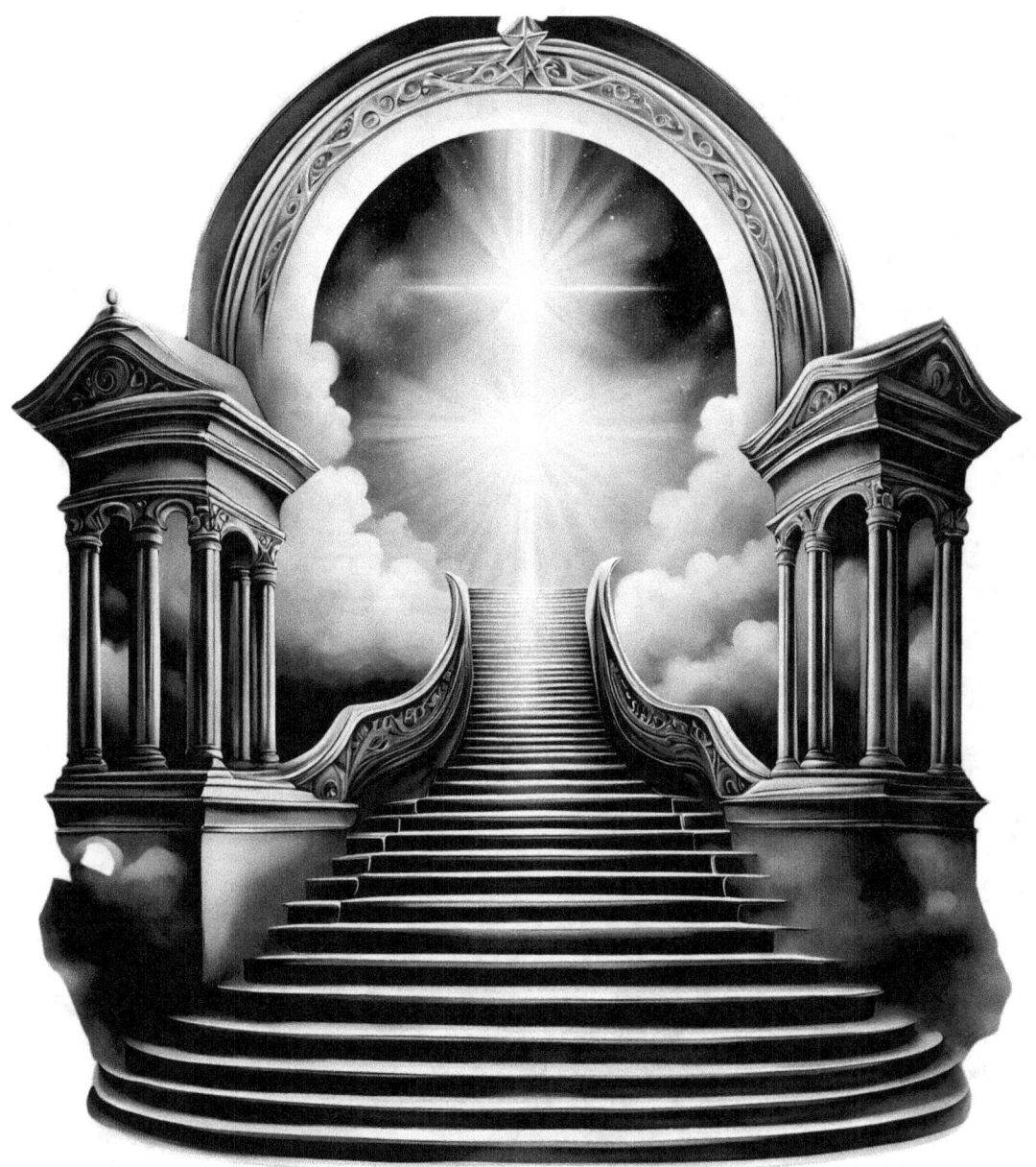

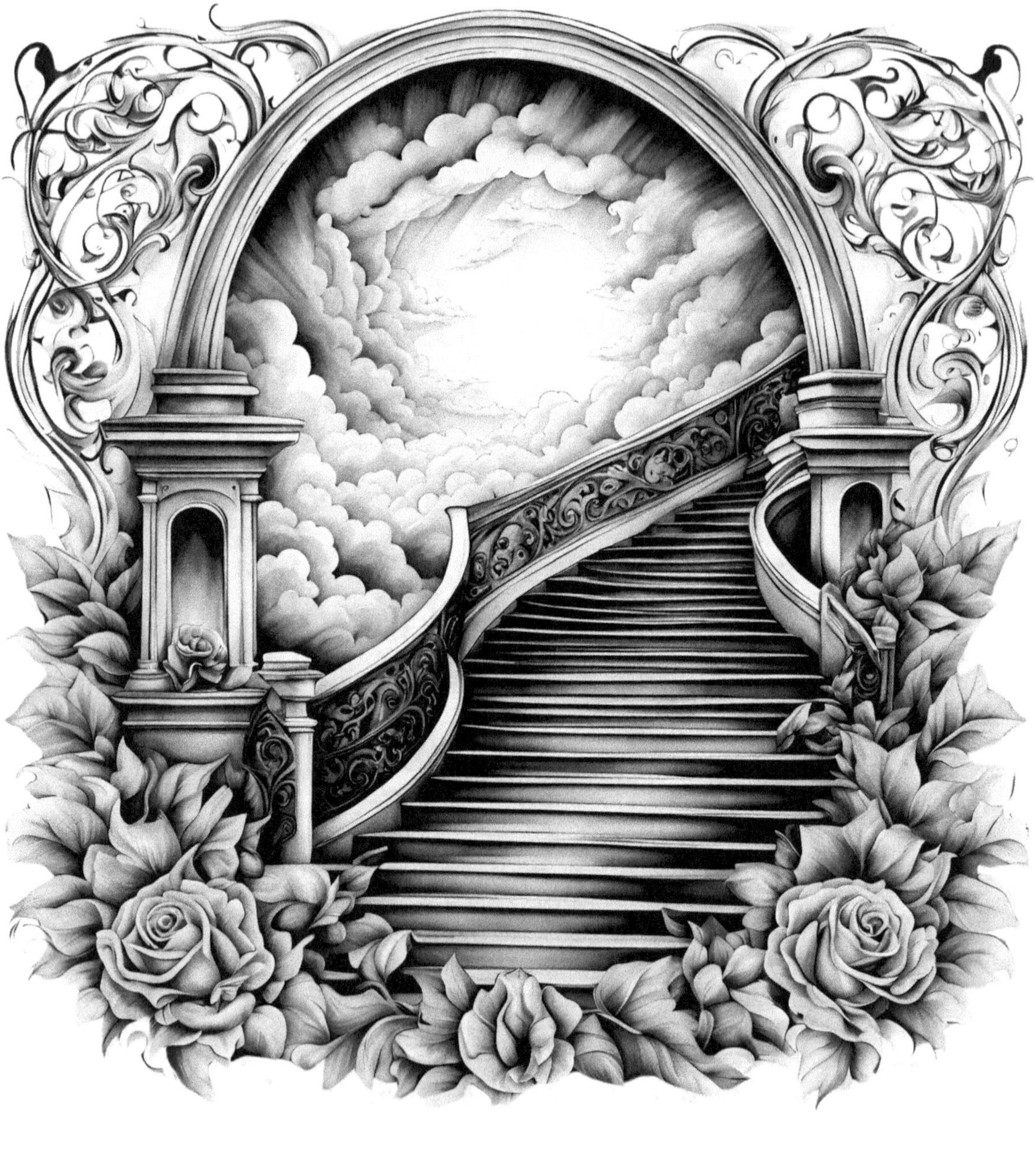

STAIRWAY TATTOOS

STAIRWAY TATTOOS

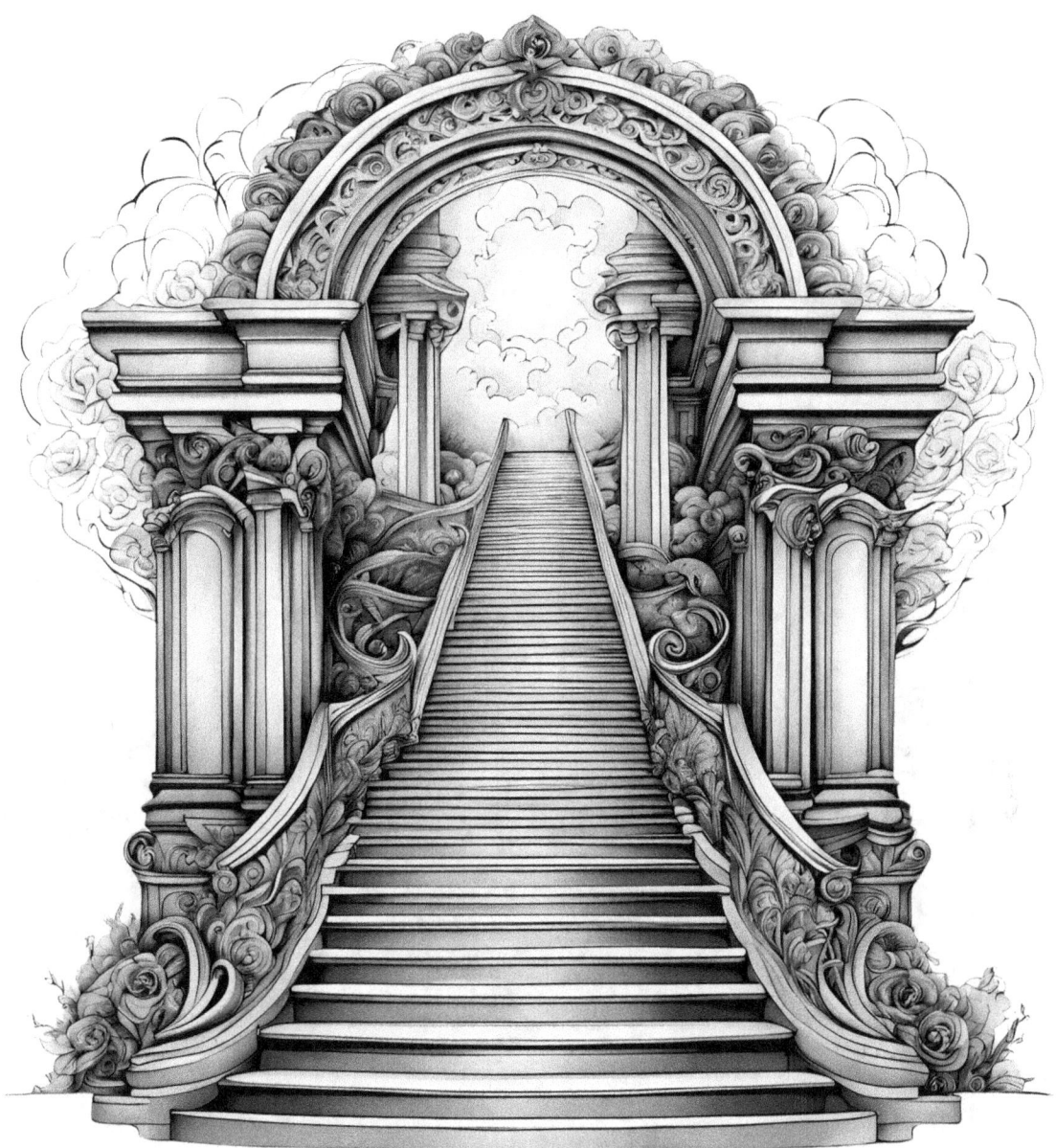

PAGE 139

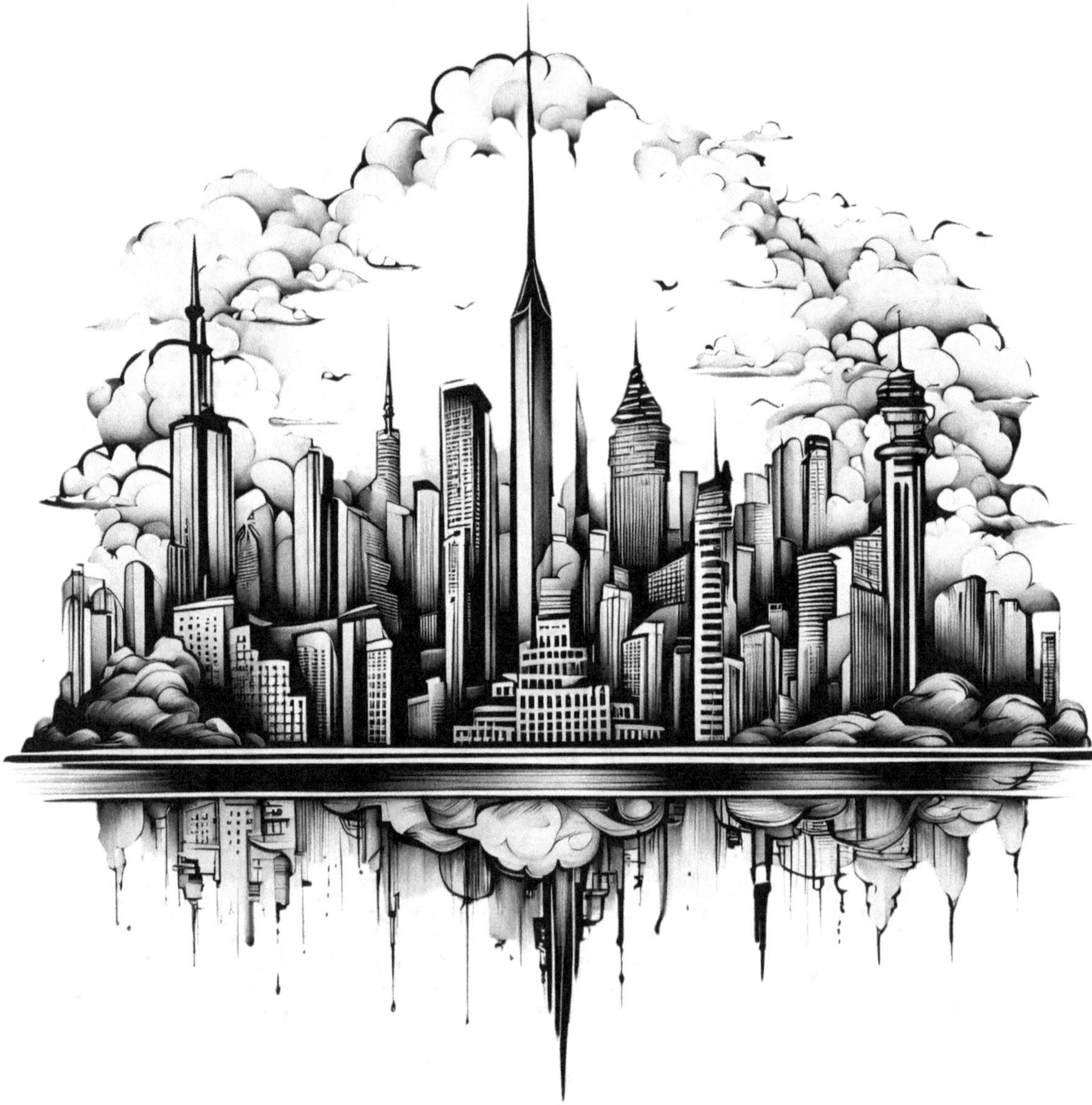

CITYSCAPE TATTOOS

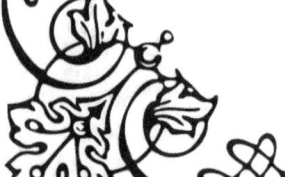

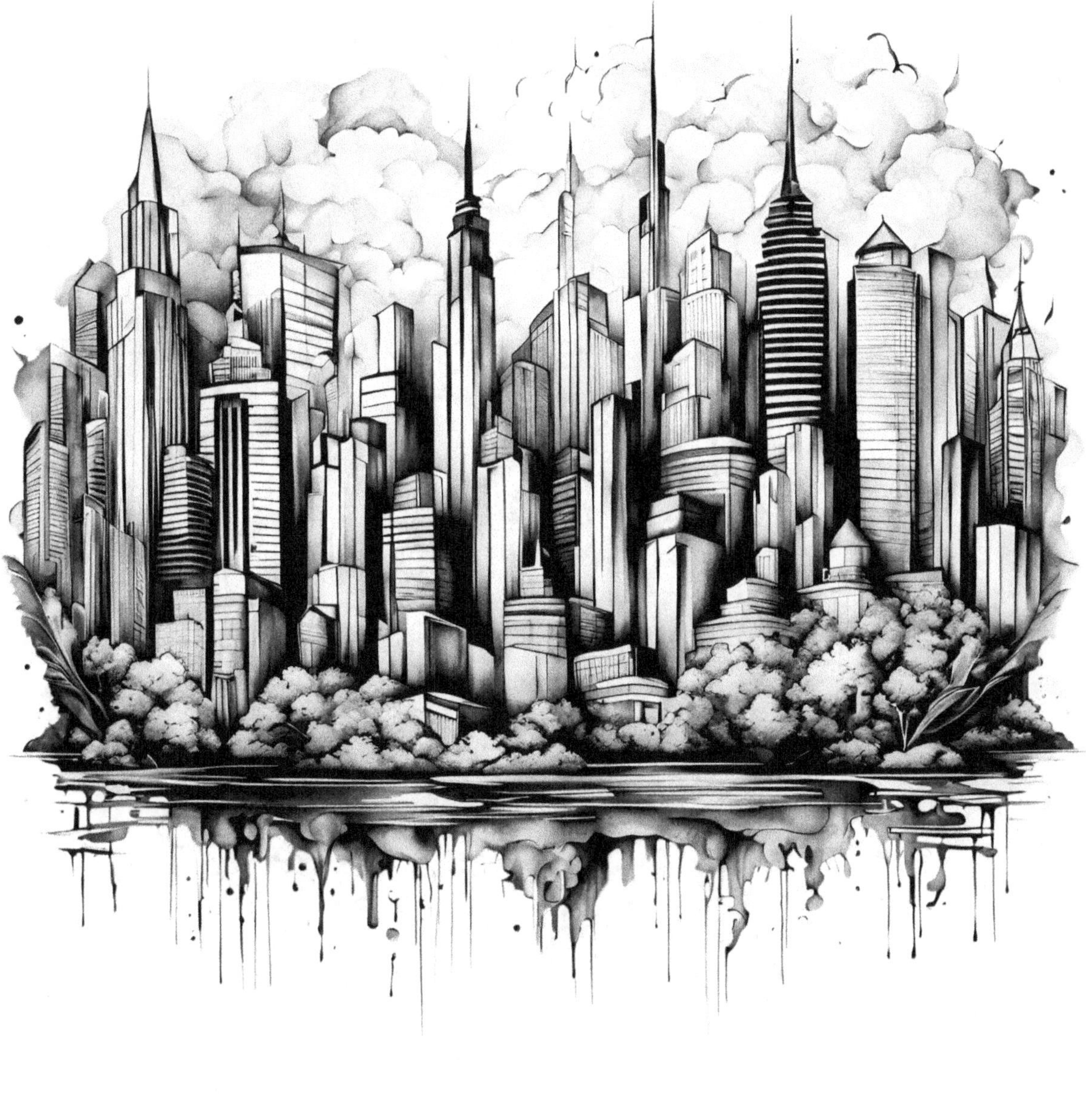

CITYSCAPE TATTOOS

PAGE 141

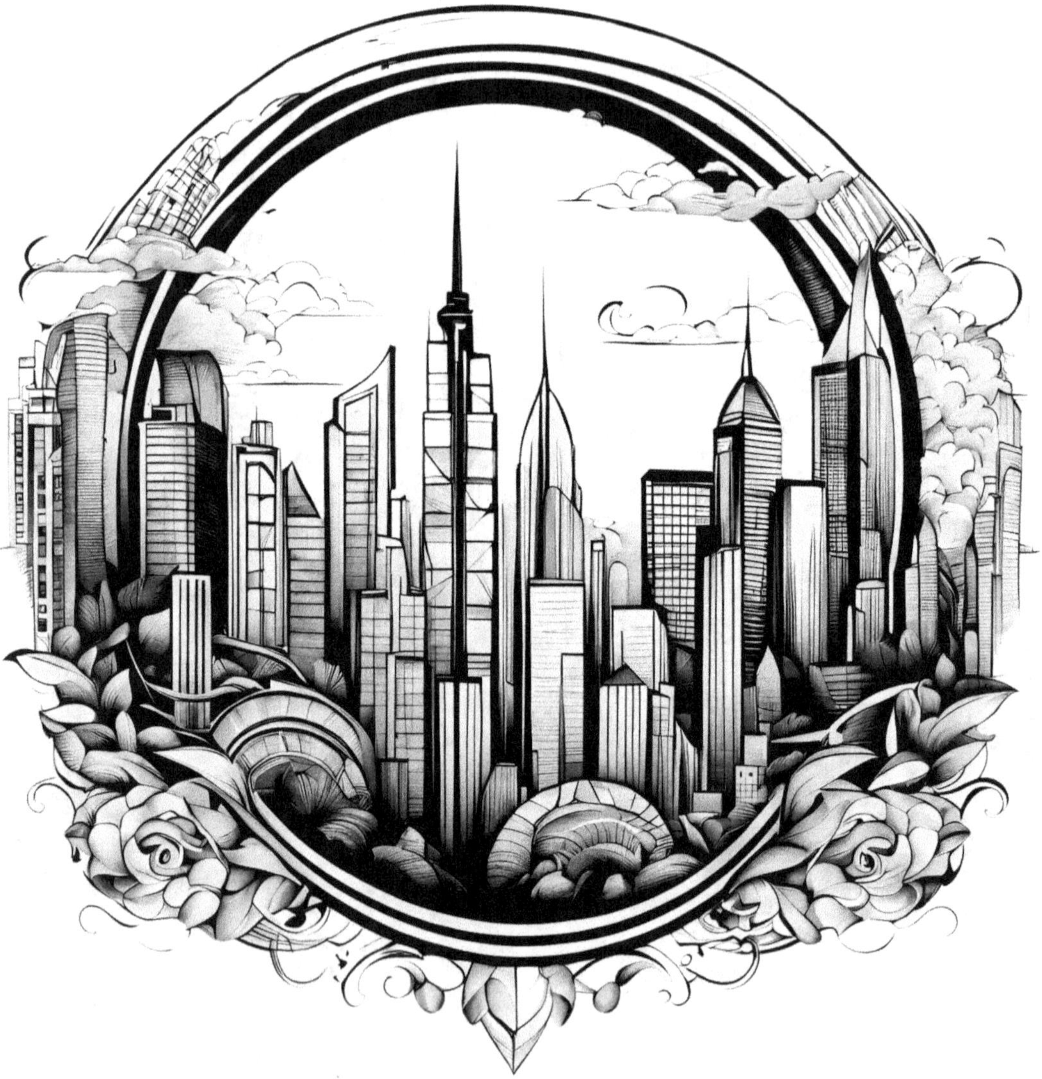

CITYSCAPE TATTOOS

CITYSCAPE TATTOOS

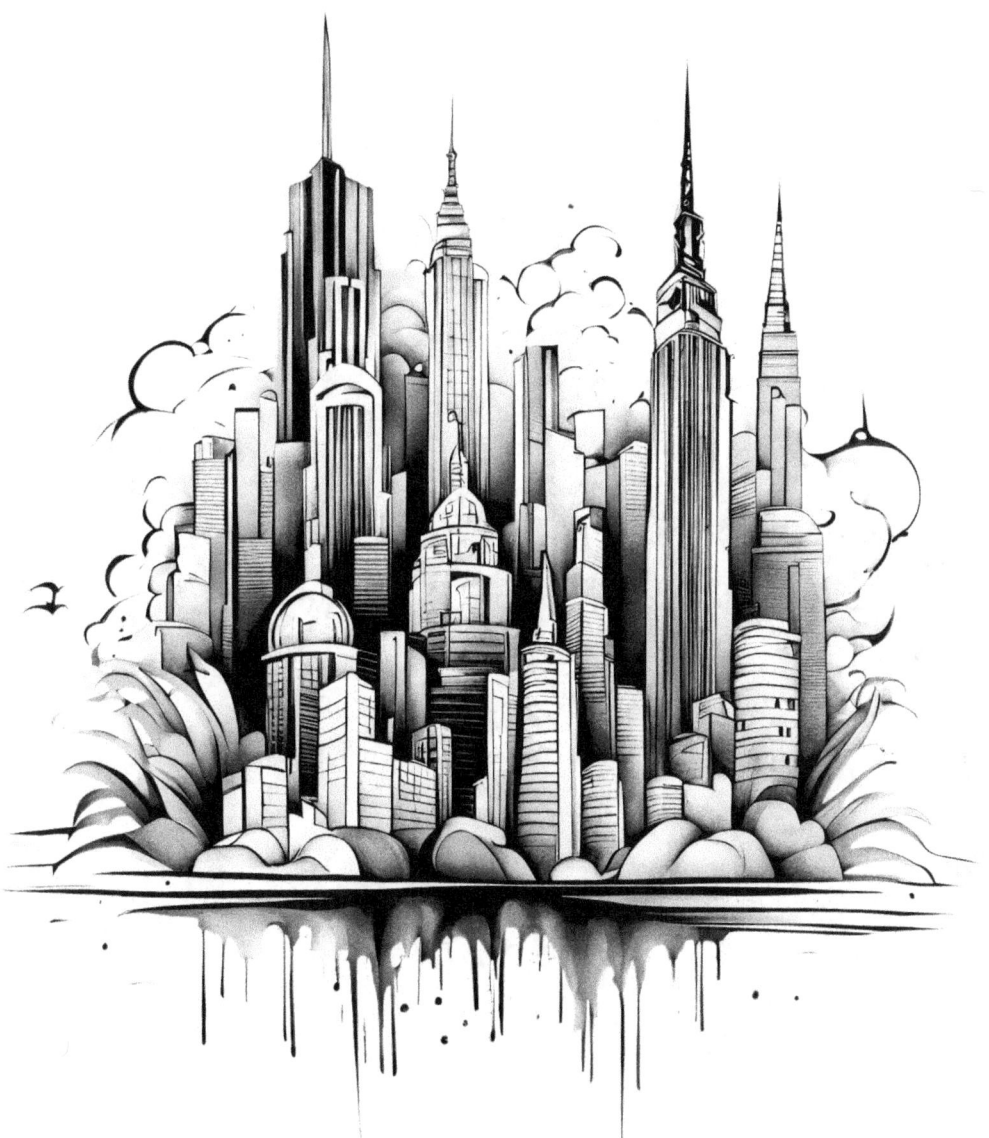

CITYSCAPE TATTOOS

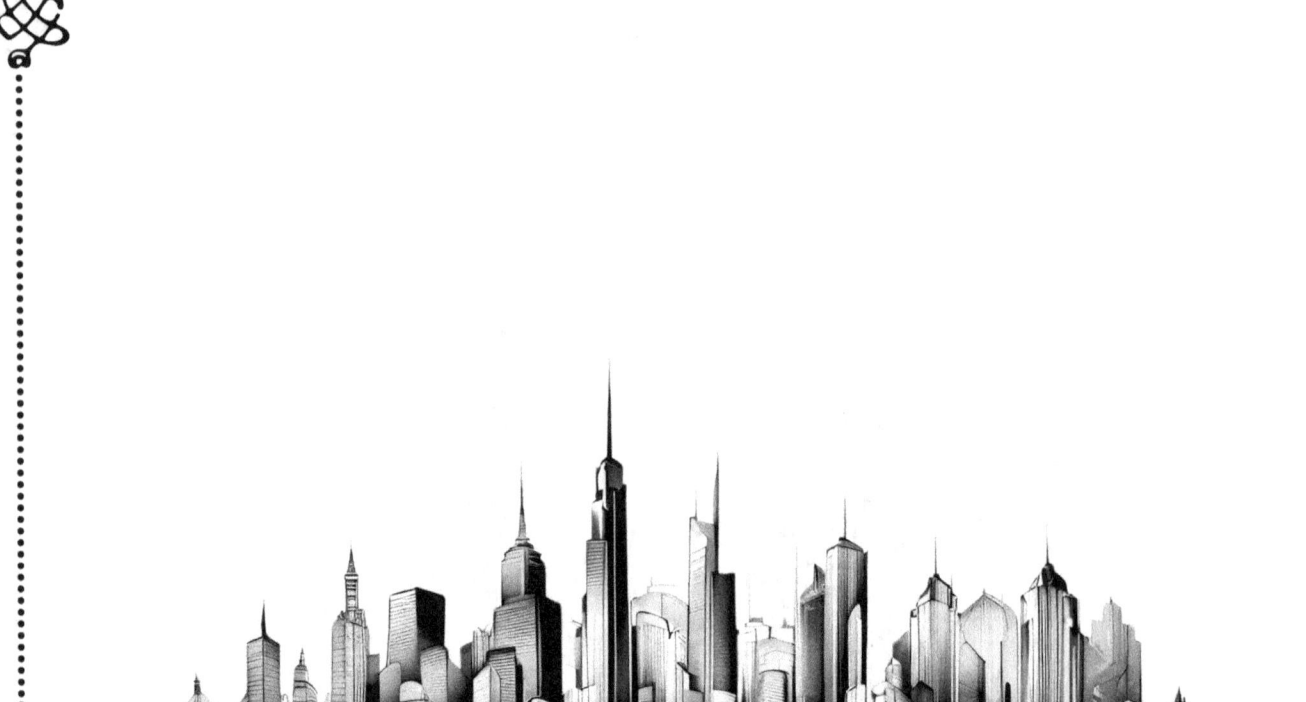

PHOENIX TATTOOS

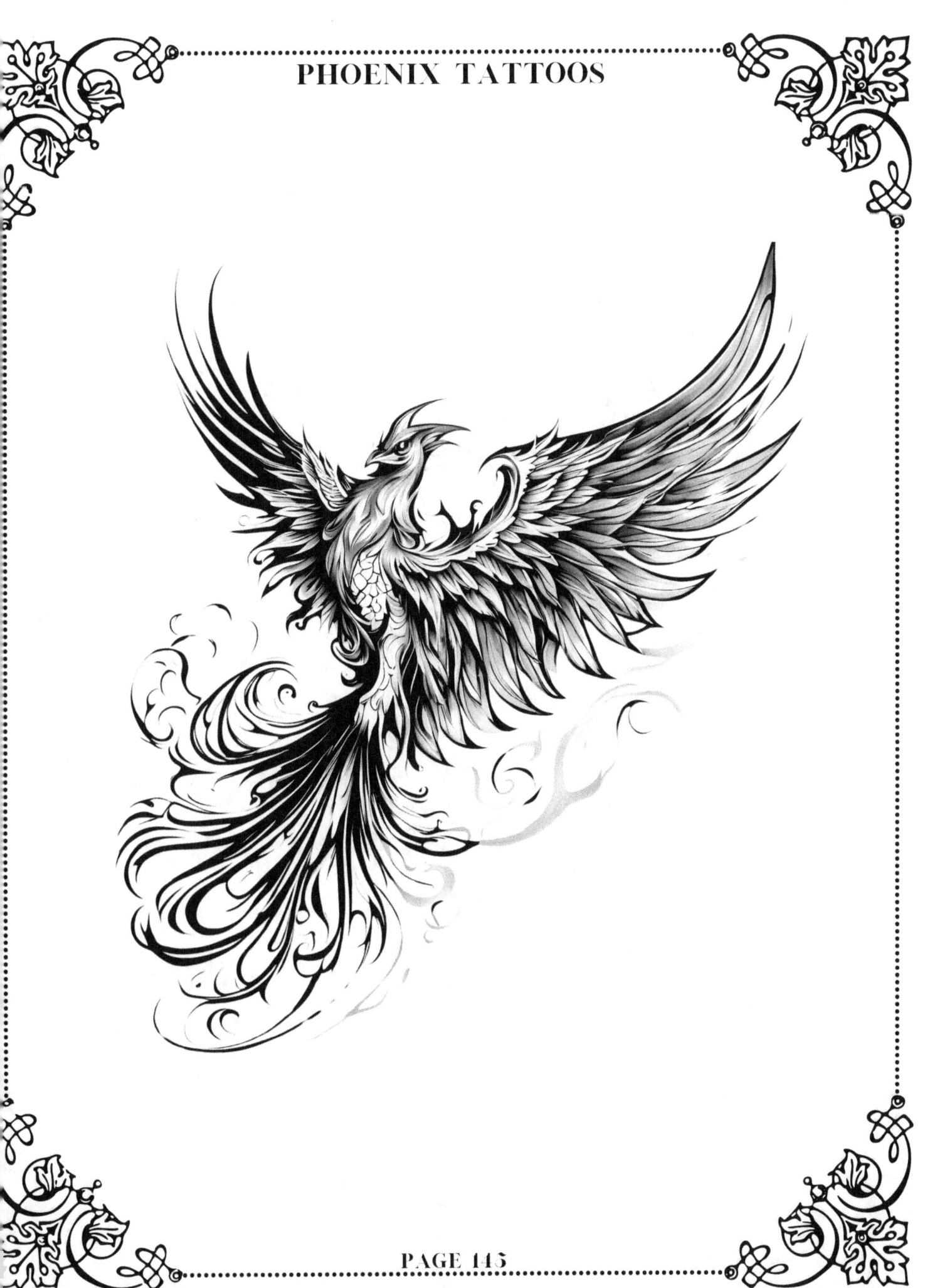

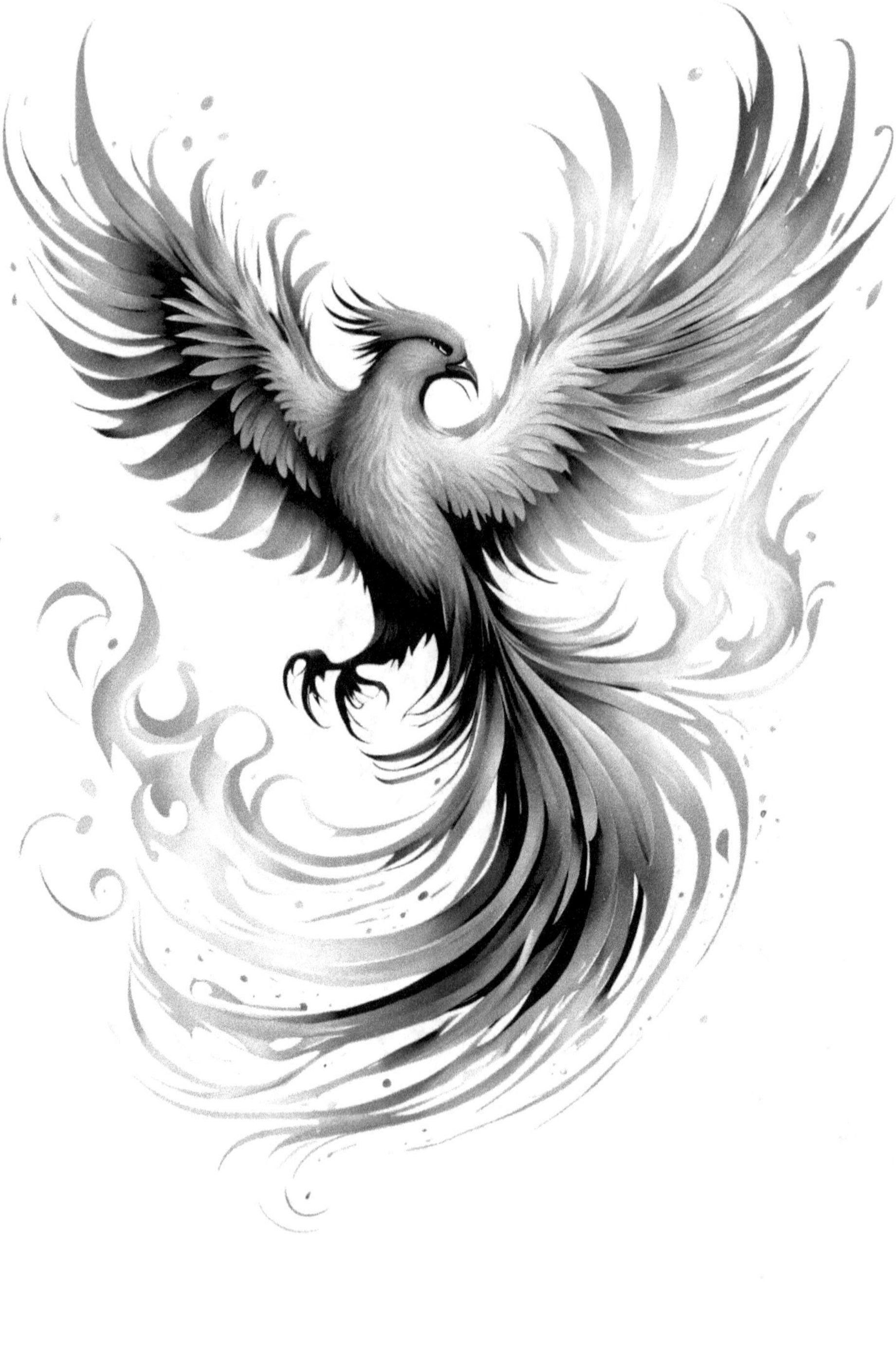

PHOENIX TATTOOS

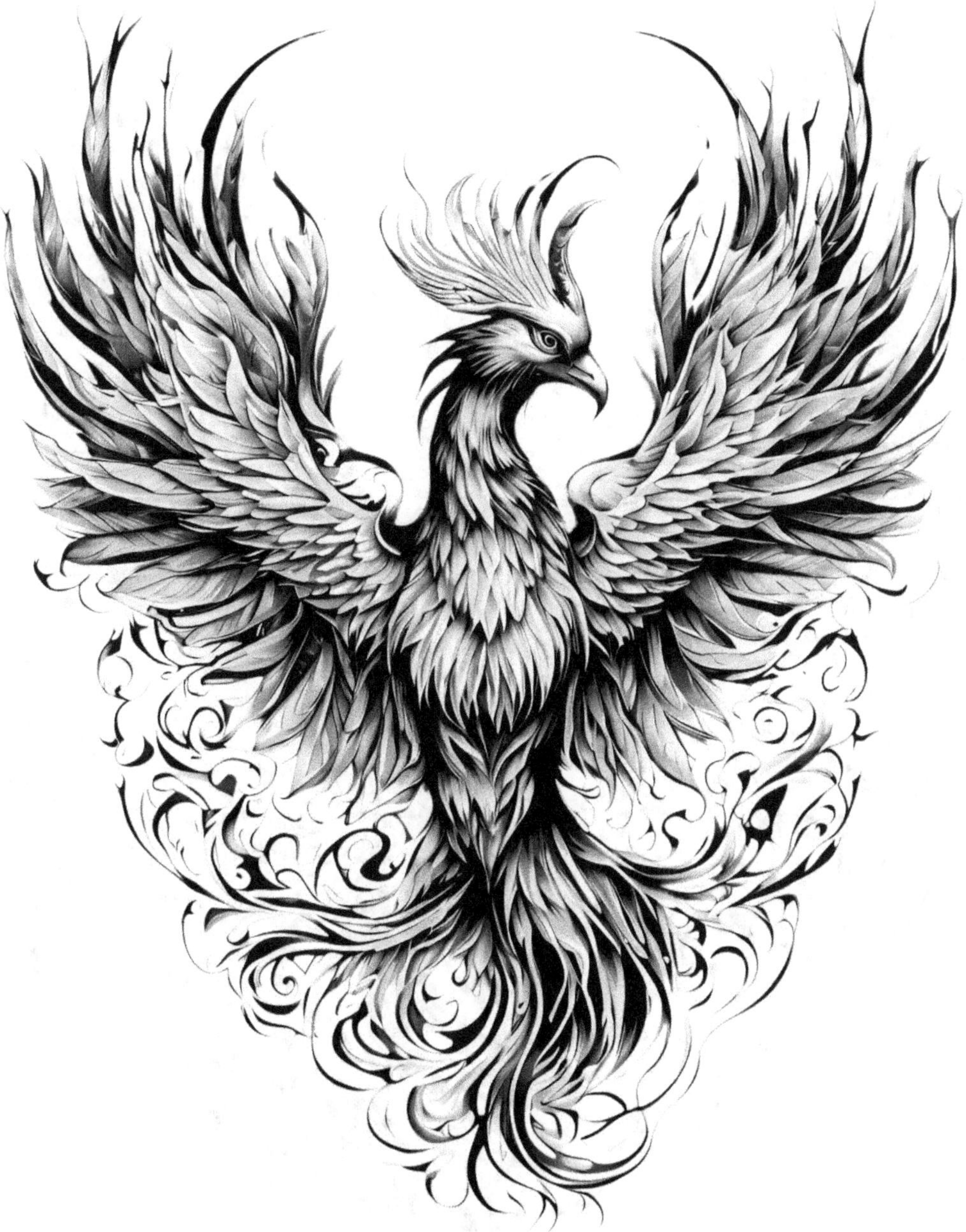

PHOENIX TATTOOS

PHOENIX TATTOOS

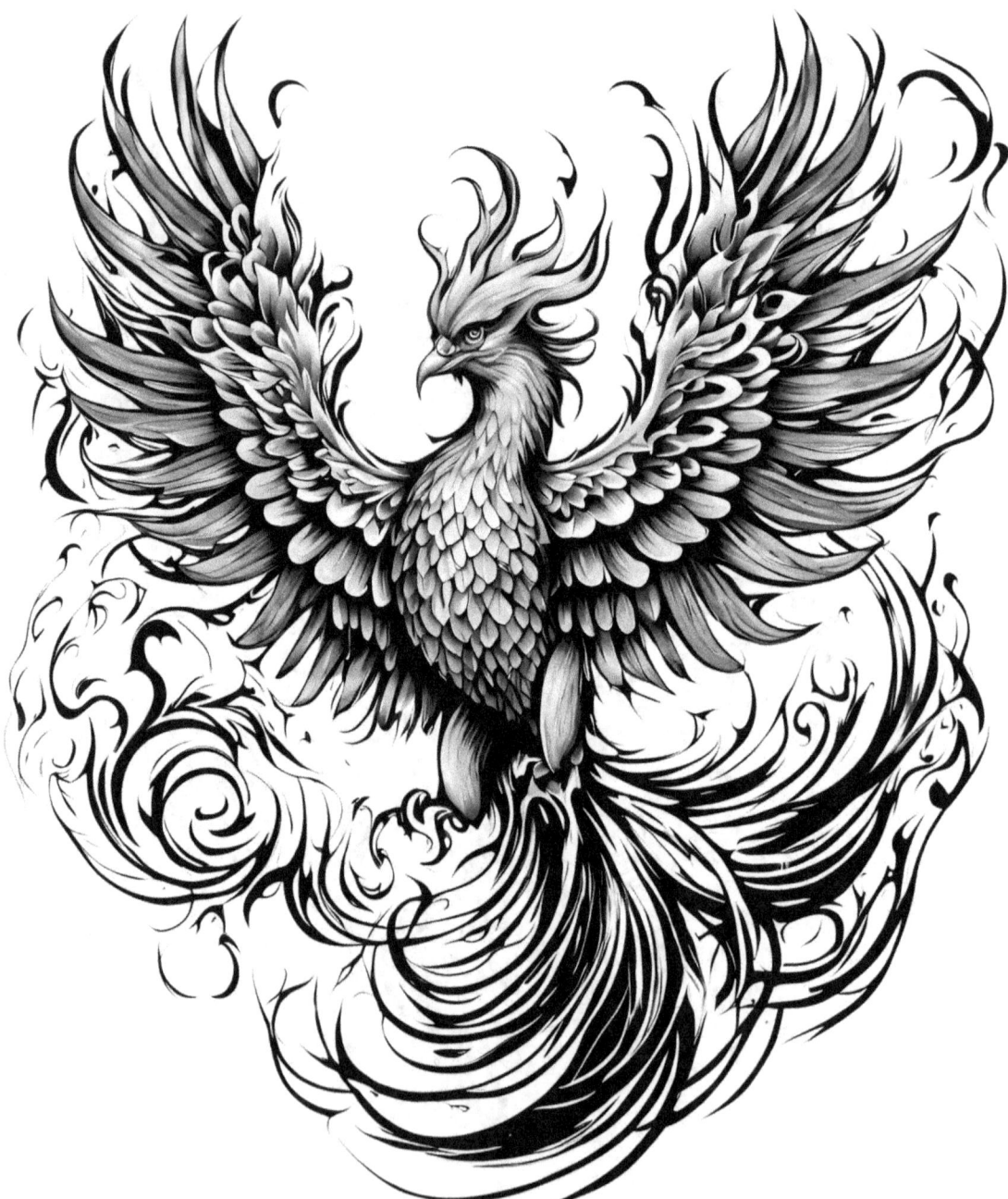

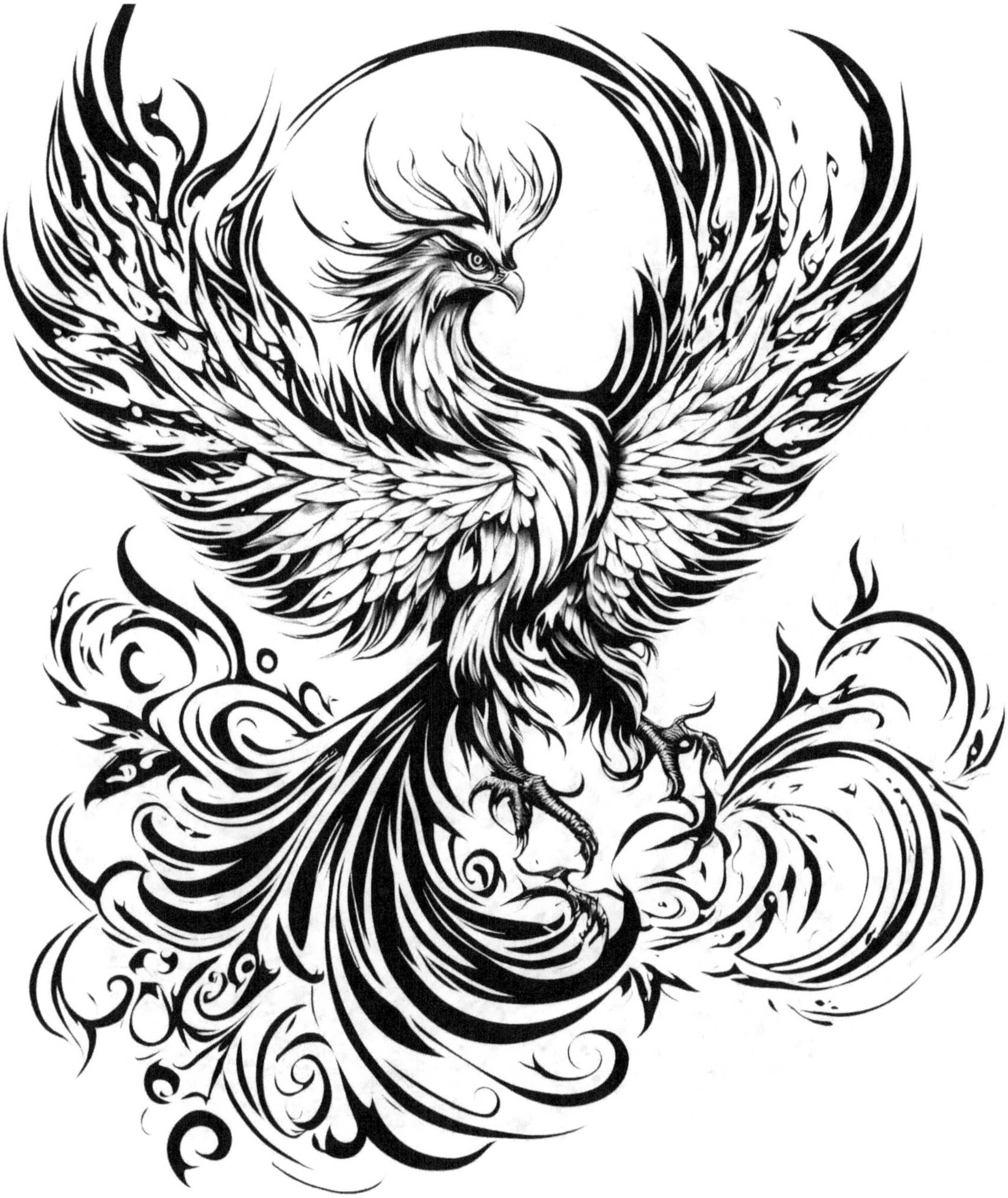

PHOENIX TATTOOS

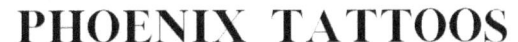

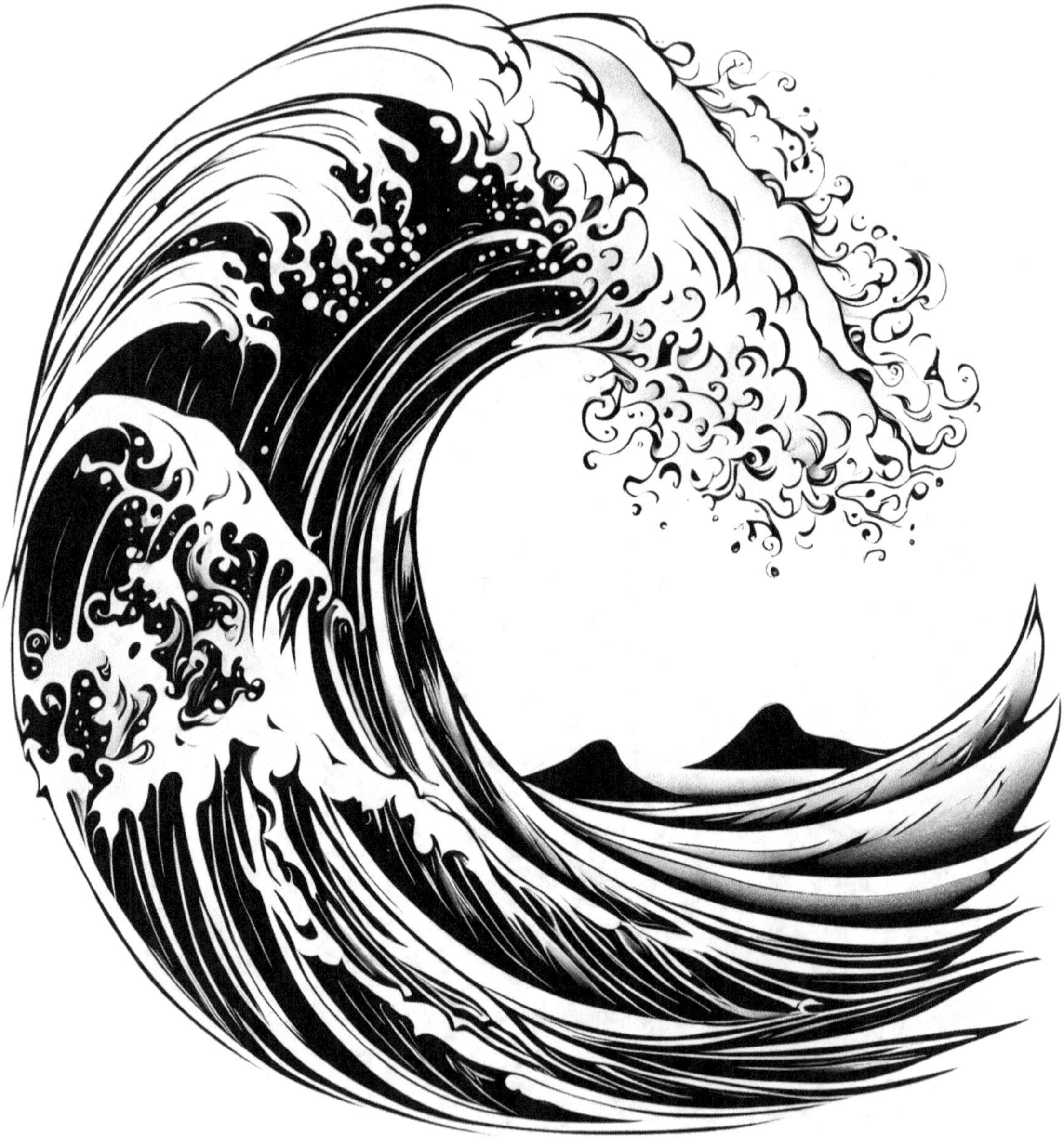

WAVE TATTOOS

WAVE TATTOOS

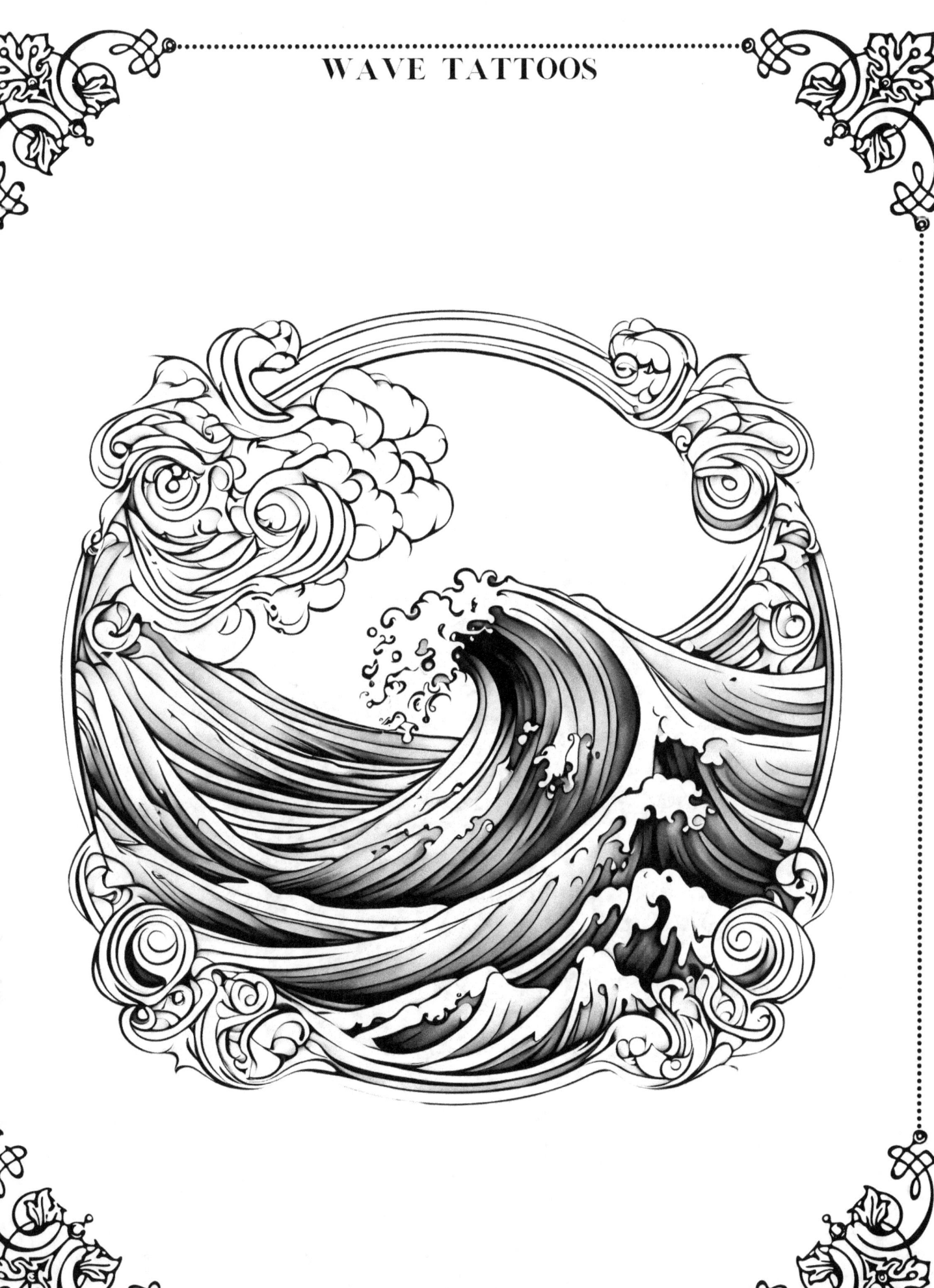

WAVE TATTOOS

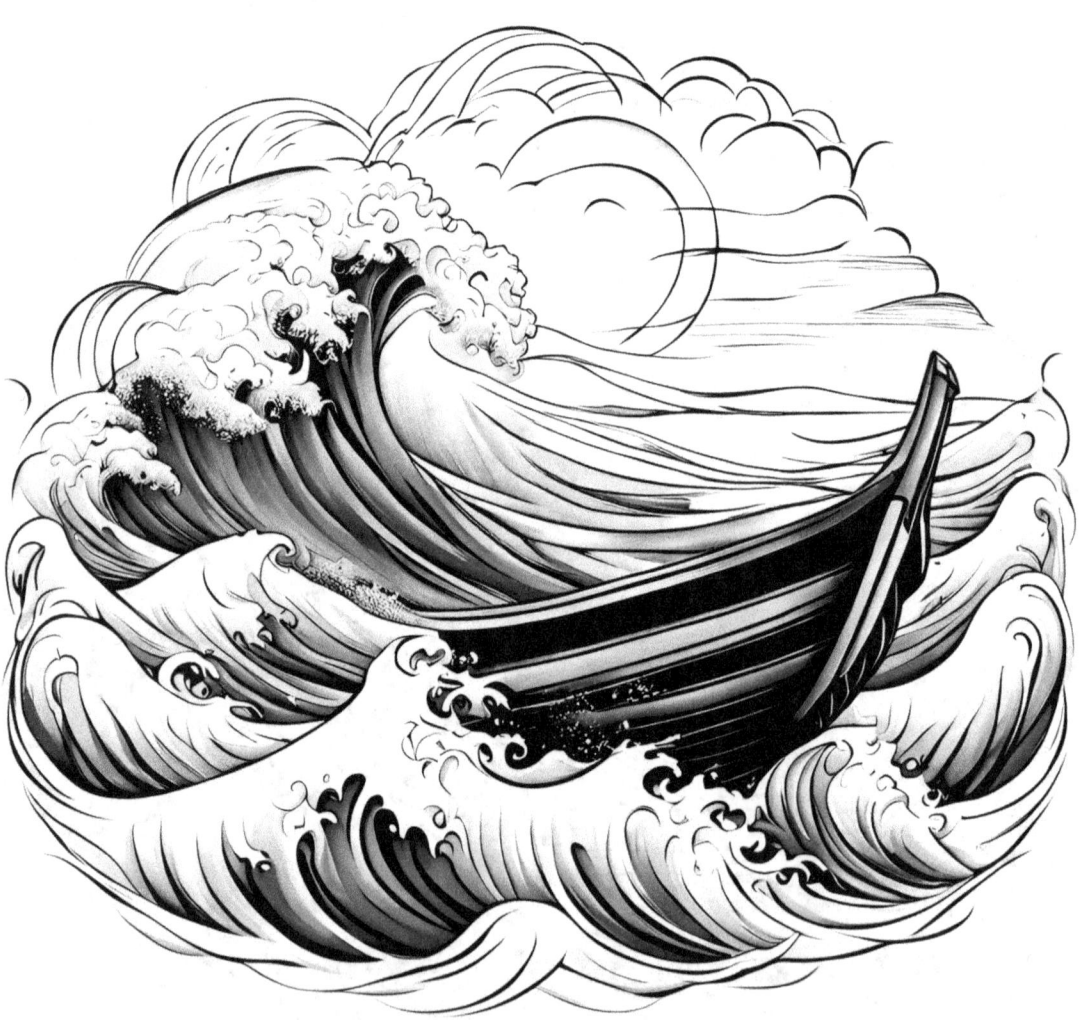

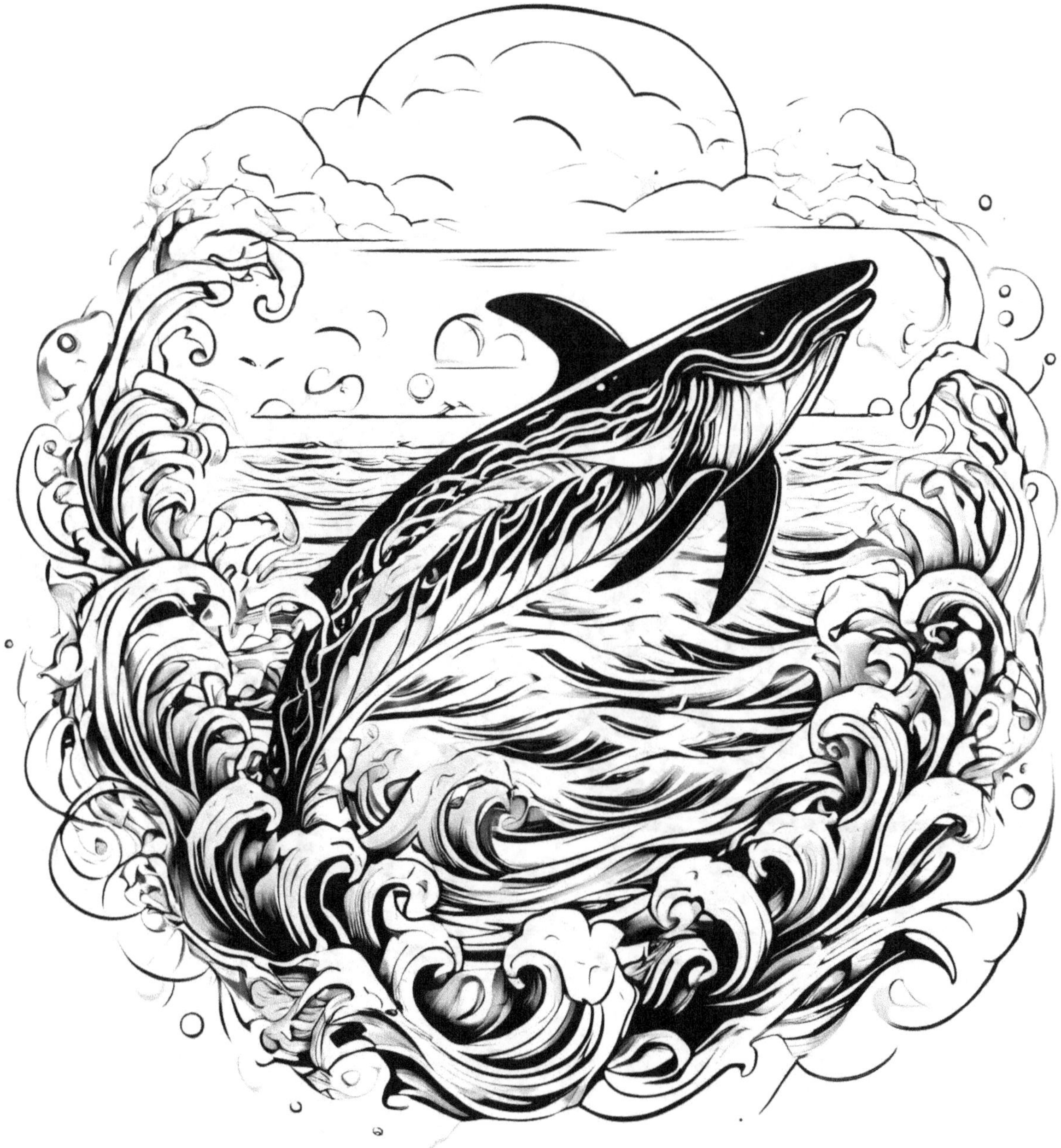

WAVE TATTOOS

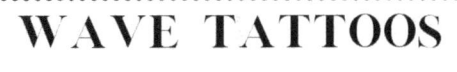

WAVE TATTOOS

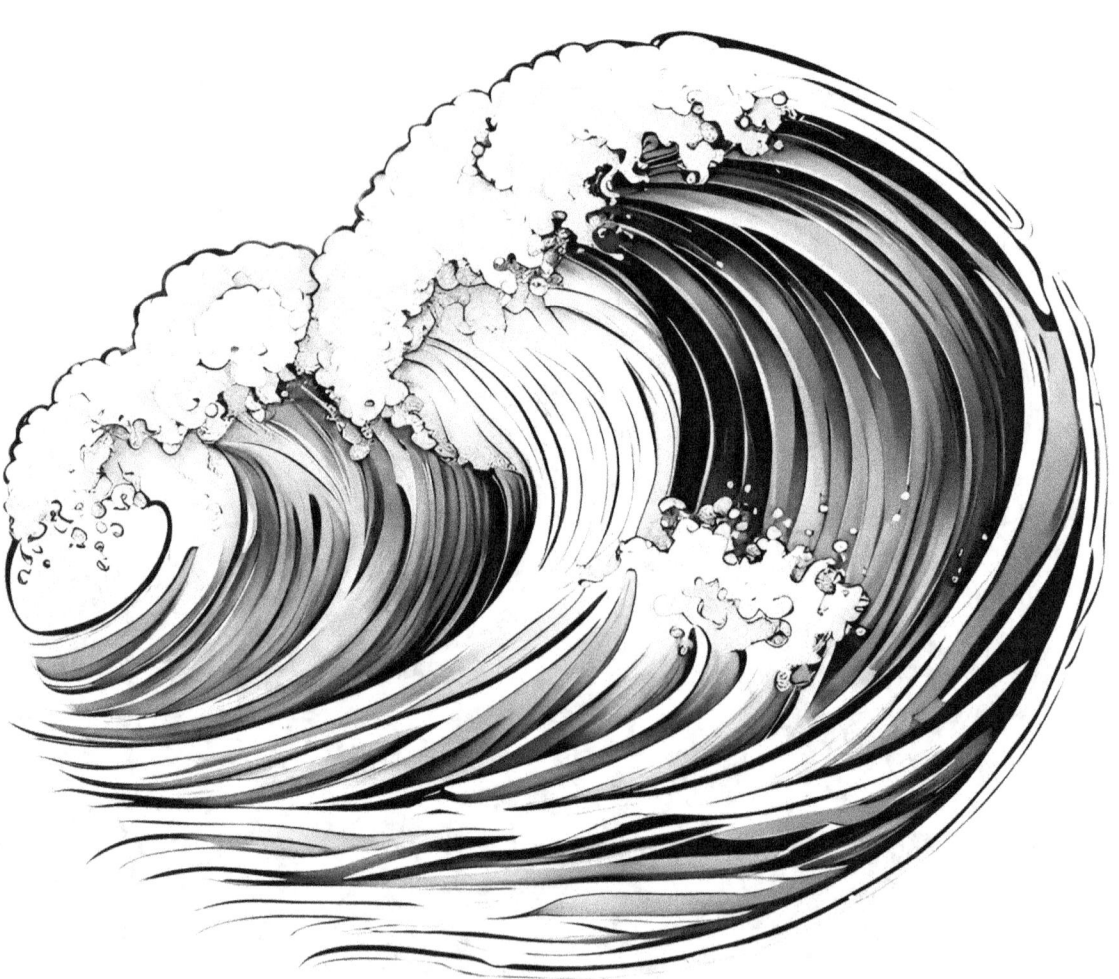

MONEY BAG TATTOOS

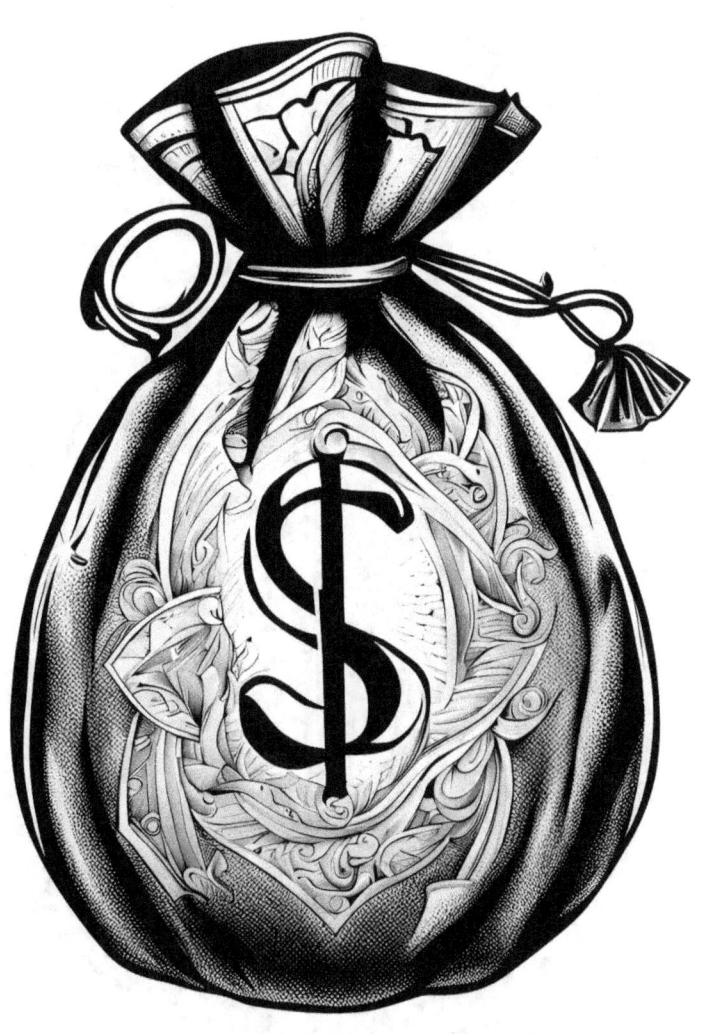

MONEY BAG TATTOOS

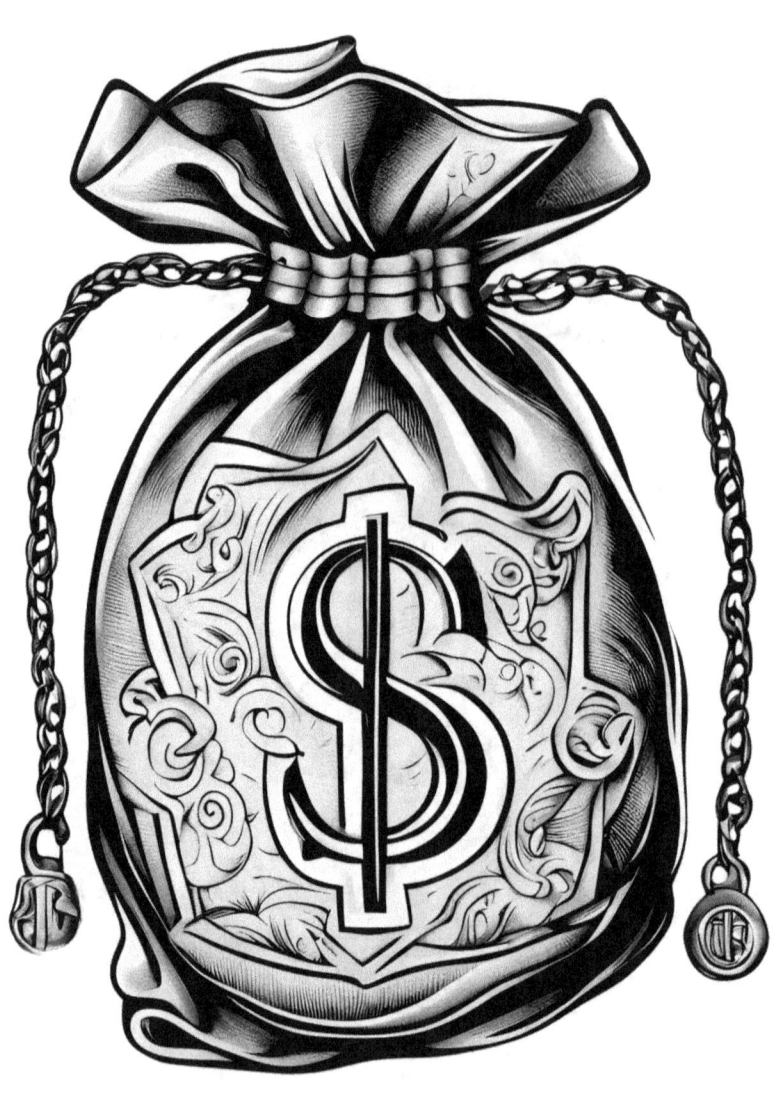

TREASURE CHEST TATTOOS

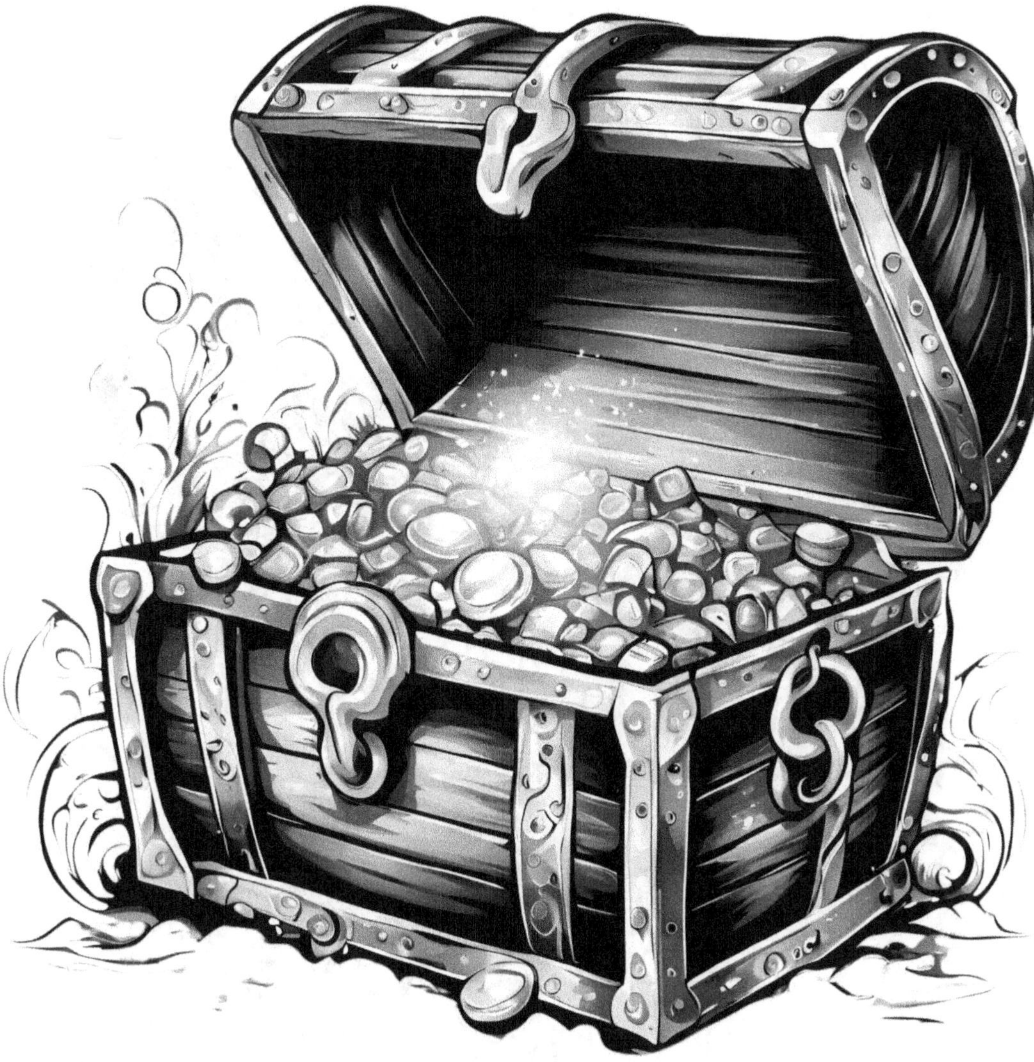

TREASURE CHEST TATTOOS

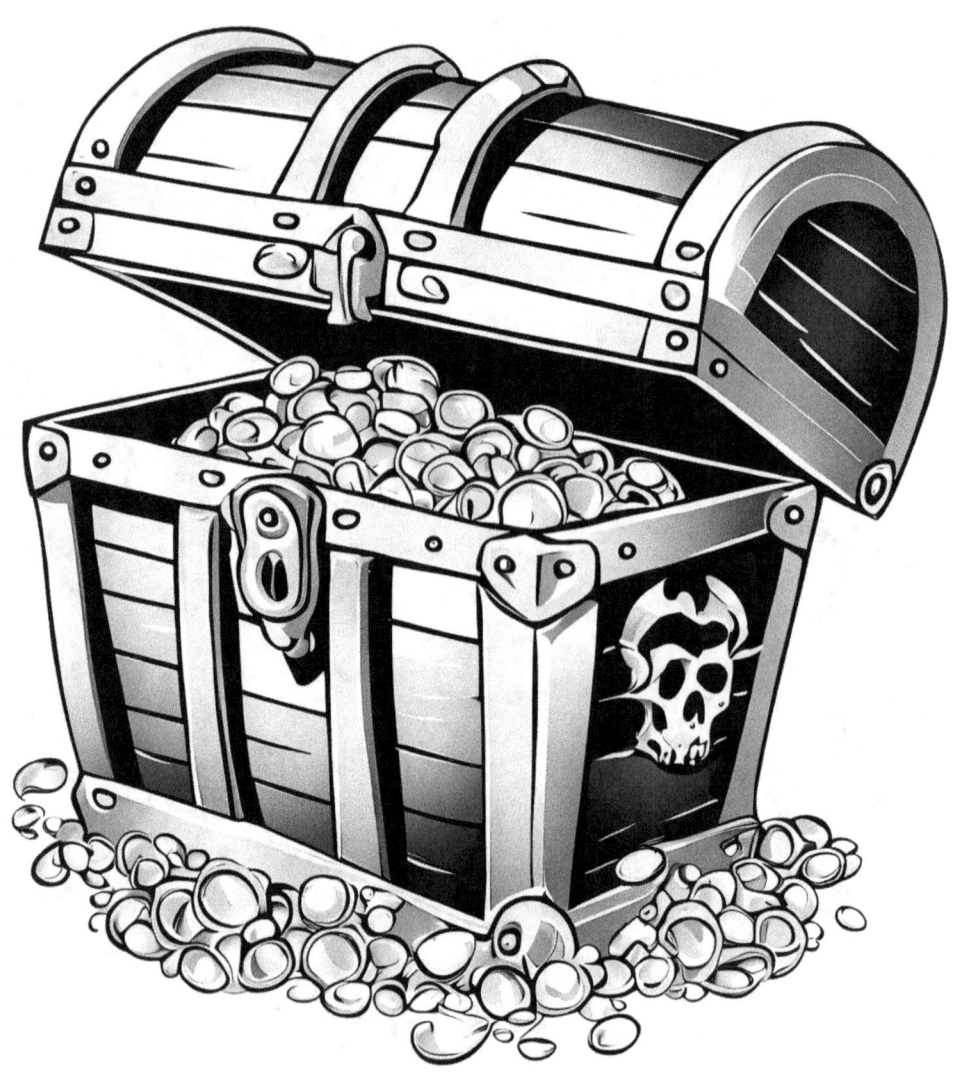

TREASURE CHEST TATTOOS

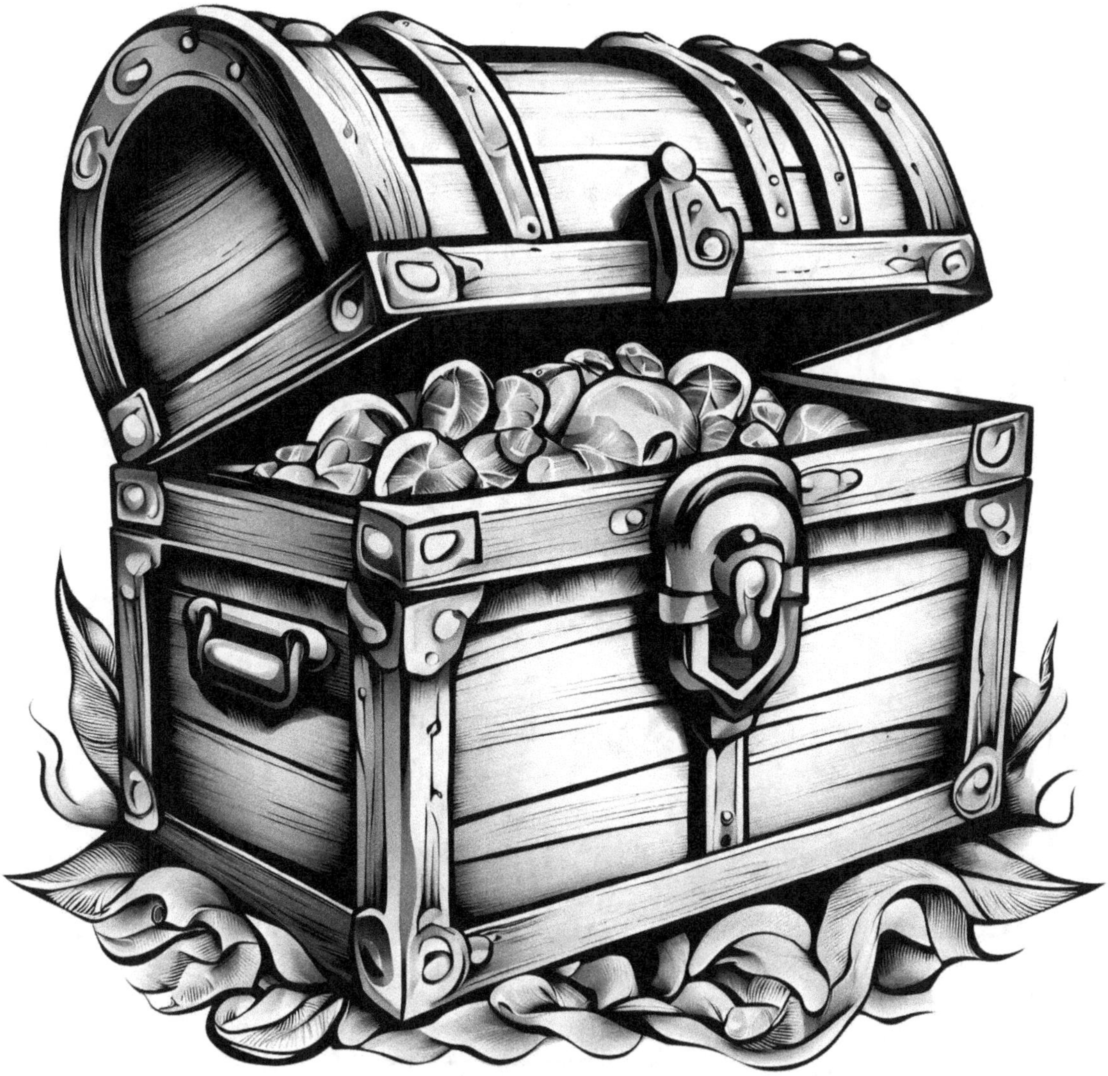

TREASURE CHEST TATTOOS

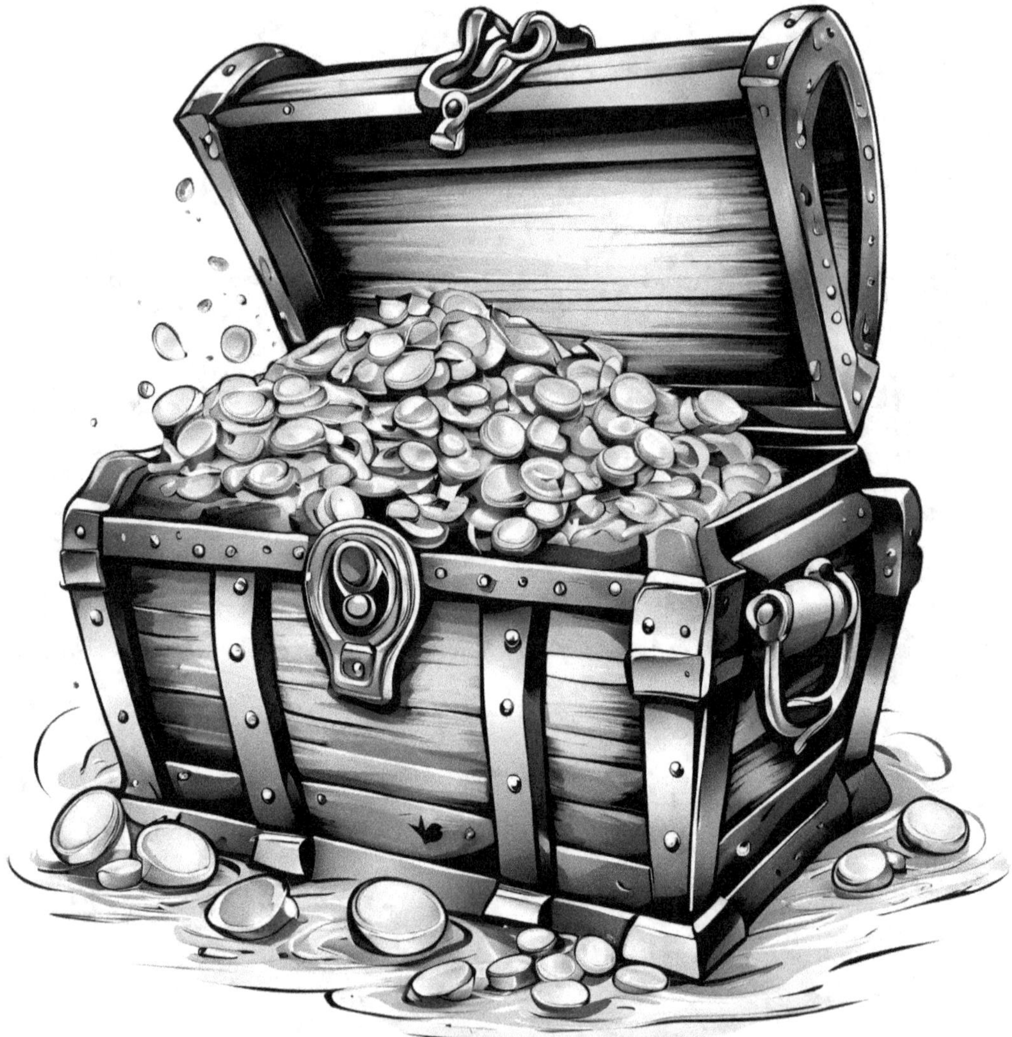

TREASURE CHEST TATTOOS

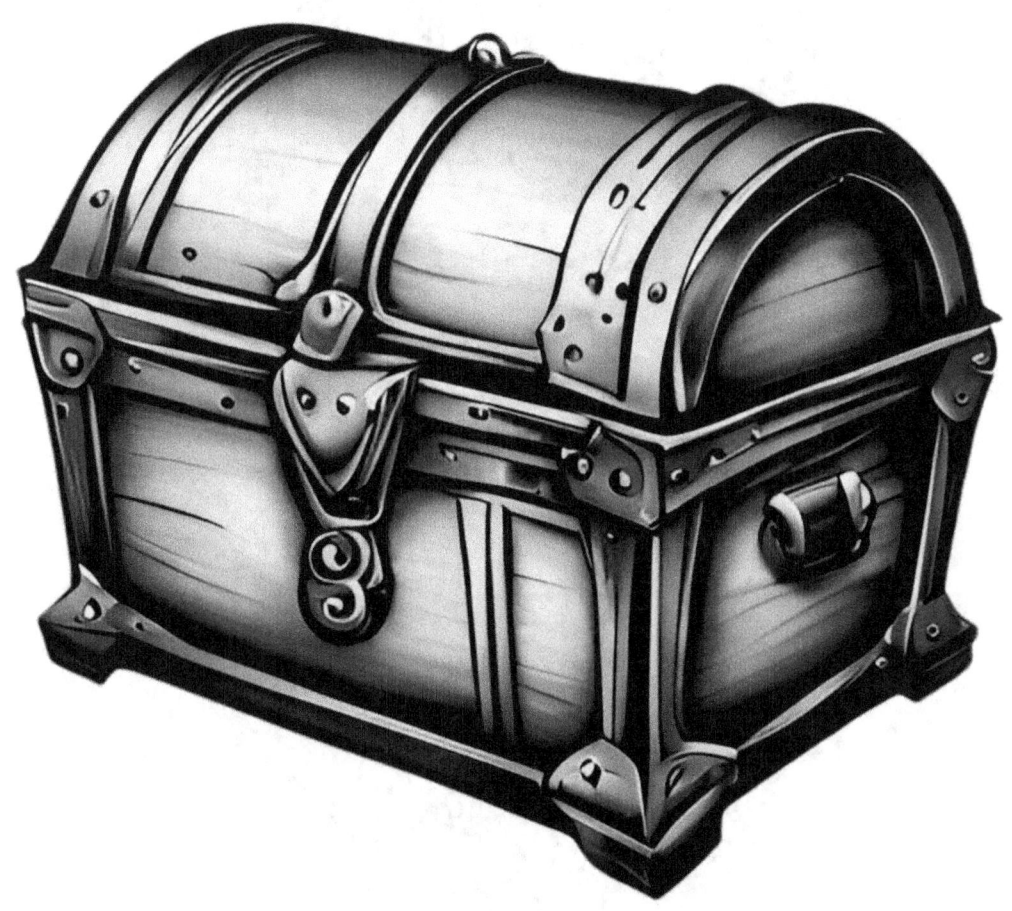

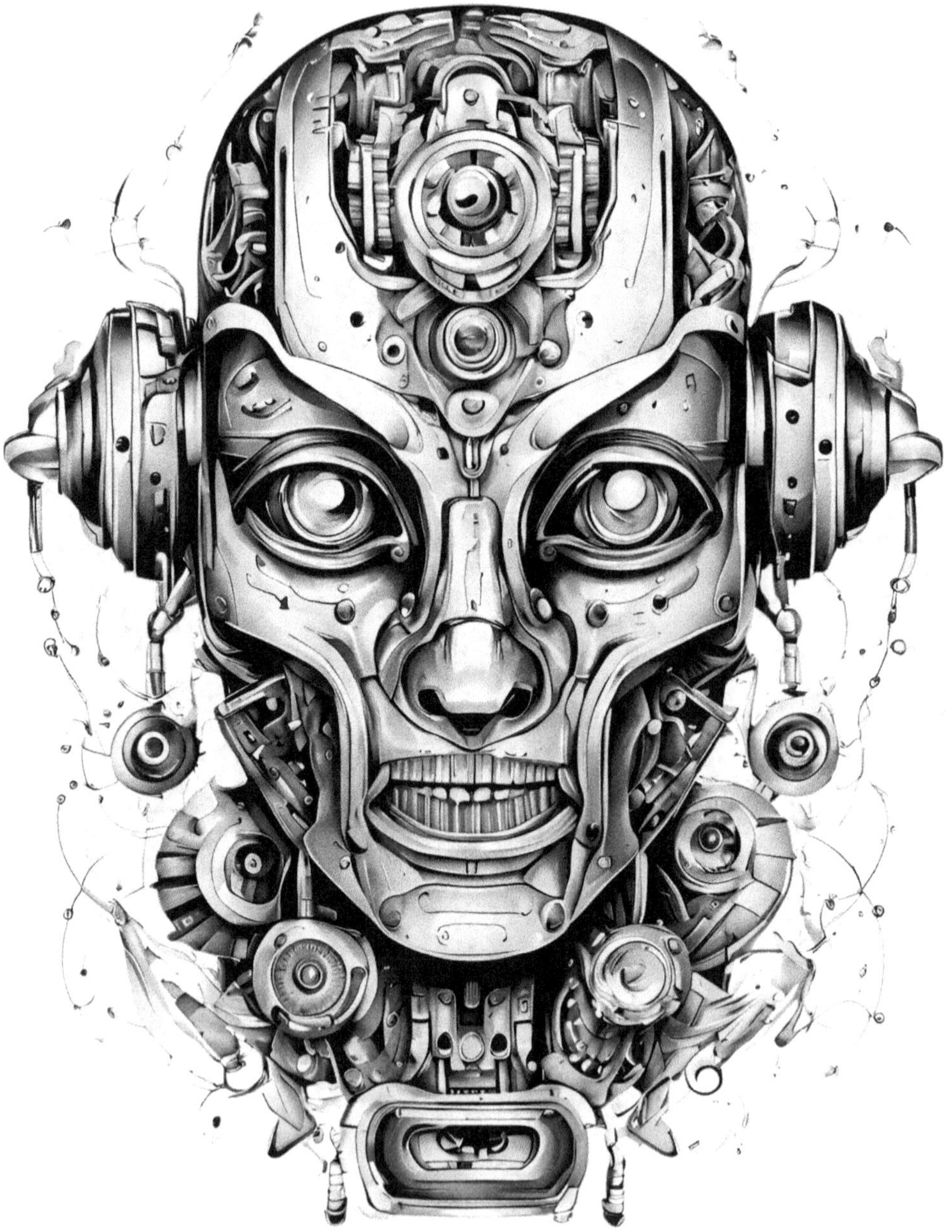

ROBOT TATTOOS

PAGE 162

ROBOT TATTOOS

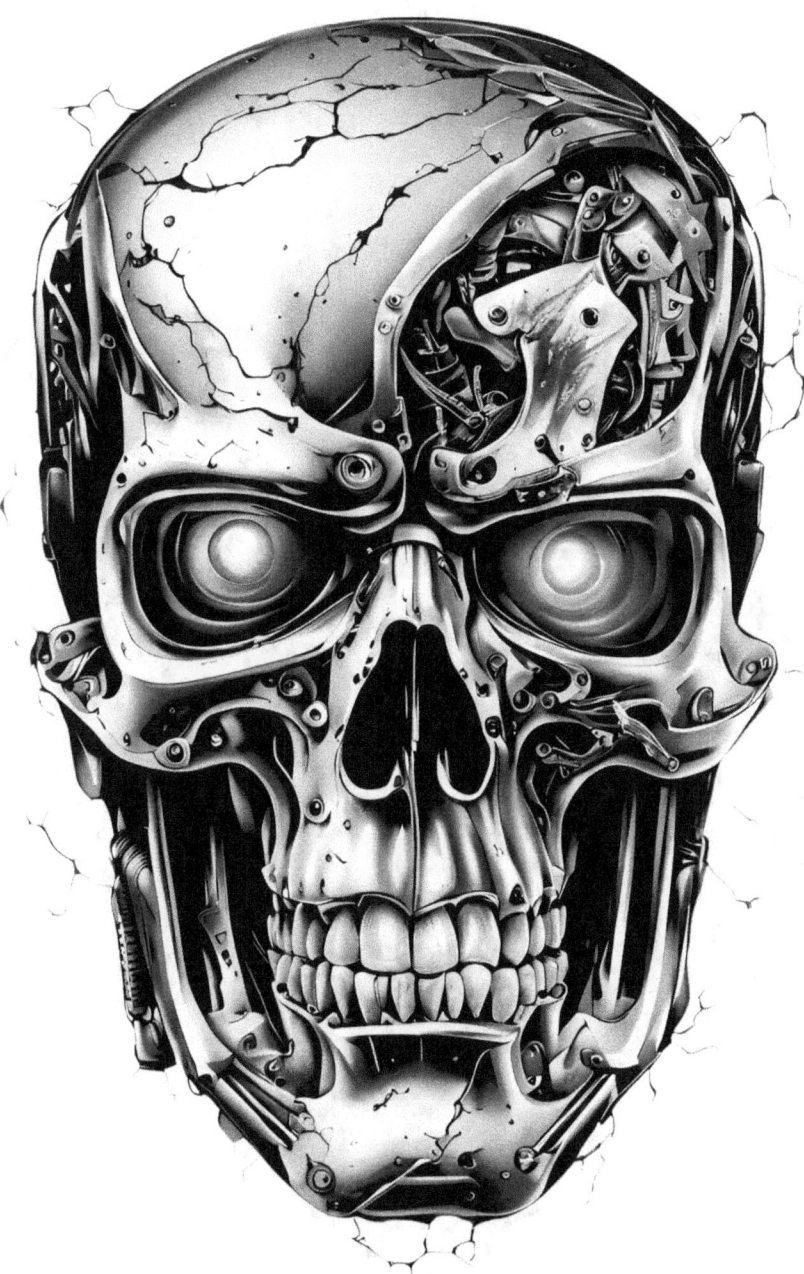

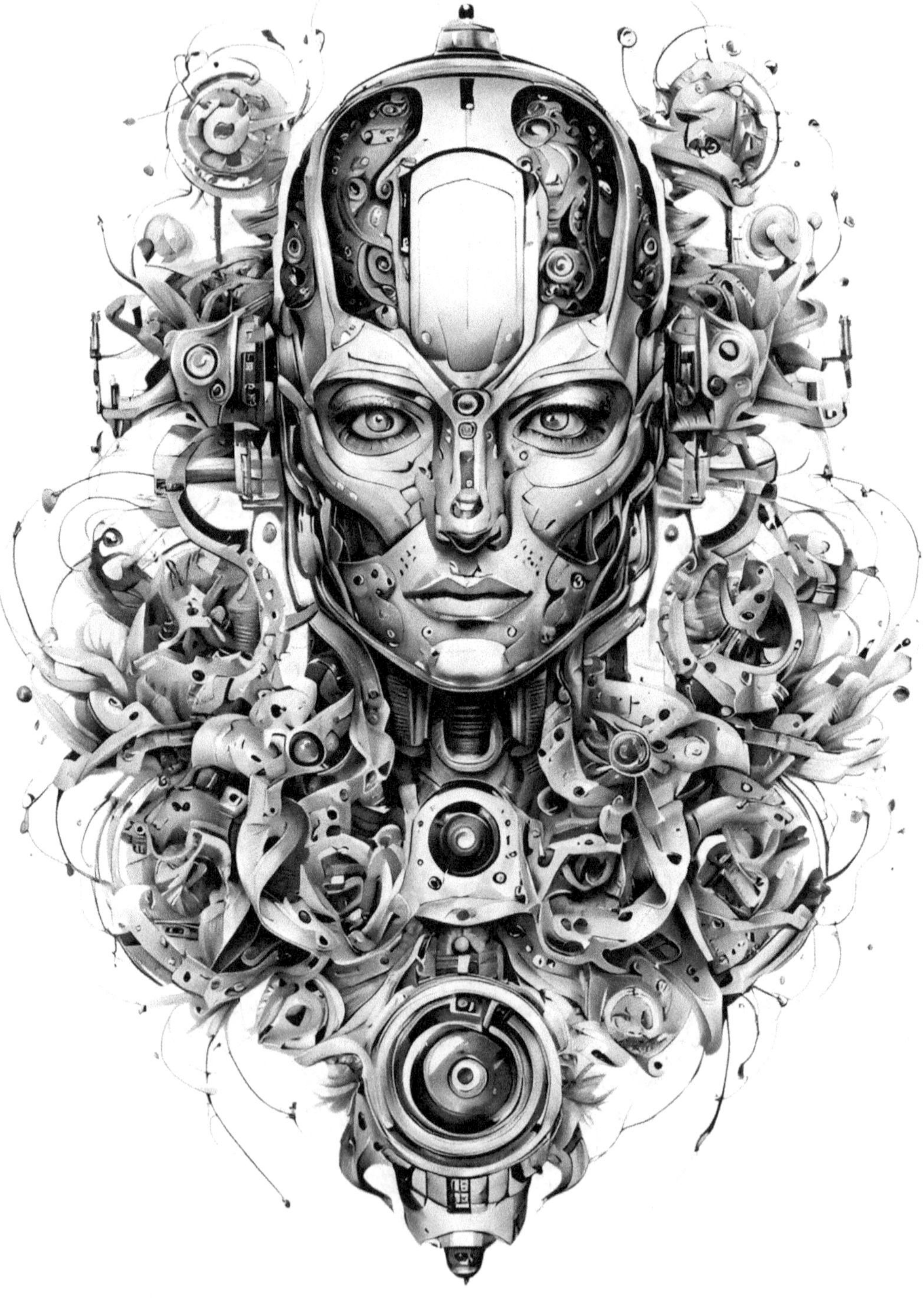

ROBOT TATTOOS

ROBOT TATTOOS

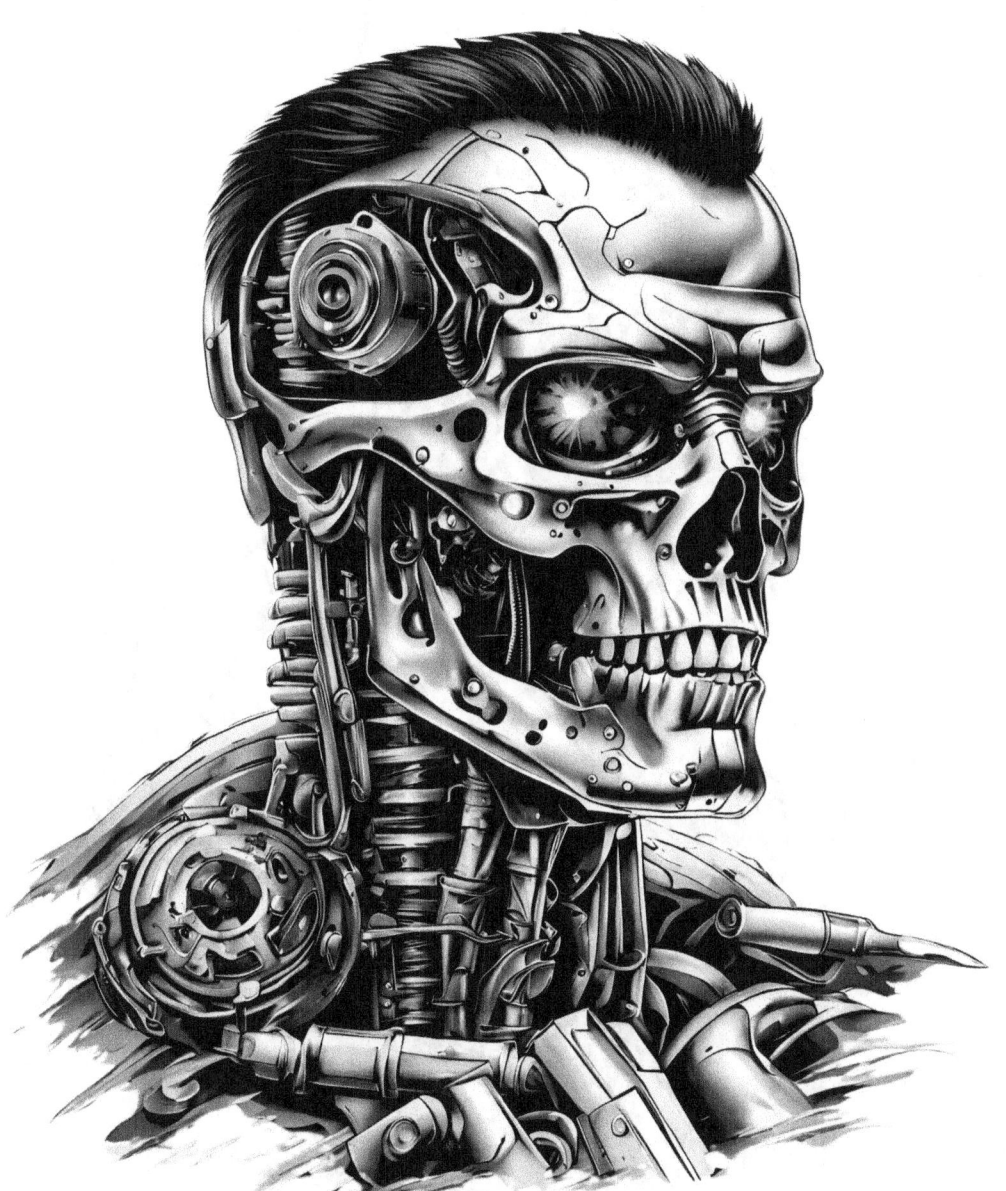

ROBOT TATTOOS

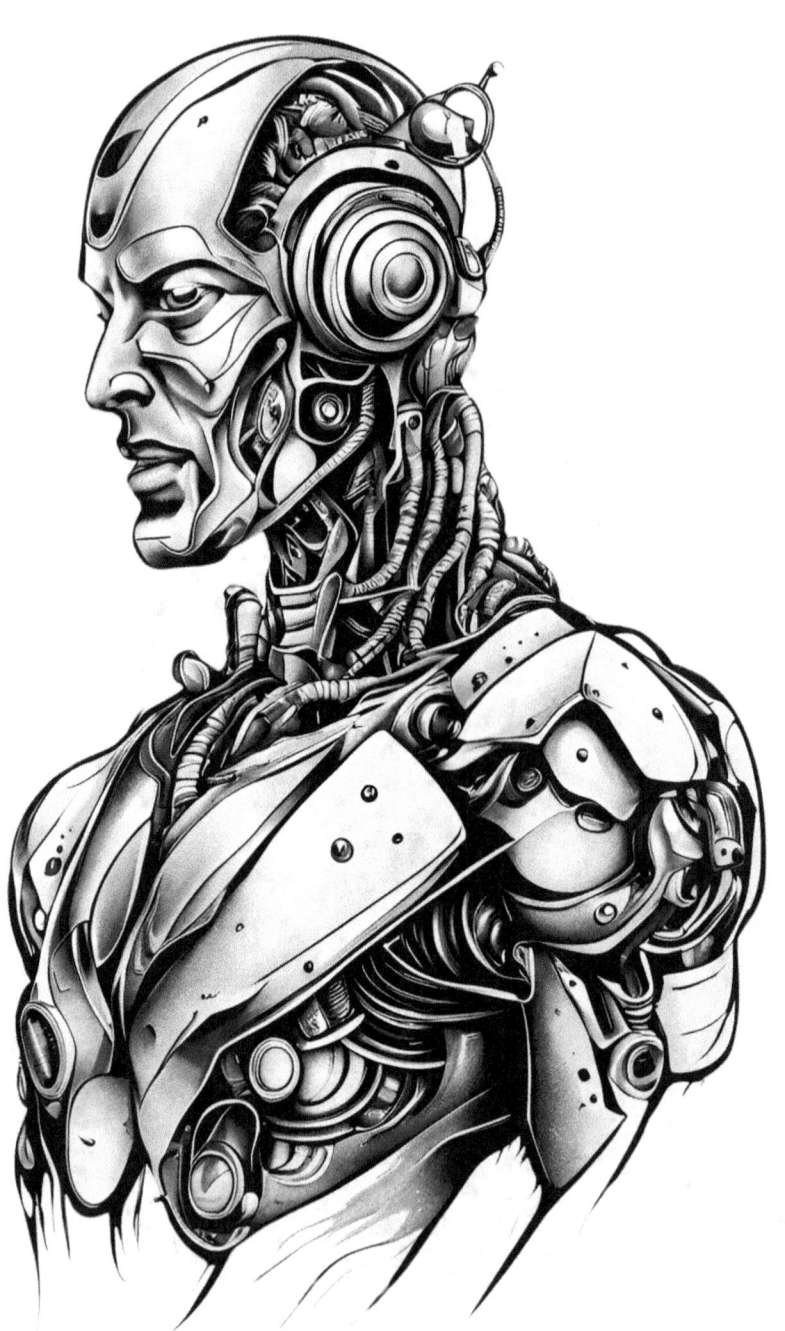

ROBOT TATTOOS

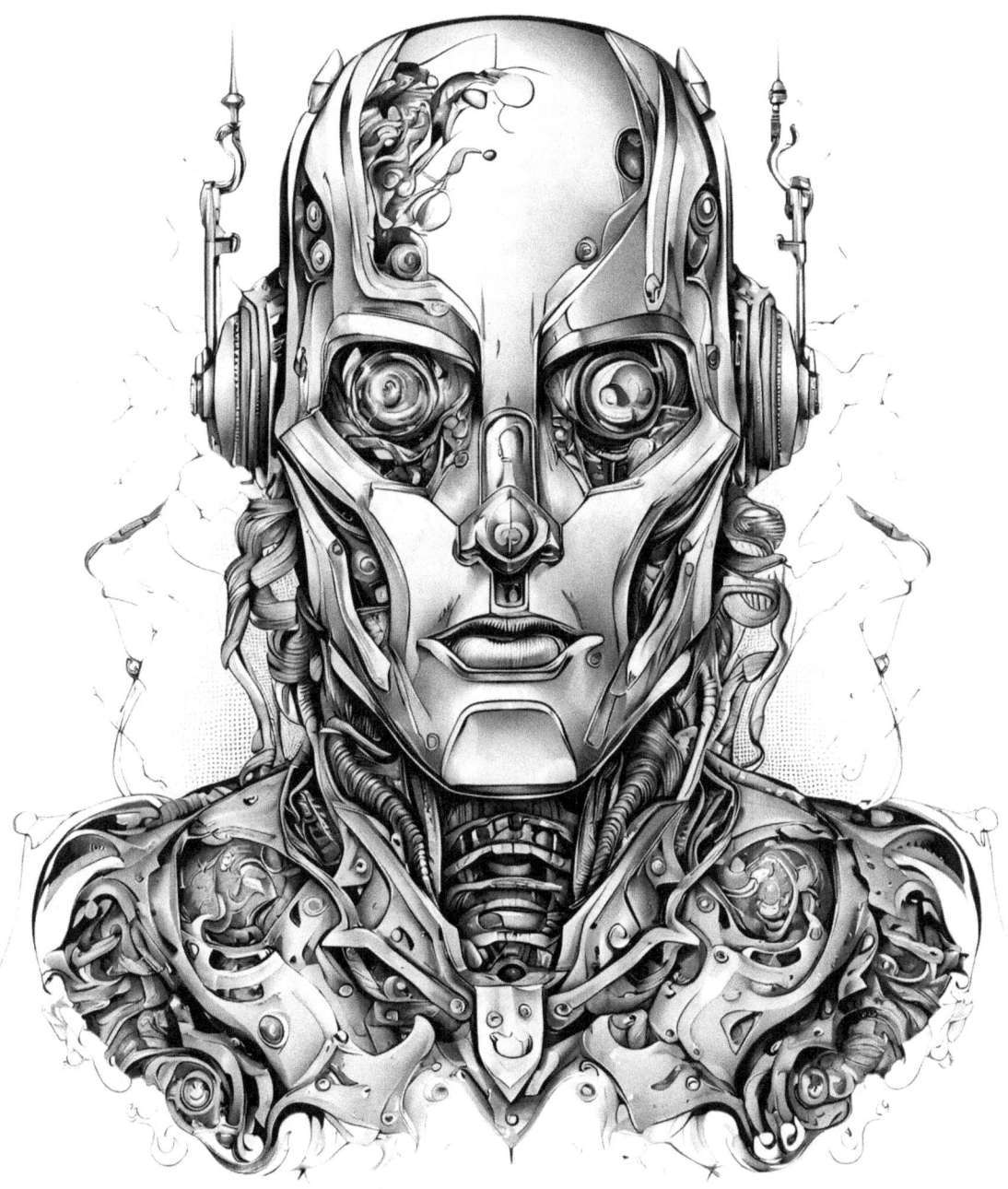

LIPS TATTOOS

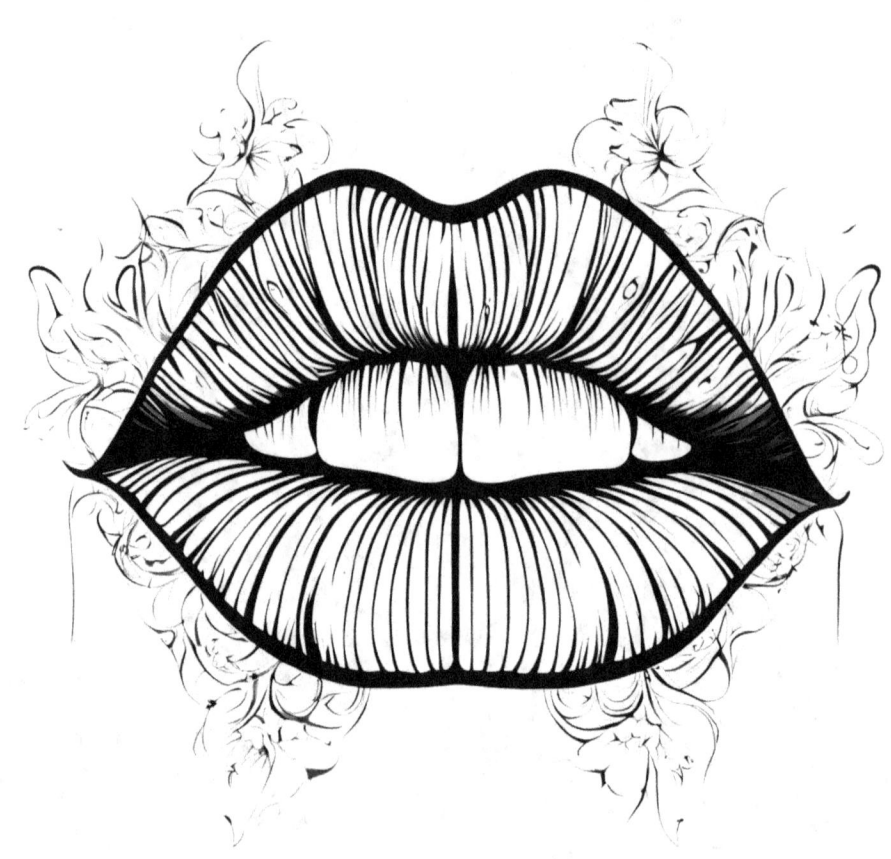

LIPS TATTOOS

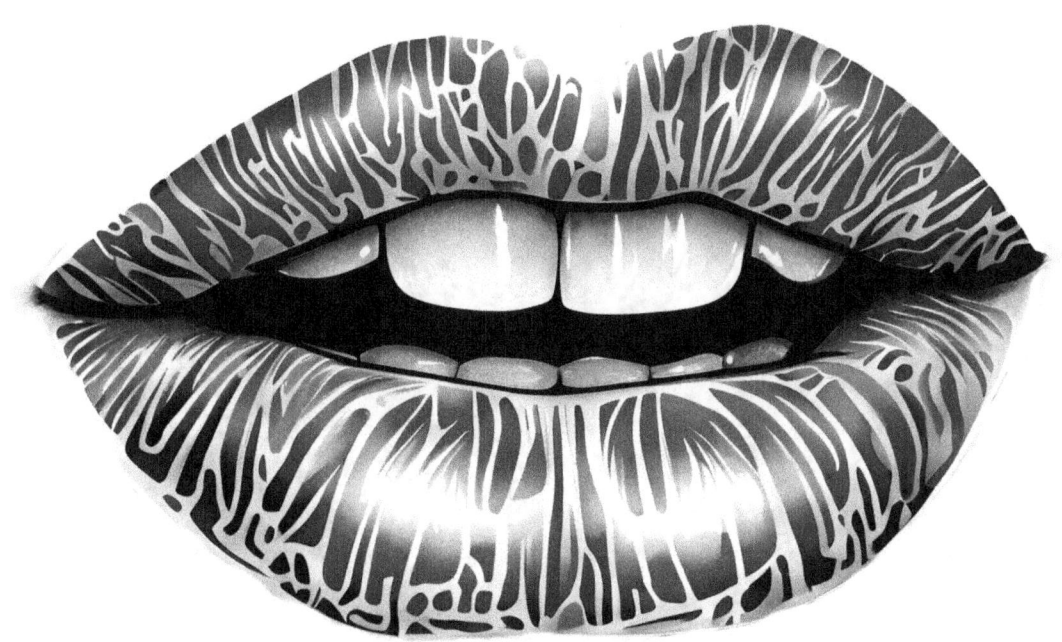

LIPS TATTOOS

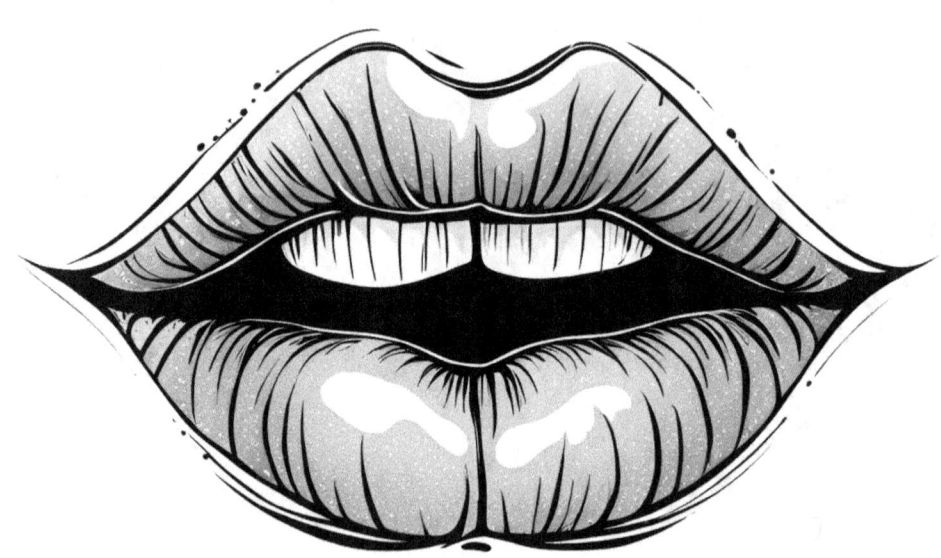

HOURGLASS TATTOOS

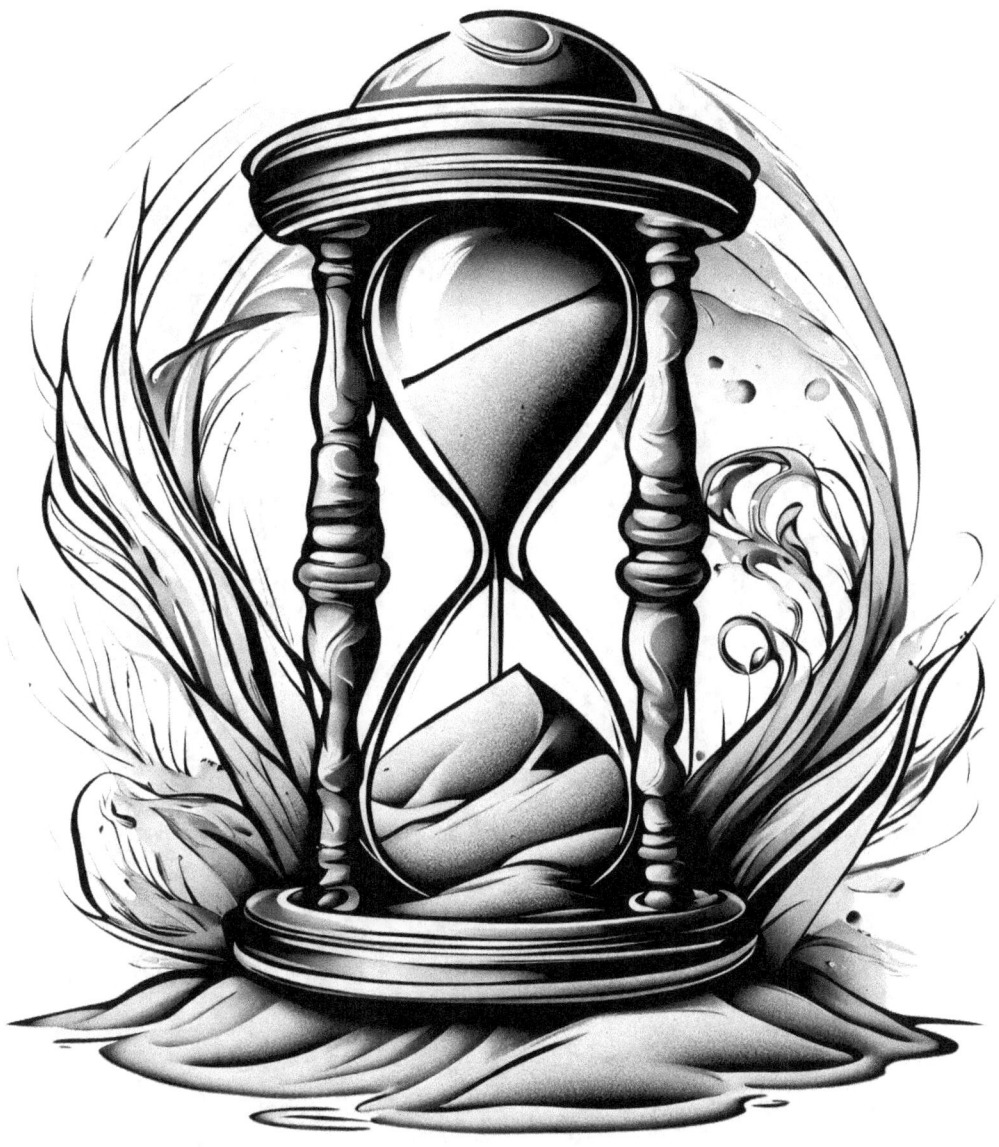

HOURGLASS TATTOOS

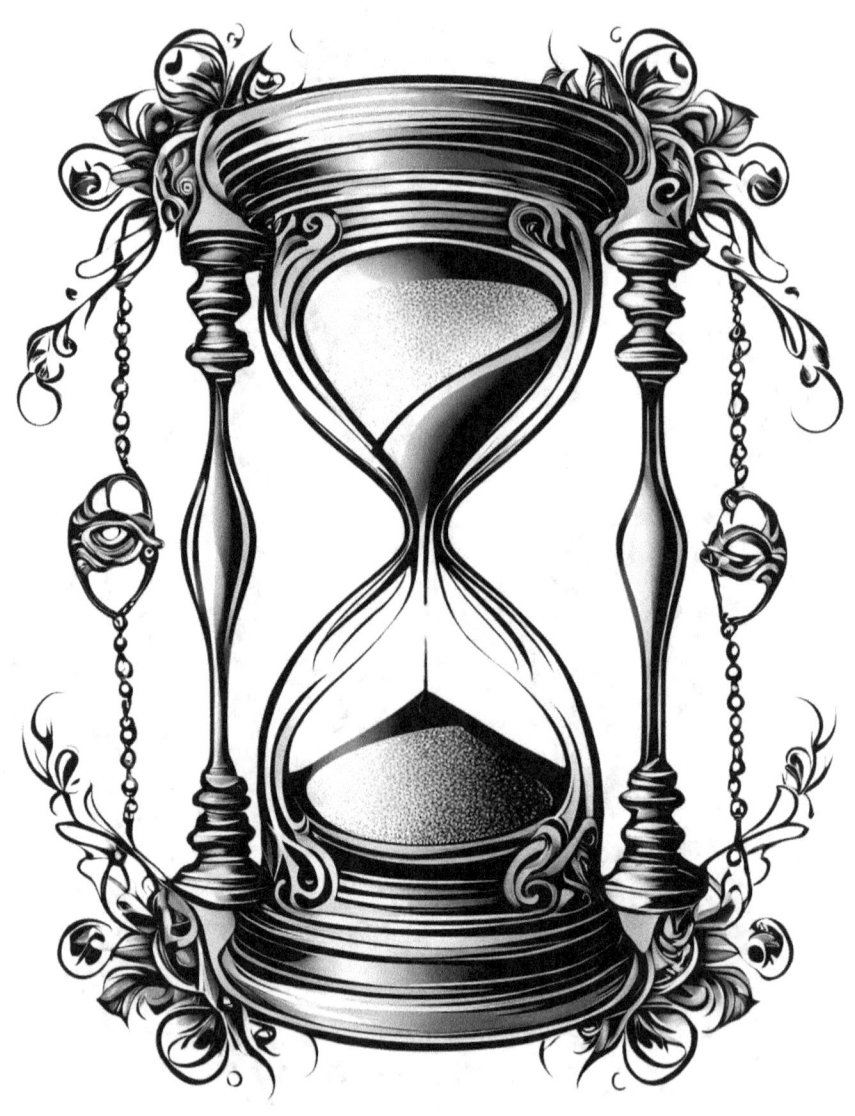

PAGE 172

HOURGLASS TATTOOS

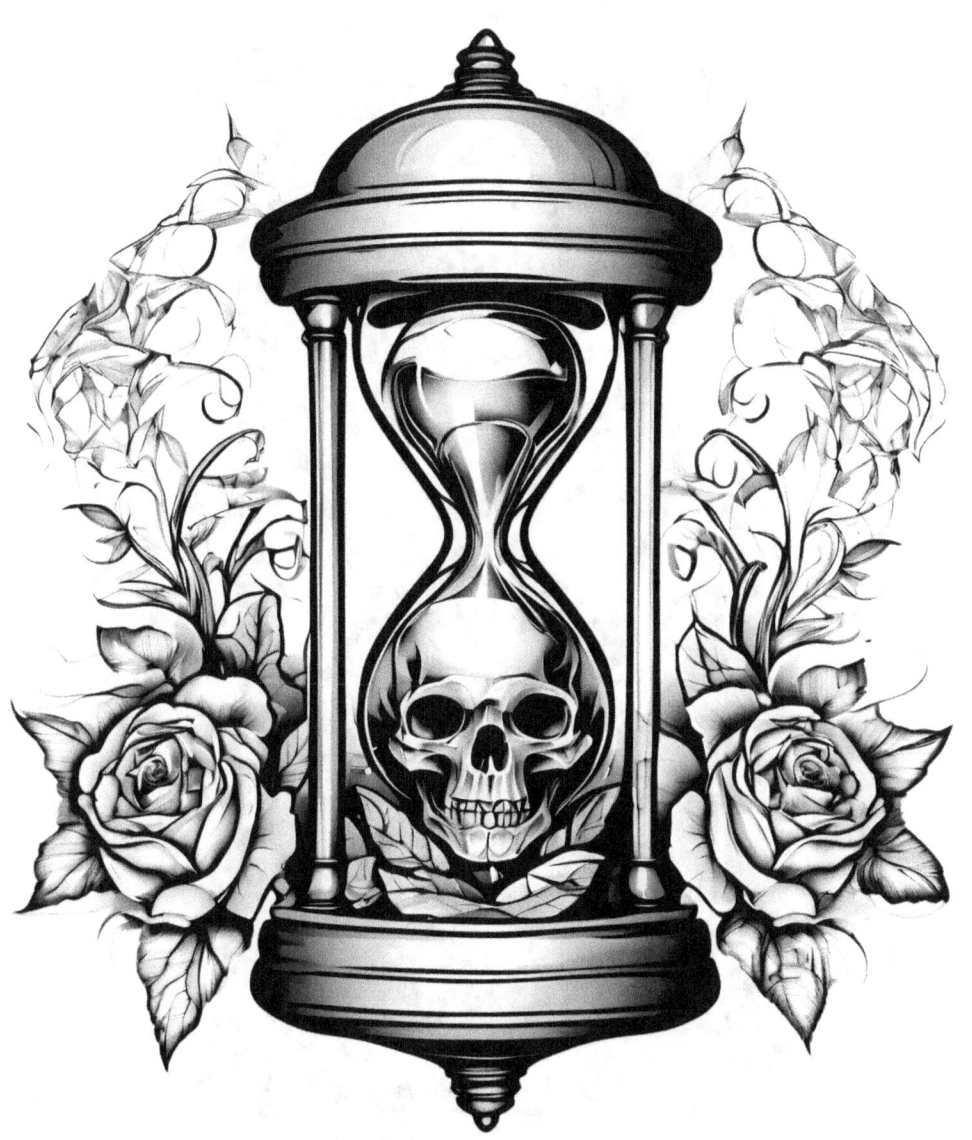

HOURGLASS TATTOOS

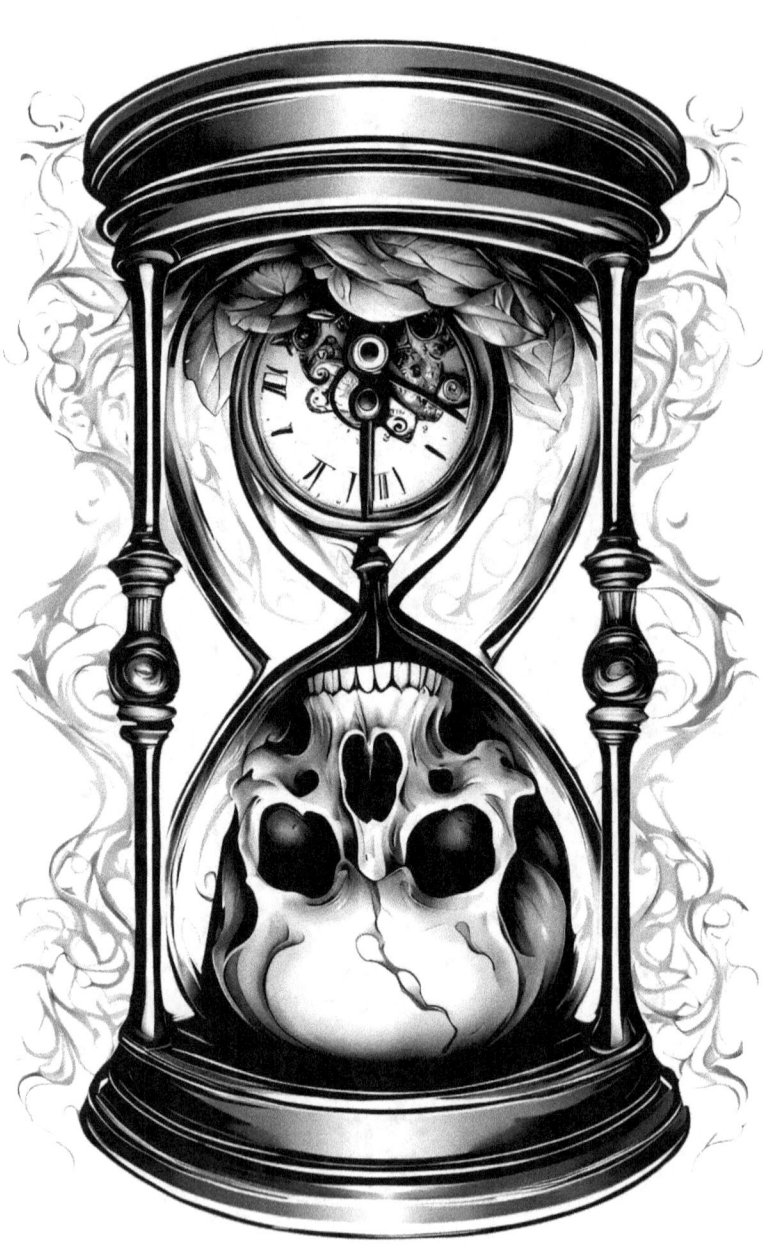

GLADIATOR TATTOOS

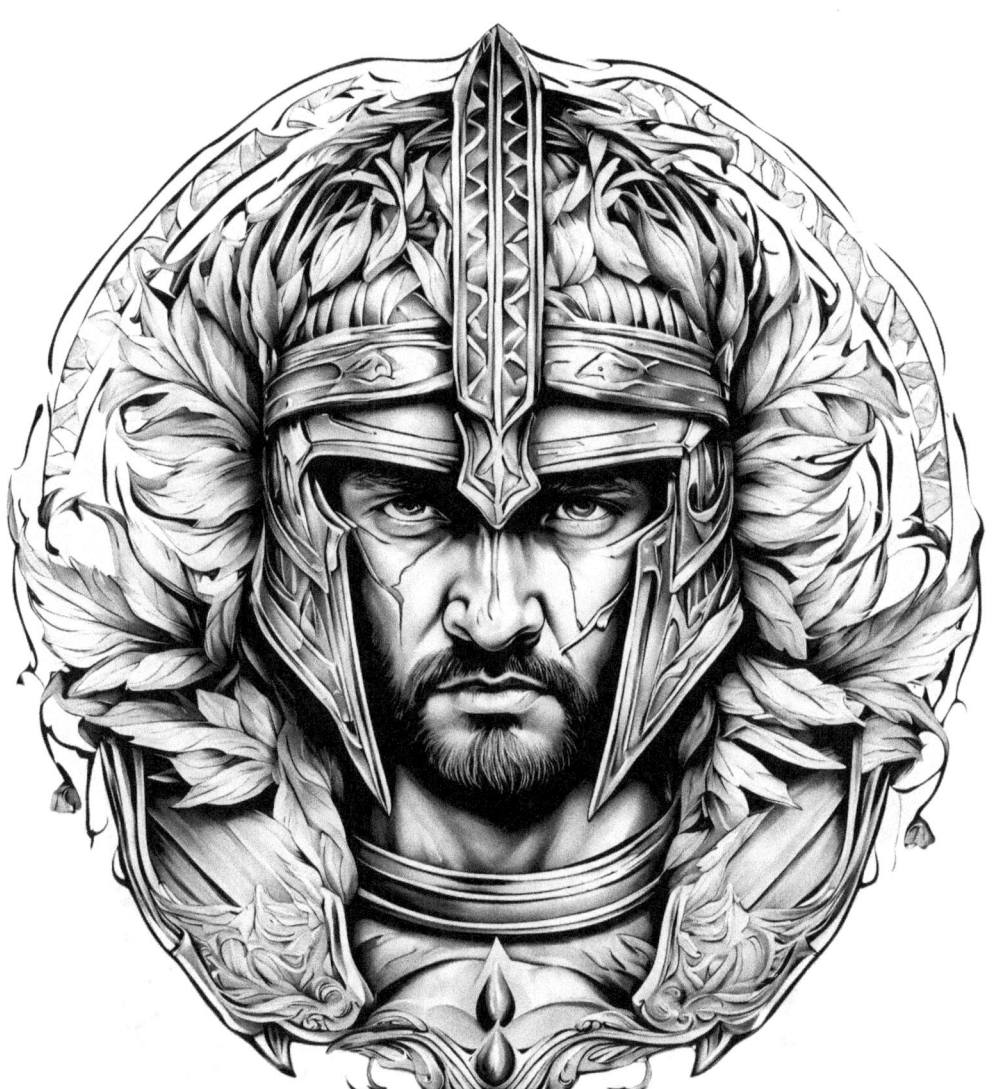

GLADIATOR TATTOOS

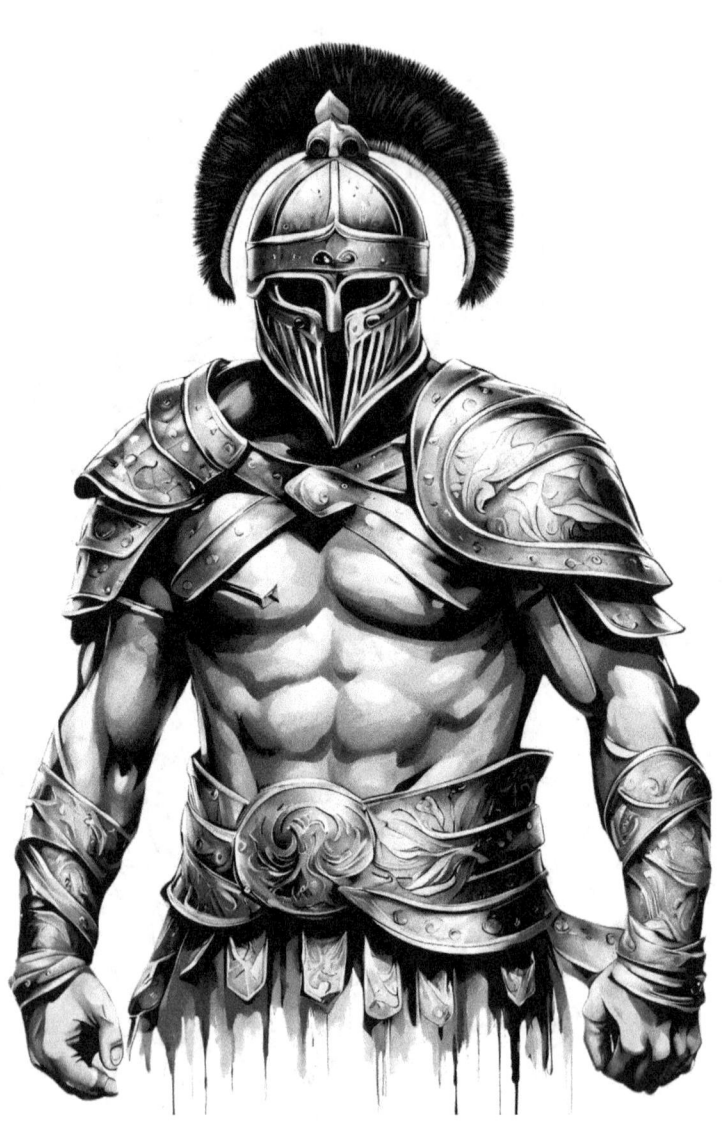

GLADIATOR TATTOOS

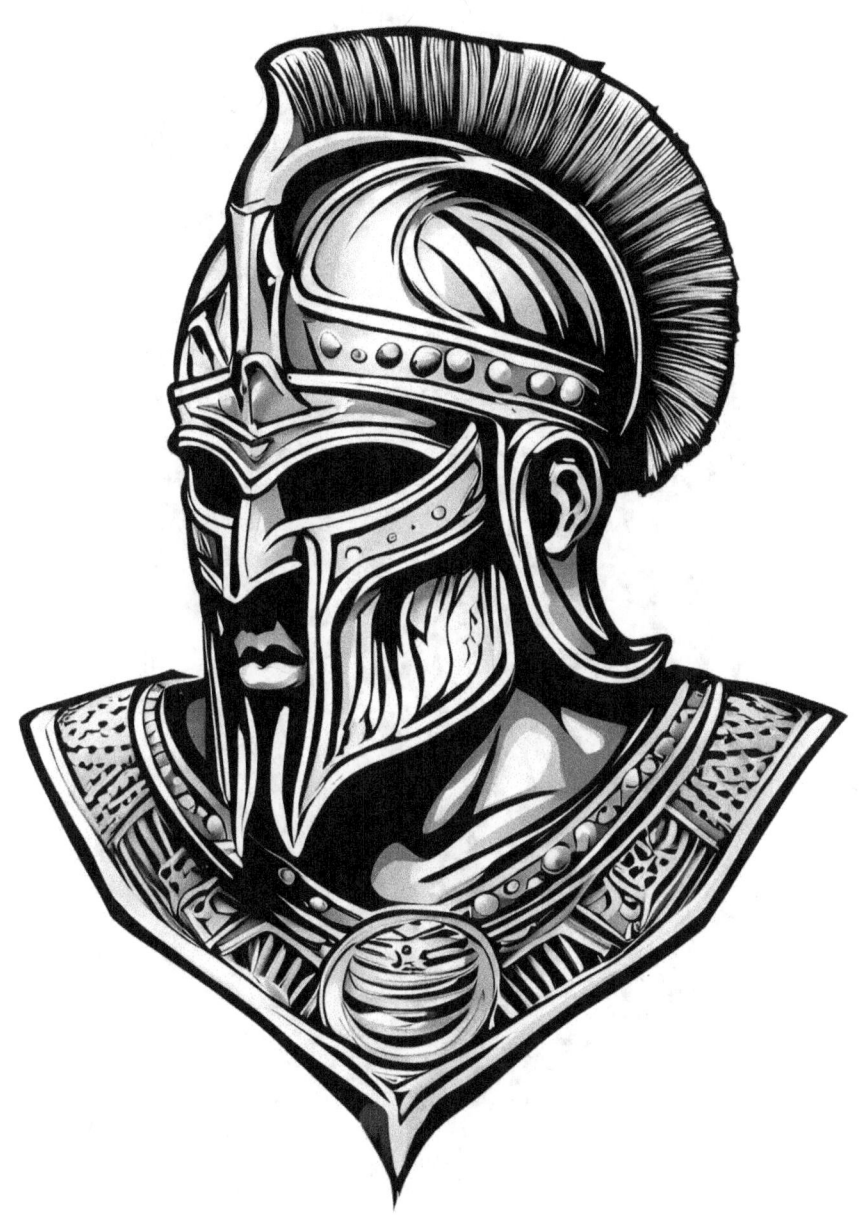

GLADIATOR TATTOOS

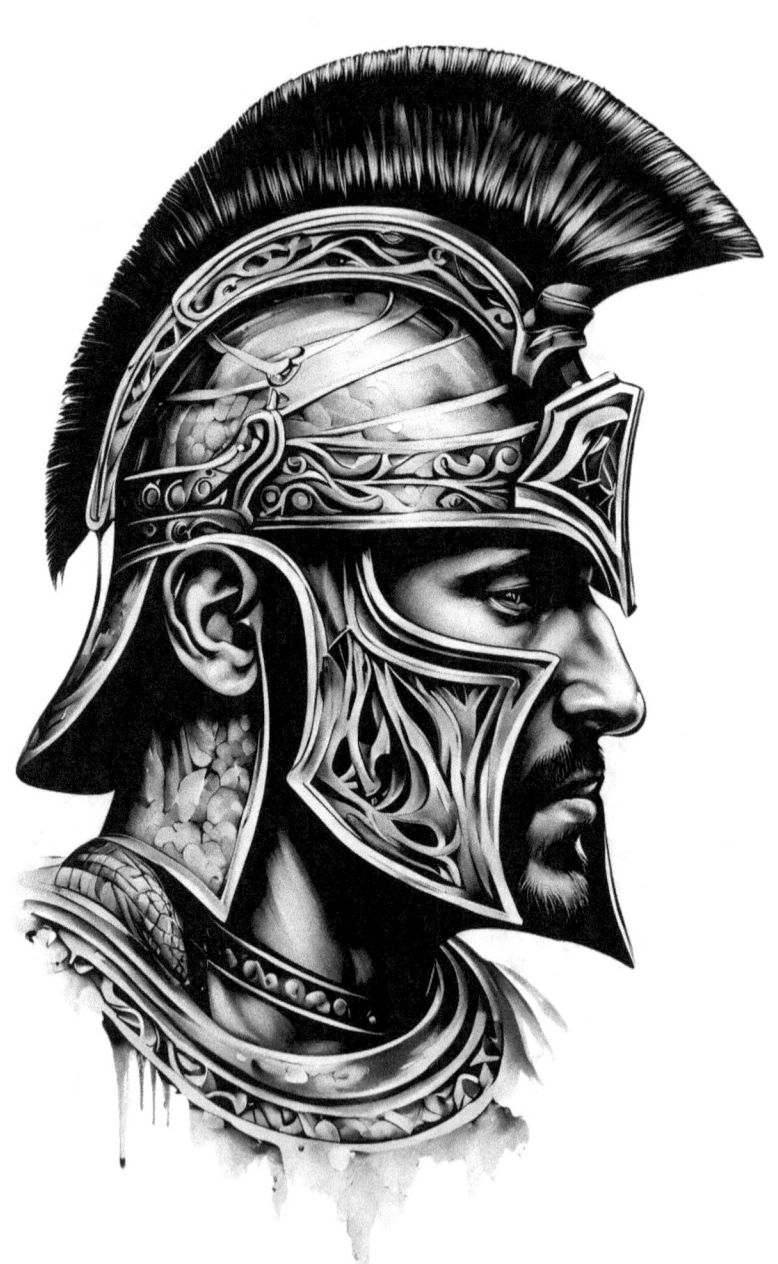

PAGE 178

GLADIATOR TATTOOS

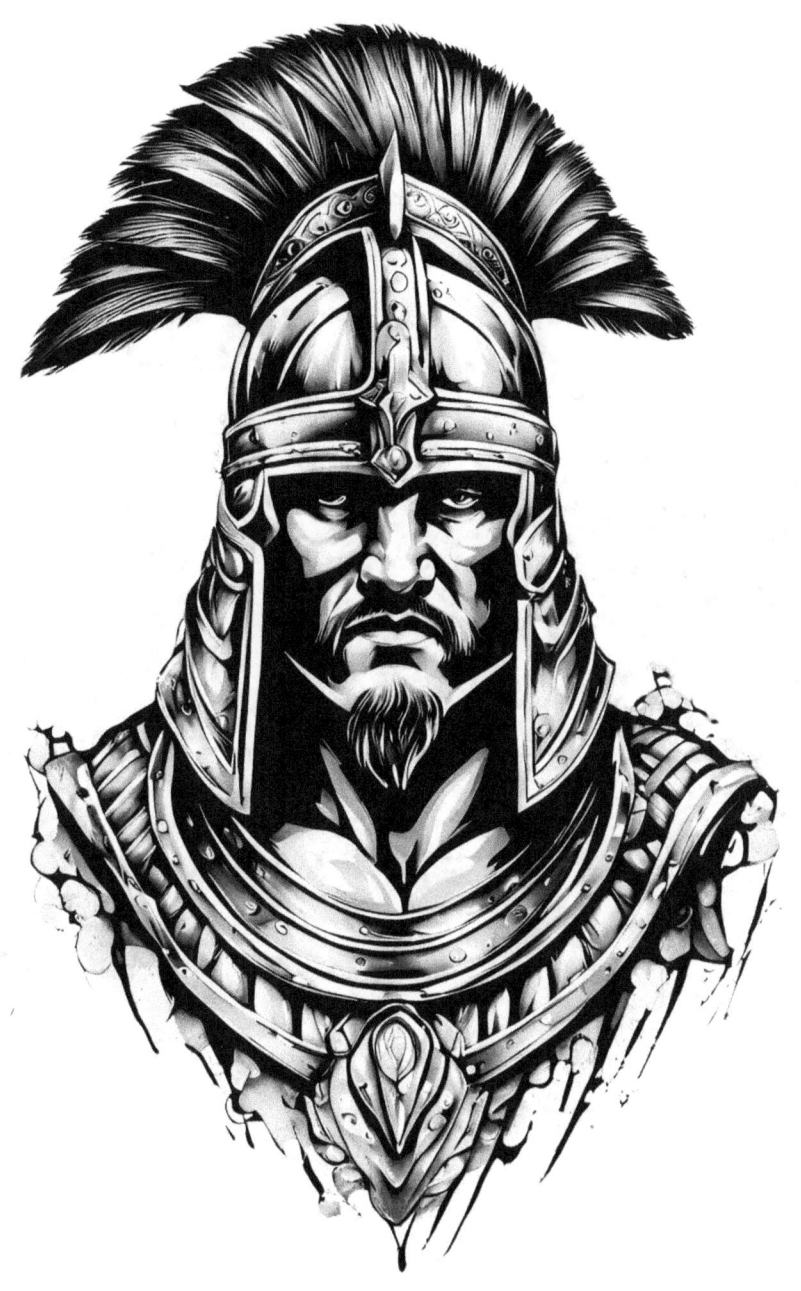

TRANSPORT TATTOOS

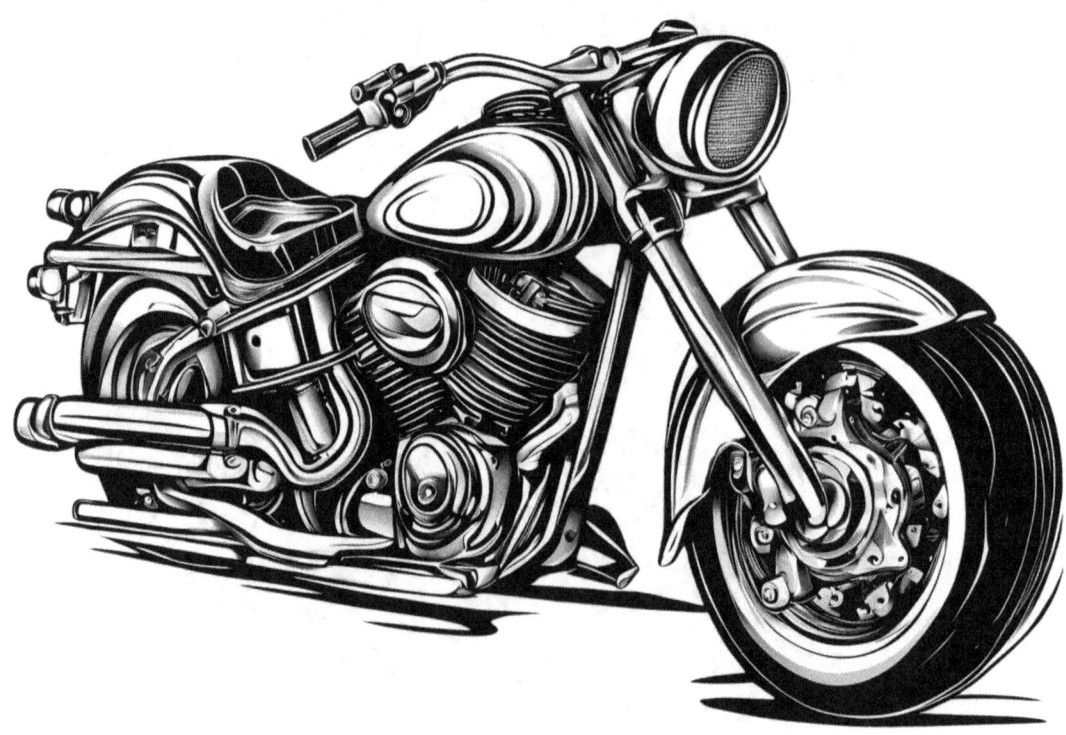

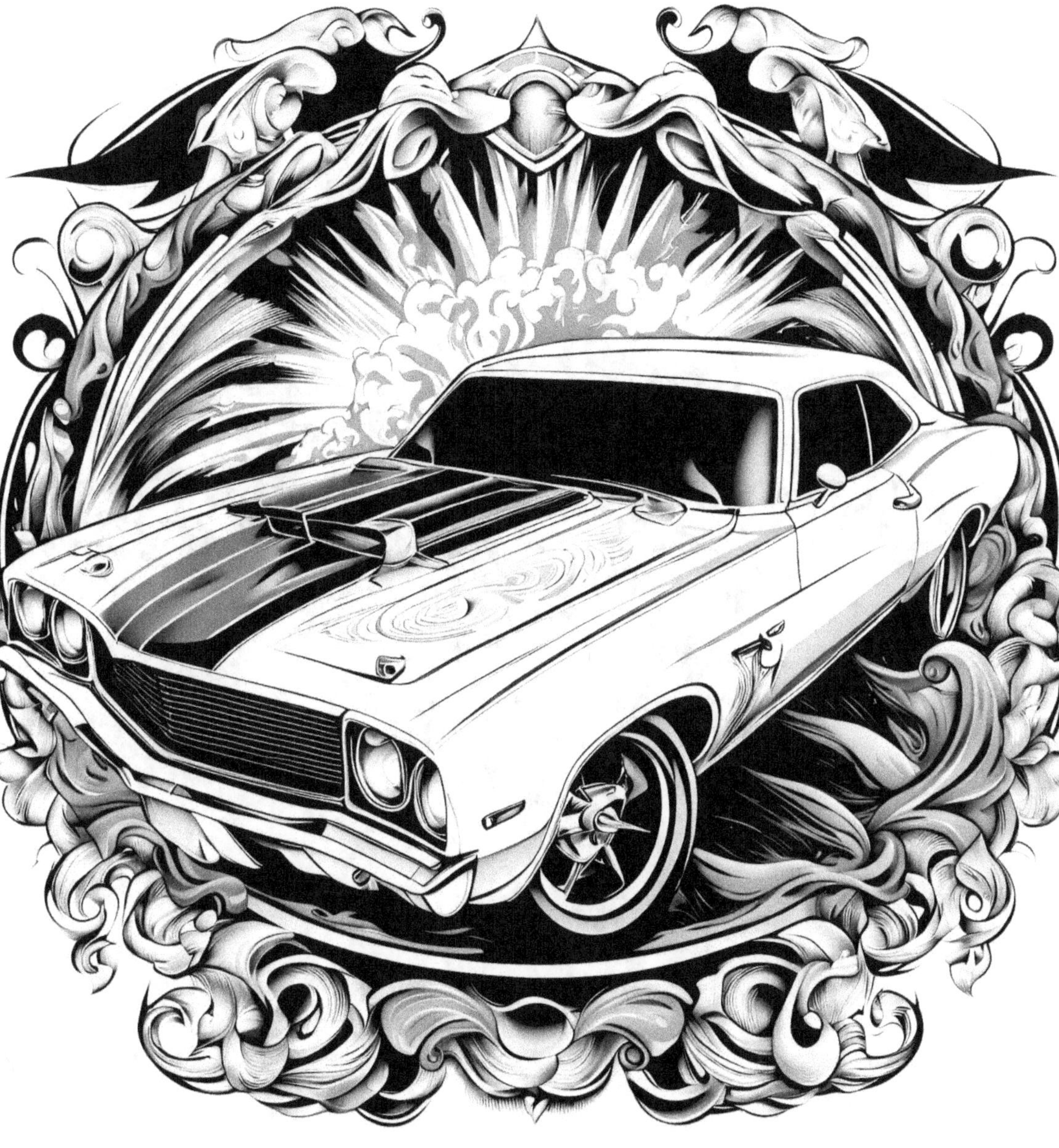

TRANSPORT TATTOOS

TRANSPORT TATTOOS

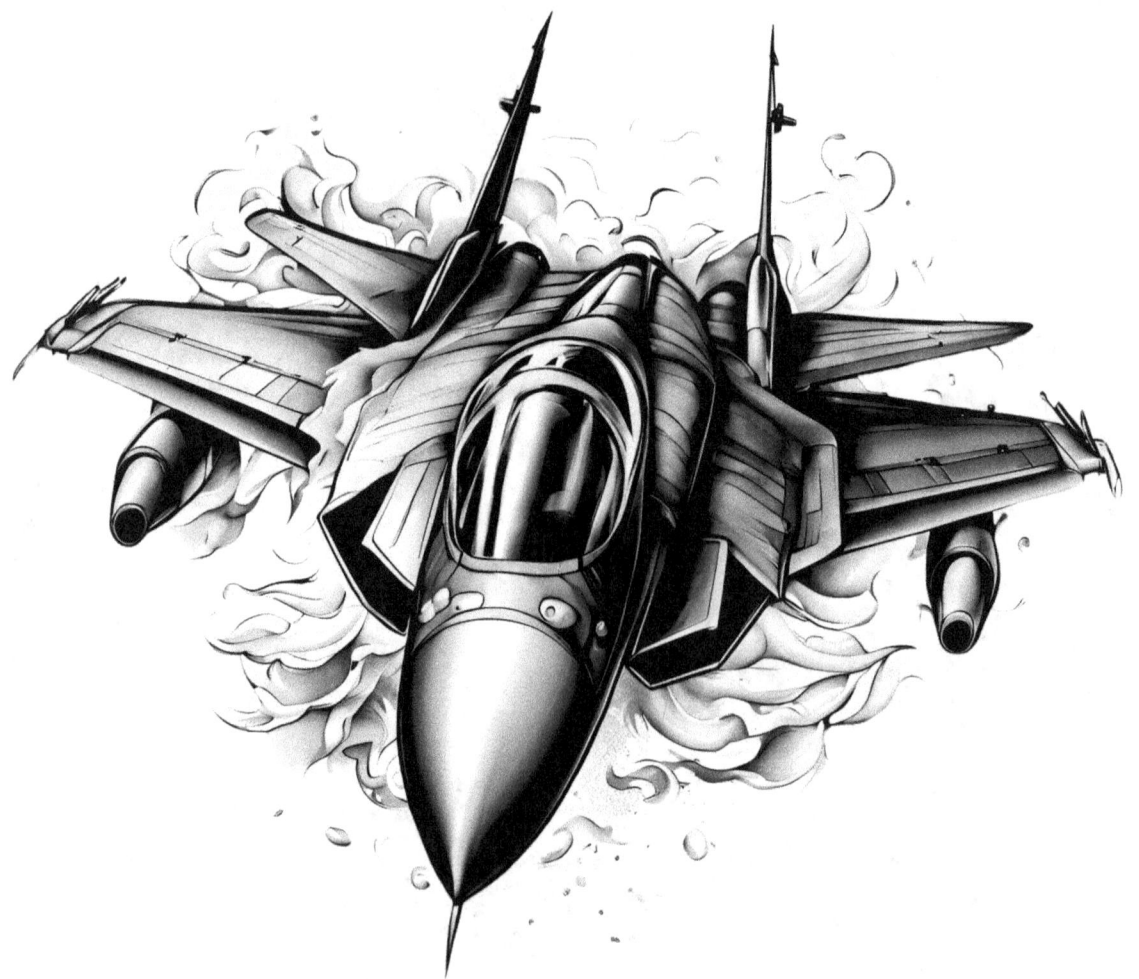

TRANSPORT TATTOOS

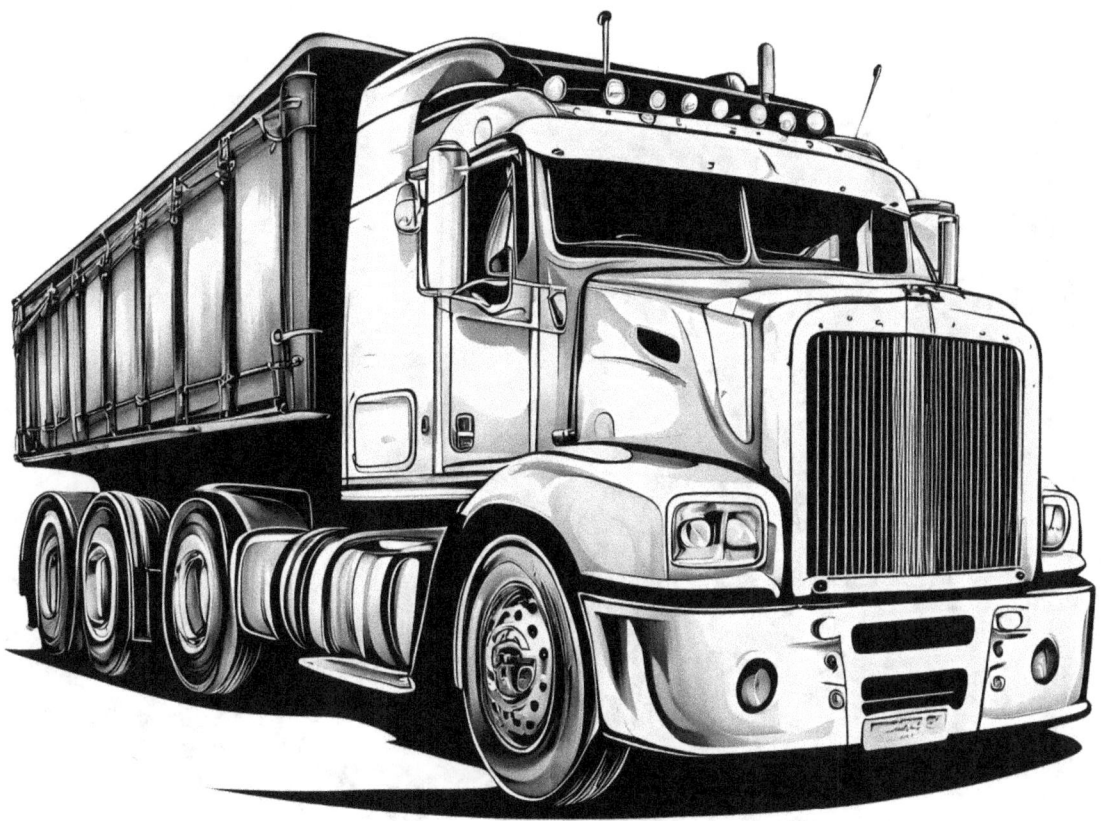

TRANSPORT TATTOOS

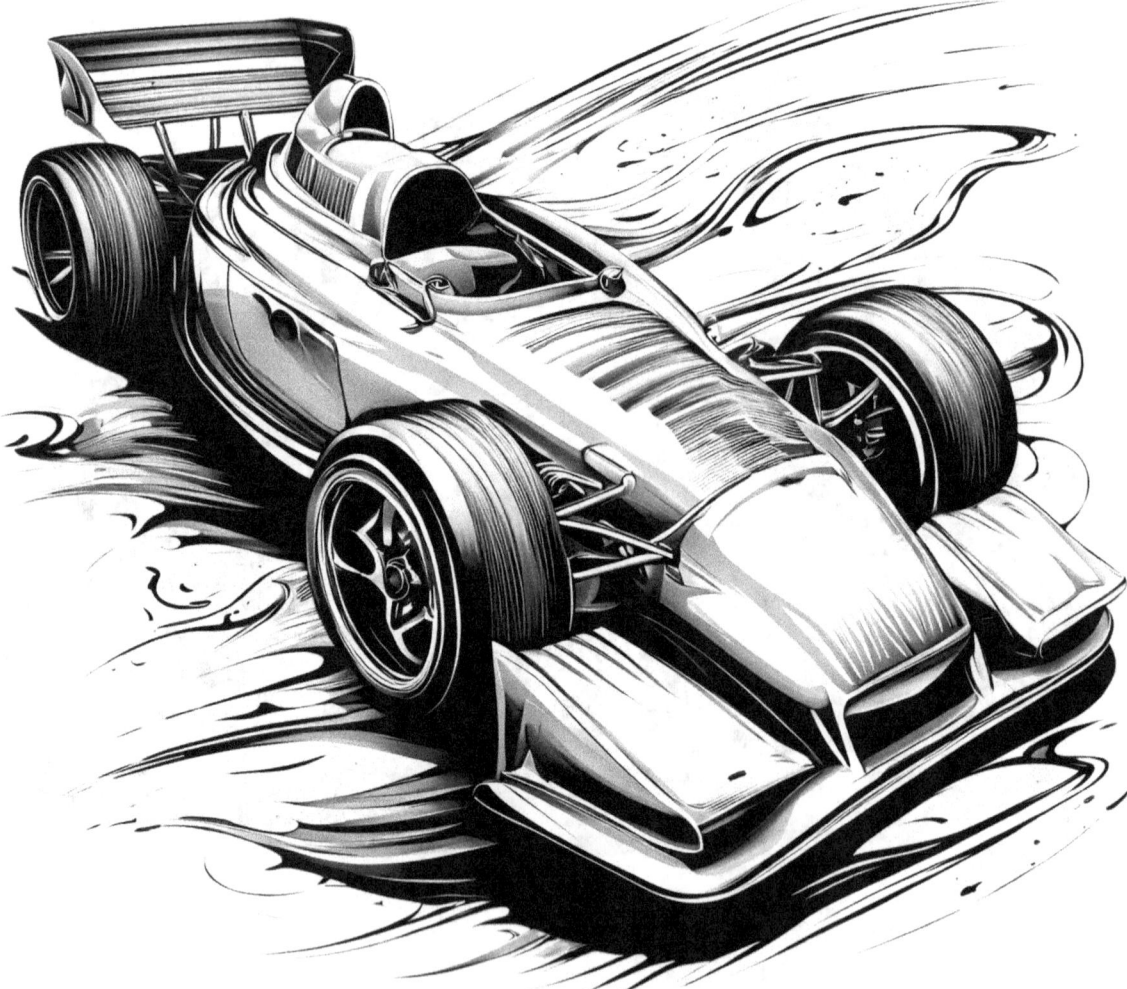

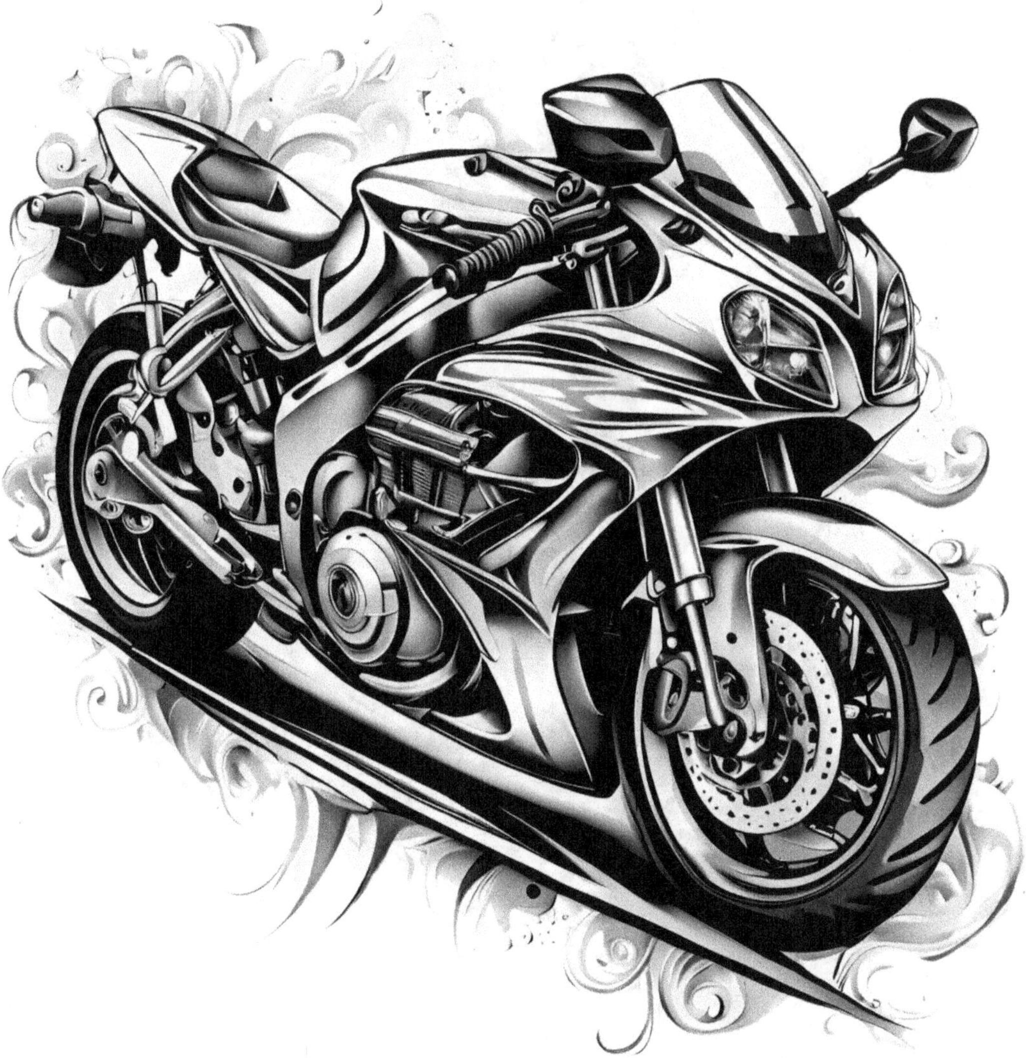

TRANSPORT TATTOOS

CHESS TATTOOS

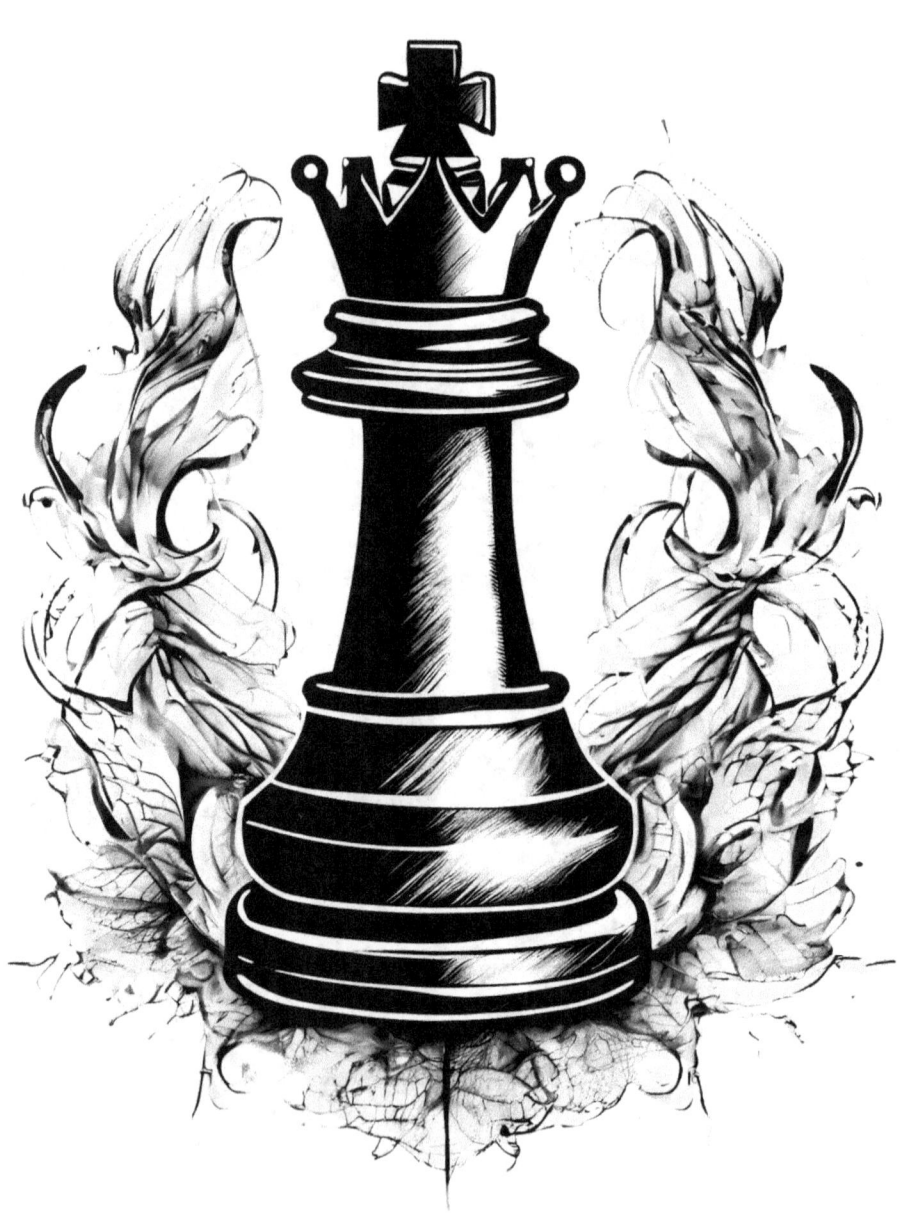

CHESS TATTOOS

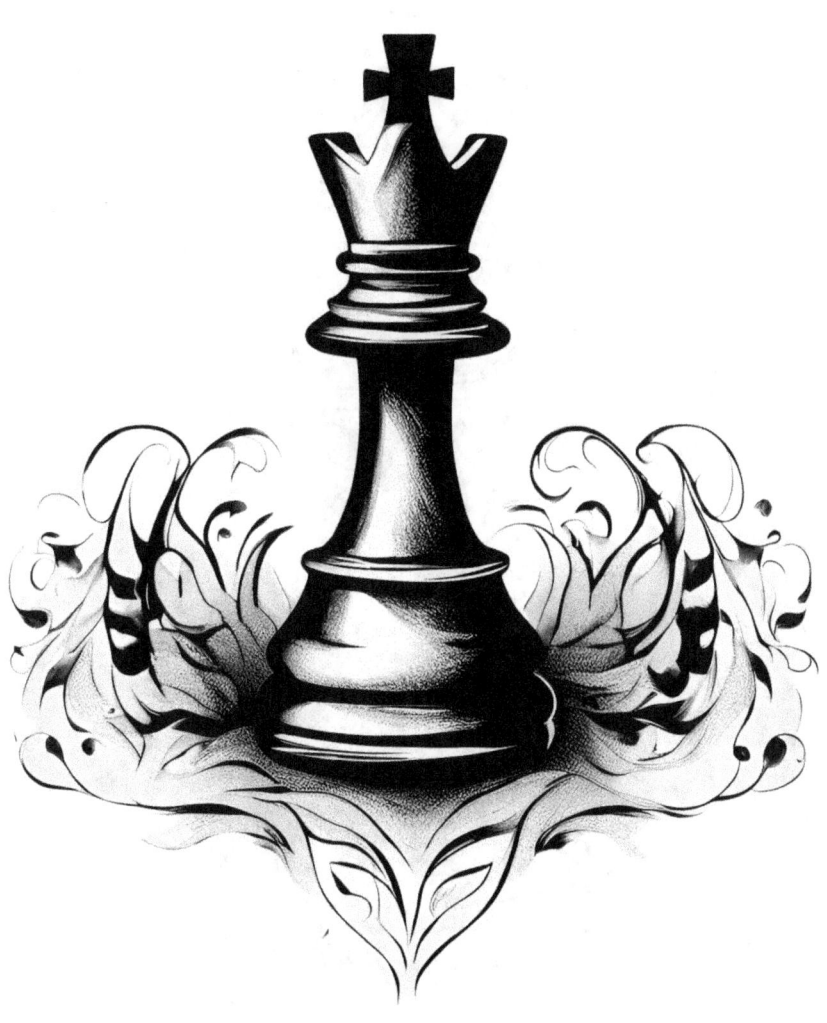

CHESS TATTOOS

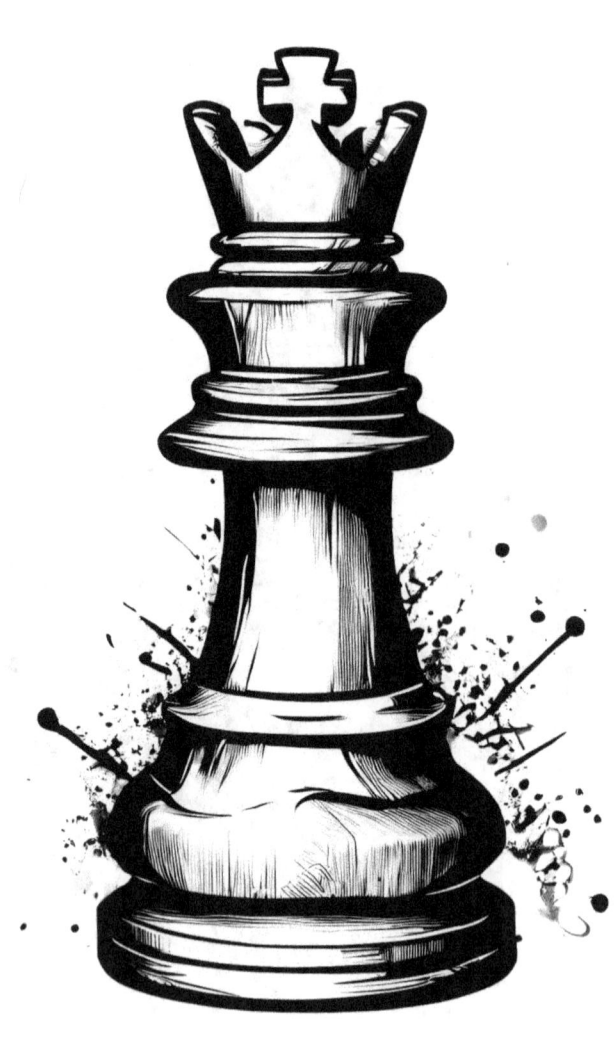

CHESS TATTOOS

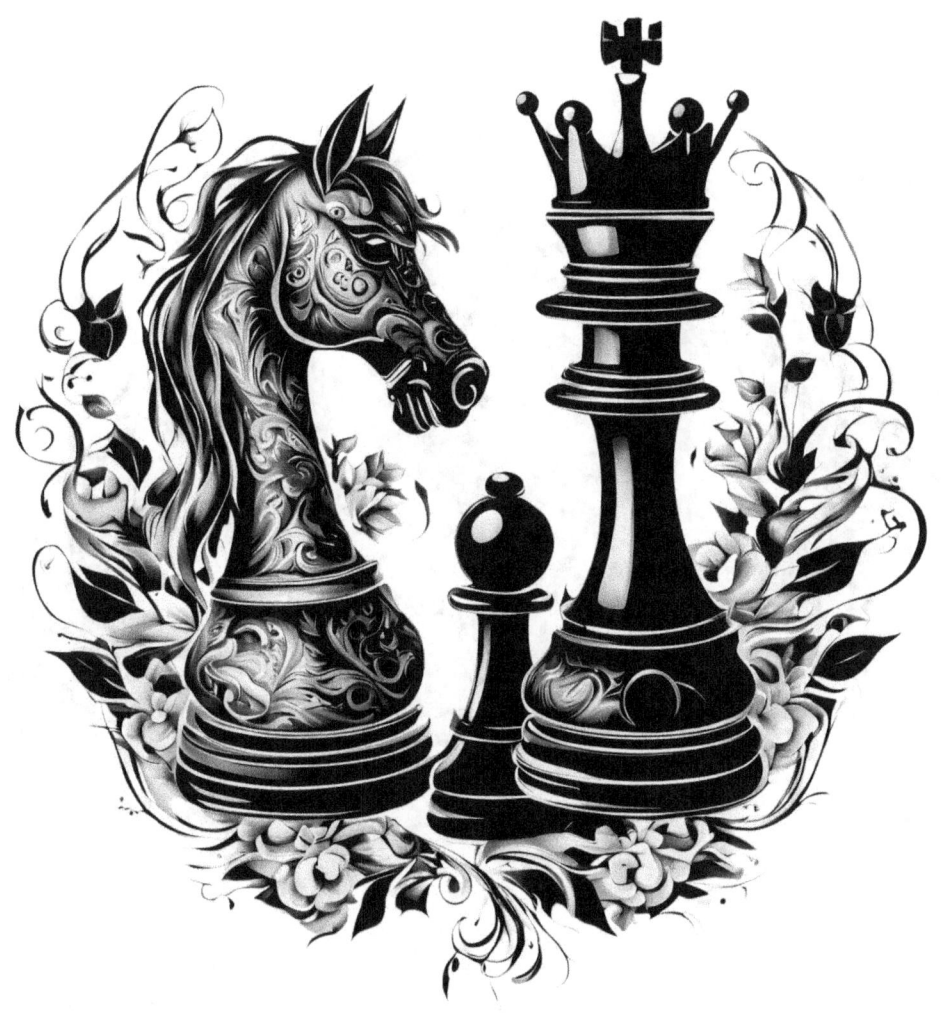

EYE TATTOOS

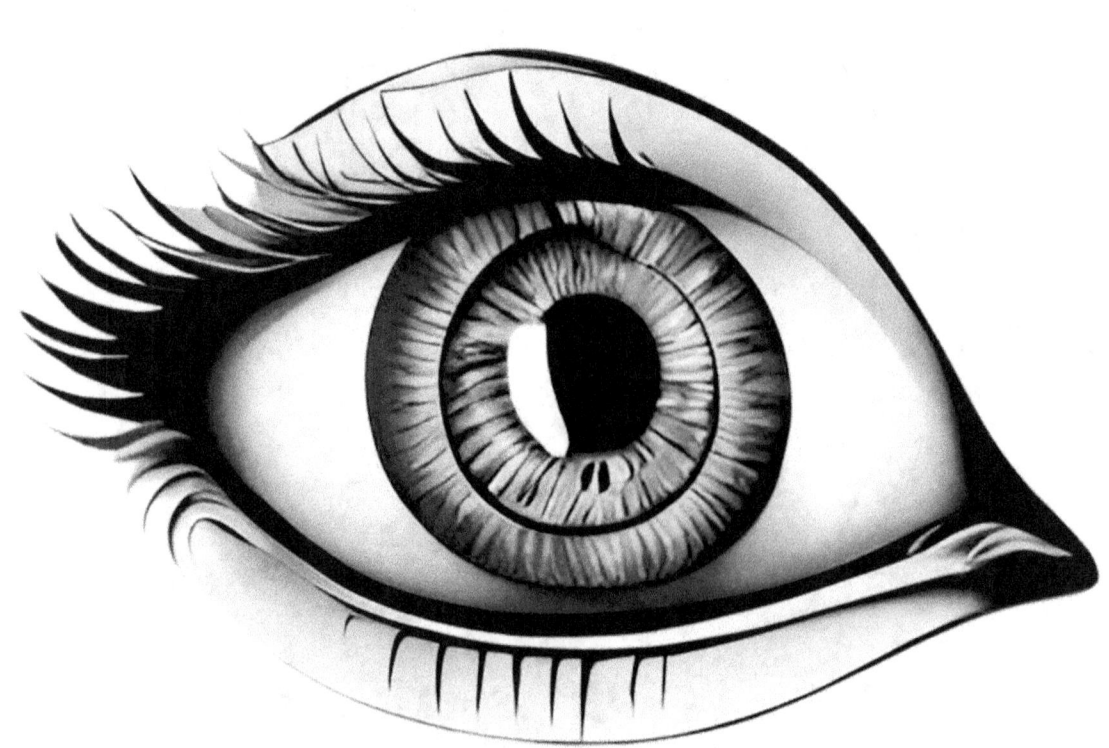

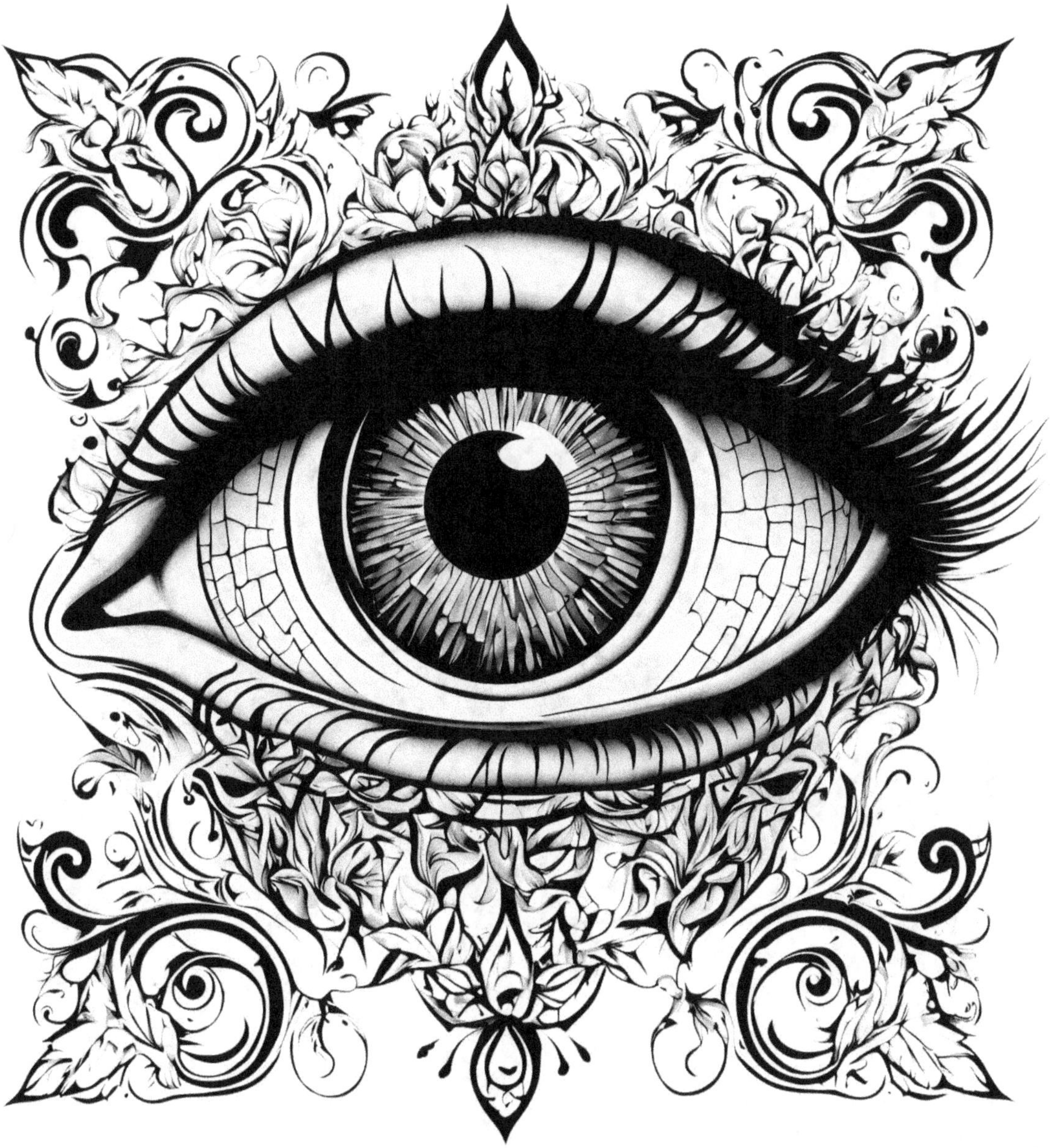

EYE TATTOOS

PAGE 191

EYE TATTOOS

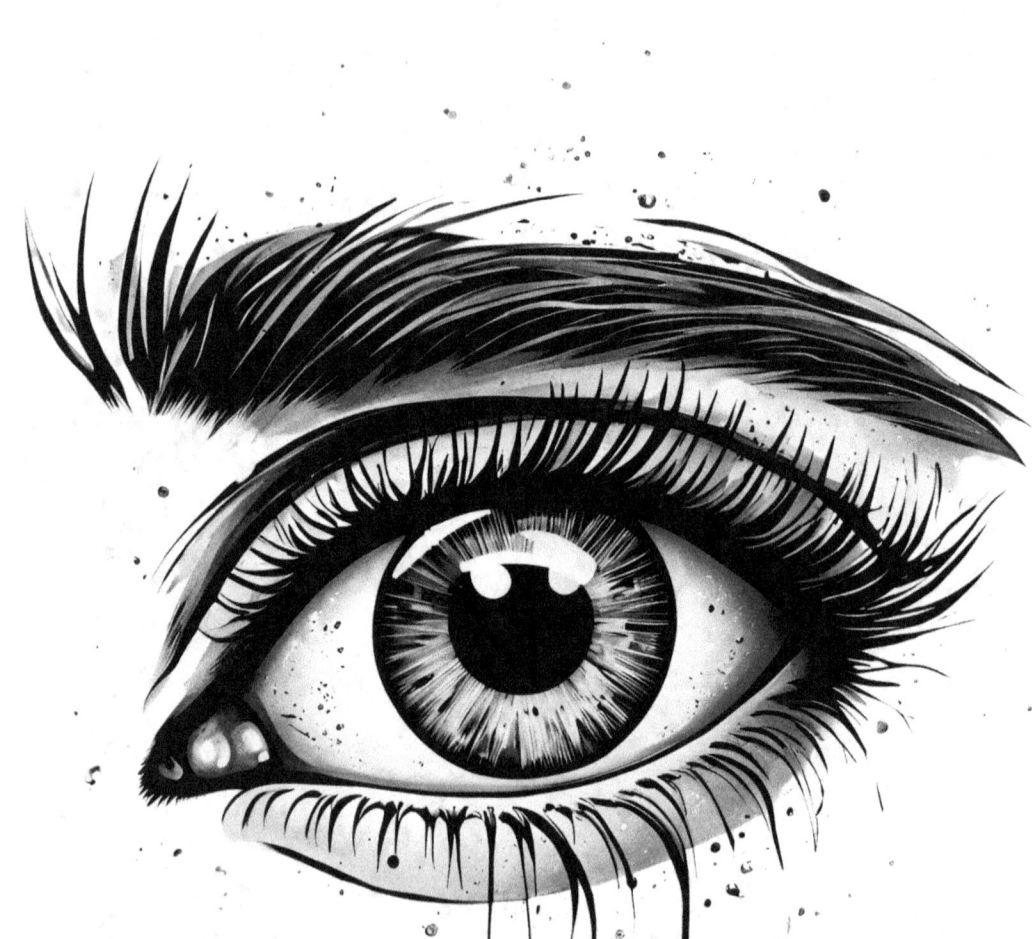

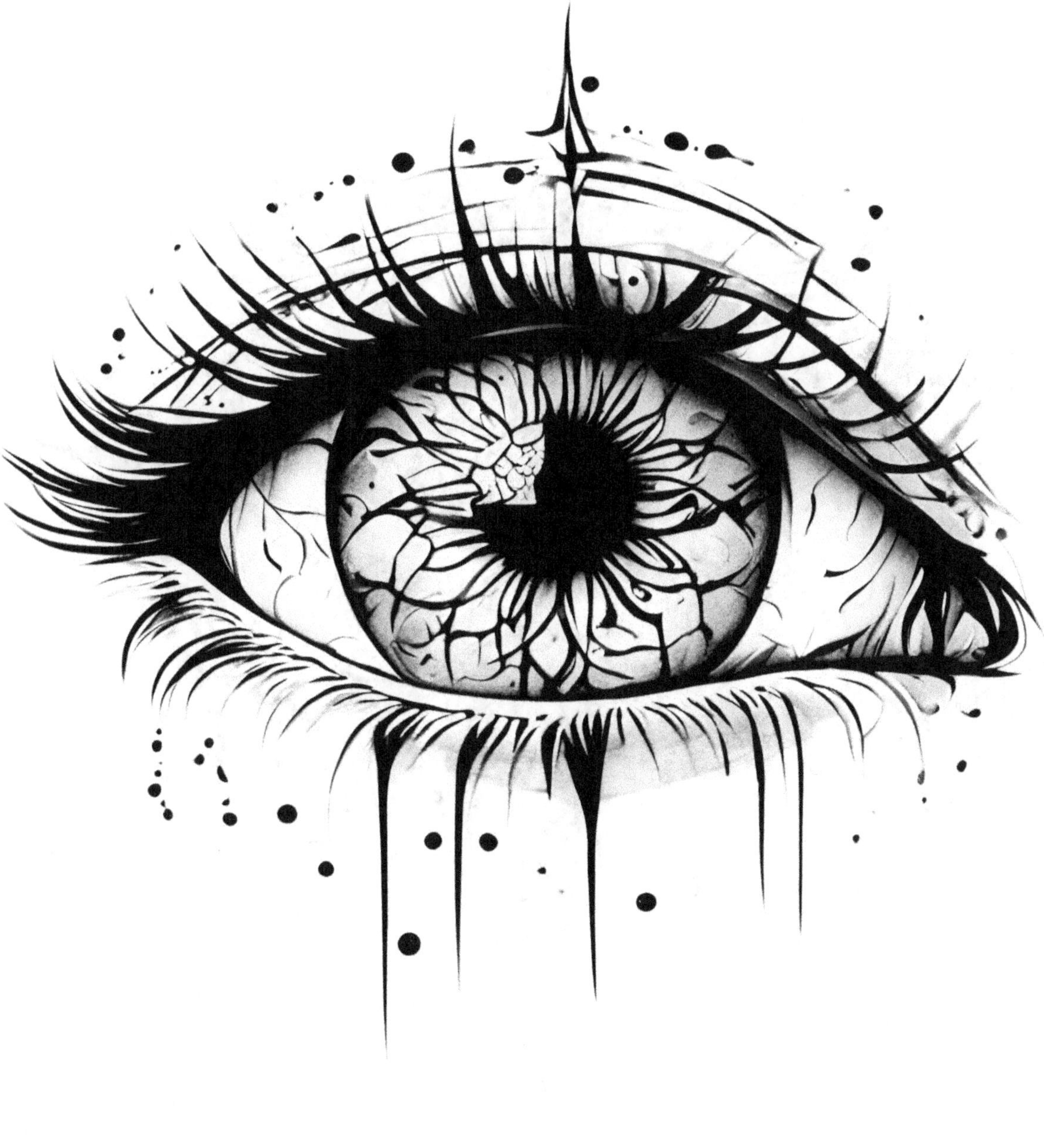

EYE TATTOOS

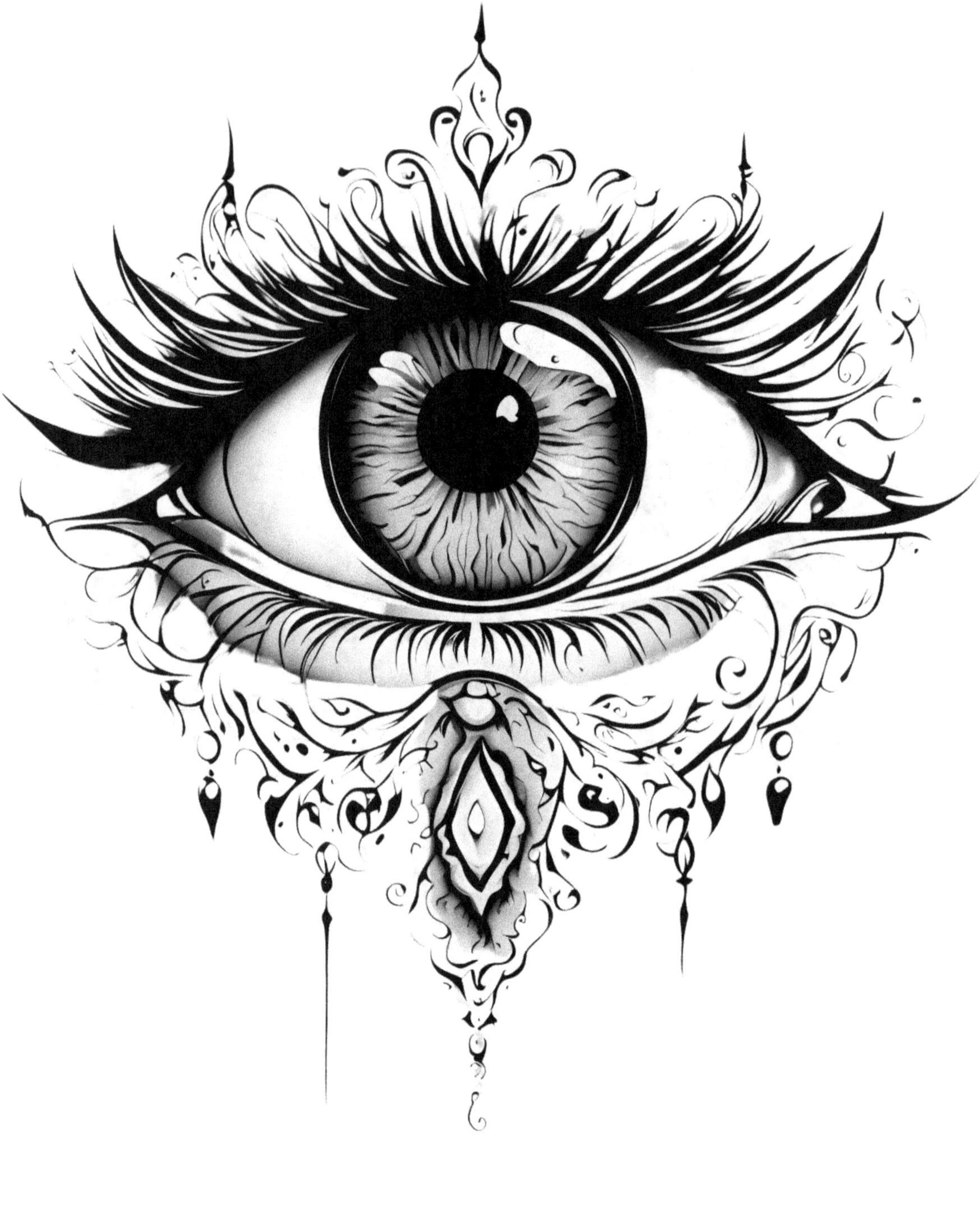

EYE TATTOOS

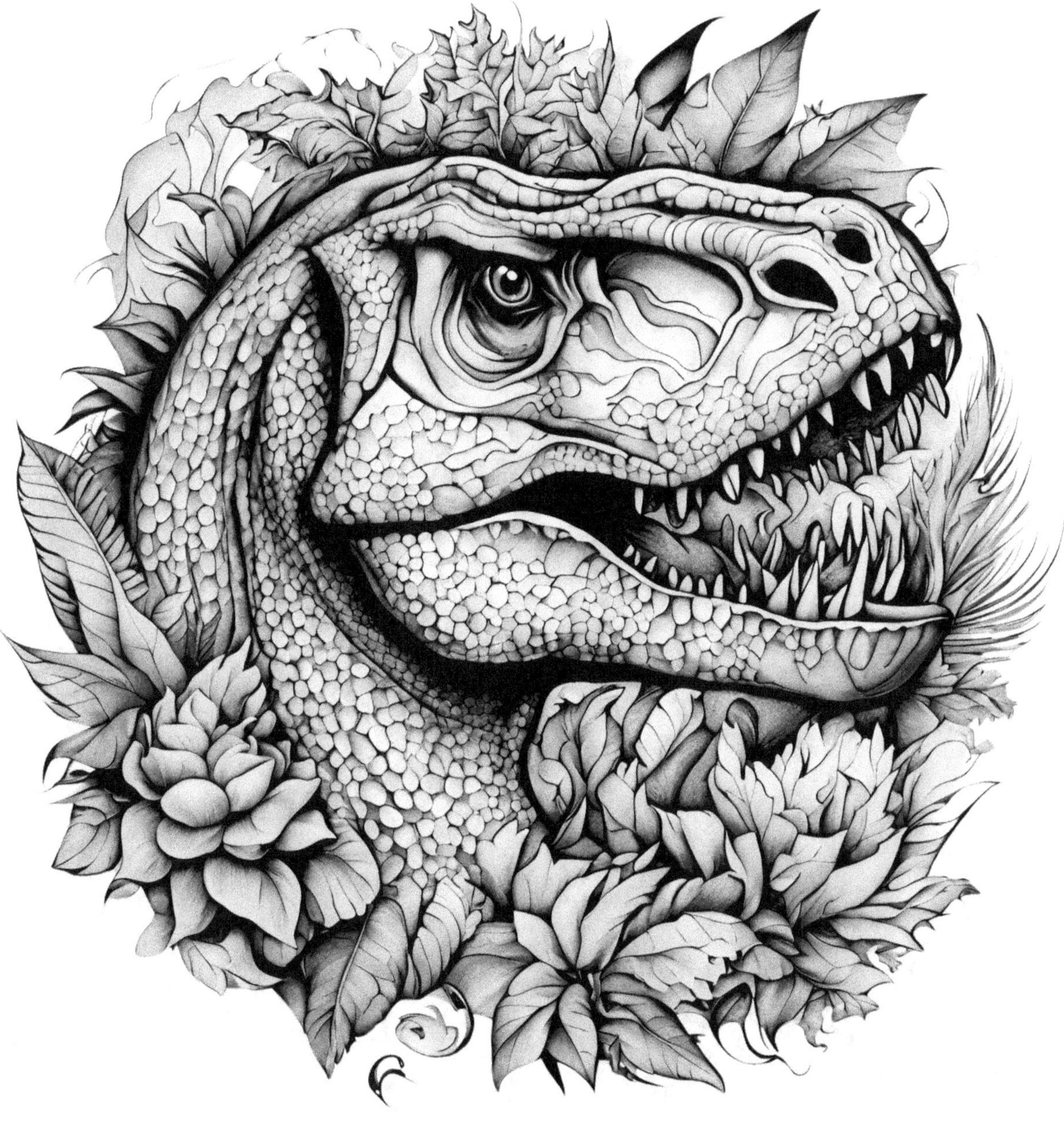

DINOSAUR TATTOOS

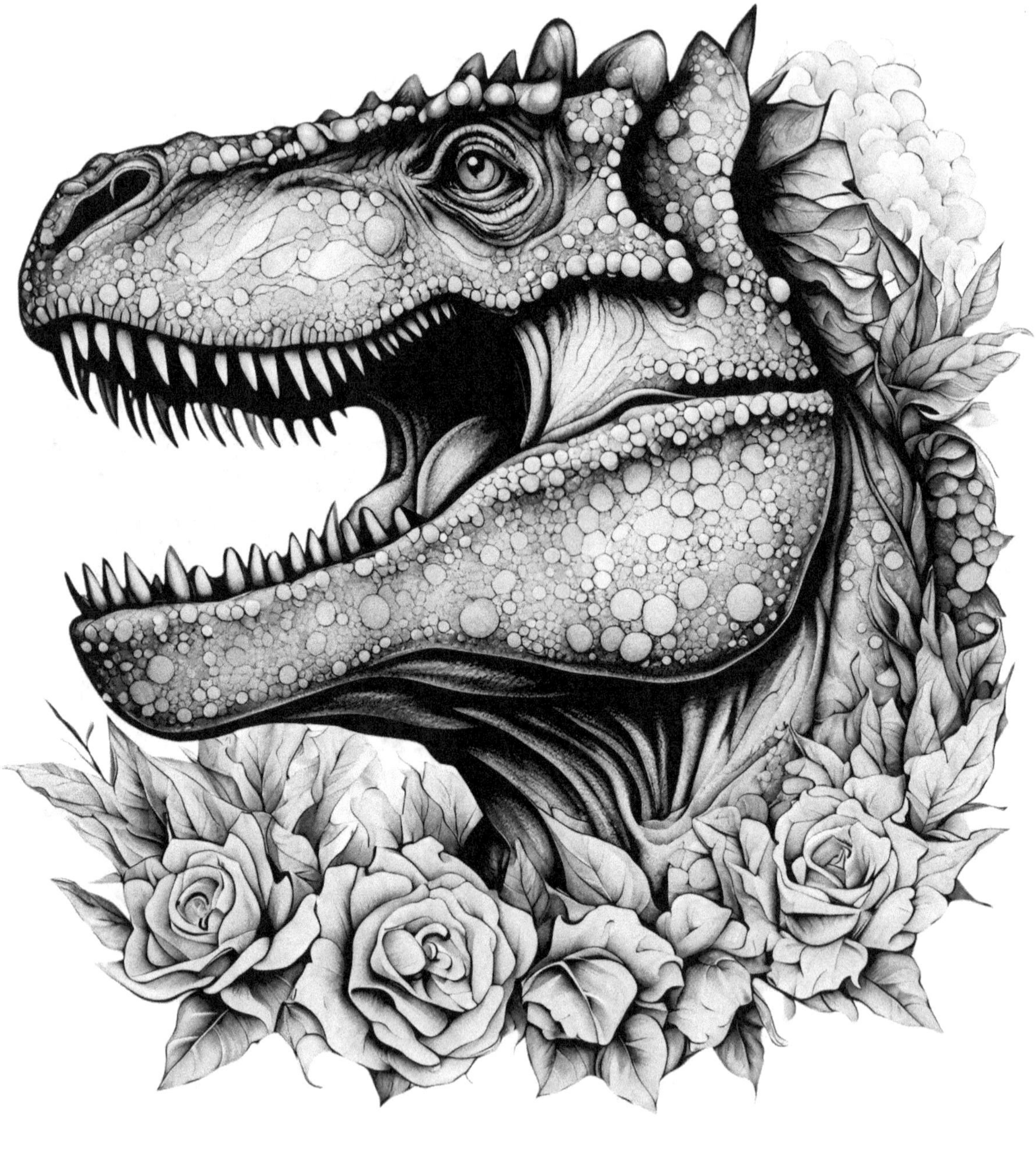

DINOSAUR TATTOOS

DINOSAUR TATTOOS

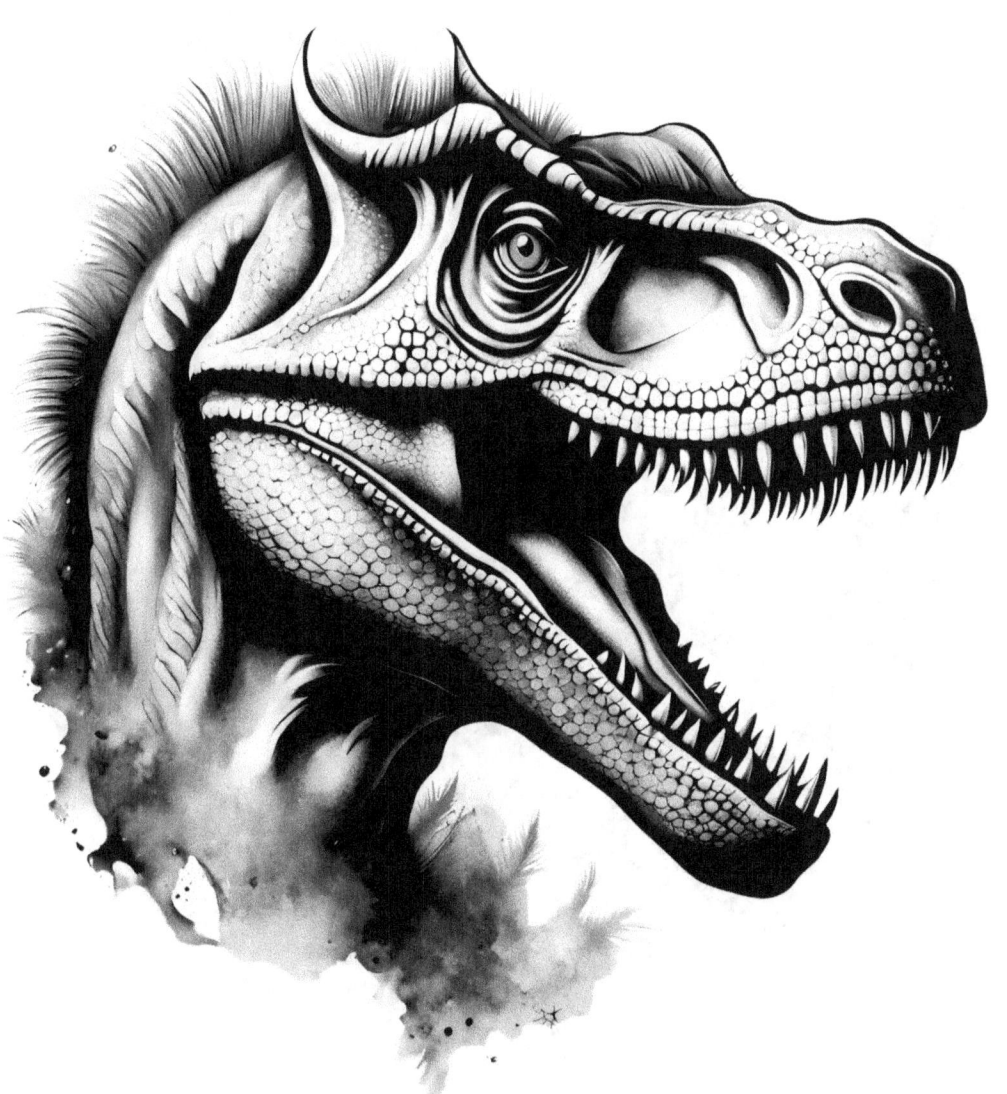

PAGE 197

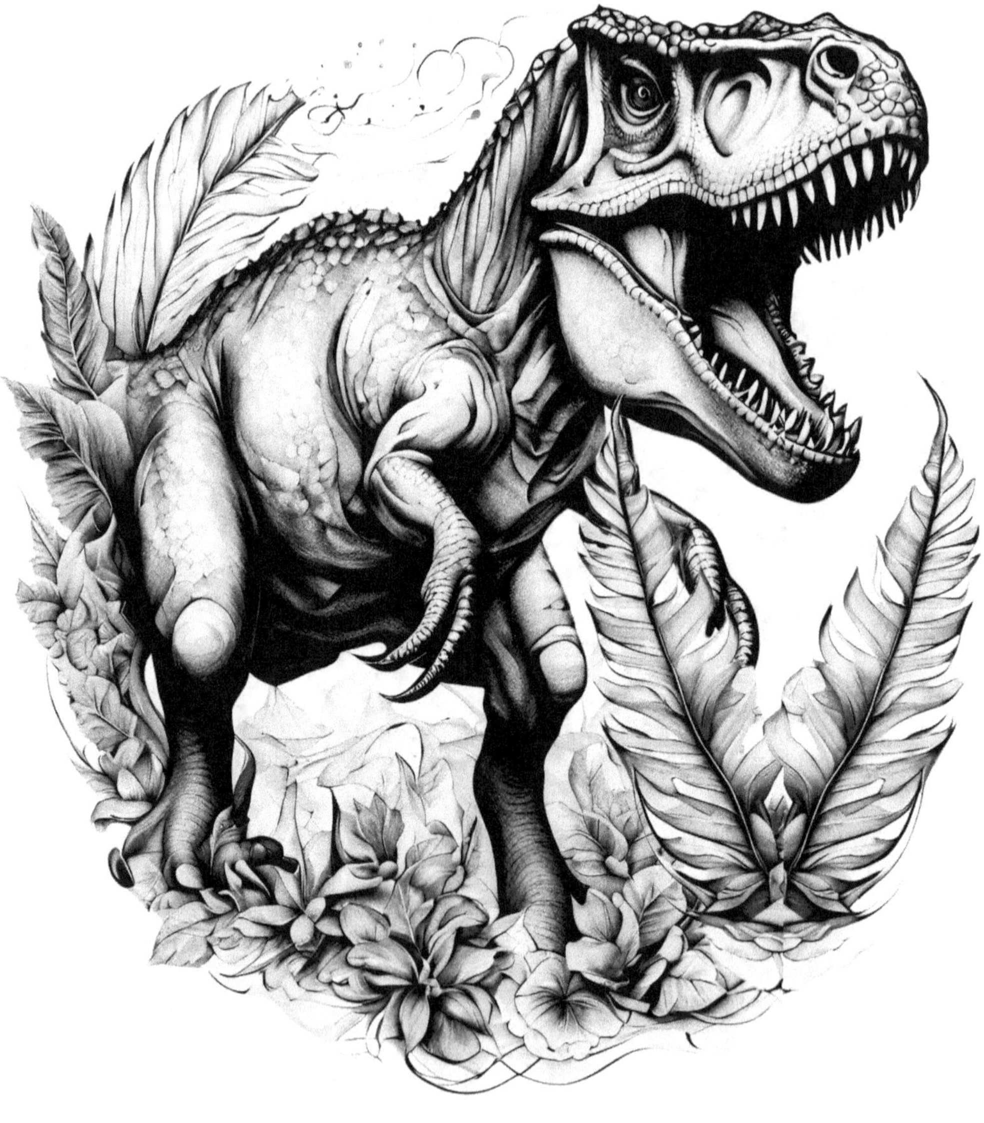

DINOSAUR TATTOOS

PAGE 198

LOCK TATTOOS

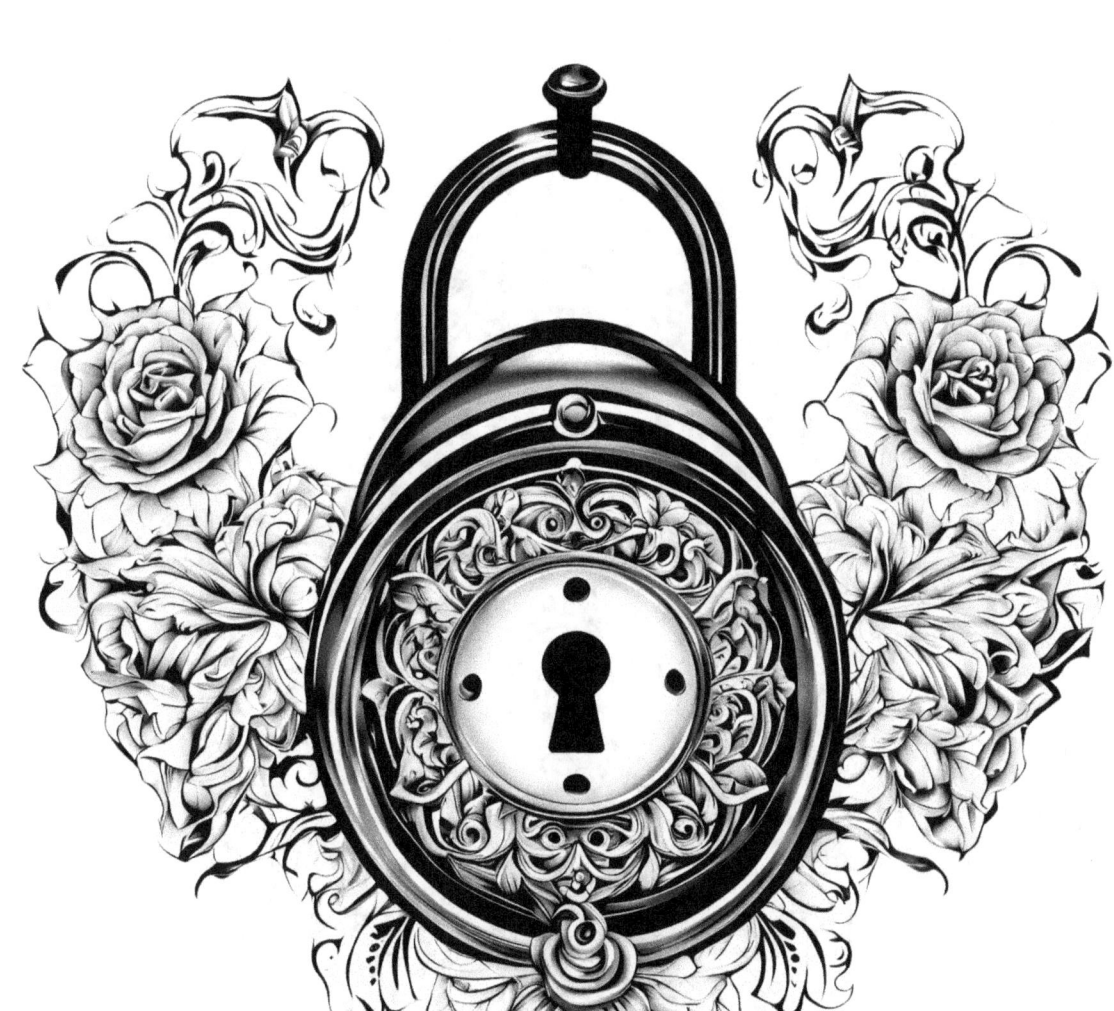

LOCK TATTOOS

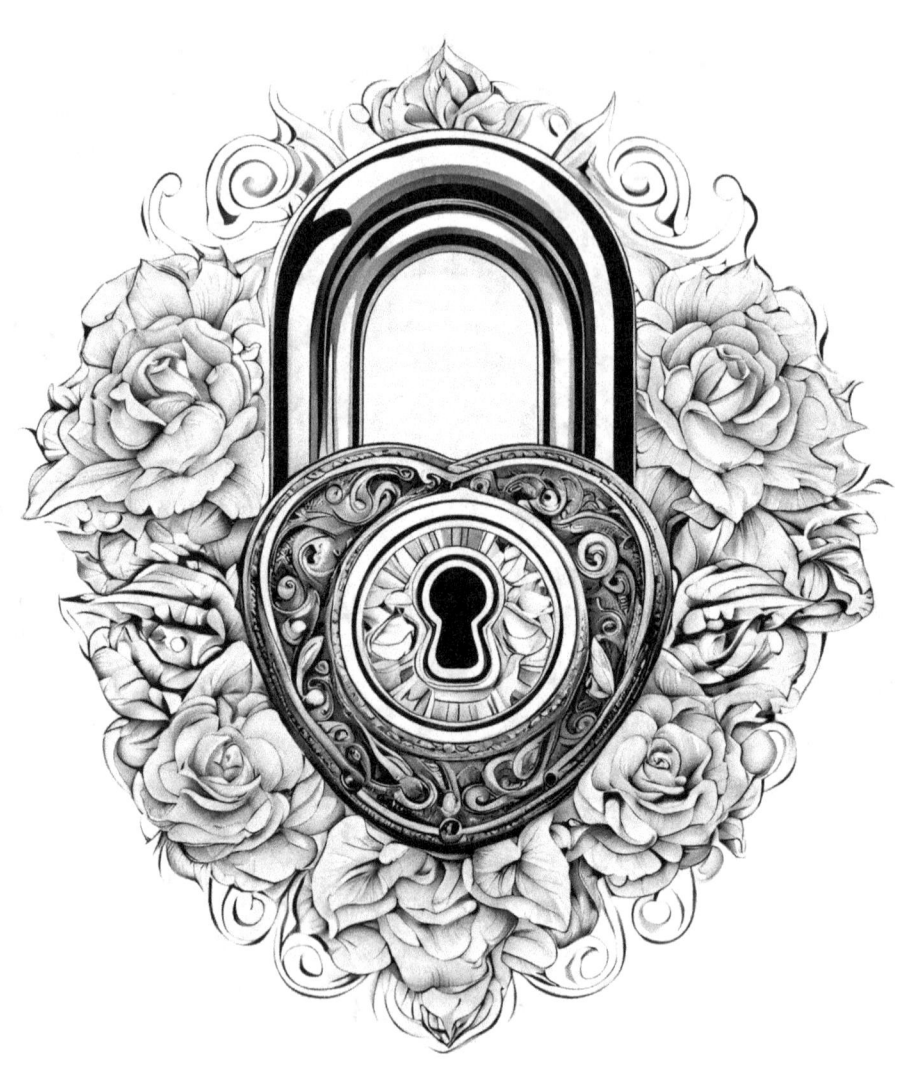

LOCK TATTOOS

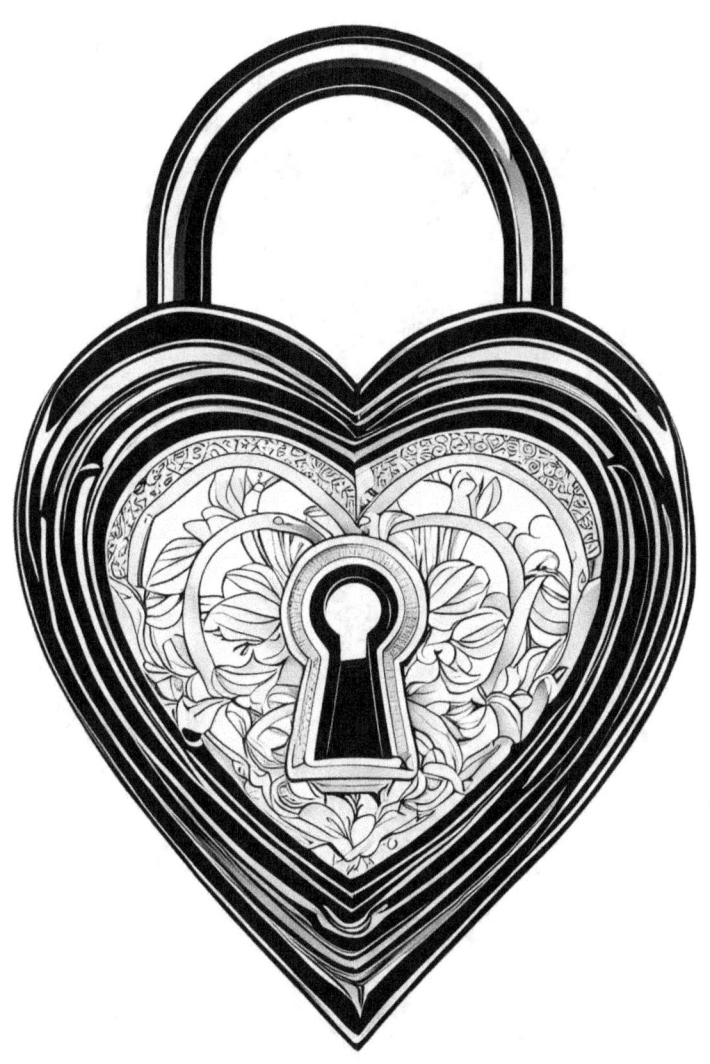

KEY TATTOOS

KEY TATTOOS

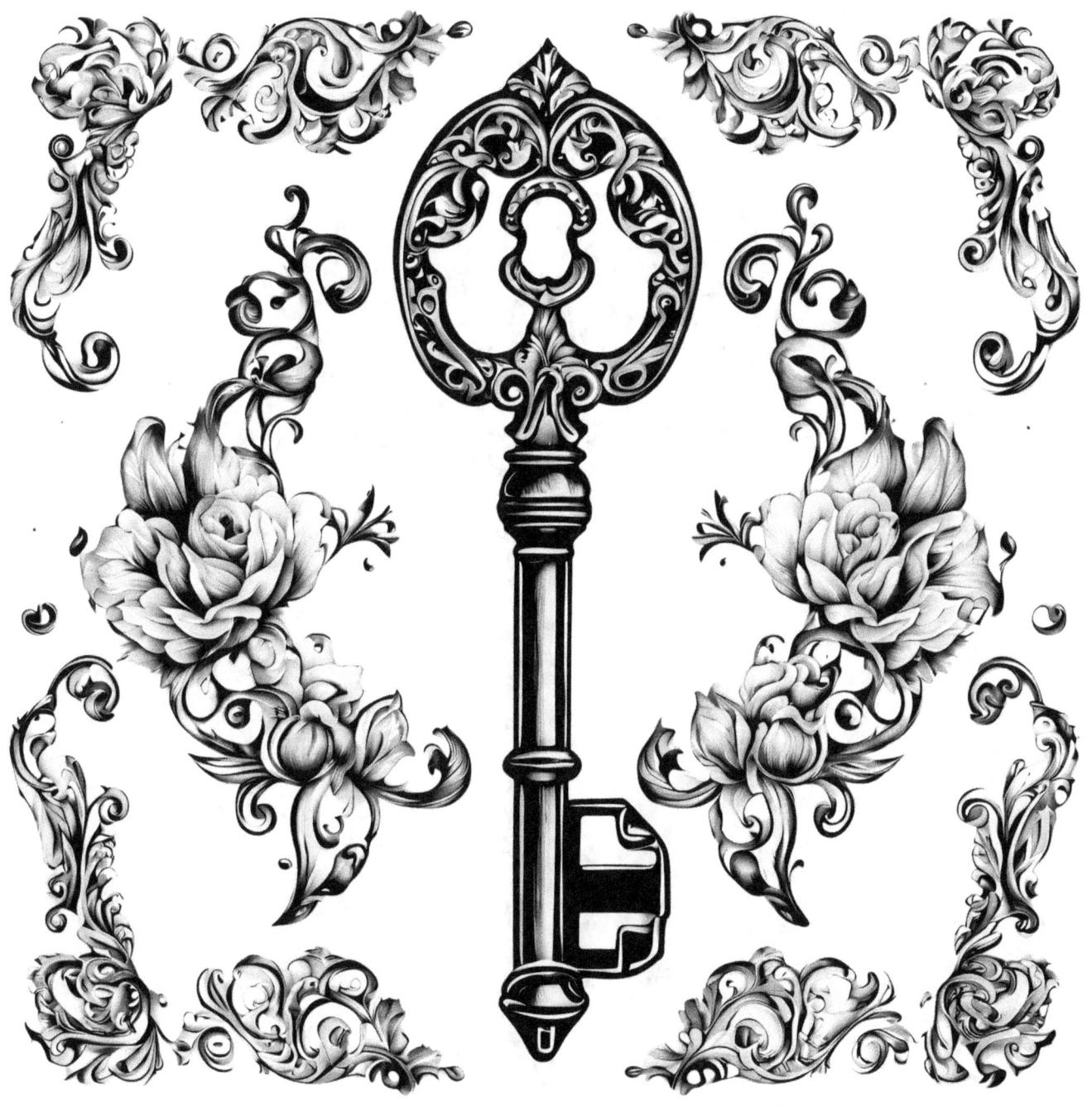

PAGE 203

KEY TATTOOS

KEY TATTOOS

FINAL THOUGHTS

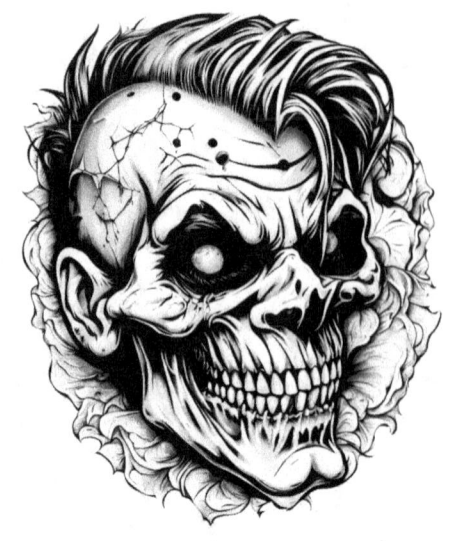

Thanks for purchasing this book, be sure to check out my other books on my author page including;

1. BLACK AND WHITE TATTOO DESIGN BOOK
2. SKULL TATTOOS: OVER 200 SKULL TATTOO DESIGNS

If you enjoyed this book I would greatly appreciate a positive review.

Many thanks

Harley Ray

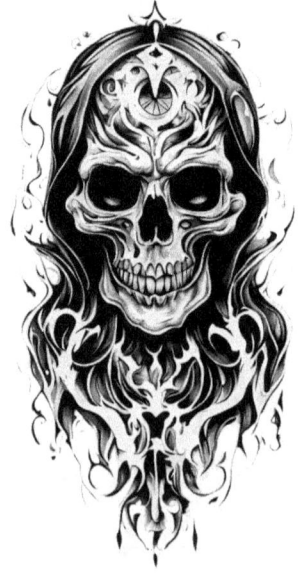

www.ingramcontent.com/pod-product-compliance
Lightning Source LLC
Chambersburg PA
CBHW062102220526
45471CB00010B/3578